Fiction in the Historical Present

Fiction in the Historical Present

FRENCH WRITERS AND THE THIRTIES

Mary Jean Green

Published for Dartmouth College by
UNIVERSITY PRESS OF NEW ENGLAND
Hanover and London, 1986

© 1986 by Trustees of Dartmouth College

Printed in the United States of America

LIBRARY OF CONGRESS CATALOGING-IN-PUBLICATION DATA
Green, Mary Jean Matthews.
Fiction in the historical present.
Bibliography: p.
Includes index.
1. French fiction—20th century—History and
criticism. 2. Politics in literature. 3. Social
problems in literature. 4. Novelists, French—20th
century—Political and social views. 5. Literature
and history—France. I. Title.
PQ673.G74 1986   843'.912   85–40933
ISBN 0–87451–364–2

To Ronnie

Contents

Preface

Acknowledgments

This project had its inception in my graduate work at Harvard. It is the long-ripened fruit of reflections begun in a course on the political agitation of the 1930s given by Fredric Jameson during the equally agitated 1960s. My thinking on the relationship of history and literature has also been shaped over the years by an ongoing dialogue with W. M. (Brick) Frohock. One phase of that dialogue ended at Brick's death in August 1984, but it continues as I, like many other students on whom he left his mark, persist in testing my own interpretations against his now classic readings of Malraux. While I regret Brick did not live to see the finished book, I am gratified that he read the manuscript and that a small part of it appeared in the *Festschrift* presented to him at the 1984 MLA conference not long before his final illness.

My understanding of the fiction of the 1930s has been developed through my teaching at Dartmouth College and has benefited from discussions with those colleagues in the Department of French and Italian who have read the manuscript—in particular Steve Nichols, Colette Gaudin, and Neal Oxenhandler. I am grateful for a Faculty Fellowship from Dartmouth, which made possible an essential term of research in Paris.

This book would never have reached completion without the understanding and support of my children, Matthew and Julie, and, above all, of my husband, Ronnie. It is in gratitude for the long hours he spent learning how to get around Paris with a toddler while I worked at the Bibliothèque Nationale that this book is dedicated to him.

Translations

I am responsible for the translation of quotations from critical and historical sources that appear in my text, except in the few cases where a published translation is listed as a reference. Quotations from the fiction analyzed appear in French in the text, with English translations in alphabetically keyed footnotes. When I have used a published translation, I have cited it in the first reference to the book, and page numbers appear at the end of each translation. Where no page number appears, the translation is mine.

Hanover, New Hampshire   M. J. G.
October 1985

Fiction in the Historical Present

CHAPTER 1

A New Consciousness of History

*A partir de 1930, la crise mondiale, l'avènement du nazisme, les
événements de Chine, la guerre d'Espagne, nous ouvrirent les
yeux. . . . Notre vie d'individu, qui avait paru dépendre de nos
efforts, de nos vertus et de nos fautes . . . était gouvernée jusque dans
ses plus petits détails par des forces plus obscures et collectives et que ses
circonstances les plus privées reflétaient l'état du monde entier. Du
coup nous nous sentîmes brusquement* situés.[a]

JEAN-PAUL SARTRE,
Qu'est-ce que la littérature?

The sudden awakening to history of which Sartre speaks was the
experience of a significant number of French writers in the 1930s.
André Malraux corroborates Sartre's judgment when he writes that
it was precisely this consciousness of history that separated his own
generation from that of André Gide. In his preface to *Les Cahiers de la
petite dame,* a book of reminiscences about Gide, Malraux states
openly, "We are separated from Gide and his world by our relationship with History."[1] This new awareness of history is at the root of a
profound change in the French literature of the 1930s, a literature
that sought to confront the chaos of the era's political and social reality. Perhaps never before in French literary history had so many
writers been possessed by what Paul Nizan, quoting Dostoevsky, was
to call "the passion for the present."[2] Flaubert had written about the
events of 1848, but he had allowed himself years of distance, as did
Zola when he wrote on the decline of the Second Empire. Unlike
their nineteenth-century predecessors, French writers of the 1930s
brought into their fiction a history still in the making.

[a]From 1930 on, the world depression, the coming of Nazism, and the events in
China opened our eyes. . . . And our lives as individuals, which had seemed to de-
pend upon our efforts, our virtues, and our faults, . . . seemed governed down to
their minutest details by obscure and collective forces, and their most private circumstances seemed to reflect the state of the whole world. All at once we felt ourselves
abruptly *situated.*

Their new attitude toward history was a response to a change in the nature of historical events themselves in the years around 1930, which have been justly termed pivotal ("années tournantes"[3]). These were the years of transition between the uneasily calm aftermath of World War I and the agitated prelude to World War II. And these were the years that brought into the general consciousness the crisis of European civilization announced by the Great War.

The effects of the four years of World War I had been felt in even the most isolated French hamlets, whose *monuments aux morts* bore the evidence of the million and a half dead. Many more men returned from the trenches bearing permanent physical or emotional scars, and the country as a whole found the recovery of Alsace-Lorraine an uncertain compensation for the destruction of industrial and agricultural productivity in the vast regions that had served as battlefields or been occupied by the enemy. The grave threat to French economic equilibrium was matched by what the most sensitive observers saw as a danger to the whole of European bourgeois civilization, whose highest values had been exemplified by French culture. One of the most significant analyses of this situation was made by Paul Valéry, a central figure of the prewar intellectual milieu. Writing in the *Nouvelle Revue Française* in August 1919, less than a year after the armistice, Valéry proclaimed a major "crisis of the mind." Beginning his article with an abrupt announcement of cultural mortality—"We civilizations are now aware of our mortality"— he goes on to enumerate the intellectual casualties of the war: "There are the thousands of young writers and artists who have died. There is the lost illusion of a European culture and the demonstration of the impotence of knowledge to save anything whatever; there is science mortally wounded in its moral ambitions, and as if dishonored by the cruelty of its applications; there is idealism, which has won with great difficulty, but deeply wounded, responsible for its dreams; realism disillusioned, beaten, laden down with crimes and errors." Summing up the bankruptcy of the nineteenth-century confidence in the power of humanity to control its own destiny, Valéry concludes, "The rolling of the ship has been so great that the most firmly hung lamps have finally been overturned."[4]

Other intellectuals shared Valéry's perception of a cultural debacle. Many of them, born in the first decade of the century, were too young to have fought in the war. They were joined in their dissatisfaction by those of their elders who were not content to sink into the extreme conservatism of the veterans' organizations and who found the postwar world a bitter disappointment after the suffering and sacrifice of the front.[5] The feeling that the war had dealt a decisive blow to an already decaying society was most evident in the frantic activity of the dada and surrealist groups. Others found an outlet in recording the extent of French postwar decadence, creating a "literature of decadence," of which Drieu la Rochelle's fiction of the 1920s is the most representative. Still others fled a crumbling European civilization in search of exotic sources of renewal: Nizan left for Aden, Malraux for Indochina, Paul Eluard for the far-off islands of Oceania.

Some of these young rebels, particularly the surrealists, did attempt to point the way to cultural regeneration. As Claude-Edmonde Magny points out, their activities were received with amused tolerance by the reigning bourgeoisie.[6] Furthermore, as Sartre suggests with respect to the surrealists, they often participated in the spiritual inertia of the world they professed to transform.[7] In any case, their activity, which was largely confined to the realm of artistic creation, had little real effect on the structure of the society. They did succeed in founding a number of small journals, such as the constantly rebaptized surrealist publication, Drieu la Rochelle's significantly named *Les Derniers Jours*, and the Marxist *Philosophies* group, of which Nizan was a part. But these journals proved not only ephemeral but plainly ineffective in awakening the consciousness of the population. As Nizan's students in *La Conspiration* discover on publishing their own journal in this era, "it was a success, but you couldn't say it effected a major change in the direction of French thought."[8]

While these small groups of young rebels tried to deal with the French cultural decline, most Frenchmen lucky enough to have survived the war devoted their energy to denying the effects of the historical cataclysm. In the politics of the conservative Chamber of Deputies (called the *Chambre bleu horizon* because it was overwhelmingly composed of conservative returning veterans) as well as in the flourishing literature of entertainment and evasion, the central effort of the 1920s was to return to the stable, prosperous prewar world and its values. And indeed, by the late 1920s, this prewar stability seemed to have returned. On the international scene, peace seemed assured, having been only briefly disturbed by an uprising in Morocco in 1925. The efforts of the foreign minister, Aristide Briand, to bring about European cooperation seemed to be succeeding, and the League of Nations in Geneva promised peaceful settlement of any disputes that might arise. In domestic politics, the ironically mis-named Radical party (which was, in fact, the mouthpiece of the moderate bourgeoisie) was more firmly than ever in control of the Chamber of Deputies in the wake of a brief flirtation with a left-wing coalition that was widely blamed for the 1925 crisis of the franc. Extremist groups, like the Communists and the right-wing "leagues," which had flared up briefly in the 1925 crises, could boast only small memberships by the end of the decade. Describing this period from the point of view of a group of rebellious students, Nizan writes: "Things seemed in general to be calming down, in economics and politics. There was a moment when European history seemed as calm as the sea at low tide, when you forgot war and peace, the Ruhr, Morocco and China."[9]

In the euphoria of the prosperous 1920s, the literary domain shared in the general effort to avoid confronting the deep problems revealed by the war. Like the political parties of the era, much of the important literature simply carries out to greater perfection the work of writers who had begun their careers before the war. Gide's *Faux-Monnayeurs*, the later volumes of Proust's *A la recherche du temps perdu*, the accumulating works of Colette and Valery Larbaud—these represent the crowning achievements of projects whose roots are deep in the prewar world. In a sense, the literature of this era was, as Magny puts it, living on the reserves of preceding generations.[10] As for the newer writers, their function was either to reassure the bour-geois reading public about the stability of their way of life or to make possible an amusing flight from a reality that, during the war years, had proven unbearably oppressive. In *Le Sabbat* Maurice Sachs re-lates the lack of seriousness in literature to the prosperity of the eco-nomic scene: "Unparallelled prosperity that was to give us seven years of an extraordinary euphoria, . . . Easy money put a short-lived effervescence into the arts. . . . In short it was a tacitly estab-lished rule that you had to live to the limit."[11] Robert Brasillach in 1931 was ready to comment on the literature of the decade that had just come to an end: "It was nothing but distraction in the Pascalian sense . . . we wanted to escape from the world of time."[12] Brasillach's contemporary, Jean-Pierre Maxence, sums up the vocabulary most frequently used by other critics when he calls the literature of the

1920s "a welter of creations, of daring, of madness, a magnificent abundance, a bursting forth of fireworks."[13]

In the flourishing literary production of the 1920s, there was little evidence of a desire to help readers face up to the crisis touched off by the war. As Magny has noted, "In the fifteen years that followed the war there was a disparity between literature, as it continued to live off its past (despite innovations in form and changes in sensibility) and the new task obscurely felt."[14] It was not until the 1930s that the literary mainstream, along with much of its readership, turned to face the chaotic events of contemporary history. This new consciousness of reality was awakened by a series of historical events that indicated to many observers that the crumbling edifice of Western civilization, shored up temporarily during the 1920s, was finally about to collapse. This moment of historical turnabout may be dated as early as 1929, the year of the infamous Wall Street crash that triggered a worldwide depression. In France, 1929 was also the year of the retirement of the conservative leader Raymond Poincaré, who had long epitomized governmental and financial stability. The crucial date may be set later—in 1931, for example, when the effects of the Depression began to make themselves felt on a heretofore prosperous and seemingly invulnerable France. This was also the year in which Briand, the architect of peace and European unity, was defeated in a bid for the French presidency, a defeat that coincided with the apparent failure of his projects. The decisive date may even be placed as late as 1933, when Hitler, whose Nazis had profited from Germany's economic disarray, was finally made chancellor of the Reich. German withdrawal from the League of Nations in that same year dealt the final blow to the concept of an international peacekeeping organization, already weakened by its powerlessness in the face of the Japanese invasion of Manchuria. However, it is clear, whichever date is chosen as the crucial one, that the series of events that led to the collapse of France in 1940 began in the years around 1930.

The changes in the economic and political climate found an immediate reflection in the domain of the intellect. By 1931 Brasillach, then a fledgling literary critic for the *Action Française* and other publications, was ready to signal "the end of the postwar era" in literature.[15] The eminent literary historian Albert Thibaudet, writing just before his death in 1935, was also clearly aware of a change in literary climate, which he dated in 1930.[16] Later critics and intellectual historians have tended to agree with the retrospective judgments of Sartre and Malraux that 1930 marked the beginning of a new intellectual era.[17] The philosopher Emmanuel Mounier, a contemporary, called it a "total crisis of civilization."[18] The political scientist Jean Touchard, in his important article, "L'Esprit des Années 1930" ("The Spirit of the 1930s"), attributes the intellectual crisis of that time to causes anterior to the economic collapse, causes that dated, as we have seen, from the war itself. Nevertheless, he sees the economic crisis as a significant factor: "The economic crisis abruptly accelerated the development of the intellectual crisis, it showed that delay was no longer possible."[19] The essential characteristic of this new era was a willingness on the part of intellectuals and writers to confront historical reality, rather than attempting to flee it, as the writers of the previous decade had done. Magny says of what she calls the second generation of postwar writers, "They face up to their situation before the world, the historical moment."[20] As Sartre has noted, it was the movement of history itself that suddenly forced itself into the intellectual consciousness.[21] And Maxence, in his memoirs, echoes this feeling: "Events came to seek us out. They forced us to weigh them. The world seized us, swept us up."[22]

With its new concerns, the new literature immediately appeared less frivolous, less flamboyant, than that of the 1920s; Pierre-Henri Simon terms it "more serious, less egoistic, less playful than that of its predecessors."[23] As individuals felt themselves swept up in historical and societal problems, there was a turning away from introspection and concern with the isolated individual and a movement toward the larger society. It was accompanied by a rejection of fantasy and a return to concrete reality. Brasillach, in his 1931 article, had already noted these concerns of the new literature: "the existence of others and openness to the real."[24] Maxence emphasizes, in particular, the new attitude toward reality: "to return to the object is to return to the world, to events."[25]

In response to their new feeling of involvement in the world of contemporary history, French writers and intellectuals threw themselves into political activity with a fervor that, in intensity and duration, surpassed even that of 1848 or the Dreyfus Affair. An article in *Marianne* in June 1934 stated: "There is no longer an intellectual in France whose pen is not in the battle; at the very least, he signs manifestos. The most detached spirit no longer feels it his right or even his wish to be absent and to isolate himself from the times."[26] Maxence calls the phenomenon a "mobilization of intelligence."[27] Intellectuals of the 1930s chose to ignore the warnings against political involvement that had been delivered by Julien Benda in *La Trahison des Clercs*, a book written in 1927, only a few years before. But by 1937 Benda himself could be heard delivering speeches in support of the Spanish Republicans in an embattled Madrid.[28]

Like Benda, even the most determined of nonparticipants were pulled from their ivory towers. Martin du Gard's correspondence, for example, reflects his often losing struggle to remain free of political entanglements in order to concentrate on his writing. His close friend Gide had long since accepted the role of an *écrivain engagé*. Gide's public condemnation of the French colonial regime in the accounts he had written of his travels to the Congo and Chad in the late 1920s had ultimately resulted in important reforms in colonial policy. In the years around 1930, perhaps intuitively sensing the winds of change, Gide became deeply concerned with the problem of social injustice and was fascinated with the apparently successful Marxist experiment in the Soviet Union. The pages from his journal that he published in the 1932 *Nouvelle Revue Française* contained extreme statements of commitment: "Indifference, toleration are no longer acceptable when they give aid and comfort to the enemy and bring prosperity to what you consider decidedly evil."[29] Always open to new experience, Gide was among the first to participate in what would prove to be the spirit of the decade.

The intense involvement of writers with the problems of the moment was, quite naturally, reflected in their artistic creation. Rare were the artists who, like Bernanos and Mauriac, reserved their polemics on current issues for essays and journalism, although many did not hesitate to express themselves in these media as well. Poets wrote about the bombing of Spanish cities and the beauties of Soviet industry; filmmakers spoke of the hopes for world peace and the fight against social injustice; painters used their brushes to protest the bombing of innocent civilians.

But the most important artistic medium for the discussion of contemporary events was the novel. This genre had flourished in France with the development of the nineteenth-century bourgeoisie and thus had been identified with the society it had created. For this reason, many of the young radicals of the 1920s, the surrealists in particular, had rejected the novel, at least in its traditional form. Aragon, in his surrealist period, had in fact been criticized by the other members of the group for his attraction to this form of expression. Nevertheless he, as well as the surrealist leader André Breton, did write prose works that attempted to break with the established conventions of the genre. In the 1930s, in contrast, prose fiction became the preferred form of expression, even for those in revolt against the dominant bourgeois society. Magny calls the decade "the golden age of the novel," and Nizan noted that the novel was for his own time what tragedy had been for the classics.[30] Converting from surrealism to Communism in 1930, Aragon began to devote the major part of his artistic effort to an immense series of novels that observed most of the conventions and that he himself labelled realistic. Younger writers, just beginning their careers, seemed naturally attracted to fiction. Malraux, Sartre, Nizan, and Brasillach began their literary careers by writing prose rather than poetry, and their prose soon took novelistic form. Céline, Guilloux, and Dabit began immediately by writing novels.

Despite its identification with the bourgeois society, which many of these writers hoped to change, the novel was, in many ways, a form appropriate to the needs of the time. In contrast to poetry, prose seemed to offer the possibility of direct communication with the reader,[31] as Sartre would later remark.[32] Many writers abandoned even the constraints of novelistic structure for the direct expression available in the pamphlet or essay. Important examples of the genre were Bernanos's *Les Grands Cimetières sous la lune*, Nizan's *Aden-Arabie*, Céline's *Bagatelles pour un massacre*, Drieu la Rochelle's *Socialisme fasciste*. But fiction offered, in addition to this communication, the possibility of imaginative reconstruction of reality, as a character of Malraux's would later say, a "rectification" of this reality. This possibility corresponded to the widely expressed need not only to describe but to transform contemporary reality.

Another attractive characteristic of the novel was its traditional concern with concrete reality. "The Real World," the title Aragon chose for the cycle of novels he began in the 1930s, might serve to sum up the era. Close ties to reality had characterized the novel from its beginnings, and, as Erich Auerbach has insisted, these ties were drawn tighter when Stendhal situated the life of his protagonist in the most concrete kind of contemporary history,[33] launching a trend continued by the other great nineteenth-century French realists. Of course, there have always existed "poetic" novels, where the links with reality have seemed more tenuous; there were symbolist novels and, despite the surrealists' professed aversion to the genre, even surrealist novels. In the 1930s, however, such novelistic fantasy became rare. A telling example of its fate is provided by Georges Limbour's surrealist novel, *La Pie voleuse*, which he began writing in 1936. The novel's first part, set in a Spanish seaside town, is composed of strange, magical characters and events. In the second part, written after the outbreak of the Spanish Civil War, Limbour uses similar surrealistic techniques to treat an extremely realistic subject matter, the fascist bombing of the town and the banding together of its inhabitants in mutual defense. Even the world of imagination found it hard to resist the encroachments of real events in this era.

With their new sensitivity to contemporary history, writers of the 1930s began consciously to use their fiction as a means of exploring the time in which they lived. They evidenced a desire to paint contemporary society reminiscent of Balzac and Zola, to whom they often pointed with approval. But their interest in contemporary events went beyond the portrayal of modern social types and the recording of large movements of social change. They quite characteristically included in their works direct reflections of specific historical phenomena, like the riots of February 1934, the effects of the economic crisis, the rise of fascism. Important contemporary events, of which the Spanish Civil War is certainly the outstanding example, were responsible for the immediate generation of literary texts, which appeared within a year or two of the event in question. Malraux's *L'Espoir*, for example, was written upon his return from Spain and published within a year, while the war was still in progress.

Aragon saw the abundance of historical events as a direct cause of a flourishing novelistic production: "(I consider, on the contrary) our era a flourishing one for the novel, and that is explained precisely by the extraordinary richness, the rapidity of the historical transformations of our society, which give the novelist an abundance of subjects, an almost unheard of stimulant for writing, which forces novels into being." [34] The fictional treatment of current events was a phenomenon that seemed to arise spontaneously. There were, however, those who explicitly advocated it. Drieu la Rochelle claimed as his major contribution to French literature his portrayal of the society in which he lived. [35] And the Association des Ecrivains et des Artistes Révolutionnaires, a broadly based writers' organization of the Left, made the treatment of contemporary issues an article of belief. In a manifesto of 1934, it declared, "The writer who, living in a time like our own, when one society is ending and another rising, finds a way of giving his artistic activity an object other than this formidable event is some sort of eunuch."[36]

It was Nizan, however, who, in his numerous critical writings became the most important theoretician of this literature of the present. He was all too aware of the difficulties presented by this effort to write about a rapidly changing world: "For a novelist grappling with the problems of the present, everything makes his task difficult—the confusion of events, the absence of clear definitions of human types, secrets still kept, ideas not made clear by their consequences, ignorance of the future."[37] But, he insisted, "you must take the greatest risk." He took heart from the example of Dostoevsky, another writer possessed by the "passion for the present," and he offered himself and other writers Dostoevsky's method: "Guess and . . . make mistakes."[38]

Of the vast literature that responded to these exhortations to explore contemporary reality in the 1930s, the work of at least ten novelists has endured to the present: Louis Aragon, Robert Brasillach, Louis-Ferdinand Céline, Eugène Dabit, Pierre Drieu la Rochelle, Louis Guilloux, André Malraux, Roger Martin du Gard, Jean-Paul Sartre, and, of course, Nizan himself. These writers will form the basis of this study. Some of these figures are better known than others: the works of Aragon, Malraux, Sartre, and, more recently, Céline have achieved the status of classics of the era. Martin du Gard's reputation has declined since the 1930s, but he remains the most admired of the creators of the *roman-fleuve*, and he has been the subject of sustained critical interest. The work of Nizan, despite the damage done to his literary reputation by his former colleagues in the Communist party, enjoyed a rebirth of critical interest in the 1960s, when it spoke directly to a new generation of young people. Guilloux's fiction also benefited from this climate of political activism. More recently, there has been a significant renewal of interest in the life and work of Drieu la Rochelle,[39] and Brasillach has become increasingly important as the martyred predecessor of a renascent European Right. The work of all these writers is still in print and continues to generate critical commentary. It may thus be said to have successfully answered Nizan's anguished question, "How to describe a changing world with a technique and strategies that might give the description of this change a possibility of lasting?"[40]

These ten writers were not by any means the only ones who treated contemporary reality in the 1930s. The list does not include Tristan Rémy, for example, who wrote an interesting account of the 1936 factory occupations, *La Grande Lutte.* And it has completely neglected Trilby, author of such timely series novels as *Bouboule et les Croix de feu* and *Bouboule et le Front populaire.* But most of these works no longer merit serious critical attention. On the other hand, as this study will attempt to show, the fact that a work of art is produced in direct response to a historical event does not condemn it to oblivion in advance. Susan Suleiman has commented on the way in which the term ideological novel (*roman à thèse*) has been commonly used in a derogatory sense.[41] The same might be said of works classified as "committed." Yet many historically inspired works form part of our literary and artistic heritage: an important example is furnished by Picasso's "Guernica," which he painted immediately after the bombing of the Basque capital.

There will be no attempt to assert that the ten writers selected form a "generation" in the traditional sense, a category under which many commentators have attempted to classify the historically conscious writers of the 1930s.[42] It may indeed be possible to use the term generation for the group of socially concerned British writers of the same historical period, as various critics have done.[43] These were men of similar age and social background who displayed a real commonality of culture and attitudes on important issues. But the ten French writers selected here show wide differences among themselves. In age, they range from Martin du Gard, a contemporary and close friend of Gide (thus born around 1880), to Sartre, Nizan and Brasillach, all born near the end of the century's first decade. In between these two extremes of youth and age are those who participated in World War I as young men—Drieu, Aragon, Dabit, and Céline—and an intervening generational group, Guilloux and Malraux, just too young to have taken part in the fighting.

These ten writers also represent widely divergent political attitudes. Aragon and Nizan were members of the Communist party, while Drieu and Brasillach were avowed fascists. Céline, too, eventually became identified with the Right, while the remaining writers in the group chose to ally themselves with various segments of the Left.

Many of them were involved in extraliterary political activities, a form of *engagement* Nizan saw as essential to the writing of political fiction. Political novelists, he asserted, like those who write of love, should benefit from direct experience: "The problem of the novelist today is perhaps to find an alternating rhythm of action and creation that would enable him to pass from involvement in politics to a narrative about politics."[44] Without specifically making *engagement* a requirement, most of the other writers on the list agreed on the need for uniting action and the intellect, a theme that was a particular favorite of Drieu and Malraux. All the left-wing writers in the group participated in the long series of antifascist meetings and manifestos that became more and more frequent as the decade progressed. In the course of their work for the Communist party, Aragon and Nizan edited literary journals, reported on current events, and wrote theoretical articles. In his native province of Brittany, Guilloux was responsible for much of the aid to unemployed workers and, later, refugees from the Spanish Civil War. Malraux was an active antifascist organizer before undertaking the direction of a squadron of foreign aviators for the Spanish Republicans. Even Dabit enrolled as a member of the activist Association des Ecrivains et des Artistes Révolutionnaires and spoke at its functions. On the Right, Drieu gave his support to the fascist Parti populaire français and wrote regularly for its newspaper *L'Emancipation Nationale*, while Brasillach gave talks for the profascist group clustered around the bookstore *Rive gauche* and wrote for the right-wing newspaper, *Je suis partout*. On the other hand, both Martin du Gard and Sartre attempted to resist political involvement, although their sympathies were not far distant from those of their actively involved left-wing friends. Céline, too, refused to participate in political groups, although he made his position clear in a series of antisemitic pamphlets.

Unlike the many British writers who had proceeded from well-known public schools through Oxford or Cambridge, their French contemporaries did not come from similar backgrounds nor did they share a common level of culture. Martin du Gard had always enjoyed an independent income, but the younger men were forced to support themselves through journalism or other professional activities, like Céline's medical practice or Sartre's teaching. Guilloux and Dabit were sons of the working class with limited formal education, while Sartre, Nizan and Brasillach were products of the prestigious Ecole Normale Supérieure. Céline and Aragon, both from families with limited financial means, had studied to be doctors rather than writers.

Nevertheless, all ten of these writers did share at least one common experience in their sensitivity to contemporary history. For those who had begun their careers in the 1920s or earlier, the awakening to history around 1930 had marked a change in direction. Aragon's dual conversion to Communism and the realistic novel has already been mentioned. Drieu la Rochelle, whose "decadent" novels of the 1920s had served to characterize the fate of an entire "lost" generation in France, began to incorporate into his fiction the themes that had already formed the center of his political essays. Even a member of the prewar generation like Roger Martin du Gard was forced by the pressure of historical events to effect a radical change in the direction of his Thibault series, begun in the 1920s, and to introduce the political preoccupations of the 1930s into the last two volumes. But such a preoccupation with history seemed natural to the others, who began their novelistic careers in the late 1920s and early 1930s, when the tide had already begun to change.

These writers were also united by their anguished experience of the postwar world, a community of experience that enabled them to see their own intellectual dilemmas and even their personal evolution in the work of a colleague. In the Paris of the 1930s, they read and commented upon each other's books and were conscious of their common concerns, which transcended the barriers of age, temperament, and political allegiance. Even the much older Martin du Gard served as a particular friend and mentor to younger writers, while the reclusive Céline, overtly hostile to the Parisian literary scene, found companionship in Dabit, a fellow painter of the poor districts of Paris. The political cleavage that characterized the decade eventually split these writers, like all French intellectuals, into separate groups of Left and Right. Those at the extreme ends of the political spectrum, especially Brasillach on the Right, had little direct contact with the others, but despite the political divisions, apparent ideological opposites like Drieu and Malraux, Céline and Dabit, often found they had much in common.

In studying the relationship of these ten writers to the historical phenomena of the 1930s, I will limit my attention to those works published in the course of the decade that treated current events and problems in Western Europe. The fiction many of these authors wrote about World War I would thus appear to lie outside the scope of the study. This is not really the case, however: for the writers in question, re-creating the atmosphere of World War I becomes a way of examining the reality of their own time. A similar phenomenon occurs with Sartre's novella, "L'Enfance d'un chef," where a story ostensibly set in 1924–25 is designed to reproduce events of 1936.

The limitation of this study to works of a single decade would appear to be somewhat arbitrary, since, in general, reality has a way of overflowing the artificial divisions established by decades or even centuries. In the case of the 1930s, however, we are dealing with a period that, in terms of both political and intellectual history, is clearly distinguishable from that which preceded and that which followed. As I have pointed out, major historians and literary critics are in agreement that the year 1930 marked the beginning of a new era. And there is even less disagreement on the moment when this era came to an end: along with the Third Republic and the familiar world of most French citizens, it collapsed under the advance of German Panzer divisions in May of 1940.

The object of this study of an admittedly limited number of works—which, however, include many of the finest and most enduring productions of the decade—is not to obtain a sort of "writer's eye view" of history. It is true that eminent historians have quoted Malraux on the Spanish Civil War or Drieu on the February riots, as sources illuminating this history from a special angle. But there already exist many excellent histories of the 1930s that, in fact, take into account this personal perspective in their use of memoirs and diaries as well as fiction. And fiction itself does not provide an adequate historical record of an era: relatively little fiction, for example, deals with the disillusioning experience of the Popular Front, and it was not until 1948, with the publication of Sartre's *Le Sursis*, that a major French novel was written about the crucial period of the 1938 Munich agreement.

Nor will an attempt be made to arrive at a sociological overview of the period, although I find myself in sympathy with Lucien Goldmann's hope that the study of particular literary works might lead to an understanding of the structures of the intellectual life of the period and its relationship to the structures of the economic, social, and political life of Western Europe.[45] While the results of this study may point to some common elements in the work of the writers under consideration and thus contribute to a sociological understanding, such is not its primary object.

Rather, the analyses of individual novels or stories will tend to illuminate the ways in which these writers of the 1930s attempted to make artistic sense of the historical chaos of their decade. These writers are not known primarily as the originators of new techniques. With a few exceptions—Céline's invention of a new literary idiom based on popular speech, Sartre's creation of a metaphysical realism—they relied primarily upon literary tools forged by their immediate predecessors, Gide and Proust, or, to a lesser extent, Barrès and Romains. They also consciously sought new inspiration in the tradition of French realism—Stendhal, Balzac, Flaubert and Zola—as well as in the work of the great nineteenth-century Russian novelists, Dostoevsky and Tolstoy, whose subjects were close to their own preoccupations. Under the pressure of events, the writers of the 1930s were forced to adapt these techniques to the portrayal of a rapidly changing historical reality. In depicting such a reality in ordered fictional form, they were attempting to explore its meaning, a meaning often obscured in the undifferentiated onslaught of events in the newspapers. Fiction in such a situation became, as Nizan conceived it, an exploration, one designed to help both writer and reader achieve some understanding of the present and of themselves: "The true function of the reader is to want to learn to live, thus to consider the novel, literature in general, . . . as an instrument of knowledge."[46]

CHAPTER 2

Writing About War Between Two Wars

La guerre n'est pas un contraire, ni un moment, mais une suite. . . .
je ne crois pas aux 'circonstances,' sauf, pourtant, qu'elles m'ont per-
mis de comprendre plus tôt un monde qui, sans elles, me serait encore
resté longtemps caché. [a]

LOUIS GUILLOUX,
Dossier confidentiel

In the early 1930s many writers began to develop a consciousness of living in a period "between two wars." Hitler's rise to power and subsequent German rearmament gave substance to a threat of renewed war that hovered over the entire decade and, more than any other political or social development, gave it its tone. Not unexpectedly, the theme of war is a major one in the literature of the 1930s, and the war that appears most often in the fiction of the period is World War I. The Great War had left its mark on French writers, many of whom had been combatants. Of the ten writers in this study, five (Céline, Drieu la Rochelle, Martin du Gard, Aragon, and Dabit) were old enough to have had direct experience with the front.

Even those too young to be veterans recognized that the war had initiated a new historical reality. Attempting to define his concept of the present era, Nizan saw it as beginning with the Great War: "It is very difficult for writers of the present generation not to consider, for example, the prewar years as a historical era. . . . For them, the present begins in 1918." [1] Most writers saw World War I as the point of departure for the era in which they were living, and it is therefore

---

[a] War is not a contrary nor an episode, but a continuation . . . . I do not believe in "circumstances," except as they allowed me to gain an earlier understanding of a world that, in their absence, would have long remained hidden from me.

not surprising that so many of them found it necessary to come to terms with the war in their fiction.

The entire period of *l'entre-deux-guerres* saw a substantial output of war literature, as Maurice Rieuneau has so thoroughly documented.[2] The type of war literature produced in the 1930s is, however, strikingly different from that of the previous decade. The immediate postwar period and even the war years themselves had witnessed the publication of a long stream of works that were often little more than fictionalized memoirs. These examples of *témoignage* were closely related in both form and content, and many of their characteristic features were to have important consequences for French fiction in general. Most of these works, for example, adopted the limited perspective of a single soldier or that of a small combat group. This narrative strategy might seem somewhat surprising, in view of the fact that World War I, in contrast to previous wars, was a mass phenomenon. The nations involved could call upon the resources of broad-based conscription to put into uniform the large numbers of men necessary to maintain the long battlefronts. Masses of infantrymen were also needed for the large-scale attacks against murderous new weapons like the machine gun, which produced massive casualties.

It was precisely the unprecedented scale of the combat that produced an impression of chaos and confusion among the participants. It is not at all certain that even the French General Staff was able to comprehend the events on the battlefield at any given moment, and from the perspective of the average infantryman in his trench, blinded and deafened by shelling, things were sheer chaos. Having experienced this reality, the combatants were almost unanimously disgusted by the old-fashioned rhetoric of individual heroism that was still being used to describe the war to civilians, usually by writers too old to fight themselves. Many of the early war novels depict soldiers on leave from the front who are literally struck dumb by the civilians' false concept of the experience. Such scenes are echoed in the work of Céline, Guilloux, and Drieu. The primary effort of the early war novelists, then, was simply to communicate to those who had not experienced it the reality of combat in this new type of war and to present it as they themselves had known it, not from the panoramic perspective of a general but from the point of view of the man in the trenches.

This effort had a number of important stylistic implications. It obviously encouraged the use of a limited narrative perspective. The abandonment of the omniscient narrator was, of course, already a characteristic of twentieth-century literature, reflecting the new century's diminished confidence in human ability to understand an increasingly complex universe. The war was an extreme form of this incomprehensible modern world, and it drove even novice writers, unaware of literary trends, to adopt the limited perspective. René Pomeau has suggested that these combat narratives themselves played an important role in reinforcing the predilection of the modern novel for subjective narration.[3]

The early war novels also tended to take as their protagonist a common soldier or a typical infantry group, since, in this war of the masses, only generals and perhaps the privileged aviators did not share in the common experience. This tendency to view reality from the perspective of the humble infantryman, oppressed both by the indifference of his commanders and the violence of enemy weapons, helped focus literary attention on the peacetime existence of the same "common man," who becomes an important figure in the socially oriented fiction of the 1930s (see Chapter 3).

As a reaction against the outmoded and artificial rhetoric that sought to describe the war in heroic images and meaningless abstractions, the combat novelists emphasized the unpleasant physical realities of mud and blood, disease and death, introducing a vision quite different from the elegant world of Proust and Gide. In addition, these realities were often referred to not in the academic language of established literary prose but in the obscene slang adopted by the men in the trenches. The acceptance of this language in the domain of the war novel paved the way for many subsequent experiments with popular speech, most notably those of Céline.

Because of their mistrust of the writers who had attempted to describe the war without knowing what it was like, the early war novelists implicitly advocated a realism based on "lived experience" ("expérience vécue"). This concept was carried over to the fiction of the 1930s, which, in theory and practice, valued close adherence to the writer's first-hand knowledge. Certain novelists, like Nizan, advised writers to participate in the events they wished to describe. Much of the fiction of the 1930s was based on the authors' journalistic activity. Historical reconstructions, like those of Aragon and

Martin du Gard, were thoroughly documented and, in addition, animated by the writers' knowledge of their own time.

The war novels of *témoignage* tended almost uniformly to stress the horror of the combat experience. A work like Roland Dorgelès's *Les Croix de bois*, one of the best-known of its genre, does not move beyond this perspective. Other combat novels, however, are clearly intended to persuade the reader of the writer's ideological point of view, ranging from revolutionary pacifism in the case of Henri Barbusse's *Le Feu* to the glorification of war in Philippe Barrès's *La Guerre à vingt ans* or Henry de Montherlant's *La Relève du matin*. These works are thus not exempt from moral or even social concerns, but they are centered upon the combat experience itself, and they attempt, above all, to communicate this experience to the reader.

While such personal accounts of combat continued to be published in the 1930s, the major war fiction of the decade is of a radically different sort. Life in the trenches, which had formed the setting for most of the *témoignages*, is pushed into the background or driven entirely out of the novel. The war is the primary subject of the three novels of Aragon's cycle *Le Monde réel*—*Les Cloches de Bâle*, *Les Beaux Quartiers*, and *Les Voyageurs de l'impériale*—but these novels are not set in the war years themselves. Only in the last pages of the third volume of the series, pages written after the declaration of war against Germany in 1939, is the reader introduced to the outbreak of hostilities. Similarly, Martin du Gard's *L'Eté 1914* focuses on the period immediately preceding the mobilization, and a glimpse of combat appears only in the last chapters. Guilloux's *Le Sang noir*, which does take place during the wartime period, is set in a small Breton town well away from the front lines. Even Céline's *Voyage au bout de la nuit*, which describes the experience of a soldier, devotes only 145 of the 632 pages in the Folio edition to the topic. And Drieu, in *La Comédie de Charleroi*, gives as much attention to the postwar setting of the story as to the battle itself. Clearly, all these writers have other interests in mind.

In all these works, the analysis moves beyond the events on the battlefield to consider the entire society, sometimes even the universal human condition, of which the war is only the visible expression. Pomeau was among the first to record the war novel's shift in emphasis: "After 1930 the accusation against the war is aimed beyond the war itself. . . . It entails the indictment as bearers of endemic plague either of the civilization, or of the society, or of man himself."[4] Rieuneau's exhaustive analysis echoes and supports Pomeau's judgment.[5] There continues to be in these works an important pacifist tendency, expressed most clearly in Jean Giono's 1931 novel, *Le Grand Troupeau*, where the horror of war is set against the creative forces of a peaceful agricultural community. There is also, as Rieuneau points out, a growing historical consciousness, a desire to understand the horror of the trenches in its widest possible historical context.

' The most complete of these historical studies of the war is Jules Romains's novelistic cycle, *Les Hommes de bonne volonté*, whose 27 volumes treat the period from 1908 to 1933. Romains had conceived the series in the 1920s as an application of his unanimist techniques to large social masses. The volumes published during the 1930s, however—the best-known of which are the two centering on the battle of Verdun—do not attempt to deal with issues of the postwar period. The rest of the series was published after the beginning of World War II, when the problems of working out postwar peace were no longer particularly relevant, and when Romains's original historical vision had been seriously challenged by subsequent events.

To a much greater extent than *Les Hommes de bonne volonté*, many war novels of the 1930s are directly related to events of the time in which they were written. In these novels, the violence of the war is seen as a symptom of the destructive forces concealed within society itself, which is not only that of 1914 but that of the postwar period as well. For these novelists, consideration of the Great War is essentially a means of approaching the problems of their own era. Guilloux and Céline both connect the destructive effects of the war to the oppressive institutions of civilian society, institutions that, in their view, produced the war and nevertheless continue to exist virtually unchanged at the time they write their novels. For Drieu la Rochelle, the war both prefigures the failings of the postwar world and provides a moment of authentic existence against which the extent of postwar social decadence can be measured. Writing later in the decade, both Aragon and Martin du Gard, in their analyses of the events leading to the outbreak of war, are intensely conscious of the possibility of a second war with Germany. Aragon points up specific parallels between historical phenomena of the prewar years and more recent events, while Martin du Gard uses the summer of 1914 as a setting for his meditations of the late 1930s on war and peace, political isolation and commitment. These novels of World War I are thus not primarily historical studies at all but expressions of the desire, widely felt in the 1930s, to use fiction as a means of understanding contemporary events.

All these authors tend to portray the world of their fiction as that of a dying social order. While Céline characteristically sees little hope of change, Guilloux and Drieu yearn for a renewal of this outmoded order through the forces of youthful rebellion, thus participating in the political outlook that certain commentators have called the "spirit of 1930" (see Chapter 4). Yet these two writers, like Céline, focus their attention primarily on the world they would reject, and their hopes for social renewal are only vague dreams, if not frustrated altogether. The inability of their fictional youth to change a world dominated by a hypocritically self-serving older generation reflects a widespread frustration in France at the beginning of the 1930s. Many attributed the stagnation of political life to the fact that the generation of men lost in the war was not available to enter into and renew the sources of political and social power, as they would normally have done. All the war fiction of the 1930s I have examined reflects a feeling of existence between two social orders, two worlds,"one dead, the other powerless to be born."[6]

There is a clear inability on the part of these writers to portray the regenerated society for which they yearn. Aragon attempts to provide a vision of life in a world reborn in the short concluding section of *Les Cloches de Bâle*, but he gives us a lyrical vision of a woman rather than a concrete picture of society. Aragon's second volume, reflecting the emergence of the Popular Front in 1936, places greater hope in the growing political consciousness of the French proletariat, an optimism that gives way to a renewed attack on moribund bourgeois individualism as immediate political hopes fade. Martin du Gard, writing in the second half of the decade, also links the cause of peace with hopes for social justice. But by this time, he can only treat both aspirations with heavy irony, born of his knowledge of the past and his tragic understanding of the present.

Voyage au bout de la nuit

Voyage au bout de la nuit (1932)[7] opens with the protagonist's war experiences, which in many ways mirror Céline's own. This first section, taken by itself, could easily be classified among the novels of *témoignage* that had emerged from the war and appeared in quantity during the 1920s. Céline's denunciation of war was an important factor in gaining his first novel one of its earliest favorable reviews, in the pages of Henri Barbusse's *Monde*, a left-wing journal of pacifist sympathies. Barbusse's own war novel, *Le Feu*, had long been for the French the great classic of pacifist protest, and Céline himself saw Barbusse as a predecessor.[8] *Voyage au bout de la nuit* does make use of many of the conventions of novels of the Great War, but Céline uses them to effect radically different ends.

The combat experiences in *Voyage* are much like those of the author and thus possess the ring of *expérience vécue*. Céline had volunteered for the cavalry in 1912 and saw action in Flanders as soon as the war broke out. Like his protagonist, Bardamu, he was wounded, cited for bravery, and invalided out because of his wounds. Bardamu is, however, not wholly to be identified with the young Céline; his creator seems to take pleasure in denigrating through Bardamu his own proven heroism. Bardamu's own heroic act and concomitant wound are never described. Instead, he is shown cowering behind trees and even seeking to be taken prisoner in order to escape further combat duty. When a wound finally does get him away from the front, he stages a complete mental breakdown in order to avoid being sent back. *Voyage* thus describes the war not as Céline himself had lived it, but as he saw it from the vantage point of the 1930s.

In the novel, the experiences are placed within the structure already established by such classic World War I novels as *Le Feu* and *Les Croix de bois*: the protagonist loses his innocence under fire, witnesses the bloody and horrifying deaths of officers and comrades, participates in the nighttime drudgery of supply details, undertakes a solitary scouting mission near enemy lines, is wounded and finally evacuated to a hospital in the rear. Indeed, the episodic nature of *Voyage* may owe as much to the combat novel as it does to the picaresque tradition to whose influence it is often attributed;[9] the novels of the Great War commonly relate a series of different episodes joined together only by the presence of the war in its various manifestations and, generally, by the constant presence of a narrator.

The language of the trenches, used in the combat novel to discuss the everyday realities of putrefying corpses, bodily disorders, and defecation, is not dissimilar in vocabulary and subject matter to the literary language created by Céline.[10] The acceptance of this slang within the genre of the combat novel must certainly have paved the way for Céline's more radical use of the popular idiom. Of course, his predecessors in the use of popular urban slang also include Zola. But in Zola's works, the language appears as the mark of a group that is observed as a curious sociological phenomenon. In the combat novel, even when it is not adopted by the soldier-narrator, the language is the idiom of a group with whom the narrator identifies and for which he speaks. From here it is only a short step to the more pervasive use of slang to be found in *Voyage*, where Céline incorporates it into the voice of the narrator himself.

Céline's use of the vocabulary of *argot* is, as has been pointed out, statistically much less important than a first impression would suggest.[11] Particularly striking is Céline's use of the syntax of popular speech, especially the *rappel* (for example, "j'aurais bien voulu le voir ici moi, le Déroulède" [b] [p. 23]), so well analyzed by Leo Spitzer and more recently by Julia Kristeva.[12] This creation of popular speech, however, often gives way to passages of great lyric beauty in quite conventional poetic language.[13] Nevertheless, it was Céline's irreverent use of language that so shocked his contemporaries and, in all probability, accounted for the unwillingness of the Goncourt jury to award him the prize he richly deserved.[14]

The shock value of the language he had chosen to adopt came as no surprise to Céline, who later told an interviewer he preferred this idiom because it was a language born specifically from a need to express a denunciation of the accepted social order: "It's hatred that makes slang. Slang is created to express the real feelings of poverty. . . . Slang exists to allow the worker to tell his boss he detests him: you are living well and I'm not, you exploit me and drive around in a big car, I'm going to do you in."[15] Many of the words drawn from popular speech that Céline repeats to the point where their repetition becomes thematic are words of vituperation and insult, particularly the often reiterated "la vache" (as in "Faut être à peu près seul devant elle [la guerre] comme je l'étais à ce moment-là pour bien la voir la vache" [p. 25] [c]).[16]

When not used as a direct insult, slang often serves to denigrate the thing to which it refers; thus it contributes powerfully to the vision of the world Céline is trying to convey. Even the use of the most common slang terms—*bouffer* for *manger*, *baiser* for *faire l'amour*,

---

[b] I myself would have liked to see him here, Déroulède (translation mine).
[c] You've got to be pretty much alone with her [war] as I was then to get a good look at her, the slut (p. 10).

crever for *mourir, trimarder* for *travailler*—drains these basic human activities of eating, sex, dying, and work of any dignity they might have. As the war itself has done, Céline's language tends to reduce humanity to the status of "meat" ("viande") or of "guts" ("tripes"); Bardamu continually claims that his major interest is to "save my guts" ("sauver mes tripes"). The opening passage of *Voyage*, which serves to present the themes of the novel as a whole, makes effective use of Celinian slang to deflate a number of sacred cows of French culture. The ideal of "la race française" emerges as "ce grand ramassis de miteux dans mon genre" (p. 16),[d] and "nos pères" are described as "violés, volés, étripés et couillons toujours" (p. 16).[e] Céline's slang expresses his distrust of the abstract ideals of the dominant culture, an attitude he shared with many writers of this disabused postwar period, and serves as the appropriate medium to communicate his vision of a blackened[17] and debased world.

It is not merely the constant use of slang that renders it so effective as a weapon for deflating the accepted ideals, but Céline's carefully orchestrated counterpoint of *argot* and conventional language. As Yves de la Quérière points out, a slang term is often used in unexpected juxtaposition with a thing held in some respect by the reigning culture. For example, a slang term may be used in combination with a rare grammatical form, like the imperfect subjunctive: "bien que nous *fussions* occupés à battre en retraite depuis plus d'un mois, il *engueulait* tout le monde quand même" (p. 35, italics mine).[f] Here it serves to deflate the pomposity of the academic discourse. Or it may be juxtaposed to a word signifying something commonly viewed with respect, as when the mayor of Noirceur attempts to persuade Bardamu and Robinson that their "devoir était bien de foutre le camp" (p. 64).[g] [18]

Much of the specific slang vocabulary used by Céline is connected with bodily functions: words such as *merde, pisser, chier, dégueuler* ("shit," "piss," "throw up"), all in their multiple grammatical variations, occur again and again. Use of such terms is not wholly unexpected in the war section, because such physical realities had as-

---

[d] a collection of riffraff like me (p. 4)
[e] raped and robbed, mangled and witless (p. 4)
[f] even when we'd been busy retreating for more than a month, he'd chew everybody out (p. 17)
[g] duty was to get the hell out (translation mine)

sumed great importance for the men in the Great War and had been discussed in the war fiction. But Céline's use of this vocabulary is not incidental nor is it confined to the war section of the novel. References to defecation, for example, become even more important in the passage set in New York, where Céline indulges in a long description of the underground camaraderie of the clients of a public restroom (or "fecal cavern") and, especially, in the sections set in Paris, where multiple references to defecation and urination crowd the opening descriptive passage: "Mais quand on connait depuis vingt ans la cabine téléphonique du bistrot, par exemple, si sale qu'on la prend toujours pour les *chiottes*, l'envie vous passe de plaisanter avec les choses sérieuses et avec Rancy en particulier. On se rend alors compte où qu'on vous a mis. Les maisons vous possèdent, toutes *pisseuses* qu'elles sont. . . . Un rebut de bâtisses tenues par des *gadoues* noires au sol . . . . Au bout du tramway voici le pont poisseux qui se lance au dessus de la Seine, ce gros *égout* qui montre tout. Au long des berges, le dimanche et la nuit les gens grimpent sur les tas pour faire *pipi*" (pp. 304–5, italics mine).[h]

The imagery of bodily function, often expressed in slang terminology, must be connected with a larger category of images of putrefaction and viscosity, which Julia Kristeva has analyzed, with particular reference to Céline, as participating in the phenomenon of abjection.[19] Such imagery emerges naturally from the mud and *merde* of the war. Bardamu meets with this viscous vision as he is initiated into the nature of modern warfare by witnessing the deaths of his colonel and a messenger. The blood of the decapitated messenger resembles simmering jam: "du sang dedans qui mijotait en glouglous comme de la confiture dans la marmite" (p. 29).[i] And, of course, both bodies are immediately reduced to the status of bloody *viandes*. Later, in the hospital Bardamu's neighbor Princhard provides him with a graphic vision of the continuation of this process, the reality behind the myth of a noble wartime death: "A trois pieds

---

[h] But when you've known the telephone booth of the corner café for twenty years, so filthy you always mistake it for the *crapper*, you lose all desire to joke about serious things and about Rancy in particular. Then you realize where they've put you. These houses are your prisons, *pissy* within. . . . Cast-off buildings bogged down in black *muck*. . . . There at the end of the streetcar line a grimy bridge spans the Seine, that enormous *sewer* which displays everything that's in it. Along the banks, on Sunday and at night, men climb up on piles of garbage to *take a leak* (p. 205).

[i] with blood in it bubbling and glugging like jam in a kettle (p. 12)

dessous, moi papa, ruisselant d'asticots et bien plus infect qu'un kilo d'étrons du 14 juillet, pourrira fantastiquement de toute sa viande déchue" (p. 91).[j]
This process of dissolution of human flesh continues to function thematically in the novel. Even the *glouglou* of the sticky, viscous blood recurs in the Parisian abortion to which Dr. Bardamu is later called.[20] It is most prevalent, however, in the African section, where the climate seems literally to dissolve the unresisting Europeans, destroying whole armies, as in the war: "Sous le climat de Fort-Gono, les cadres européens fondaient pire que du beurre. Un bataillon y devenait comme un morceau de sucre dans du café, plus on le regardait, moins on en voyait" (p. 189).[k] The women melt away in interminable menstruation, the children are drained by diarrhea, and the men are eaten away by a variety of tropical diseases. Even the constructions of the Europeans are dissolved by the climate: Tandernot's roads are consumed by the encroaching vegetation, and Grappa's dock is eaten away by mollusks so quickly that it must be rebuilt for the arrival of each monthly supply ship. Even Bardamu's hut is slowly devoured by insects and melted away by the rains. Such dissolution of humanity in a hostile environment may be a physical feature of the war and even of the tropical colonies, but when this process continues even in the rancid Parisian suburb of Rancy, it is clear that Céline is pointing to a deeper psychological and spiritual reality.

It is quite possible that Sartre, who makes heavy use of viscous imagery in his fiction of the 1930s, was influenced by Céline, whose work he received with great interest.[21] The threat of dissolution Céline finds in the viscous is indeed part of Sartre's understanding of it. The analysis of the particular qualities of the viscous in *L'Etre et le néant* illuminates both Sartre's own use of it and Céline's. Sartre sees the viscous as a halfway state between the inert solidity of Being In-Itself and the fluid freedom of the For-Itself. But in this ambiguous state it represents a trap, threatening to engulf the For-Itself, dissolv-

---

[j]while three feet under papa, that's me, dripping with worms and infinitely more disgusting than ten pounds of turds on the Fourteenth of July, will be rotting stupendously with all my deluded flesh (p. 56)
[k]In the climate of Fort-Gono the European cadres melted faster than butter. A battalion was like a lump of sugar in your coffee; the longer you looked, the less you saw (p. 123).

ing it into slime: "I suddenly understand the snare of the slimy: it is a fluidity which holds me and which compromises me."[22]

Of 632 pages in the Folio edition of *Voyage*, only 45 are directly concerned with Bardamu's combat experience, and a total of 145 encompass his entire contact with the military, including the long convalescence. These statistics alone make it clear that *Voyage* is not merely a war novel. The war is for Bardamu—as it was for Céline—a revelation of certain realities of life in society. Céline has confessed: "It's in the war that I first had the feeling of revolt. . . . That's where I understood. I said to myself, 'It's no good any more.'"[23] As is the case with the language and imagery, the situations that Bardamu first encounters in the war are repeated in the novel's subsequent sections until they become emblematic of life itself.[24]

The narration of Bardamu's war experience opens with a naive but nervous Bardamu receiving orders from his colonel in the middle of a road under a hail of German bullets. He manages to take shelter behind a tree, but the colonel continues to pace back and forth unperturbed, as the Germans switch from rifles to machine guns. The introduction of heavy artillery, however, proves too much for the noble tradition of military heroism: a shell reduces it to a bloody pulp. In addition to rendering the increasing mechanization of the war, this episode presents for the first time an experience that will come to symbolize Bardamu's situation in both war and peace: he is characteristically a target for an inexplicably hostile world.

The full significance of this situation bursts upon Bardamu much later when he is on leave in Paris recovering from his wounds. Wandering through the parc de Saint-Cloud with his American girlfriend, he comes upon a carnival shooting gallery, aptly named *Le Stand des Nations*. This shooting gallery reappears at two other significant moments in the novel—shortly before Bardamu discovers his friend Robinson's abortive attempt to assassinate an old woman and again just prior to Robinson's own murder at the hands of his rejected fiancée. It offers as targets a bride and groom complete with wedding party, standing in front of a city hall, whose windows open to provide additional targets, and a regiment of soldiers. It thus embodies the principal institutions of society. When Bardamu first sees the booth, temporarily shut down because of the war, he realizes that the same people who had found their amusement there in peacetime are now off at a new kind of fair, fixing their sights on living targets like himself: "Et puis sur le régiment . . . sur moi on tirait" (p. 80). Shortly afterward, entering a restaurant with Lola, he suddenly sees that all the people there have become targets in the great shooting gallery of the war: "Tous ces gens assis en rangs autour de nous me donnaient l'impression d'attendre eux aussi que des balles les assaillent de partout pendant qu'ils bouffaient . . . . partout un tir immense, dont on ne sortirait pas" (pp. 80–81).[1]

It is when he is fevered or delirious, as he is in this scene, that Bardamu's vision of reality is most penetrating. His intuitive awareness that society is a vast shooting gallery not only sums up his experience in the war but points ahead to the subsequent sections of the novel. In the various hospitals where he is placed for observation, Bardamu is surrounded by threats to his life, from the concierge who sleeps with the patients in order to betray their confidence, from the pretty nurses, who, like Lola, get their excitement from sending men off to die, and even from his fellow patients, whom he cannot dare to trust, although they share a common desire to save their skins. In Céline's world, unlike Malraux's, facing death together does not bring about a sense of solidarity. On the contrary, it seems to exacerbate the homicidal passions. This is equally true of the old men who share a wing of one of Bardamu's hospitals: "Ils ne se servaient de leurs ultimes et chevrotantes energies que pour se nuire encore un petit peu et se détruire dans ce qui leur restait de plaisir et de souffle" (p. 117).[m] Although the old men are unaffected by the war, the atmosphere of hostility among men facing death is the same in both wings of the hospital.

Bardamu is ultimately released from service, but he does not therefore cease to be a target. On the ship that carries him to the French African colonies, he unwittingly draws upon himself the hatred of the other passengers, which is fostered by the stifling hothouse of the ship. It is here that he comes to see that this situation is, in fact, a reality of daily life: "D'ailleurs, dans la vie courante, réfléchissons que cent individus au moins dans le cours d'une seule

---

[1]And they'd shot at the regiment . . . and now they were shooting at me (p. 48). . . . I got the idea that these people sitting in rows around us were waiting for bullets to be fired at them from all sides while they were eating. . . . There'd be shooting from every side, no one would escape (p. 49).

[m]They employed their last quavering energies in hurting each other a little more, in destroying what little pleasure and life they had left (p. 74).

journée bien ordinaire désirent votre pauvre mort, par exemple tous ceux que vous gênez, pressés dans la queue derrière vous au métro, tous ceux encore qui passent devant votre appartement et qui n'en ont pas, tous ceux qui voudraient que vous ayez achevé de faire pipi pour en faire autant, enfin, vos enfants et bien d'autres. C'est incessant. On s'y fait" (pp. 153–54)." As the passengers provoke a final confrontation, Bardamu can save himself only by the technique he has learned during his wartime convalescence: he hides his cowardice behind a screen of patriotic rhetoric, instantly producing a false feeling of solidarity.

Bardamu is even more subject to the hostility of his fellow men in the mythical African colony where he goes to escape the bloodshed of Europe. The world of la Brambola-Bragamance (based on the Cameroons, which Céline had visited on two occasions) contains obvious echoes of the war in the absurd spectacle of Alcide's black recruits conscientiously going through a pantomime of military drill without clothing or rifles. But the colony mirrors the European slaughter in more ways than this. As Céline constantly reminds us, it is itself a war, "la guerre en douce" (p. 167).ᵒ The Europeans are surrounded by hungry crocodiles, victimized by insidious tropical diseases, and attacked by the omnivorous African insects, which eat away at the houses and men and demolish entire piers in a single month (on the battlefield, Bardamu had compared German bullets to swarms of wasps; here the insects are compared to the wartime weapons). But even more lethal than the natural environment are the European whites, whose rapaciousness mercilessly exploits the black population before turning upon itself: "Et les hostilités particulières et collectives duraient interminables et saugrenues entre les militaires et l'administration, et puis entre cette dernière et les commerçants, et puis encore entre ceux-ci alliés temporaires contre ceux-là, et puis de tous contre le nègre et enfin des nègres entre eux. Ainsi, les rares énergies qui échappaient au paludisme, à la soif, au soleil, se consumaient en haines si mordantes, si insistantes, que

---

ⁿAnd besides, when you stop to think about it, at least a hundred people must want you dead in the course of an average day, the ones in line behind you at the ticket window in the Métro, the ones who look up at your apartment when they haven't got one themselves, the ones who wish you'd finish pissing and give them a chance, your children and a lot more. It happens all the time (p. 99).

ᵒa quiet war (p. 108)

beaucoup de colons finissaient par en crever sur place, empoisonnés d'eux-mêmes, comme des scorpions" (pp. 165–66).[p]

The scenes Bardamu witnesses in the colonies never fail to remind him of the war. In the shop of a merchant whom he observes cheating a native of the fruits of several months' labor, Bardamu is reminded of the wartime supply convoys. The flames of his burning hut in the jungle evoke the villages of the war, and the boastful little civil servants make him think of his old captain, Ortolan. When he goes deep into the jungle to take up the isolated post being vacated by his old wartime acquaintance Robinson, they spend a long time debating whether their present existence is better or worse than the war. Although Robinson assures Bardamu that the war was worse, he nevertheless deserts his post, as he had earlier sought to desert the army. There is a certain irony in the company director's proud insistence on the civilizing mission of the French, who have rescued the natives from a useless existence of hunting, fishing, and massacring each other. His vision of their cannibalism—"cent paniers de viande humaine bien saignante pour s'en foutre plein la lampe" (p. 185)[q]—reminds us of the much more abundant human meat that had resulted in Bardamu's vomiting on the Flanders battlefields. But civilized or not, men destroy each other; Céline, while showing sympathy for the victimized blacks, is far from subscribing to the myth of the noble savage.

In New York Bardamu is no longer surrounded by the overtly murderous forces of the previous two sections. Yet he feels America is even worse. It is indeed the absence of active hostility, illustrated by the absence of the vituperative French concierges, that he finds disconcerting. There are, as he had observed much earlier, two ways to die at the hands of your fellow men: "Il existe pour le pauvre en ce monde deux grandes manières de crever, soit par l'indifférence absolue de vos semblables en temps de paix, ou par la passion homicide

---

[p]The consequence was private and collective quarrels, preposterous and interminable, between the military and the administration, between the administration and the traders, between these two in temporary alliance and the military, between the whole lot of them and the black population, and finally between blacks and blacks. The little energy that hadn't been sapped by malaria, thirst, and the heat was consumed by hatred so fierce and deep seated that it wasn't uncommon for these colonials to drop dead on the spot, poisoned by themselves like scorpions (p. 107).

[q]more than a hundred baskets of bleeding human flesh to stuff their bellies with! (p. 120)

des mêmes en la guerre venue" (p. 109). [r] America provides for Bardamu a case study of death from indifference in the dehumanized world of a mass society. After wandering lost in the streets of New York, Bardamu finds himself working in the Ford factory, whose metallic noises recall those of combat. Having survived the destruction of the war and the decay of the tropics, he is on the point of succumbing to the inhuman indifference of a society dominated by the cold metal of gold and machines.

Although he is rescued from this fate by Molly, a Detroit prostitute who is a radiant source of human warmth, Bardamu decides to return to France, thus inaugurating the second major division of the novel. Back in Paris with his eyes now fully open, he loses no time in seeing that urban peacetime existence has all the symptoms of a continued war, with its oppressive nocturnal anguish and sudden outbursts of violence. As a doctor, he is allowed to penetrate to the hidden homicidal passions of families: the mother whose jealousy allows her attractive daughter to die from a failed abortion, the woman who schemes to assassinate her mother-in-law to save the cost of her board. As in the war, many of the victims of this violence are children. The little boy Bardamu had encountered in Flanders, who is shot by the Germans for no apparent reason, finds his counterpart in the various child-martyrs of Rancy, injured in the explosion of familial rather than military hatreds.

An increase in violence is signaled by the return of Robinson, who is not afraid to give full expression to the homicidal wishes that remain under some constraints in the case of other men. In his abortive attempt to accomplish the murder of old Mme Henrouille so desired by her greedy son and daughter-in-law, Robinson only succeeds in blinding himself in the premature explosion of a home-made bomb (his wounds are later passed off as having occurred in the war). This episode ultimately leads to two real deaths, that of old Mme Henrouille, who does not escape a second time, and that of Robinson himself, shot by his enraged fiancée. She kills him as they return home from a carnival in which a featured attraction has been the recurrent shooting gallery, which points up the continued relevance of Bardamu's original wartime vision.

[r] A poor man in this world can be done to death in two main ways, by the absolute indifference of his fellows in peacetime or by their homicidal mania when there's a war (p. 68).

Bardamu also develops in the war scenes his characteristic response to the shooting gallery experience, that of retreating quietly to a secure place. In the first scene, he is tempted to emerge from behind his tree in order to convince the colonel of the futility of the war. Had he done so, he too would have been pulverized by the shell. Returning to camp with the news of the colonel's death, Bardamu is rewarded for his initiative by being designated for supply duty, a task that subjects him to the nauseating sight of freshly butchered meat, only too reminiscent of what he has just seen on the battlefield. The lesson to be drawn from these experiences is obvious: it pays to remain as silent as possible[25] and to seek a safe retreat. Bardamu at first dreams of the relative tranquillity of a prison, and he and Robinson later seek unsuccessfully to be taken prisoner by the Germans.

Bardamu ultimately finds his long-sought shelter from the war not in a prison (as Princhard's case proves, even common criminals are being sent to the front) but in the hospital where he is placed after his mental breakdown. Finally released by the army medical authorities, Bardamu spends the rest of the novel seeking to regain this refuge.[26] In the stifling and deadly atmosphere of Africa, he again seeks the liberation of a feverish illness that would gain him entry to the hospital, "seul armistice à ma portée dans ce carnaval torride" (p. 188).[s] And, in the end, it is a severe attack of fever that brings about his escape to America. The same pattern repeats itself in the Paris section. As a doctor, Bardamu cares for tubercular patients who seek only to maintain their illness at a level sufficient to ensure their receiving a government pension, and Bardamu himself finally takes refuge as a doctor in a mental hospital, where he paradoxically feels less threatened by the insanity of those around him. He has lived out the truth of his wartime revelation, which is summed up by Robinson: "Parce que, tu vois, les hommes quand ils sont bien portants, y a pas à dire, ils vous font peur. . . . Surtout depuis la guerre. . . . Quand ils sont debout, ils pensent à vous tuer. . . . Tandis que quand ils sont malades, y a pas à dire, ils sont moins à craindre" (pp. 387–88).[t]

---

[s] the only happiness within my reach [in this torrid carnival] (p. 124)
[t] Because people with nothing wrong with them, you can't get around it, are frightening. . . . Especially since the war. . . . As long as they're up, they think about killing you . . . but when they're sick, no two ways, they're not as frightening (p. 264).

In the novel's second wartime passage, Bardamu serves as a liaison officer with the aptly named General des Entrayes, who cares greatly for the welfare of his own intestines but little for those of his men. As the general busies himself with ministering to his own material needs, Bardamu and his colleagues, as common soldiers, are sent out into the night to rejoin their own regiment. If they succeed in this almost hopeless venture, they are rewarded by spending the night laboring hopelessly under heavy sacks of provisions. If they do not reach the regiment, they wander aimlessly, waiting to be shot down by the French sentries if they manage to avoid the Germans. This is, in fact, the fate of Bardamu's companion, the little Breton Kersuzon, whose almost mute incomprehension of the wartime world is reflected in his characteristic comment, "c'est tout noir comme un cul" (p. 42).[u]

The repeated descriptions of men wandering lost in the night are typical of the novels of World War I,[27] where much activity seems to have indeed taken place under cover of darkness. In Céline's novel, however, these scenes lay the foundation for an understanding not only of the war but also of all Bardamu's subsequent wanderings. The night to whose end he journeys is one that he first experiences, in a literal and figurative sense, during the war and in which he continues to wander—against the background of African drums, in the dark and labyrinthine streets and corridors of New York, and through the empty boulevards of the Parisian suburbs. Allusions to blackness and night are frequent, and they become progressively detached from literal reality to become symbolic of life itself. One particularly long night metaphor, extending over two pages, occurs in Bardamu's description of the introduction of a priest into the already involved situation of the Henrouille episode. He envisions them all wandering together in the night, holding hands to keep from falling, passing back brief counsels or commands, much like the nighttime movements of troops in the trenches of the war novels: "Il apprendrait à marcher dans la nuit, le curé, comme nous, comme les autres. Il butait encore. . . . On arriverait au bout ensemble et alors on saurait ce qu'on était venu chercher dans l'aventure. La vie c'est ça, un bout de lumière qui finit dans la nuit" (p. 430).[v] In this image of human beings wandering in the night, Céline has taken a situation that had

---

[u] It's as black as an asshole (p. 21).

[v] The priest would have to learn to walk in the dark like the rest of us. He was still unsteady on his pins. . . . We'd get to the end together, and then we'd know what

become associated with the war and extended it to vast areas of peacetime reality, to life itself.

The war also reveals to Bardamu the exploitive nature of society, which had formed the content of the image introduced in the opening passage. There, Bardamu had prophetically envisioned society as a ship in which the people, as galley slaves, row frantically for the benefit of the rich men who stroll on the deck with their beautiful, perfumed women. Those below are allowed to emerge into the air only when they are sent to attack, for no apparent reason, an identical galley that represents an enemy country. This division of the world into exploiting rich and victimized poor corresponds to what Bardamu subsequently observes in his various adventures, and, from the first pages of the book, Céline makes it clear that it is intimately related to war. It was through the war that Céline himself, according to his own testimony, became aware of social injustice. Before, he claims to have accepted the social order without question, but the war caused him to see things more clearly: "What opened the eyes of even the stupidest ones were the profiteers. It was clear. The ones who didn't go off to war got rich. We were always the suckers."[28]

In Bardamu's war, the Germans are not the only enemies nor those most to be feared. The real threats to Bardamu's well-being in the war seem to come from the general, from the self-seeking mayor of the village of Noirceur-sur-la-Lys (whose name suggests it is a blot on the landscape), and from the materialistic civilians who gladly take time out from their mourning to provide Bardamu with exorbitantly priced wine. These contacts only foreshadow the cast of characters who await Bardamu in wartime Paris, an entire society that lives by exploiting the suffering of the victims at the front, from the meat-selling Argentinians, to the revealingly named Mme Herote, who runs a brothel out of the back room of her little shop, to the rich American Lola. Already among the privileged classes, Lola reaps no material profit from the war. She merely enjoys the opportunity to play a featured role in the chief entertainment of the era while using her job as a volunteer nurse to acquire a string of lovers. Yet she is the major target of Céline's ridicule. He lingers over the details of her mock-heroic contribution to the war effort: the improb-

---

we'd been looking for in our adventure. That's what life is, a bit of light that ends in darkness (p. 294).

able task of tasting the *beignets* made daily for the veterans' hospitals.[29] Lola's horrified reaction on gaining two kilos as a result and her distress at having missed the prewar elegance of the Longchamps racetrack forms an ironic contrast to the very real suffering of the men at the front. In making Lola the chief recipient of his invective about the war, Céline is, in fact, pointing to the forces that have profited from the war in the long run: the expanding American industrial economy that has thrived at the expense of a debilitated Europe. It was World War I that marked the emergence of the United States as the major world power, and American influence would, in the 1920s and 1930s, profoundly change the face of French life. In France during the war Lola is seen only as the most active of the forces that try to push Bardamu back to the front, but, in the section on America, Céline places her more clearly in the context of Wall Street bankers, who had more recently involved France in their downfall, and Detroit industrialists, originators of the production line. In making Lola the chief war profiteer, Céline is really indicting the increasing materialism and dehumanization of life in the modern capitalist society that postwar France was becoming.

Exploitation, as Bardamu soon discovers, is not unique to the wartime situation. The African colony offers a crude but clear caricature of the French social hierarchy, from the company director and governor to the white-collar employees right on down to the unclothed natives, mercilessly exploited by white tax collectors and merchants alike. Despite their dark skin and scanty clothing, Bardamu realizes, the natives are "en somme tout comme les pauvres de chez nous mais avec plus d'enfants encore et moins de linge sale et moins de vin rouge autour" (p. 186).[w]

In America Bardamu sees a social structure whose polarities are marked by the affluent New Yorkers and the physical misfits who are preferred as workers in the Ford plant. As Bardamu is told even before debarking in New York, "C'est tout millionnaire ou tout charogne: Y a pas de milieu" (p. 240).[x] This two-tiered society is, of course, still a feature of French life on Bardamu's return, but by now the have-nots are no longer the men at the front but the poor of La Garenne-Rancy, who are terrorized, like the fleeing rabbits of their

---

[w] Actually, they're just like our poor people, except they have more children, less dirty washing, and less red wine (p. 121).

[x] They're either millionaires or skunks! There's nothing in between! (p. 161)

place of residence, by the constant threat of unemployment brought on by "la crise."

Céline constantly relates these deep divisions within society to the wartime situation in which he first became aware of them. Society as a whole is in a constant state of warfare, the social divisions setting not only rich against poor but also the poor against each other in the struggle to survive. In fact, Céline speculates, war itself may simply be a device used by the powerful to release this hostility when its buildup begins to threaten them.

The language, imagery, and situations of the war segment form the basis of the larger vision of reality presented in *Voyage au bout de la nuit*. Bardamu's experiences in the war open his eyes to the truth of reality and shape his response to his subsequent encounters with life. Not surprisingly, Céline himself seems to have been indelibly marked by his war experience. On the eve of World War II, he confided to a departing soldier, "without Sergeant Destouches [Céline's real name and military rank], there would never have been Céline. You'll see, when you get back, you'll never be the the same again."[30] Indeed, Céline had come to feel that the war had brought with it an altered vision of human possibility, a radical pessimism that he expressed in the strange "Hommage à Zola"[31] he delivered at the writer's former home in Médon in October 1933, only a year after the publication of *Voyage*. Céline used this speech not to extol the merits of naturalism but to explain why a literature like Zola's was no longer possible in the hopeless world of modern man, "as we have understood it for the last twenty years"—that is, since the Great War. Changing times had brought with them a changed vision of the human soul: "We have learned strange things about souls since he left." The new vision of humanity that replaces Zola's relative optimism is centered on violence: Our civilization "seems caught up in an uncurable warrior psychosis. We live only for this sort of destructive repetitions." The Zola speech makes apparent Céline's feeling that World War I had inaugurated a new era of civilization, one characterized by increasing totalitarianism and continual warfare. Thus the structure of *Voyage au bout de la nuit*, which introduces the reader directly into the world of the war, and the preponderant importance in the novel of images drawn from the war are explained by the impact of the war on Céline's personal vision. World War I was an event that had shaped his own response to reality and, he felt, had radically altered this reality itself. Thus the novel he wrote about contemporary France begins with the war and uses it as a means of understanding the whole of modern life.

Le Sang noir

Le Sang noir[32] is a case somewhat unusual for this period, a war novel written by a noncombatant, since Guilloux had been too young to be called to the front. Nevertheless, in keeping with the tradition of eyewitness accounts, the novel is a reflection of his own wartime experiences, which took place far from the front lines in the Breton city of Saint-Brieuc. Here, as in all Guilloux's novels, his native city functions as a microcosm of French society.[33] A provincial town like thousands of others, it brings together the essential elements of French life and shows the impact made on such previously isolated areas by the events of the twentieth century. In *Le Sang noir* Saint-Brieuc is portrayed at a moment of crisis, perhaps the greatest crisis France had to face during the Great War. The events of the novel, like those of James Joyce's *Ulysses* and Virginia Woolf's *Mrs. Dalloway*, take place in a single day, and that day is set in November 1917.

Like many of his contemporaries, Guilloux chooses to depict World War I not in its triumphant moments but at a time of threatened collapse. In 1917, for the first time in the war, widespread mutinies occurred among the French frontline troops. In May and June soldiers spontaneously protested the purposeless slaughter that had resulted from General Nivelle's ill-conceived policy of repeated unsuccessful infantry attacks. The mutineers succeeded in getting Nivelle replaced by the more humane Pétain, but at a cost to themselves: a number of men were brought to trial and condemned, and 49 were finally executed.[34] Nineteen seventeen also saw the first serious wartime strikes by civilian workers, and in June, Annamite troops fired on striking women in Paris. Discontent on both the military and domestic fronts exacerbated the disorganization of the government. Cabinets fell in quick succession until, on November 13, President Poincaré was forced to call in his old enemy Clemenceau as the only man capable of restoring order.

The French were threatened from abroad, not only by the Germans but also by their Russian allies. The popular uprisings in Russia of February-March 1917 were based, like the French mutinies, on impatience with the interminable war and a desire to assert the dignity of the individual soldier against an often cruel and indifferent officer caste. The unrest led to the Bolshevik seizure of power (November 3–7) and, ultimately, to the Soviet Union's complete withdrawal from the war. As Guilloux commented in his *Carnets*, the year 1917 marked a point of change; it was "the last year of the nineteenth century, the first of the era of assassins."[35]

All these events are mirrored in Guilloux's provincial town; they are not merely reported but woven into the fabric of the novel. The slaughter in the trenches is rendered present in the wounded being cared for in a wing of the lycée, the men leaving for the front, the crippled and disfigured veterans, the grief-stricken mothers. A link between this town and the deaths at the front, the mayor is forever scurrying through the streets on his way to notify families of the war's latest victims. The death toll is so high that he is forced to grab meals on the run and, even then, cannot keep up to date.

The songs of the Soviet soldiers interned in the local camp are a constant reminder of their Revolution, and the characters' frequent allusions to the great nineteenth-century Russian authors suggest parallels between the two societies. *Le Sang noir* has been termed "the first novel of purely French texture that can be directly related to the works of the great Russian novelists,"[36] and Guilloux shows himself quite conscious of the Russian literary tradition. His protagonist, Cripure, constantly refers to his fellow citizens as "dead souls," and the reference to Gogol is an obvious one amid Guilloux's collection of grotesque characters. The influence of Tolstoy, important to Guilloux's earlier work, is evident here in the effort to present a panorama of wartime society, and there are touches of Dostoevsky, particularly in the portrayal of the divided, guilt-ridden Cripure, who possesses the Idiot's gift of penetrating each person's hidden source of anguish. The minor character of the Polish Jew Otto Kaminsky seems to have stepped from the pages of *The Possessed*, and indeed, Kaminsky, who has lived in St. Petersburg, is the one best able to point out the parallel between the moribund French society in which he finds himself and that of pre-Revolutionary Russia: "'Dans la ligne générale, dans le fond social, dans le psychologique, eh bien, nous sommes ici en pleine Russie impériale, mes chers amis. Votre petite bourgeoisie chrétienne, c'est la bourgeoisie de Tolstoi. Et vos paysans sont de vrais moujiks. Mais oui. Croyez-moi,' poursuivit-il, 'les plus beaux personnages, disons par exemple de Tchékov, je les ai retrouvés ici trait pour trait à un samovar près" (p. 353).[y]

The short-lived riot of returning soldiers at the railroad station (such riots did, in fact, occur in 1917) is the reflection in the limited world of the novel of both the Russian Revolution and the French army mutinies, related in their desire to reject a repressive, death-dealing social order in order to open new possibilities for human life. It is in the course of this riot that Cripure slaps Nabucet, the supreme incarnation of the reigning order of "bastards" ("salauds"), as Guilloux had labeled them even before Sartre's *La Nausée*. Revealing his profound sympathy with the rebellious soldiers, Cripure's slap, "an extraordinary, global slap," sums up in an act his years of intellectual condemnation of the rotting society in which he had, nevertheless, consented to lead his daily life. The initial rejection displayed in the slap leads almost inevitably to Cripure's suicide, his supreme refusal of his share in the universal corruption.

Nabucet, the recipient of the slap, is Guilloux's incarnation of the society that has given birth to the war. Neither a munitions maker nor an arbiter of economic power, Nabucet (Napoléon Poucet) is nevertheless a war profiteer, taking advantage of the disorder of the war to become the leader of local social and cultural life. Thoroughly espousing the reigning materialistic ideal of bourgeois security, he asserts in his speech that the soldiers are giving their lives so that future generations will be able to enjoy French culture in its material abundance. It is, therefore, fitting that he should act as host to the representatives of the major social forces—the school, the Church and the army—that gather to present the Legion of Honor to a local volunteer nurse, Mme Faurel.

There Nabucet's hypocrisy is displayed in all its splendor. Despite his praise of the heroic *poilus*, the reader has already seen his contempt for the real war-wounded, whom he does not deign to invite to the party. In contrast to his rhetorical tributes to the glory of French culture is his hatred of real intellect, as represented by Cripure, the only intellectual of any stature in this provincial lycée.

---

[y] "In a general way, socially and psychologically, we might be in the midst of imperial Russia, my good friends. Your little Christian bourgeoisie is Tolstoy's bourgeoisie. And your peasants are real moujiks. Yes, they are. Take my word for it," he continued, "the finest characters in Chekhov, let us say—well, I've found them right here, trait for trait, everything but the samovar" (p. 396).

Nabucet, more than any other character, embodies the hypocrisy that permeates the social order and alone permits it to maintain a hold on its victims. Mme Faurel is its perfect heroine: although she has allegedly cared for soldiers with typhoid, she has done little more than everyone else, and certainly much less than the crippled veterans. It is clear to all that she is receiving the award primarily because she is the wife of the local *député*. Even her appearance of youthful beauty is, like everything else about her, deceptive: "Son visage était rose comme celui d'une jeune fille: émaillé de frais. Elle paraissait trente ans à peine! Quelle joie éperdue dans ses yeux bleus, pâteux de khôl! Et ses cheveux blonds, son beau sourire trop rouge sur les dents fausses" (p. 252).[z]

It is this hypocrisy that, more than anything else, incites the rebellion of the young soldiers, to whom the experience of combat has revealed the truths behind the patriotic platitudes. Hypocrisy constitutes the major charge made against the lycée professors, who incite the young to volunteer for combat. This sentiment is expressed in the poem dashed off by the young bohemian lycée assistant, Francis Montfort, in whom Guilloux has offered a humorous portrait of himself:

> Vous m'avez trompé
> Menti
> Vestons
> Binocles
> Souliers vernis
> Chapeaux melons
> Qui le preniez de si haut!
> Montrez voir un peu votre âme immortelle?
> A présent
> Rien que le vent
> Qui tombe
> Sur cent mille cadavres.
> (p. 140)[a]

It is again hypocrisy that forms an element of Cripure's indictment of his world in a statement that Guilloux chose as the *bande* of the

---

[z]Her face was as rosy as that of a young girl: freshly enameled. She did not look a day over thirty! What a rapturous enthusiasm in her heavily penciled blue eyes! And her blond hair, her smiling lips, which were too red for her false teeth behind them (p. 280).

[a]You have deceived me / Lied / Coats / Eyeglasses / Polished shoes / Derby hats / With your high and mighty ways! / Let's have a little look / At that immortal soul of

original edition: "La vérité de cette vie, . . . ce n'est pas qu'on meurt, mais qu'on meurt volé" (p. 201).[b] Cripure's observation, like Montfort's poem, makes clear the real danger of hypocritical lip service to traditional social values that serve to mask the reality of death. It has taken the war to impress this truth on many people, and the first to learn are the young men who have gone off to the trenches. The truth is also brought home to their parents, as it is to the Marchandeaus when they hear of the impending death of their son Pierre, who is to be executed in the name of social order for his part in the army mutinies. Upon realizing his powerlessness to save his son, his father also realizes his own complicity in his son's death because of his failure to protest against this social order.

But the war is not the chief source of death in *Le Sang noir*. Of the various deaths in the novel, only one takes place on the front lines. The others occur as a direct result of the normal course of life in this society. This is indicated by the "black blood" of the title, which, as Guilloux has explained, refers to the oxygenless blood of those who are slowly asphyxiated.[37] Thus Guilloux emphasizes the theme of asphyxiation used as an image of societal oppression by other authors of the period, such as Céline, Nizan, and Malraux. The two characters who best embody the perspective of the younger generation, Lucien Bourcier and Simone Point, have come to understand this process of repression. Simone runs off to Paris with Kaminsky in order to escape the certainty of a bourgeois marriage typified by her parents, a future she knows will destroy her: "Car ils savaient très bien assassiner et ils n'avaient besoin pour cela ni du couteau ni du poison: leurs moyens étaient plus subtils" (p. 180).[c] Lucien, returning from combat, is able to see equally destructive forces in his home life. The war had only speeded up a process of repression that had been operating throughout his life: "La vérité, c'est qu'il avait été comme tous les enfants, un enfant écrasé, puis un jeune homme et un homme écrasés, à qui on avait commencé de voler la vie en détail avant de tenter le grand coup de la lui voler en bloc" (p. 104).[d]

---

yours? / Now / There is only the wind / That blows / Over a hundred thousand corpses (p. 151).

[b]The truth in this life . . . is not that one dies but that they rob you before you die (p. 221).

[c]For they knew how to kill, you could be sure of that; they needed neither poison nor dagger; their methods were more subtle (p. 198).

[d]The truth was, he had been like all children, browbeaten, then a browbeaten

The death-dealing nature of the society described by Guilloux is summed up in the surrealistic vision that appears to Cripure as he approaches a church set in a square of typical bourgeois dwellings. In his eyes this ugly, squat little church suddenly takes on the qualities of an ox: "Deux courtes tours, nues et carrées, péremptoires comme deux commandements quelconques du décalogue, figuraient assez bien les cornes aveugles de la bête et, entre les tours, le porche bas—c'était pourtant bien un porche—ne pouvait signifier autre chose qu'un front immense, épais, carré, obscur, avec, au dessous, des piliers énormes, seules rondeurs dans cette carrière, ce qui évidemment étaient les pattes" (pp. 313–314).ᵉ Since he knows the church has been built on the site of a former cemetery, Cripure imagines that the dead, driven out by the Ox, have come to live in the surrounding houses. Associating the Ox with death, Cripure recognizes it as a symbol not only of the Church but of the entire society, which constantly attempts to deny life: "Non. Le boeuf disait toujours non. Le boeuf et toute sa charmante petite famille de préfectures et de casernes, de lycées et de banques, etc., le boeuf disait toujours non, jamais oui" (p. 135).ᶠ It thus embodies the multiple aspects of the society presented in the novel—a society that engenders murderous wars and, even in peacetime, makes love and happiness impossible.[38]

The Ox's chief victims in the course of Guilloux's eventful day are Mme de Villaplane, the owner of a small local boarding house, and Cripure himself. Mme de Villaplane, abandoned by her husband and alienated from her children by quarrels over the inheritance, has seen her charming boarder Kaminsky as her last hope of love—and life—and begs him to take her away from her empty existence. Her plight is similar to that of many other women in the novel, whose desire for love is frustrated by the loss of husband or child and who are left to live out their lives in lonely misery. These

---

young man and a man, whose life they had begun stealing piecemeal, before they made the final attempt to rob him of it in the bulk (p. lll).

ᵉA pair of abbreviated towers, square-hewed and barren, and peremptory as a couple of the Ten Commandments, could very well pass as the blunted horns of the beast; and that low portico there between the towers—for it was a portico, right enough—could not be anything other than an emormous, square, thick-set and somber forehead; while those great pillars down below, their roundness standing out against the squareness of the whole, were quite obviously the animals's legs (p. 353).

ᶠNo. The ox always said No. The ox and all his charming little family of prefectures and barracks, banks, schools, etc.—the ox always said No (p. 354).

women are summed up in the figure of the *bossue*, an old hunch-backed woman who wanders through the streets with her beloved little dog, singing arias from Carmen. In the square of "dead souls" she appears to Cripure as a singular source of life, "l'unique survi-vante d'une catastrophe" (p. 315).[9] But the *bossue*'s love is left with-out object, as is that of Mme de Villaplane, who, rejected by Ka-minsky, swallows a dose of poison.

It is by making love impossible that the Ox-dominated society most effectively stifles its victims. There is no happy couple in the novel: even the Marchandeaus, who seem to share deep mutual af-fection, are isolated from each other by the death of their son. Fam-ily life, as described in the Bourcier and Point households, is a fa-çade of social respectability that masks cruelty and indifference. Even communication is lacking in this alienating world. Social classes are driven apart: Mme Marchandeau, as wife of the *proviseur* at the lycée, is criticized for trying to cheer the legless son of the concierge; Cripure is unable to communicate with his illegitimate son Amédée, who has been raised by his chambermaid mother; Maia, Cripure's illiterate common-law wife, can speak easily with Amédée but, despite her deep affection for Cripure, cannot begin to give him the understanding he needs. Generations are also sepa-rated. Symbolically, parents with sons at the front receive no letters and find that the trains are not running when they try to go to see them. The young people experience again and again the impos-sibility of talking with their elders, even with Cripure, who at least shares their contempt for the social order. Lucien walks out on his family because of his inability to make them understand his refusal to wear his uniform; Etienne Couturier leaves for the front without the longed-for talk with his father; and Simone Point hurls insults at her parents in English, a language they do not understand. When the young try to speak the truth, the confrontation with the reigning hypocrisy can only result in violence: the young soldiers to whom Babinot tries to read his mediocre patriotic verse finally have to hit him to make him understand their rejection of his falsehoods, just as Cripure is driven to slap Nabucet.

The most tragic victim of this asphyxiating society is Cripure, the central character, who has been for many readers the book's most memorable feature (on meeting Guilloux in Russia, Boris Pasternak

---

[9] the sole survivor of a catastrophe (p. 354)

reproached him for letting Cripure die [39]). This many-faceted character was based on a real model, a philosophy professor in Guilloux's
lycée, Georges Palante.[40] Author of several well-known books on his
philosophy of individualism, Palante was, like Cripure in the novel,
a man of unusual intellectual stature for a small provincial lycée.
Also like Cripure, he suffered from a strange deformity, a hyper-
development of the extremities that resulted in grotesquely large
feet. Cripure's deformity, which causes him difficulty in walking, is
used in the novel to suggest his inability to function normally in the
world. Also like Cripure, Palante shot himself after the peaceful resolution of a projected duel with a rival philosopher.

But Guilloux has expanded the portrayal of Cripure beyond the
limits of the man Georges Palante, until he becomes, as Victor Brombert has termed him, "the Intellectual Hero,"[41] the embodiment of
the philosophy of this society. The deputy Faurel, a former pupil, describes him as "ce que notre civilisation peut donner de meilleur"
(p. 433).[h] Thus he is a figure much like Nizan's Professor Lange in *Le
Cheval de Troie*. Cripure's stature is further defined as Guilloux places
him in the context of his fellow philosophers: Socrates, because the
townspeople consider his caustic spirit subversive to youth; Rous-
seau, because of his persecution complex and inability to function in
society, as well as his illiterate mistress and abandoned offspring;
Nietzsche, because of his contempt for the herd; and Kant, because
his *Critique de la raison pure*, which Cripure is fond of citing, has
been perverted by the students to form his nickname. Providing
additional commentary is the fictional local philosopher Turnier,
based on the real Jules Lequier,[42] who had died mysteriously by
swimming out to sea after losing his true love. Cripure had written
his thesis (rejected, of course) on this enigmatic figure to give expression to his own feelings on losing Toinette, his first wife and only
real love. Like Sartre's Roquentin, Cripure becomes entangled in the
contradictory aspects of the subject of his biographical research.
Turnier, in this respect, too, provides an illuminating parallel to Cripure himself.

Cripure is a character so torn apart by internal conflicts that he
can only destroy himself. He is, as Guilloux has described his characters, in contradiction with himself and with life.[43] His lucidity
gives him tragic dignity: more than any other character, he is ca-

[h] all that is best is our civilization (p. 484)

pable of piercing through the façade of societal respectability to the anguish it attempts to conceal. But he is unable to move beyond universal condemnation to find a positive source of value. Thus he is rendered incapable of positive action and, in his daily life, ends up going along with the societal values he professes to despise (he is contemptuous of the houses around the Ox, for example, but reveals he is their proprietor; he hates patriotic rhetoric but has made patriotic speeches himself). As Trotsky had observed in his analysis of Céline's *Voyage au bout de la nuit*, a total pessimism paradoxically leads to acceptance of the status quo,[44] a judgment later echoed by Nizan (see Chapter 4).

The complexity of Cripure's characterization poses a real stylistic problem for Guilloux, who wants to use Cripure's disabused lucidity to expose the corruption of society but needs to move beyond this perspective, to place it at an ironic distance as itself a part of a collapsing world. A similar problem faced Flaubert in writing *Madame Bovary*, and he exercised an acknowledged influence on *Le Sang noir*. Flaubert's caricatures are clearly the ancestors of several of Guilloux's characters: the young professor Moka, who spends his free time pasting stamps on dinner plates, is compared to Binet and his lathe, and both Babinot, with his military mania, and Nabucet, with his vicious social climbing, are clearly descended from Homais. But Flaubert's great contribution to *Le Sang noir* was in his technique of avoiding direct authorial intervention by adopting the point of view of his characters, varying the perspectives so that each, especially his protagonist, appeared in various lights. Guilloux adapted this technique to his own purposes, moving easily back and forth between third-person statements, *style indirect libre*, and interior monologue or even interior dialogue, as Cripure conducts imaginary conversations with himself in the mirror.

Cripure's own perspective is dominant: it is through his eyes that we are introduced to the Ox, that we see the award ceremony as a dramatic performance. And it is through his mind that we strip away the comforting surface of social custom with which men absurdly attempt to conceal their fundamental nature. Cripure anticipates Sartre's Roquentin[45] in conjuring up a horrifying vision of human mortality while observing a colleague: "Rien de ce que disait, de ce qu'était Babinot ne prêtait plus à rire, dès qu'on le regardait ainsi non plus dans son visage qui n'était qu'un masque en carton, mais dans sa vraie chair tendre qui commençait à se défaire, à se décoller et à pendre sous les maxillaires, à se gonfler comme se gonfle la chair des cadavres. Bientôt d'ailleurs . . ." (p. 262).[i] And in a passage that evokes Camus's *Myth of Sisyphus,* Cripure wonders how men can lead their trivia-filled lives in the face of their common anguish: "Avec ce noyau de plomb au fond du coeur, comment pouvaient-ils être aussi durs et secs, jeter leurs fils au charnier, leurs filles au bordel, renier leurs pères, engueuler leurs femmes qui pourtant les maniaient—bataille sans fin—rogner ses gages à la bonne qui sortait trop, était trop 'prétentieuse,' tout cela en pensant au cours de la rente et au prochain film comique qu'on irait voir au Palace, si on avait des billets de faveur?" (p. 274).[j] Cripure's particular understanding of the human condition clearly places him within the context of existentialist thought, which was influencing the fiction of Malraux and Sartre.

But Cripure is not only tragic: if he were, his philosophy would be the final message of *Le Sang noir.* He is also a figure of ridicule. Thus he appears to the townspeople, with his oversized feet and his perennial fur coat, generating frequent allusions to large hairy animals (he is variously called a porcupine, a bear, a giant boar, an orangutan). He becomes comic, too, through the repeated contrasts between the loftiness of his thoughts and aspirations and the sordid reality of his life. This disparity is brought home to Etienne Couturier, a former student who seeks Cripure's wisdom on the morning of his own departure for the front. Mildly surprised by the disorder of Cripure's peasant mistress and cluttered study, Etienne is profoundly disillusioned by the hysteria that replaces Cripure's former philosophical detachment when he finds that his life has been threatened by a student prank. Another contradiction is revealed by

---

[i]The things that Babinot said, the person he had become, were no longer a subject for laughter, when one no longer looked him in the face, which after all was but a pasteboard mask, but when one rather regarded his flesh, his true and feeling flesh, that flesh which was beginning to crumble, to become undone and to sag down over the jaws, puffing out as the flesh of corpses does. Soon enough, for that matter— (p. 293).

[j]With this leaden weight, this core of lead down deep in their hearts, how could they go on being so hard and unfeeling; how could they send their sons forth to the slaughterhouse, their daughters to the brothel; how could they disown their fathers, berate their wives, who for all of that led them around by the nose (an endless battle, this), and cut the wages of a maid who went out too often or who "put on too many airs," while all the time thinking of the rise and fall of profits and the next comic film they were going to see at the Palace, if they got complimentary tickets? (p. 307)

Cripure's considerable financial activities, which belie his stated contempt for the social order.

Perhaps the gravest criticism of him, however, is provided in the figure of the *Cloporte*, who, along with the Ox, is one of the novel's central images. Cripure classifies the townspeople as *cloportes* (woodlice), an image surely taken from Flaubert, whose *Bouvard et Pécuchet* was originally titled *Histoire de deux cloportes*. As Cripure defines them, *cloportes* are creatures who, much like his fellow citizens, cower in the false security of a decaying world: "Animaux essentiellement terrestres (régions tempérées) vivant . . . dans les endroits humides et obscurs: caves, celliers, sous la mousse et les vieilles écorces. Plusieurs ont la faculté de se rouler en boule à la moindre apparence de danger" (p. 119).[k]

The idea of the *cloporte* is epitomized for Cripure by a crippled old man who walks the streets at night. In his physical appearance and pathetic solitude, the *Cloporte's* resemblance to Cripure is unmistakable. Perhaps for this reason, Cripure tries to avoid identification with him and even comes to fear his appearance. The *Cloporte's* strange midnight encounter with the *bossue* on the night of Cripure's death mirrors, in an allegorical ballet, Cripure's attainment and subsequent loss of Toinette, and Cripure himself climbs out his window to pick up the *Cloporte's* cheap scholar's medal that the *bossue* has thrown away. Through the figure of the *Cloporte*, as well as through many of his own actions, Cripure is shown as part of the society collapsing around him, whose inadequacy his intellect recognizes. Unable to create a new mode of life for himself or for others, he can free himself only by ceasing to exist. And, as Lucien recognizes, it is necessary for Cripure to disappear, because his philosophy is no longer adequate to the needs of the younger generation.

Youth, the source of hope in the novel, is represented most articulately by Lucien, who is set up from the beginning to provide a counterweight to Cripure's impotent pessimism. He appears in the first pages as the young lieutenant whose optimistic faith in humanity Cripure cannot bring himself to share. When Lucien appears to speak in his own right, Guilloux's presentation is an exceptional case

---

[k] Distinctly terrestrial (temperate zone), these animals sometimes live . . . in dark, moist places, such as caves, cellars, or under moss and old tree-bark. Some of them have the faculty of rolling up into a ball at the slightest sign of danger (p. 128).

of direct authorial intervention: "Le visage était extrêmement jeune encore—Lucien n'avait pas vingt-cinq ans—et bien qu'il ne fut pas question d'y découvrir la moindre ride, il y avait pourtant quelque chose autour des yeux qui n'appartenait ni à la jeunesse ni à la vieillesse: les traces subtiles, devinées plutôt qu'aperçues, des acquisitions de la douleur et de l'intelligence" (p. 97).[l] Perhaps because his character is not illuminated from any other angle, Lucien does not display the complexity and human depth of a Cripure and thus cannot really counterbalance Cripure's domination of the novel. This is why critics at the time thought Guilloux's book was essentially pessimistic, and Guilloux felt called upon to defend himself against this charge: "It is too easy to speak of despair and to overlook all this book wants, would like to translate of hope."[46] Certainly, the presence of Lucien is meant to provide this element of hope, which is absent from the otherwise very similar social criticism of Céline. The ideal Lucien embodies is only sketchily defined and is not given the detailed attention of Cripure's more pessimistic viewpoint. But Lucien's doctrine is less thoroughly articulated precisely because he does not spend his time talking about it: he characteristically says little and believes, above all, in the necessity of action. As he states, "La question n'était pas de savoir quel était le sens de cette vie, la vraie question, la seule, était de savoir: que pouvons-nous faire de la vie?" (p. 135).[m]

Lucien's relationship to Cripure is much like that of Kyo and old Gisors in Malraux's *La Condition humaine*: the older man has provided the theoretical analysis of the existing order, but an excess of condemnation has resulted in paralysis. The younger man must cut through the intellect's web of contradictions and act in order to give real content to ideals such as life and human dignity. In his vague aspirations, Lucien has much in common with the protagonists of other antiwar writers of this decade: like Giono's characters in *Le Grand Troupeau*, Lucien affirms the value of life over death; like Drieu's narrator in *La Comédie de Charleroi*, he asserts the spirit of youth over decadent old age.

[l]His face was still quite young—Lucien was but twenty-five—and while there was not the slightest sign of a wrinkle, there was, nevertheless, something around the eyes which did not go either with youth or with age: the subtle traces, to be divined rather than glimpsed, left by suffering and the lessons it had brought (pp. 103–104).

[m]The question was not what direction this new life would take; the real question, the only one, was: What can we make of life? (p. 146)

Such generalized concepts are given some concretion in Lucien's ultimate departure to join in the Russian Revolution. The Revolution, however, is only in its initial stage and, as it functions in the novel, stands simply for a revolt against the war and the social oppression that had produced it. There is no evidence of a specifically Marxist analysis in *Le Sang noir*, and Guilloux in 1935 was not a member of the Communist party. His personal disillusionment with Stalinism is made clear in his 1949 novel, *Le Jeu de patience*, where Lucien reappears, disgusted with politics. While Guilloux seems to have shared in the wave of sympathy toward the Soviet Union that characterized French left-wing intellectuals during this era of Popular Front spirit,[47] it would be a distortion of the novel to tie the Russian Revolution in *Le Sang noir* to specific points of Soviet policy. It is primarily a symbol of hope, a proof that human beings can revolt against a repressive social order to create possibilities for human existence.

Like Céline and Drieu, Guilloux has focused his attention in *Le Sang noir* on the society whose hypocrisy and corruption lay behind the slaughter on the battlefields. But the social analysis of *Le Sang noir* is not directed only, or even primarily, toward the condemnation of the prewar status quo. It is rather a commentary on the time in which Guilloux is writing, just as the character of Cripure is at once a portrait of an admired teacher and a reflection of Guilloux's own feelings: "To Palante's protest, I have added my own. Our two hatreds have come together in a poetic creation."[48] In an article written shortly after the publication of *Le Sang noir*, Guilloux specifically refers to the state of affairs he has described in that novel as a phenomenon of the present: "When I was writing *Le Sang noir*, I saw around me only confused and disoriented men. . . . Everything was false, contradictory, and, to begin with, they were in contradiction with themselves. They were no longer in agreement with the values that had made their civilization, created the customs to which they still remained obedient."[49] The atmosphere Guilloux creates of a decaying and collapsing world is one in which many intellectuals of the 1930s felt themselves to be living. Paul Nizan, for example, using terms similar to those of Guilloux, writes in 1932, "A civilization stifled by the contradictions it engenders itself, victim of its own poisons, has begun to die."[50] This contemporary relevance was noted by many commentators, including Guilloux's friend Dabit, who declared at the meeting held by the Association des Ecrivains et des

Artistes Révolutionnaires to protest the refusal of the Goncourt to Guilloux's novel, "*Le Sang noir* is about a total revolt, a refusal of a world that was ours, that today is still ours."[51]

Even the attack Guilloux levels at the philosophers of Cripure's generation is relevant to the 1930s, when the official philosophy of the Sorbonne and other leading institutions was still dominated by the men who had established their reputations in the *Belle Epoque.* Nizan's *Les Chiens de garde* is a bitter attack, from a Marxist perspective, on the abstract idealism of the reigning thinkers of the day, whom Nizan calls the defenders—"the watchdogs"—of a liberal bourgeois society in its last stages of decline. In many ways, Nizan's attack is similar to Guilloux's criticism of Cripure, who is clearly identified with the Kantian perspective Nizan sees as dominant. Like Nizan's comfortable bourgeois thinkers, Cripure has thoroughly compromised himself by accepting the financial inducements of bourgeois society, and, although he does not make ludicrous statements of support for the war, as Nizan's targets do, his very silence is a form of complicity. The accusation hurled at him by his former student Matrod, whose face has been shot away, is clearly meant to be shared by the reader. Cripure is, of course, far superior to the ridiculous stick figures castigated by Nizan. Unlike them, he does not support the social order; unlike them, he has suffered and is sensitive to suffering in others. Yet, in his inability to provide a basis for positive action, his unwillingness to participate in social change, he is clearly a member of the philosophical establishment, which continues to dominate the 1930s.

Guilloux's need to express in *Le Sang noir* the hopes and anxieties of his own troubled times is certainly understandable in terms of his preoccupations during the time of its writing. He had assumed the position of regional *responsable* for the effort to aid the Spanish refugees fleeing the failed uprising at Oviedo in 1934. In addition, he was heavily involved in helping the local unemployed. As he wrote in his journal, "I am, then, at each moment under the necessity of going either to the police or the prefecture for the refugees; or to a meeting at the 'Maison du peuple' for the unemployed."[52] Concern with the Nazi menace was not absent from his thinking, either, for in June 1935 he acted as secretary for the Congress of Writers in Defense of Culture. Yet all these activities, seemingly unrelated to a historical study of 1917, did not seem to interfere with the development of *Le Sang noir*. Supporting an argument that would also be made by Nizan, Guilloux sees political activities as contributing positively to literary creation: "Far from leading to sterility, on the contrary, they refertilize the domain of creation. Everything works together."[53] Guilloux's own experience with the victims of social oppression during the years in which he wrote *Le Sang noir* had furnished him with the profound reality of his fictional world.

La Comédie de Charleroi

The experience of leading a charge in the Battle of Charleroi was for Pierre Drieu la Rochelle the brief incarnation of an ideal that was to dominate his life. Even in the worst moments of the Nazi occupation, when he had lost any illusions he might have had about Hitler or the efficacy of his own role as collaborator, he would write in his journal: "Lord, what has my life been? A few women, the charge at Charleroi, a few words, the contemplation of a few landscapes, books, statues, paintings and that's it."[54] While Drieu dismisses his own voluminous and wide-ranging literary production of the 1920s and 30s as "a few words" and the great loves of his life as "a few women," the charge at Charleroi retains its preeminent position.

Drieu wrote about the experience of Charleroi at two moments in his life. While convalescing from the wounds he had received in combat, he published a collection of poems, *Interrogation*, which gave expression to his youthful enthusiasm and exaltation of war. Almost twenty years later, he returned to the subject in his story, "La Comédie de Charleroi," published as the title piece in his collection of short fiction about the war. Its very title points to a change in perspective. In the story the lyrical moment of the charge appears once again, but its presence only serves to emphasize the dissolution and decadence of the context in which it is embedded. The youthful fervor of the voice in the early poems gives way in the stories to the pessimism of a mature narrator, who, much like the Céline of *Voyage au bout de la nuit*, submits the adventures of his youthful incarnation to ironic analysis.

The change in narrative voice seems to reflect a modification of Drieu's own attitudes about the war during the intervening years. In 1929, in an open letter to Benjamin Crémieux, Drieu admitted that his feelings about the war had changed since his composition of the poems. On rereading his own war poetry, he wrote, "These reflections end up in a complete reversal: I do not believe *Interrogation* is an equitable statement about the war."[55] In 1931 he underlines his new attitude toward war by asserting that he would refuse to serve if mobilized.[56]

As also witnessed by Drieu's many published works during this period, the postwar years had deflated the exuberance of the young bourgeois intellectual to whom the war had suddenly offered the possibility of being a man of action. Action did not seem so simple in the peacetime world of the 1920s, where Drieu felt himself immersed in decadence. Unable to lead meaningful lives, his fictional heroes of this era, many of them loosely autobiographical, drown themselves in women, drugs, and alcohol (*L'Homme couvert de femmes*, *Le Feu follet*). While he was reflecting a decadent world in his fiction, in his political essays Drieu was trying to suggest to his contemporaries a way out of their morass. Unlike those who complacently viewed the French victory as the guarantee of a return to prewar stability, Drieu recognized that France had emerged from the war dangerously weakened, as had the other European states. He was also painfully aware that the war had provided the occasion for the emergence of America as the dominant world power, rivaled only by the youthful Soviet state. Under these conditions, Drieu urged Europeans to abandon their outdated nationalisms, which could only lead to still more destructive wars, and to create a strong, unified Europe. It is a sad irony that Drieu, who, from the early 1920s had so clearly seen the approaching European debacle, nevertheless allowed it to sweep him to his own destruction. Yet this was a consequence of his decision, unlike that of the deserter whom he portrays in one of the stories in *La Comédie de Charleroi*, to tie his own destiny to the threatened European world.

By 1934, the year in which he published *La Comédie de Charleroi*, Drieu felt he had found the political credo around which this long-desired European unity could be created, a unique blend of ideologies from Right and Left that he called *socialisme fasciste*. The year 1934 represents, in many ways, a turning point in his work. In his writing of fiction, he abandoned the short novels of decadence for the major novels in which he makes lengthy studies of his own background and life experience, *Rêveuse Bourgeoisie* and *Gilles*. In the domain of politics, he had now clearly defined his doctrines and was soon ready to turn from the medium of the theoretical essay to active involvement in a real political party, Doriot's Parti populaire français. It was at this critical moment of his life that Drieu felt called upon to reexamine his experience of the Great War. Frédéric Grover, author of some of the most perceptive studies of Drieu, contends that Drieu's political evolution was intimately related to his war experience and that his turning back to analyze the meaning of the war at this point in his life was not merely fortuitous.[57] Like others of his contemporaries, Drieu saw in the experience of the Great War the key to understanding the postwar moment he was then living. His experiences on the battlefields of Charleroi and Verdun had revealed to him the summits of human possibility, as they had made clear the abject condition of modern man. The latter was an aspect of the war that he had brushed aside in his youthful exuberance of 1917 but that had apparently returned to haunt him in the intervening years.

The title story of *La Comédie de Charleroi*,[58] also the longest, contains within itself all the contradictory feelings and insights of the narrator's war experiences: "Dialogue entre les courages: courage de rester, courage de partir. Dialogue entre la politique et la vie: arabesque de la légende franco-allemande, enlacée à ma destinée d'Européen qui pressentait le harassement du fer. Dialogue de la vie et de la mort: efficacité du trépas à vingt ans, efficacité du trépas à cinquante ans" (p. 118)." It also introduces the major themes that the succeeding stories will develop. As the narrator walks through the battlefield of Charleroi in 1919, he relives for himself the experiences of that day in 1914, which had contained elements of the various faces of the war. Shortly before the battle, unnerved and depressed by the "marches and countermarches" that had led to no significant action, he had toyed with the idea of committing suicide. This atmosphere of stagnation, which Drieu seems to blame on the unpreparedness for modern warfare of the French military, also provides the background for a later story in the collection, "Le Voyage des Dardanelles." After he has been wounded and the battle lost, the

---

"Dialogue between two courages: the courage to stay, the courage to leave. Dialogue between politics and life: arabesque of the Franco-German legend, interwoven with my destiny as a European who foresaw the torture of iron. Dialogue of life and death: efficacy of death at twenty, efficacity of death at fifty.

protagonist is tempted to abandon the weakened, perennially defeated French and to seek his own salvation in America, a plan of action that has been carried out by the character in "Le Déserteur." The narrator's first experience of shelling at Charleroi introduces him to the reality of mechanized warfare, which will be heavily reinforced by Verdun ("Le Lieutenant de tirailleurs") and by his participation in an American unit at the moment of victory ("La Fin d'une guerre"). It is this negative vision of war that emerges as dominant in the collection of stories and even in the title story itself, where the inhumanity of modern war provides a point of contact with the peacetime world portrayed in the framing episode.

This frame provides a concrete picture of the postwar world, which has brought about Drieu's modified vision of the war itself. The story begins by insisting upon the context within which the war experience must now be placed. "La Comédie de Charleroi" is, in fact, narrated in a double retrospective. Returning to Charleroi after the war, the narrator tells the story of the battle to the mother of his fallen comrade, Claude Pragen, whose body they have come to reclaim. Scenes set in 1919 open and close the story, and conversations of 1919 continually interrupt the narrative of 1914. Events of both 1914 and 1919 are recounted in a past or pluperfect tense, but becoming increasingly evident in the story is a present tense that expresses the observations of a narrator somewhat vaguely situated in the 1930s.

The story is structured around a series of oppositions: [59] the two time sequences of the narration; the two embodiments of the central character, as both youthful protagonist and mature narrator; the contradictory principles of unity and disintegration within the protagonist (who is meant to be representative of European man) and within the larger society; the two moments of the attack and its collapse; the narrator's ideal of war ("la Guerre") and the modern war in which he finds himself ("cette guerre"); and the two theatrical genres, tragedy and the *comédie* of the title. In all these opposing pairs, an ideal is contrasted to a reality that represents its dissolution and decadence. The ideal of heroic action, of personal and social integration, which is incarnated in the attack led by the protagonist in 1914, begins to disintegrate almost immediately. By 1919 this process of dissolution seems to have reached its final point, like the bodies of the soldiers at Charleroi, already reduced to butchered "meat" by the wartime shelling, which finally dissolve into the formless, viscous substance, "ce miel d'horreur" (p. 97),[o] found in the coffins unearthed in the military cemetery.[60]

The contrast between the circumstances of the particular Battle of Charleroi and the concept of war itself, in its eternal dimensions, a contrast reiterated again and again, is summed up by Drieu in the formula: "Il y a ici deux questions différentes: la question de l'homme sur le champ de bataille moderne, et la question du chef dans l'action" (p. 88).[p] In his description of men in the battle Drieu suggests several ironic contrasts between the wars of a heroic past and their modern manifestation. The name of Richard the Lion-Hearted is evoked, only to be applied to a conscripted soldier who is suffering from inflammation of the testicles: "De le voir portant ses bourses comme un saint sacrement de douleur, me faisait penser dans les hallucinations de la marche forcée, à Richard Coeur-de-Lion qui, sur un livre de mon enfance, portait des têtes de Sarrazins attachés au poitrail de son cheval" (p. 48).[q] The procedure is like that used by Drieu's good friend André Malraux, who, in his descriptions of war in *L'Espoir* and *Les Noyers de l'Altenburg*, commonly makes connections between the humble combatant of the twentieth century and heroic or historical figures. But while Malraux uses this type of imagery to place his characters within a context of eternity, to endow their actions with a cosmic dimension,[61] Drieu clearly intends to emphasize the pathetic disparity between the heroic images of the past and their modern counterparts.

He makes a similarly ironic contrast between the heroic image of the Roman phalanx (*carapace*) and its modern version in which groups of soldiers band together, forming a shield of their knapsacks, to protect themselves against shelling. A technique that worked well for the Romans with their simple weaponry is rendered totally ineffectual by modern artillery: "Nous formions, selon la règle rédigée dans un bureau placide, un tumulus de viandes, toutes prêtes pour le hachis. Comme ça, les Allemands feraient quarante victimes d'un coup" (p. 55).[r]

[o]that honey of horror

[p]There are two different questions here: the question of man on the modern battlefield, and the question of the leader in action.

[q]To see him carrying his "purses" like a holy sacrament of pain made me think in the hallucinations of the forced march, of Richard the Lion-Hearted who, in a book from my childhood, carried the heads of Saracens attached to his horse's chest-piece.

[r]We formed, according to the rule drawn up in a quiet office, a tumulus of meat, ready for the grinder. This way, the Germans would get forty victims at a shot.

This bathetic collapse of "eternal War" into the modern mechanized battlefield appears most strikingly in the two moments of the central episode in the story, an account of the heroic but ill-fated charge led by the narrator. In an élan of heroism he galvanizes the immobilized men of his unit into a single force capable of advancing against the German lines. The narrator suddenly discovers what for Drieu will remain the summit of human possibility, which he identifies as the experience of being a *chef*: "Qu'est-ce qui soudain jaillissait? Un chef. Non seulement un homme, un chef. . . . Un chef, c'est un homme à son plein; l'homme qui donne et qui prend dans la même éjaculation" (p. 70).[5]

This concept of the *chef*, with its multiple connotations, was, of course, not without its effect on Drieu's political philosophy and seemed to lead inevitably to fascism. However, he was often to express his reservations about the possibility of the embodiment of this ideal in any real political figure. His play *Le Chef*, first produced in the same year as the publication of *La Comédie de Charleroi*, expresses the conflict between an idealistic intellectual and his best friend and former comrade-in-arms who has become a political dictator. Here, although it is the dictator who emerges victorious, the reader senses that Drieu's sympathies lie more with the idealist. Similarly, in his political writings, as in "La Comédie de Charleroi" itself, he often lumps together both Communist and fascist dictators as targets for his contempt. Yet the ideal of the *chef*, the man of action become political leader, never ceased to fascinate Drieu: this figure is central in the last novel published during his lifetime, the allegorical *Homme à cheval*. And in Drieu's own biography, it was his failure to find such a *chef* behind the public image of the French fascist Doriot or, later, of the Nazi fuhrer himself, that lay at the root of his political disillusionment.

Drieu's imagery links the experience of the charge at Charleroi to dimensions of reality that surpass it. Its significance borders on the religious: the narrator sees the plain of Charleroi as a "place of judgment" (p. 69) that reveals to him the meaning of "grace and miracle" (p. 70). Comparisons with the great battles of history suggest themselves, and in this passage Drieu is able to use them without irony, seeking to place this "moment of eternity" in its proper con-

---

[5] What suddenly burst forth? A leader. Not only a man, a leader. . . . A leader is a man in his highest form; the man who gives and takes in the same ejaculation.

text. He sees the battle as part of an archetypal struggle between two peoples, "la Gaule et la Germanie. Inchangeables, éternelles comme l'Egypte et Babylone. Incapables de vaincre, incapables d'être vaincues. C'était l'éternelle bataille dans la plaine" (pp. 71–72).[ᵗ] The charge is also explicitly connected with the experience of sex: "Je me suis donné deux ou trois fois dans des batailles—deux ou trois fois dans des lits" (p. 72).[ᵘ] The entire passage is described in the images of ejaculation. In the beginning there is the "bouillonnement du sang jeune et chaud—puberté de la vertu" (p. 70),[ᵛ] followed by the "bursting forth" of the leader and the connection of his action with that of ejaculation, a process that eventually leads to "exhaustion." This description of war in sexual terms is occasioned not merely by Drieu's need to express the short-lived emotional intensity of this climactic moment but also by the intellectual vision granted him by the experience, the sudden realization that all the various activities of human life, commonly viewed as separate and even contradictory, are united in a single stream: "Même geste pour manger et pour aimer, pour agir et pour penser, pour vivre et pour mourir. La vie, c'est un seul jet" (p. 73).[ʷ] Before the charge, the narrator had been aware only of contradictions: "Réflexes croisés, principes contradictoires: 'Un homme est fait pour vivre' et: 'Un homme est fait pour mourir.' 'Quand il n'y a pas de chef, il faut qu'il y en ait un' et 'Je ne veux pas de chef'" (p. 30).[ˣ] The "slender bourgeois intellectual," as the narrator describes himself before the battle, has discovered he is also capable of becoming a man of action, just as Drieu's own war poems exalted his discovery of the possibility of unifying "dream and action."[62]

In "La Comédie de Charleroi," however, the brief moment of exaltation is immediately followed by one of disillusionment, as the French advance is checked, first by the shock of finding no enemy troops rising up to meet it and then by a resumption of fire by the still-concealed Germans, which forces the narrator to seek shelter in a shell hole. Drieu's description of the moment of collapse exactly

---

[ᵗ]Gaul and Germania. Unchangeable, eternal like Egypt and Babylon. Incapable of overcoming, incapable of being overcome. It was the eternal battle on the plain.

[ᵘ]I have given myself two or three times in battle—two or three times in bed.

[ᵛ]bubbling of the young warm blood—puberty of power

[ʷ]A single gesture to eat and to love, to act and to think, to live and to die. Life is a single stream.

[ˣ]Reflexes at odds, contradictory principles: "A man is made to live" and: "A man is made to die." "When there is no leader, there must be one" and "I want no leader."

mirrors the account of the previous moment of exaltation. As the
charge had been depicted as an ejaculation, its disintegration is described as a failed sexual encounter: "Ils ne se sont pas rencontrés,
ils ne se sont pas heurtés, enlacés, étreints" (p. 75).[y] The mounting
enthusiasm of the charge had been expressed in terms of reiterated
short verbs of action, alternating the singular and plural first-person
pronouns and eventually expanding to include the third-person plural: "Je me levai. . . . Nous criions. . . . Je criais, je courais, j'appelais. . . . Je criais, j'avançais. . . . Je criais. J'agissais. Nous avan-
cions. . . . Des hommes étonnés se levaient. . . . Ils se mettaient à
courir" (pp. 71–74). Similarly, the verbs in the subsequent passage
reflect the gradual cessation of this forward movement, ending the
series of verbs in the *imparfait* with a definitive *passé simple*: "Je
courais, je trébuchais, je criais. . . . Ils couraient. Nous courions,
nous trébuchions, nous tombions. . . . Et pourtant, je me relevais, je
courais, je criais, j'appelais. . . . On s'appelait, on ne se répondait
pas. . . . Je ne faisais plus que gesticulailler, criailler. Je n'avançais
plus guère. Je trébuchais, je tombais. Ils trébuchaient, ils tombaient. . . . Je gesticulaillais, je criaillais. Je trébuchais, je tombais. . . .
Nous tombâmes dans un trou" (pp. 74–77).[z]

The failure of this charge at Charleroi becomes for the older narrator emblematic of the collapse of French society when confronted
with the world of modern industrialization and the anonymity of
mass society revealed in the experience of the Great War: "Nous y
sommes encore dans ce trou, nous n'en sommes jamais repartis. Il y
a eu un élan dans cette guerre, mais il a été tout de suite brisé. Il n'a
jamais abouti. Trop inhumain cet élan, trop chargé d'acier et trop
battu par l'acier, se heurtant à une résistance trop inhumaine"
(p. 77).[a]

[y]They did not meet, they did not run into, clasp, embrace each other
[z]I got up. . . . we were shouting. . . . I was shouting, running, calling. . . . I was
shouting, going forward. . . . I was shouting, I was doing something. We were moving
forward. . . . Astonished men were getting up. . . . They were beginning to run. . . . I
was running, stumbling, shouting. . . . They were running. We were running, stumbling, falling. . . . But I was getting up again, running, shouting, calling. . . . We were
calling each other, not replying. . . . I was no longer doing anything but gesturing
wildly, shouting wildly. I was no longer making any progress. I was stumbling, falling.
They were stumbling, falling. . . . I was gesturing wildly, shouting wildly. I was stumbling, falling. . . . We fell into a hole.
[a]We are still in that hole; we never got out of it. There was a certain momentum in
that war, but it was immediately broken. It never went anywhere. Too inhuman that
momentum, too overburdened with steel and too beaten down by steel, meeting up
with a too inhuman resistance.

Human values of virility and individual courage, embodied in the figure of the *chef* and in the heroic figures of the past, have, in Drieu's view, been destroyed by "this war of an advanced civilization" (p. 75). Like Céline, Drieu is acutely aware of the connection between the mechanized slaughter of the war and the American-style mass production that has contributed to the dehumanization of European life. The narrator can even feel sympathy for the Germans against whom he is ostensibly fighting, for they, like all Europeans, will be defeated by American industry: "J'ai vu ça en 1918 cette chère vieille infanterie allemande crever décidément sous le flot de l'industrie américaine" (p. 81).[b] The war has provided the brutal revelation of one of the central problems of modern society: "Il faut que l'homme apprenne à maîtriser la machine, qui l'a outrepassé dans cette guerre—et qui maintenant l'outrepasse dans la paix" (pp. 75–76).[c63]

With the collapse of the charge comes the disintegration of the unitary vision that the protagonist has momentarily attained. Before the attack, he has been very conscious of the divisions between social classes, which the promiscuity of life in a conscripted army has not been able to overcome. As a frail bourgeois intellectual, the protagonist has felt a sentiment bordering on contempt for the "paysans abrutis" and "ouvriers tous sournoisement embourgeoisés" (p. 36)[d] who surround him. He has felt a particular hostility to his officers, who respond by looking down on him as a pampered bourgeois but who themselves offer neither leadership nor even an elementary understanding of the tactical situation: "Sortis du rang, c'étaient des ronds-de-cuir qui attendaient leur retraite" (p. 36).[e] The protagonist's repeated challenges to the obtuseness of his superior officers testify to his desire to revolt against the established social hierarchy, which he calls idiotic, in order to institute the true hierarchical order of a *chef* and his natural followers, which he discovers during the charge: "J'étais un chef. Je voulais m'emparer de tous ces hommes autour de moi, m'en accroître, les accroître par moi et nous lancer tous en bloc, moi en pointe, à travers l'univers" (p. 70).[f] Only at this

---

[b]I saw it in 1918, the dear old German infantry absolutely finished off under the onslaught of American industry.
[c]Man must learn to master the machine, which got the better of him in this war—and which now is getting the better of him in peacetime.
[d]moronic peasants, workers who had all sneakily gone over to the bourgeoisie
[e]Risen from the ranks, they were penpushers waiting for retirement
[f]I was a leader. I wanted to take possession of all those men around me, expand

point in the narrative can he make extensive use of the pronoun *nous*. But this momentary integration quickly falls apart. The protagonist finds himself again alienated from his companions, confronting another obtuse officer and about to be captured by the Germans: he decides to take off on his own. Once again, he finds himself in the situation of isolation that has seemed to characterize both the war and the society of which it is a reflection: "L'armée commençait à se disloquer. Sous les premières fureurs du feu, ses parties se séparaient les unes des autres. Déjà elles se voyaient à peine; bientôt elles ne se verraient plus. Et pendant quatre ans, leurs efforts et leurs souffrances s'en iraient, parallèles, sans jamais se rencontrer. Artillerie et infanterie se cherchaient et ne se trouvaient pas. Et les généraux étaient ailleurs. Déjà nous n'étions plus que des groupes perdus dans l'abominable solitude du champ de bataille moderne, chaque homme creusant sa tombe" (p. 53).⁹ The dream of an almost mystical social unity—between Right and Left, bourgeoisie and working class—that Drieu himself had glimpsed during the riots of February 1934 ⁶⁴ again proves the impossibility of its realization.

Drieu expresses this failure in theatrical terms: "La troupe des acteurs s'est mal agrégée à moi, le protagoniste qui soudain est sorti de son sommeil et s'est avancé sur la scène; le choeur n'a pas suivi. Et, en face, l'antagoniste ne s'est pas levé" (p. 84).ʰ The ideal has failed to take form in reality. The tragedy has failed and in its failure has turned into *comédie*. This collapse of tragedy into comedy is certainly one of the meanings of the title.⁶⁵ From the moment of the failure of the charge, the narrator's perception of events is increasingly expressed in terms of theater. His own actions during the charge now appear to be the empty gestures of an orator. The com-

---

my being with them and theirs with me, and launch ourselves together with me leading, across the universe.

⁹The army was beginning to break up. Under the first onslaughts of fire, its parts separated from each other. Already they could hardly see each other; soon they would not be able to see each other any more. And for four years, their efforts and their suffering would move on, parallel, without every meeting. Artillery and infantry sought but did not find each other. And the generals were elsewhere. Already we were no more than groups lost in the abominable solitude of the modern battlefield, each man digging his tomb.

ʰThe troop of actors did not play along with me, the protagonist who suddenly woke from his sleep and walked out on stage; the chorus did not follow. And, facing me, the antagonist did not rise up.

bat death of a fellow soldier turns into a gruesome *comédie*, with both captain and dying soldier playing stereotyped roles that depart grotesquely from their normal reality. Slipping away from the group trapped in the shell hole, the narrator describes himself as "un acteur qui est sorti dans la coulisse" (p. 109), and when he is wounded, he sees himself as playing the role of a wounded man, "maquillé avec mon sang, . . . mon costume, mon sang" (p. 111).[i]

The impression of unreality, of hypocrisy, of theatricality is even more pronounced in the scenes set in 1919 that form a frame for the narrator's memories of the battle. The character to whom these theatrical images are attached is no longer the narrator but the mother of his dead friend, for whom he now works as a personal secretary. Metaphors of theatricality cluster around Mme Pragen's entry on the scene. She arrives at the station "costumée en infirmière-major, toutes décorations dehors" (p. 10).[j] In the train she speaks and acts for the public, dazzling the properly impressed fellow passengers with her political connections. She stops only to close her eyes in order to "ajuster sur son visage un maquillage moral" (p. 13).[k] But, the narrator makes clear, her whole life has been an "éternelle co-médie" (p. 13), beginning with the ploy she had used to snag her rich and well-connected husband: she had parodied the fate of a lovelorn woman by fasting to the point of emaciation. Mme Pragen has spent so much of her life in vain social performances that the narrator wonders whether it is still possible to distinguish true feelings from false, since she expresses both in the same theatrical manner. Even her grief at the loss of her son is so conventional that the narrator is surprised by the thought that her sentiments might, after all, have some element of sincerity.

But such falsity is an essential part of the characterization of Mme Pragen, who expands beyond the figure of Drieu's own mother-in-law[66] to incarnate the extent to which her society represents a perversion of what Drieu sees as the natural social order. She plays the role of comforting nurse, which Drieu sees as an appropriate traditional feminine function, but she can provide no real curative power. She revels in her status as a bereaved mother, but the narrator doubts she has ever really cared for her son, whom she has pushed

[i] an actor who has gone into the wings, . . . made up with my blood, my costume, my blood.
[j] costumed as a nursing officer with all decorations on display
[k] adjust on her face a moral makeup

beyond his capacities in order to further her own ambitions. It is even harder to imagine her nursing her son at her breast: "Elle semblait ignorer déjà—mais plutôt il en avait été toujours ainsi—qu'elle eut des seins, un ventre" (p. 13).[j] In contrast to the ideal feminine qualities of warmth and life, she is repeatedly described as cold, dry, and prematurely aged by false, modern illnesses, neuroses, and drugs.

The Belgians whom she visits at Charleroi see in Mme Pragen the personification of Parisian elegance and nobility, but the narrator is quick to recognize her flaws—long feet, large toes, and, even more damning in Drieu's increasingly antisemitic perspective, signs of Jewishness. Just as she is a false aristocrat, she is a false Catholic, despite her large contribution to the Belgian parish where a memorial mass is said for her son: she is only a recent convert.

Worst of all, this false and unnatural figure is placed at the very top of the social structure, exactly where she should not be in Drieu's ideal system. Her control over French society, through her money and political connections, is emphasized again and again. She even dominates the narrator, who, in 1919, seems to have lost the qualities of courage and independence he had displayed so lavishly in the war. Mme Pragen's position of dominance is made clear from the first words of the text: "Madame Pragen décida que nous partirions" (p. 10).[m] The narrator is not enthusiastic about her decision but is powerless to change it. And, in contrast to his fearlessness in battle, he spends a bad night before the departure in fear of arriving late at the station.

If the natural social order is summed up in the image of a *chef* leading his men in battle, then Mme Pragen clearly epitomizes its opposite. She is not even a man, and Drieu's vision of what is natural seems to relegate women to a rather hazy "eternal feminine." Inferior even to the incompetent officers and generals who wield power on the battlefield, Mme Pragen, as a woman, is incapable even of making the effort to understand the reality of combat. She misuses language (for example, by referring to the Charleroi battlefield in the plural, as "*les* champs de bataille" [p. 15]) and constantly interrupts the narrator's reminiscences with absurd questions and comments. He finally despairs of making her understand: "Elle ne

[j]she seemed already to be unaware of the fact—but rather it had always been like that—that she had breasts, a womb.
[m]Madame Pragen decided we would leave.

savait pas ce qu'était la guerre et elle ne voulait pas le savoir. Cela faisait partie de ce domaine des hommes pour lequel les femmes ont si peu de curiosité" (p. 58)." If she values the qualities embodied in the narrator—youth, physical courage, virility—it is only as a façade for her own cynical efforts at political manipulation: the story ends with the narrator's rejection of her offer to finance his campaign for a seat in the Assembly.

Unlike Drieu's wartime poems, "La Comédie de Charleroi" is far from being a celebration of war. The protagonist's moment of mystical revelation, which plays an important role in the war poems, is also the lyrical high point of the story, but it is preceded and followed by long passages that describe military and social disarray. The decadent world of 1919 is clearly only a continuation of the process of disintegration begun in the war. The real outcome of the war, in Drieu's view, can be equated with the French defeat at Charleroi, and this is certainly one of the reasons he has chosen to emphasize this lost battle rather than later, militarily more successful encounters in which he had also participated. Indeed, in an essay written in the same year as *La Comédie de Charleroi*, Drieu expresses his ultimate rejection of modern warfare and urges that man's combative instincts, which he continues to view positively, be cultivated instead through competitive sports.[67]

In "La Comédie de Charleroi" Drieu is able to place the charge at Charleroi in a new context, that of the postwar years. Through his narrative structure, which embodies both the ideal of human life and its debasement in modern society, he uses his war experience to condemn the decadence of the world in which he lives.

Le Monde Réel

The first three volumes of the cycle Aragon chose to entitle *Le Monde Réel*[68] were written and, except for *Les Voyageurs de l'impériale*,[69] published in the 1930s. They all ostensibly concern the period preceding World War I, *Les Cloches de Bâle* and *Les Beaux Quartiers* concentrating especially on the years just preceding the conflict, while *Les Voyageurs de l'impériale* extends back into the nineteenth century and ends with the outbreak of war in 1914. Like *Les Hommes*

"She did not know what war was and she did not want to know. That was part of the world of men for which women have so little curiosity.

.

de bonne volonté, these novels trace what Romains had called in his own work on this period, the *montée des périls*. Aragon's perspective on these events is, of course, somewhat different from that of the liberal Romains, because Aragon is able to apply the lessons of his Marxist ideology and, specifically, the historical judgments he found in the works of Lenin.[70] Aragon thus has no need to treat every event that contributed to the war, although he does mention several specific instances of political crisis, nor does he share Romains's need to present the viewpoints of significant political figures, like Kaiser Wilhelm.

It is not only his Marxist perspective, however, that differentiates Aragon's treatment of this period from that of Romains. It is rather that, unlike Romains, Aragon has as his primary interest not the analysis of the causes of World War I but the indication to his readers of the sources of social evil in contemporary France. Since the evils of the war had already been recognized by most sectors of the French public, Aragon as novelist has only to make clear to his readers the inescapable connection between the war and the functioning of capitalism.

In *Les Cloches de Bâle* the major historical event related to the war is the 1912 peace conference in Basel, Switzerland, which gives the work its title. The conference, however, is really important not as an element in the historical analysis—since it ultimately had no influence whatsoever on the course of events—but as an opportunity to show that the social forces already identified as evil in other contexts are also working to undermine the objectives of the conference. The spectacle of the innocent and optimistic peace marchers is treated with heavy irony, since both author and reader are in a position to know that war had not been prevented, and the scene serves as a final comment on the action of the novel as a whole.

The principal war-related event in *Les Beaux Quartiers* is the passage of the "three years law," which, by extending the period of obligatory military service to three years, is obviously a step in the preparation for war. The proposed law is debated from the beginning of the novel, and as it ends, the protagonist, Armand Barbentane, is reflecting on the defiant words uttered by Jaurès at the time of its passage. Yet this event, too, is important in the novel not for its contribution to the buildup of war but as a commentary, made in the words of Jaurès, on the divided worlds of French society, a duality that constitutes the real subject of the novel.

In *Les Voyageurs de l'impériale*, where much less attention is given to the centers of political power, a major contributor to the debacle of 1914 is seen to be the apolitical individualism epitomized by the central character, Pierre Mercadier. This attitude, rather than the war that it helps to bring about, is the real subject of Aragon's concern.

Benefiting from his Marxist overview of history, Aragon does not need to linger over the cause-and-effect relationship of various diplomatic events. His primary focus in the first two novels is the functioning of the powerful industrial cartels, supported by the politicians and police, who control French life in war and in peace. These men oppress French workers in their factories at the same time as they are maneuvering to lead them into a war designed to protect their own financial interests in the African colonies and other foreign investments. The violence that appears in all three novels results not from war but from social oppression, primarily action taken against strikers. Aragon is concerned to show that the two are intimately related.

The central fictional figures in this capitalistic cartel appear in both *Les Cloches de Bâle* and *Les Beaux Quartiers* and are mentioned in *Les Voyageurs de l'impériale*. They thus remain stable fixtures of Aragon's novelistic world while the other characters come and go. No matter what the situation, Aragon would seem to be saying, it is always ultimately controlled by the same people. Aragon's most important capitalists are the auto magnate Wisner and his friend and associate, Joseph Quesnel, who is head of the consortium of Paris taxi companies, among his other business interests. They are aided in their dealings by the vaguely outlined mediation of Joris de Houten, who is, as has been revealed in *Les Cloches de Bâle*, a police agent and a dealer in illicit drugs as well. De Houten is important because he continually makes visible the connection between the supposedly respectable capitalists and more evidently sordid financial dealings: in Aragon's view, of course, they are all the same.

This is a point first made openly through the character of Georges Brunel in *Les Cloches de Bâle*. Although he appears to be a rich financier like all his friends, Brunel actually makes his money by making usurious loans to spendthrift sons of the upper classes. This practice is frowned on by proper society, which is, however, ready to tolerate quite similar activity under another name and is willing to accept much more blatant exploitation when it concerns only the workers. When Brunel's activities are exposed by the untimely suicide of a young client, he makes a cynical defense to his friend, General Dorsch, calling his activities as a usurer the same as those of investors on the stock market: "Nous sommes tous des parasites" (p. 88).[o] This parallel is underlined in Brunel's subsequent conversations with Wisner, who is now moving on from Brunel's unsavory dealings to investment in France's burgeoning colonial empire, an enterprise that, he cheerfully suggests, will cost the lives of many like the young man who has committed suicide because of Brunel: "Moi, dans mon jeu, les Sabran par centaines sont les pions d'une partie autrement intéressante, et s'il s'en casse en route, eh bien, au moins ce n'est pas pour rien" (p. 103).[p] Aragon has already made it clear that Wisner and Brunel are birds of a feather, and now he can equate Brunel's usury with Wisner's supposedly patriotic cause. But Brunel has made the mistake of getting himself exposed, and Wisner can no longer afford to be publicly identified with him. He does, however, find his old friend a new job in the police, where Brunel appears, at the end of the novel, very much at home.

The association of Wisner with Brunel is typical of Aragon's strategy: he causes the reader to question the respectability of his rich capitalists by constantly associating them with financial dealings of dubious morality. The central figure in the section of *Les Cloches de Bâle* that deals with the moneyed classes is not one of the male industrialists but Diane Brunel, née de Nettencourt. She supports herself and her entire aristocratic family with the funds she obtains from a series of men, Georges Brunel being only the latest. Like her highly respectable family, who refuse to discuss the source of their income with her as long as she sees that their expenses are met, society is unwilling to call her activity by its proper name. But Aragon, through his protagonist, Catherine, makes clear the nature of Diane's real occupation: "Enfin qu'est-ce que vous voulez qu'une femme devienne, si ce n'est pas une ouvrière? Une cocotte, mariée ou non" (p. 113).[q] A prostitution to material goods like Diane's is the animating force of the entire class that she represents, and Aragon places this activity on a level with the more identifiable forms of prostitution that Catherine discovers in the Bois de Boulogne.

[o] We are all parasites.

[p] In *my* game, hundreds of Sabrans are pawns in a game that is incomparably more interesting, and if any of them break their necks at it, well, at least it's not for nothing! (p. 79)

[q] After all, what do you expect a woman to beccome, if she is not a worker? A prostitute, whether married or not (p. 86).

Prostitution is also a central theme in *Les Beaux Quartiers*. The provincial town of Sérianne, which forms the setting of the first part of the novel, seems to revolve around its brothel, while the central figure in the Paris sections is Quesnel's beautiful mistress Carlotta, Aragon's reincarnation of Zola's Nana. Through Carlotta the reader is also introduced to the world of an elite gambling den, the *Passage-Club*, whose illegal activities are shown to mirror those of the nearby stock exchange. The gambling of the *Passage-Club* is not only similar to the dealings of capitalist high finance but an integral part of its structure, a connection that Aragon reveals when the club and its habitués become pawns in a struggle between rival gambling cartels, run, of course, by the same industrialists whom the reader has already met. Like the preparations for war and the attempts to repress strikes, the activities of the capitalists behind the *Passage-Club* result in the destruction of human lives.

Both prostitution and gambling increase their importance in *Les Voyageurs de l'impériale*, where these activities stand for what Aragon has come to see, in the last years of the 1930s, as a capitalist order in the throes of death. The young and beautiful women who have dominated the first two novels in the cycle are here replaced by almost lifeless hags who seem to embody the dominant features of an entire society. Pierre Mercadier encounters one of these women at Monte Carlo, where he goes after abandoning his family and his confining bourgeois existence, realizing that his disastrous passion for playing the stock market can be fully realized only at the gambling tables. There he finds the casino dominated by the almost allegorical figure of an old British millionnairess, the last survivor of her family, who exists only for her nightly visit to the tables: "Tandis que tout périssait autour d'elle, la vieille femme qui s'était ridée à chaque malheur, se trouvait au bout de son âge, avec, entre ses mains résumée, la toute-puissance de la maison, la monstrueuse richesse dont elle ne savait que faire" (p. 380).[r] She has become completely insensitive to the life that goes on around her, existing only for the next turn of the card. As Aragon's lingering descriptions make abundantly clear, she is meant to embody a lifeless capitalist order centered on that other Monte Carlo, the stock market.

[r] While everything was perishing around her, the old woman, who had been more and more wrinkled by each misfortune, was at the end of her era, with, in her hands alone, the incredible power of the business, the monstrous riches, more than she knew what to do with.

The second of Aragon's old women is the aging prostitute, Dora Tavernier, who presides over the last days of a paralyzed Pierre Mercadier. Aragon's physical descriptions emphasize the deformation of her appearance by her sordid life, but he views her not only as a symbol but as a pathetic victim of a society that dreams of realizing the bourgeois ideals of romantic love and happy family life while it forces people to live by prostitution. Dora's brothel, Les Hirondelles, is the fitting last refuge of the bourgeois individualist, and, as the brothel is burned down at the end of the novel in order to make way for a new cartel, it indicates the fate of the whole bourgeois edifice.

In his portrayal of industrialists and their financial dealings, Aragon is most interested in exposing the basic nature of an economic class. He once described this as the primary objective in his creation of characters: "you must substitute class for the soul."[71] The capitalists shown in *Les Cloches de Bâle* do indeed seem to be mere representatives of their class; they lack not only a soul but any interiority whatsoever. This is primarily because they are portrayed, in the first section, by a narrative voice that speaks only in clichés and has no ability to penetrate appearances.[72] Later, the same figures are seen through the uncomprehending eyes of Catherine or from the unsympathetic perspective of the taxi driver Victor. In *Les Beaux Quartiers*, the character of Joseph Quesnel is portrayed with greater depth, a portrayal Susan Suleiman sees as potentially subverting Aragon's anticapitalistic thesis.[73] I would argue, however, that this type of characterization serves in fact to illustrate the theory, articulated by the character himself, of "the double man." According to this theory, the fragmentation imposed by capitalist society causes a man to lead two lives: he must rigidly separate his sentimental and human attachments from the cold, calculating personality he displays in his business dealings. Although Aragon has said the idea of "the double man" is that of a fictional creation rather than his own,[74] other characters in *Les Beaux Quartiers* do, in fact, display such a division: Joris de Houten separates his business activities from his relationship with the admirable Martha Jonghens, and Richard Grésandage has a warm and unpretentious home life entirely unrelated to his activities in the Finance Ministry. Thus the interiority suddenly accorded the capitalists in *Les Beaux Quartiers* serves only to bring out a representative feature of their class.

The working class does not come in for any less superficial treatment. Its one significant representative in this cycle of novels is Victor Dehaynin, the taxi driver who rescues Catherine from a suicide attempt in *Les Cloches de Bâle*. Victor is a reliable spokesman for the party line and sets Catherine straight on several issues, but his whole being is summed up in his rather mechanical activity as a militant. Like Catherine, Victor is given a biography, but a biography that, like that of the protagonist in Malraux's *Le Temps du mépris*, is designed to allow him to participate in much of the history of the struggling workers' movement. He has been radicalized as a member of the famous "seventeenth," the soldiers who had refused to fire on strikers as ordered. This event is later stressed as part of the working-class history related to Armand at the mass meeting in *Les Beaux Quartiers*, and it is echoed in the soldiers whom Catherine sees at the strike in Cluses, who are not eager to fire at the mob of workers. As Nizan and Malraux would later do, Aragon is attempting to construct a history of revolutionary struggle in France in order to combat the deformed perception of reality taught in the schools. As a character says in Aragon's postwar novel, *Les Communistes*, "Il faudrait leur apprendre l'histoire de France. Ils sont pour Dumouriez contre Robespierre . . . n'allez pas leur dire que c'était un traître, ce général: un général n'est jamais un traître." [s75]

The characters who assume the central positions in both *Les Cloches de Bâle* and *Les Beaux Quartiers* and who are analyzed most deeply are caught between the two opposing classes and are shown in the process of deciding where their loyalties lie. The long middle section of *Les Cloches de Bâle* is the story of the awakening to social injustice of Catherine, a beautiful young Russian émigrée who is dependent on the profits from her father's oil wells. In the course of the novel she is progressively attracted to the working-class movement, which, as Aragon clearly indicates, would provide the only acceptable solution to her dilemma. Aragon claimed that this section of *Les Cloches de Bâle* was written in opposition to the first part, in response to Elsa Triolet's comment that the story of Diane was leading nowhere.[76] Catherine's first movement of rebellion is thus against the status of women in Western society, who, like Diane, are enslaved to men by money, as her own mother had been to her tyrannical Russian husband. Catherine's primary goal is "liberation," which she

[s]You would have to teach them the history of France. They are for Dumouriez against Robespierre . . . don't try to tell them he was a traitor: a general is never a traitor.

envisions primarily as a situation in which a woman would possess a sexual freedom equal to a man's. Because of her personal dissatisfaction with society, she turns to theories of political protest, exploring and rejecting Catholic social doctrines (insipid and hypocritical) and anarchism (more critical of the workers than of their masters, oppressive to women, and in the pay of the police, to boot) before she literally plunges into the taxi strike through her meeting with Victor. Despite her attraction to the workers and their movement, Catherine is kept from participating fully by her remaining attachments to the bourgeoisie, symbolized by the monthly check she receives from her rich father. The healing contact with the workers is able to cure her of the potentially fatal case of tuberculosis she had contracted—an illness surely related symbolically to the corrupting influences of society—but Catherine is, at the end of the novel, still unable to make the final break. Aragon himself had undergone a long period of personal debate from the moment of his first attraction to the French Communist party at the time of its founding in 1920 to his public break with the surrealists in favor of wholehearted devotion to Communism in 1930. He has admitted that he put much of his own struggle to free himself from his class into Catherine: "She translated for me what had been my own difficulties."[77]

Armand Barbentane, the bourgeois protagonist of *Les Beaux Quartiers*, does finally reject his family's financial support, get a job in a factory (as a "scab"), and ultimately ally himself with the striking workers. Or, rather, it should be said that one part of the protagonist makes this positive transition, because the central characters are a pair of brothers much like Martin du Gard's Jacques and Antoine Thibault. The older Barbentane brother, Edmond, had always accepted the values represented by his father, a provincial doctor and Radical deputy; the younger, Armand, had always rebelled, first by espousing his mother's religion against his father's militant secularism and then by getting himself thrown out of boarding school for having an affair with a laundress. As the two brothers arrive in Paris, they each have an opportunity to choose the direction of their lives. Succumbing to the lure of love and material success (these two things seem inseparable in the capitalist world) Edmond ends up in the bizarre position of being paid by Quesnel to be Carlotta's lover, an arrangement that permits Quesnel some peace of mind but reduces Edmond himself to a prostitution far more humiliating than Carlotta's. In contrast, Armand joins the ranks of the workers. In

Susan Suleiman's analysis, the novel uses the elementary schema of the "antithetical brothers," juxtaposing two exemplary apprenticeship stories, one negative and the other positive.[78] The destinies of the two brothers serve as an allegorical representation of the choices available to the bourgeoisie, and Aragon declares that they, too, are incarnations of different facets of himself: "The two brothers of the book, Armand and Edmond, were really a single character doubled for the purposes of the novel; it was I, the one who knows how to please and the one who is unable to please, myself rewritten in the negative separated from myself rewritten in the positive."[79]

It is clear from this examination of the protagonists of *Les Cloches de Bâle* and *Les Beaux Quartiers* that Aragon is discussing in these two novels not only the origins of World War I but his own political evolution. In the characters of Catherine and Armand, he is tracing a path he is implicitly—and, at times, explicitly—urging his readers to follow. By the time he writes *Les Voyageurs de l'impériale*, in the face of the collapse of the French Left and the imminence of war, he can only examine the failure of the bourgeoisie to make such a political commitment.

Many other aspects of these novels, ostensibly set in the years immediately preceding World War I, reveal a relevance to the 1930s. In *Les Cloches de Bâle*, Aragon's omniscient narrator points some of these out, suddenly breaking into the narrative to introduce a brief glimpse of subsequent historical events. The world of Aragon's novels is clearly not one of those constructions of the imagination that ceases to be with the last word of the narrative; it is, indeed, "the real world," and its characters and events will continue to project themselves into the future. One of these sudden intrusions of the future has to do with the historical figure of Paul Doumer, the man who was elected president of the Republic in 1931 in preference to Briand. Doumer appears briefly in the narrative of *Les Cloches de Bâle* as a supporter of the industrialists of the "Comité des Forges," but Aragon breaks in to note that this is the same man who is to be assassinated in 1932 (just two years before the publication of the novel). Thus he establishes a link between the political figures who dominate both the prewar and postwar worlds.

But Aragon does not always have to insert contemporary references as openly as this. Much of the time he prefers to leave the job to the reader, for whom such connections would have been inescapable at the time of the novel's publication. The many suicides of

Les Cloches de Bâle, for example, could not help but evoke a more recent event. Aragon's novel appeared in 1934, not long after the February riots (see chapter 4), which were initiated by the alleged suicide of the financial swindler Stavisky. Many people accused the police of having killed Stavisky themselves in order to prevent him from exposing the important political figures involved in the scandal, disclosures that threatened to compromise the entire regime. *Les Cloches de Bâle* includes six successful suicides and one suicide attempt (*Les Beaux Quartiers* records three, but it increases the number of murders). This frequency of deaths and, especially, suicide (as well as miscarriages and abortions) must certainly be a comment, much like Guilloux's, on the destructiveness and *self*-destructiveness of bourgeois capitalist society. Some of the suicides seem suspiciously like crimes. The death of Pierre de Sabran, who supposedly shoots himself in despair over Brunel's financial pressure, is narrated from the totally uncomprehending perspective of Diane's young son Guy. What actually happened is never made clear, although several disputable versions of the facts are put forth by the characters. The death of Martha Jonghens's brother Blaise is even more suspicious. Blaise confesses to Catherine that he is about to be caught at his illegal manipulation of stock market funds; after Martha enlists the aid of Joris de Houten (who, the reader knows, is a police agent), Blaise is found by the police in a strange hotel room, where he has supposedly killed himself. There is more than a suggestion that he has been eliminated as an incompetent or possibly talkative partner in one of de Houten's schemes. The double deaths of Martha's sister Solange and her husband, who has been introduced into the family by de Houten, are also unexplained. They have ostensibly died from an overdose of drugs, but de Houten himself is questioned about the matter before the scandal is finally hushed up.

The suicides and many other incidents in the novel testify to the activity of the clandestine police network. This police underground, it is intimated, is deeply involved in financial scandals as well as in political repression. The anarchist Libertad is supposedly a police agent, but the police finally turn on him and beat him to death. And the famous anarchist terrorists, the "bande à Bonnot," are also, it is implied, in league with the police, who are in no hurry to catch them as long as their activities can succeed in terrorizing the public into accepting the need for the regime's version of law and order. At the end of the novel, Aragon hints that the assignment of Brunel to spy on the pacifist leader Jaurès may be related to the latter's assassination on the eve of war. As a beginning reporter cutting his journalistic teeth on crime stories,[80] Aragon certainly had a great deal of contact with the Police. And as a reporter for the Communist *L'Humanité*, he had the opportunity to know them as a hostile presence; in fact, he was able to use the police station where he was once himself detained as the setting for one of the scenes in *Les Beaux Quartiers*.[81] But the importance of the police in *Les Cloches de Bâle* and *Les Beaux Quartiers* is more deeply related to a major issue at the time of these novels' publication. In 1934, in particular, attention was focused on the Paris prefect of police, Chiappe. He was removed from office under pressure from the socialists, who resented his tolerant attitude toward right-wing groups, as against his more violent treatment of left-wing demonstrators. Chiappe's removal particularly enraged the right-wing leagues and contributed directly to the February riots. Beyond the particular case of Chiappe, there was a widespread belief that the police played a concealed but powerful role in French politics. This vision of the police surfaces in the fiction of Communists like Aragon and Nizan (*La Conspiration*), as well as that of the fascist Drieu (*Gilles*) and the liberal André Chamson (*La Galère*).

Aragon's choice of a taxi strike as his example of proletarian action in *Les Cloches de Bâle* certainly has to do with the fact that he himself spent a great deal of time with the striking Paris taxi drivers of 1934, whose struggle he reported on daily in the columns of *L'Humanité*. Many of the episodes in *Les Cloches de Bâle* are direct transpositions of events of 1934—for example, the death of the driver Bédhomme and the demonstrations at his funeral. Strikes of all kinds were common in the years 1934–36, while Aragon was writing *Les Cloches de Bâle* and *Les Beaux Quartiers*, and it is no mere coincidence that they play a major role in the novels. In *Les Voyageurs de l'impériale* the emphasis is rather on the repression of unionized labor that occurred in the later years of the decade after the fall of the Popular Front. The mass meetings and marches on which Aragon focuses—the taxi drivers' marches and the congress at Basel in *Les Cloches de Bâle*, the meeting at the pré Saint-Gervais in *Les Beaux Quartiers*—were also common events of the politically agitated time in which Aragon was writing.

Each of his novels of the 1930s is, in fact, designed to reflect the situation of the particular time in which it was written. *Les Cloches de Bâle*, as I have indicated, is a commentary on the events of February 1934. Its fragmented narrative form, in which each division of the work portrays a distinct social milieu, reflects the deep social divisions that had been exacerbated by the February riots, and the groping of the protagonist, Catherine, to ally herself with the workers' movement reflects the Communists' tentative effort toward gathering bourgeois support under the leadership of the proletariat. The pacifist emphasis in *Les Cloches de Bâle*, particularly in the last section about the Congress of Basel itself, is appropriate to a moment of intense French pacifist sentiment, a response to the recent signs of renewed German aggression and the observance of the twentieth anniversary of the declaration of war in 1914.[82]

Les Beaux Quartiers, which Aragon finished on June 10, 1936, was written at a very different moment of the decade. The union of the Left created in response to the February riots had become the Popular Front and was about to form its first government under Léon Blum A wave of popular enthusiasm was sweeping the country, and, under these conditions, it is no wonder that Aragon allowed his protagonist, Armand Barbentane, to declare his solidarity with the workers, as many bourgeois leftists were doing in the mid-1930s. As Garaudy points out, there is also in *Les Beaux Quartiers* a heavy emphasis on French nationalism.[83] In *Les Cloches de Bâle*, Aragon's Wisner had called the concept of the French "une façon de parler très simple, pour dire *nous*, un certain groupe d'intérêts communs" (p. 103),[1] and this is what Aragon himself had believed for a long time. But in 1936, with the Left in power, France once again seemed to have become the property of the workers, and patriotism was again an acceptable sentiment. The Communists made various attempts to encourage a new interpretation of the national history, placing particular emphasis on the French revolutionary spirit. The Communist-dominated Confédération Générale du Travail commissioned Jean Renoir to make his epic film, *La Marseillaise*, one of the highlights of which is the mingling of the royal guards with the people, a scene much like the twentieth-century mutiny of the "sev-

---

[1]a very simple manner of speaking, which means *we*—a certain group of common interests (p. 79).

enteenth," which figures importantly in *Les Beaux Quartiers*. The French Communist party in 1936 heavily stressed the policy of national unity, and it is little wonder that *Les Beaux Quartiers*, which Aragon admittedly wrote at the party's specific request, does so too.[84] The major theme of *Les Voyageurs de l'impériale* is also related to the moment of its composition. Aragon's bitter condemnation of bourgeois individualism and political indifference, in the character of Pierre Mercadier, takes on its full meaning in this end-of-the-decade period when everything seemed to be falling apart. Aragon has admitted that, through Pierre Mercadier, he was expressing his condemnation of the bourgeois liberals whose unwillingness to make a political commitment had contributed to the failure of the Popular Front and to the disastrous situation of French foreign affairs.[85] Pierre's rejection of political action is revealed in all its cruel indifference when he refuses to defend his dearest friend, a Jewish colleague, against a violent antisemitic attack at the time of the Dreyfus Affair. It is precisely at the moment of an antisemitic riot at the lycée where he teaches that Pierre chooses to turn his back on all his responsibilities, willfully failing to aid his friend Meyer and even walking out on the Jewish child who comes to him for protection. The book burning attendant upon the riot portrayed in the novel and the cries of "Death to the Jews" could not fail to evoke the resurgence of antisemitism that occurred in the France of the late 1930s, where similar cries were heard even in the Chamber of Deputies during Léon Blum's last ministry of the Popular Front.[86] Pierre Mercadier's refusal of political involvement is summed up in the metaphor of the *impériale*, the open top deck of the old Paris buses, from which Pierre obstinately refuses to descend in order to understand the mechanisms of the political machine that is carrying him and his fellow passengers to their destruction. Because he and his generation have insisted on having their individualistic freedom from responsibility, Pierre's son Pascal must spend four years at the front: as Pascal comments, his father's liberty has made his prison.

With the breakup of the Popular Front, the Communist party in the late 1930s had returned to its policy of denouncing the more moderate elements of the Left, a denunciation that Aragon eagerly takes up in *Les Voyageurs de l'impériale*, not only in his condemnation of Pierre's disdain for politics but also, perhaps, in his harsh treatment of Sarah Meyer's need to impose her concept of an ideal harmony on those around her, even when such harmony flies in the face of the real state of affairs.

The last section of the book, written while Aragon was awaiting mobilization in 1939, heavily stresses the motifs of death and corruption that had dominated the two preceding novels. The paralyzed Pierre is reduced to dependence on the care of the more and more demented proprietor of the brothel, which itself finally goes up in flames. That an innocent worker is accused of responsibility for the fire is a situation Aragon saw as not without analogy to his own at the time: he finished the last hundred pages of the novel at the Chilean embassy, in hiding from French patriots who blamed the war on the Communists and the Soviet nonaggression pact with Hitler.

Roger Garaudy has praised Aragon for his use of contemporary experience to illuminate and humanize his analysis of a moment of the past.[87] But in his depiction of the past, Aragon spends most of his time dealing with issues of direct contemporary relevance. The oppression of striking workers, suicides connected with financial scandals, protest marches, clandestine police activity, refusal of political commitment—all of these have more relevance to the 1930s than to the years preceding World War I. Rather than using the experience of the present to illuminate the past, Aragon seems to be quite consciously using the somewhat distant time frame of his novels as a vehicle for more effectively treating the issues of his own time. In his 1965 preface to *Les Beaux Quartiers*, he confirms this interpretation: "The appearance of the croupier Leroy and the policeman Columbin bring out here (as earlier, in *The Bells*, the taxi strike of 1911–12 mirroring that of 1933–34) the nature of the novels I had undertaken turned toward the future, and where I seem to be explaining 1913, when by 1913 I explain 1934 and what follows from it."[88] A major reason for his choice of a prewar setting is that these years stand clearly under a judgment of history: the events of this time had led directly to a war whose horror and destruction were universally denounced in the 1930s. Thus, for Aragon, to show that a certain type of activity led to the slaughter of World War I is an effective condemnation of that activity, in his eyes and in the eyes of most of his readers. The war serves in Aragon's novels as history's judgment on the functioning of capitalist society, a judgment even more ominous in the threatening atmosphere of the 1930s.

L'Eté 1914

Roger Martin du Gard's family chronicle, *Les Thibault,* published between 1922 and 1940, offers a particularly striking case of the sudden eruption of history into the novel in the critical period around 1930. David Schalk has argued that the unique evolution of *Les Thibault* testifies to Martin du Gard's attainment of a "historical consciousness" in the course of its composition.[89] This composition, as René Garguilo has shown through extensive documentation,[90] took place in two distinct stages, corresponding to the two major divisions of a work that, according to Claude-Edmonde Magny, too prominently displays the crack in its structure.[91]

Interestingly, the break in composition occurred at just the point where Magny herself notes a transformation of the novel, in the years 1929–33, a period when Martin du Gard began to concern himself intensely with contemporary events. He had conceived the Thibault series shortly after his return from service in World War I. It was thus the first of many examples of the *roman-fleuve* that flourished in the *entre-deux-guerres*. The *Fabulation générale* of 1920, the detailed outline of the entire chronicle,[92] projects a study of two brothers, Jacques and Antoine Thibault, whose different responses to life were, as Martin du Gard was the first to admit, reflections of opposing tendencies in his own nature.[93] Jacques, the eternal rebel, was slated to die in World War I, leaving his wife, Jenny, with a son. The older brother, Antoine, was to return from the war to marry Jenny, adopt Jacques's son, and continue his successful medical career. The projected episodes of the characters' postwar existence, which was to extend until 1940, included adulterous love affairs, blackmail, and even murder. These events, often quite melodramatic, were intended to advance the characters' psychological development, in keeping with Martin du Gard's professed intention of writing a work where people rather than ideas would be paramount.[94] His great prewar success, *Jean Barois,* had been a highly documented study, complete with footnotes, of events surrounding the Dreyfus case; *Les Thibault* had been conceived as a move away from that documentary style and an exploration of other fictional veins.

The first six volumes of the Thibault chronicle, which appeared during the 1920s, followed the general lines of the original plan.

Martin du Gard noticed, however, that as he became more involved with his characters, he had begun to slow the pace of the original development: the volume published in 1929, *La Mort du père*, had only gotten him up to events occurring in 1913. It was perhaps this factor that first gave him doubts about the wisdom of carrying out his original plan. In his own *Souvenirs littéraires* he claims that a lengthy convalescence from a serious automobile accident in 1931 gave him time to reflect on the chronicle as a whole, making him realize he had hardly completed one-third of the projected work and would have to write at least fifteen more volumes in order to finish. Appalled at the thought, he decided to destroy most of a volume already written, called *L'Apareillage*, and to alter his original plan drastically.[95] In the new scheme that he eventually conceived, he planned to have the brothers corrupted by their inheritance of the family fortune and then die in the war.[96]

As Martin du Gard went ahead with his new ending, he decided to jump right to the summer of 1914 and immediately found himself immersed in historical research, as he had been for *Jean Barois*. His plan of tracing events leading to the war through Swiss-based international socialist circles, with which Jacques had become involved in the previous volumes, demanded more and more documentation. Not content with reading quantities of studies on the period and contemporary newspaper accounts,[97] he entered into a prolonged relationship with Marcel Lallemand, a man who had known the milieux he was attempting to describe. Like other writers of the period, Martin du Gard seems to have needed some *expérience vécue*. The fascinating correspondence between him and Lallemand[98] records the author's struggle to make his characters historically accurate while remaining true to his original conception of their psychology. Jacques, in particular, became the subject of a tug-of-war between the two men, Lallemand seeing him as a thoroughgoing revolutionary in his own image and Martin du Gard insisting on preserving his fundamental antipathy to violence and his doubts concerning human perfectibility. The worst crisis in composition, however, centered on the character of Jacques's fellow socialist Meynestrel, whom Martin du Gard had already cast as the pilot of the plane in which Jacques was to undertake his suicidal attempt to drop pacifist leaflets on the frontline troops. Lallemand correctly observed that Meynestrel, a socialist of Lenin's stripe, would see the outbreak of war as a prelude to the expected revolution and would thus be far from sharing Jacques's desperation. In the face of threatened collapse of the whole project, Martin du Gard concocted an amorous betrayal for the unfortunate Meynestrel, thus allowing him to pilot the doomed plane while remaining historically and emotionally consistent.

Such concern with documentation, which even went so far as to threaten the psychological makeup of the characters, caused this work on the summer of 1914 to grow to unusual proportions. It came out in three separate volumes, each of them longer than many of those already published in the chronicle and, despite Martin du Gard's desperate need for money at this time, it was not ready for publication until 1936. It had already smothered the projected earlier volume on the effects of inherited fortune, and, after its publication, Martin du Gard felt it necessary only to add the shorter *Epilogue*, which traces the last moments of Antoine Thibault, in order to put an end to the chronicle.

L'Eté 1914,[99] the volume that appeared after the seven-year break in *Les Thibault*, showed a distinct change in style, in subject matter, and, above all, in its conception of history. Martin du Gard now saw the advent of war as overwhelming the individual lives of the characters: "In the foreground is *the war*, the exaltation of July 14, Jacques's rebellions, my characters swept up in the torment. . . . Public life very intermingled with private." [100] Such an abrupt transformation may be explained, as many critics have done, by saying that World War I was itself the occasion of just such an intrusion of historical forces into individual lives.[101] Paul Nizan, for example, praised the book for making it clear that "since 1914 all life has become public." [102] The novel would thus be merely reflecting a change that had actually occurred. But, if the change had occurred, Martin du Gard had not perceived it at the time. It was shortly after the armistice that he drew up his plan of a family destiny in which the war would bring only minor alterations. Although Jacques was to be killed, the lives of the other characters were to go on after the war— in a world that was fundamentally unchanged. As late as 1927, the war was not central to the novel; commenting on the early volumes, including those concerning the war period, he called them only a "prologue" to the "heart of the matter" that was yet to come.[103] Yet by 1932 he had come to see the war as the catastrophe that had brought to an end the stable bourgeois world of the Thibault family: "The Thibaults disappear, wiped out in the war. And it is an entire society, a whole form of the bourgeoisie that the war wipes out with them."[104] Thus a new consciousness of the significance of the Great War was fundamental to the radical changes that occurred in *Les Thibault*.

Martin du Gard's own claim that purely literary concerns were a major factor in this revision need not be disputed. Almost assuredly, a novel following the original plan would have degenerated into soap opera episodes, tied loosely together by the reader's continuing, but certainly diminishing, curiosity about the destiny of the familiar characters. The new ending substantially tightens the structure by preserving the basic polarity of the two brothers that had been the motor of the early volumes.[105] Magny's doubts to the contrary, *Les Thibault* certainly benefits, in aesthetic terms, from the changes made, and Martin du Gard was too good a novelist to have been unaware of this.

Nevertheless, it would be difficult to deny that a change had taken place in Martin du Gard's idea of history, in his concept of the individual's relationship to the events of his time. In *L'Eté 1914* the individual concerns of the Thibaults and their friends are suddenly submerged in the flow of history. Even the consummation of the love between Jacques and Jenny, a moment prepared from the very beginning of the chronicle, becomes only an episode in the swift stream of events. Where the earlier volumes had traced in great detail the sentimental conflicts and even the daily lives of the characters, *L'Eté 1914* is primarily concerned with the characters' reactions to the accumulation of events that lead to the war. As in Malraux's *L'Espoir*, this analysis takes place in carefully constructed dialogues between characters whose various points of view illuminate the central problems.

Much space is devoted to evoking the state of the prewar socialist movement through the conversations of the *parlote* at Geneva. Although these characters had not previously appeared in the chronicle, there is little attempt to evoke an interest in their personal lives, apart from the rapid presentation of the amorous triangle formed by Meynestrel, his mistress, Freda, and the English painter Paterson. But the main concern of these people is the eventual form of the Revolution and their position with respect to the maneuvering of the various European governments.

Jacques's trip to Paris, on a special mission, returns him to the world that had formed the background of the earlier volumes. But here, even the suicide of the profligate Jérôme de Fontanin, Jenny's father, provides only a momentary respite from the discussions of the war. The reader's almost constant accompaniment of Jacques's activities affords insight into the Socialists' frantic efforts to avert the war, as he keeps himself at the center of their activity. He has glimpses of real historical personages—who do not, however, become active characters, as they do in *Les Hommes de bonne volonté*— and manages to be present at certain significant historical moments, for example, the arrival of the German socialist delegates on the very eve of war and, most strikingly, the assassination of Jaurès.

Views of a different milieu are afforded by his visits to Antoine, who is completely absorbed in his medical practice and the establishment of his own small laboratory. The young members of his research team present the views of a spectrum of nonsocialist French opinion, from the militaristic zeal of a young follower of the Action française to a skeptical pacifism. The inside information of the diplomat Rumelles gives Antoine some indication of the real gravity of events and the inevitability of the war. The situation is put into a larger historical perspective by Antoine's revered teacher, Dr. Philip, whose views resemble the position later assumed by an older and wiser Antoine. Philip sees the war as the third and most catastrophic of the "somber" events that have disrupted the life of his generation, along with the loss of religious faith and the Dreyfus Affair.

But Antoine in this volume functions primarily as a demonstration of the futility of an individual's attempt to consider himself as isolated from the forces of history. Jacques's dialogues with Antoine confront the political activist with the average man, who wants to be let alone to manage his own personal affairs, leaving politics to the experts. Although Antoine's arguments that his time is completely taken up in serving his patients have some merit, they are seriously weakened by his indifference to social injustice and his preoccupation with establishing a name for himself through the scientific discoveries of his laboratory group. As his ambitions are frustrated by the outbreak of war, Antoine is forced to realize the greater realism of Jacques's concern with history. But it is only after his war experience that Antoine can come to a real understanding of Jacques's position, an understanding denied him at the time of their last meeting as Antoine departs for the front. This, in Camus's view, is the principal theme of Martin du Gard's work and the secret of his continuing contemporaneity: "It concerns the evolution that leads an individual to the recognition of the destiny of all men and the acceptance of its struggle."[106]

At this moment of separation, the brothers seem, in a sense, to exchange roles. Up to this point, it was Antoine who had defended the individual's right to pursue his own life, Jacques who had stressed his necessary involvement in historical forces. Now it is Antoine who, with resigned courage, accepts his part in the common destiny and Jacques who suddenly puts his hope in the exemplary act of a single individual. Martin du Gard's presentation of the inevitable progression of events that led from Sarajevo to the mobilization seems to accord little weight to individual intervention.[107] True, Meynestrel might have changed some attitudes by publishing the German documents stolen by his socialist agent; but this episode is one of the very few that Martin du Gard had fabricated out of whole cloth. He also accords great importance to Jaurès's leadership role, and there remains the possibility that, had he not been assassinated, the Socialists might have taken some action. However, Rumelles's accounts of the "diabolical mechanism" of events, which even the diplomats can no longer control, gives support to the thesis that no single person could have changed their course, and Antoine echoes this assumption. Certainly, by the time Jacques undertakes his last, self-imposed mission, the actual fighting has already begun, and there remains not the smallest possibility of stopping the war.

The final pages of *L'Eté 1914* offer a graphic illustration of the plight of the individual in this new era of mass warfare. The static discussions that dominate the rest of the novel are suddenly replaced by a torrent of action, as Jacques's plane crashes not far behind the French lines in the early stages of combat. The hurried gendarmes who remove him from the charred wreckage have no way of understanding the heroism of his intended gesture, and his individual suffering is lost in the panic of fleeing soldiers and civilians. Schalk has seen this ending of *L'Eté 1914* as "the ultimate confrontation of the privileged hero with the realities of twentieth-century history, as the last nineteenth-century act in a major work of French literature, and as the last possible of such acts."[108] By the time of *Epilogue*, Antoine is ready to express a disdain for individual heroism that is characteristic of the modern era.[109]

Despite his evident criticism of Antoine's initial indifference to politics, the author of *Les Thibault* has been cited as a writer who refused the role of *écrivain engagé* so prevalent in the 1930s. Like his friend Gide, who nevertheless was very actively involved before coming around to Martin du Gard's point of view, he feared participation in politics as a threat to his primary activity as a writer. Yet it is not true, as some would have it, that Martin du Gard always refused his support for political causes. Although he feared that an illconsidered signature might force him into assuming positions not really his own, Martin du Gard did, in fact, sign a number of antiwar manifestos in the 1930s.[110] In a letter to Gide in 1932, he seems to be tempted from his work by the pressure of current events: "I am finding it unbelievably difficult to reinterest myself in my little literature, so solicited is my whole attention by the sinister racket made by the world."[111] But in a letter to Marcel Lallemand, he expressed a contrary attitude: "You know that for months I have been wavering between the desire to block my ears and the temptation to get more involved. For the moment, I am the man who turns his back. . . . Taking sides is a necessity *of action* but not at all of thought, nor of art. (On the contrary?)"[112] The contradictory tendencies of Martin du Gard's own nature are thus accurately mirrored in Jacques's passionate commitment and Antoine's quiet devotion to a profession that, like that of the writer, also renders service to humanity. The extremes of indifference and militancy are both criticized, and in the end, the dying Antoine, who has absorbed many of Jacques's insights, reaches a sort of equilibrium that may ultimately have been that of his creator.

Martin du Gard's attempts to disentangle himself from involvement in political groups, none of which could overcome his basic skepticism, do not imply that he was oblivious to what was going on around him. He could hardly be so, when his dearest friends, men with whom he was in constant contact during this period, were involved up to their necks in the day-to-day political struggles. Closest of these friends was Gide, whose influence on him was great in both literary and political matters. It was quite probably Gide who, in the course of a visit to Martin du Gard's home at Le Tertre, suggested to him the possible role of the war in drastically changing the lives of his characters.[113] Gide's involvement in the World Congress of Youth Against Fascism and War in 1933 caused him to reflect on the importance of lending new prestige to the status of conscientious objectors, and this may not have been without its effect on the development of Jacques Thibault, for whom Martin du Gard was planning such a role.[114] His conception of Jacques's activities after the mobilization must certainly have been the product of the 1930s climate, because Martin du Gard was unable to find any historical model for Jacques's action. The solution he finally adopted seems to have been suggested by the fate of Lauro de Bosis, a young antifascist in Mussolini's Italy, a case with much contemporary relevance.

Indeed, the antiwar efforts that formed the center of French left-wing activity in the early 1930s corresponded to Martin du Gard's own deepest sympathies, which dated from the wartime era. Although he did accept mobilization, unlike Jacques, phrases taken from Martin du Gard's wartime letters reveal a kindred spirit: "If I die, it is in a spirit of *revolt*, I *don't accept* this war, I will be dying for an order of things totally *opposed* to all my directions." [115] In contrast to Gide, Martin du Gard did not devote a great deal of his time to public activities. He seems to have been a writer who needed real isolation in order to work, and he was, in this period, pouring his pacifist convictions into Jacques's protest in *L'Eté 1914*. As late as 1938, Martin du Gard echoed the passionate words he had earlier put into the mouth of his character: "anything, rather than war." [116] Thus he was not simply making excuses when he explained his failure to make public pronouncements by claiming that everything he had to say went into his *Thibault* chronicle. It was, as Camus has claimed, "the first of committed novels." [117]

The publication of *L'Eté 1914* furnished Martin du Gard a platform for a major public pronouncement when, largely because of the pacifist sentiments expressed in the novel, he was awarded the Nobel Prize in 1937. In his speech of acceptance, he stressed the antiwar content, with its relationship to contemporary events, as constituting the novel's deepest significance: "In these months of anxiety we have been living through . . . too many indicators show us the return of that cowardly fatalism, that general consent that, alone, permits wars to take place; in this exceptionally grave moment that humanity is going through, I wish . . . my book on the summer of 1914 would be read and discussed and that it would recall to everyone . . . the pathetic lesson of the past." [118] This "lesson" is the one he had expressed in *L'Eté 1914* in the impassioned words of Jacques: "Les autres, je ne dis pas qu'ils désirent la guerre: presque tous la redoutent. Mais ils s'y résignent, parce qu'ils la croient fatale. Et c'est la plus dangereuse conviction qui puisse s'enraciner dans le cerveau d'un homme d'Etat, que de croire la guerre inévitable" (3:141–

42).[a] Martin du Gard's horror of war was such that he maintained his pacifist feelings long after his left-wing friends had accepted the inevitability of a confrontation with Nazi Germany. Even during the Spanish Civil War he maintained a rigid refusal of war: "Am strong as iron *for neutrality*. Principle: anything, *rather than war. Anything, anything.* Even fascism in Spain. And don't push me, because I would say: yes . . . even fascism in France."[119]

Although the absurdity of Jacques's death is a criticism of his mistaken belief in the efficacy of individual heroism, it paradoxically serves to validate the pacifist ideal for which he dies. The confusion and death that dominate the Alsatian retreat prefigure the nature of the war that is yet to come. Like many of his fellow writers of this era, Martin du Gard chose a moment of French collapse as his one illustration of the experience of combat. Strangely enough, it involved the one area of the front he had not seen in the course of his own wartime service. He followed what had become a general practice of narrating battlefield events through the limited experience of Jacques (only later in *Epilogue* would the explanations of the diplomat Rumelles permit Antoine a "panoramic" view of the war). But Martin du Gard limits his outlook even more than is usual by reducing Jacques to a state of semiconsciousness after the plane crash, although the narration departs from his point of view in several instances. Jacques's confused perceptions mirror the confusion of the leaderless soldiers fleeing before what they gradually realize to be a German advance. The reader, constantly reminded of Jacques's intense pain, is made aware of the cruelty and indifference to human suffering that has been an immediate product of the wartime mentality. Thinking the wounded Jacques a German spy, ultrapatriotic civilians refuse him a drink and even burn him with a cigarette. And when the gendarme carrying his stretcher must choose between saving Jacques or effecting his own rapid escape, he quickly opts for survival. Before shooting his charge, he attempts to justify his act to himself by seeing Jacques as less than human, twice calling him "shitheap" ("fumier"). Martin du Gard's one short battle scene contains the emphasis on the inhumanity and futility of war that marks

---

[a] As for the rest of them, I won't go so far as to say they actually want war; in fact, they're mostly scared of it. But they're resigned to war, because they think it's bound to come. And no more dangerous belief can take root in the mind of a statesman than the belief that war's inevitable (p. 123).

the great antiwar novels of the 1930s. Although Jacques's sacrifice has accomplished nothing, his point of view on the war itself has been thoroughly vindicated.

The left-wing circles in which Martin du Gard found himself in the early 1930s, at least through the intermediary of his friends, were strongly under the influence of Marxist ideas and fascinated by the Soviet Union. During most of the period of the composition of *L'Eté 1914*, Gide was strongly attracted to Communism, an attachment that lasted until his disillusioned return from the USSR in 1936. Eugène Dabit, another friend, had died in the Soviet Union during the visit of Gide's group. During this period Martin du Gard was also a regular correspondent of his old acquaintance, Jean-Richard Bloch, who was cofounder, with Romain Rolland, of the review *Europe* and who operated on the margins of Communism. Although Martin du Gard was firm in his rejection of the Communist party—primarily because of its doctrinaire nature and readiness to accept revolutionary violence—he could certainly not remain immune to the Marxist influences that surrounded him.

An indication of his interest in Marxist ideas is furnished by *Vieille France*, a short novel he wrote during the very period of the crisis in *Les Thibault* (see chapter 3). Defending this somewhat iconoclastic work in a letter to Marcel Arland, Martin du Gard reiterated his novel's condemnation of the traditional French rural mentality and expressed hope in the possibilities of social progress embodied in the urban working class. Schalk has observed that at this moment Martin du Gard was "as close to a Marxist position as he would ever come."[120]

Some Marxist influence is noticeable in *L'Eté 1914*, as might be expected, but the distance is great from Aragon's more doctrinaire approach to the origins of the war. In Martin du Gard's novel the primary exponent of socialist pacifism is Jacques, and he is far from orthodox. In fact, he joins the party only when the war appears to be imminent. His views dominate all the others, and he is often allowed to speak at length in his own voice. His conversations, his speech at the end of a pacifist rally, his tract meant for distribution to the troops, all reflect a socialist perspective, marked, however, by Jacques's concern for the individual and his opposition to violence, traits that he seems to have absorbed from Jaurès and that he shared with his author. In his manifesto, Jacques, like his fellow Socialists, blames the war on the machinations of capitalists and, secondarily, on the intrigues of power-hungry politicians. But these activities are never shown in Martin du Gard's novel, as they are in Aragon's, and thus do not seem to form a central part of Martin du Gard's interpretation of history. Various aspects of socialist theory, particularly the form the Revolution is to take, are explored in exhaustive detail in the reported discussions of the *parlote* in Geneva, which accounts for twelve entire chapters. But in *L'Eté 1914* the many conversations involving large numbers of characters allow room for a multiplicity of points of view. As Martin du Gard wrote to Gaston Gallimard in 1935, "I touch on all the major contemporary problems, *in dialogue* (that is, without drawing a dogmatic conclusion) and I am going to have all sides against me at once."[121] The Marxist views expressed by Jacques and his friends come under various types of criticism. Their analyses are often shown to be unrelated to reality, particularly when the mythical pacifism of the masses fails to act as an effective deterrent to war. Not only are the socialist leaders unable to produce the much-discussed general strike, but the workers themselves are the first to respond to mobilization with patriotic zeal. Jacques himself has serious doubts about his own public positions; he even wonders about the possibility of changing mankind through social revolution: "Il demeurait sceptique sur les possibilités morales de l'homme. . . . Corriger, réorganiser, parfaire la condition de l'homme par un changement total des institutions, par l'édification d'un système neuf, oui certes: Mais, espérer que ce nouvel ordre social renouvellerait aussi *l'homme*, en créant automatiquement un spécimen d'humanité foncièrement meilleur—cela, il n'y parvenait pas" (3 : 177).[v] Maurice Rieuneau has observed that Jacques harbors anarchist tendencies within him, a trait that brings him even closer to his creator.[122] Although Jacques's revolutionary activity did draw him the unreserved praise of Marxist critics,[123] his theoretical underpinnings are not as pure as they might have wished.

In *L'Eté 1914* Martin du Gard remains faithful, with some minor exceptions, to the historical events of the summer of 1914 and to the attitudes they had called forth from people of the time. He does not choose the episodes with an eye to providing parallels with the threatening prewar atmosphere of the 1930s, nor does he interject

---

[v]He remained sceptical as to the possibilities of human nature. . . . Amend, adjust, and indeed perfect the lot of man. But he could not bring himself to assume that the new social order would renew mankind itself, and, as a matter of course, produce an intrinsically better type of humanity (p. 156).

comments on a postwar future. Yet Martin du Gard was intensely conscious of the parallel between his historical research and the time in which he was writing. Several times in his correspondence he calls this recognition "anguishing." In a letter to Gide, for example, he wrote: "I am in the midst of a mass of documentation and profoundly upset to relive those pathetic weeks, with such a strong *human* interest. A retrospective emotion that is like a harmonic to the anxieties of the present moment. The analogy is at times arresting between 1933 and 1913 – 14." [124]

Although he did not allow his awareness of these similarities to alter his account of the events themselves, the interminable discussions in which the novel sometimes threatens to bog down reflect issues of great significance to the times through which Martin du Gard himself was living. Such questions as the individual's involvement in history, the right to conscientious objection, the nature of a social revolution, and, particularly, the means of avoiding a European war were as topical in 1934 as they had been twenty years earlier. They were indeed even more pertinent to an age that had begun to understand the consequences of the Great War and that had finally absorbed at least part of "the pathetic lesson of the past." As Garguilo has suggested, Martin du Gard used his characters of the Thibault chronicle to express "the oscillations of his thought in the thirties, constantly torn between the desire to believe revolutionary promises and a fundamental skepticism." [125] It is clear that the dialogue between the two Thibault brothers was going on in Martin du Gard's own life. The rebellion against society that characterized Jacques and his attraction to revolutionary activism seem to have been attitudes that tempted Martin du Gard himself, perhaps more than is evident from the facts of his life. And he fully shared Jacques's pacifism. But Antoine's deeper skepticism, his readier acceptance of the world as it is, combined with a desire to alleviate suffering through his professional activity, represent the other pole of Martin du Gard's personality. The oscillation between these two possibilities of human action, examined at length in *L'Eté 1914* and attaining its ultimate literary resolution in the mature Antoine of *Epilogue*, sums up Martin du Gard's personal response to his own *avant-guerre*.

CHAPTER 3

A Literature of the People

*Nous en avons assez, des personnages chics et de la littérature snob;
nous voulons peindre le peuple.* [a]

LÉON LEMONNIER
L'Oeuvre, August 27, 1929

Perhaps the most characteristic element of the change that swept over literature at the beginning of the 1930s was a modification of its subject matter. Brasillach, in his famous analysis of "the end of the postwar era," was among the first to note this change. He saw in the new literature a reaction against the introspection and escapism that had characterized the writers of the 1920s: "The reaction beginning today . . . is a reaction against egoism and abstraction. What the postwar writers refused was the existence of others and a feeling for the real."[1] A growing number of writers in the 1930s was determined to examine the lives of people at all levels of society, especially the lowest, and to approach these characters and their world in the tradition of "realism," in the various ways this concept was defined.

This movement of literary interest away from the individual was not the property of any one political perspective. It was felt as deeply by the fascist Brasillach as by the Communists Nizan and Aragon; it formed a bond between the reactionary Céline and the left-leaning Dabit. But ideological factors did play an important role in determining the types of social problem considered and the perspective from which they were viewed, as well as the favored literary techniques. In particular, they had direct consequences for the chosen mode of narration. Writers of the Left like Dabit and Guilloux

---

[a] We have had enough of elegant characters and snobbish literature; we want to portray the people.

89

tended to stress the existence of lower-class solidarity and cooperation, their ideal being the collective action of a small group. Their
sympathy for their lower-class characters was evidenced by their
preferred techniques of narration: they characteristically adopted
the point of view of one or more characters or used a narrative voice
clearly sympathetic to them. Writers whose allegiances lay to the
Right, on the other hand, tended to denigrate the lower classes for
what they saw as their innate corruption, choosing to entrust the
narration to characters somewhat distanced from the people they
observe. The moral ideal put forth by both Céline and Brasillach is
not that of groups, but rather of individuals strong enough to retain
their humanity in the midst of surrounding corruption.[2]

Much of the fiction of the 1930s that treated the lower classes was
written by non-Communists. There was surprisingly little effort to
focus exclusively on the workers in the fiction of Aragon and Nizan,
the two principal Communist writers of the era. Both preferred to
use the victimized status of women as a means of exposing social
oppression, and where they portrayed workers, they showed them
as a political force actively engaged in strikes or street demonstrations. The Communist writers were interested not in portraying the
proletariat per se, but in exposing the entire structure of society
from the "proletarian point of view," an intention that led them frequently to focus on the managerial classes and to rely heavily on an
omniscient narrator capable of providing the economic analysis in-
accessible to the more limited point of view of a character.

Thus, a widespread literary concern with the economic situation
of the "people" in the Depression era resulted in quite different fictional visions, visions closely related to the ideological propensities
of the individual writers and expressing themselves in correspond-
ingly different fictional forms.

Although novels about the poor and humble were not a new phenomenon in France, as many critics hastened to point out, such
works had been out of vogue in the early decades of the twentieth
century. Novels about the lower classes had been identified with the
naturalists, whose dominance of the literary scene in the 1880s and
1890s had been vehemently rejected by the novelists who determined the mood of the new century. And in the 1920s, more than
ever, the primarily bourgeois reading public was eager to forget the
unpleasant aspects of life, with which they had had ample contact
in the war. In these "years of illusion,"[3] they were more interested in

reading about problems of the sentimental life, preferably among the rich, or indulging in a literature of travel or fantasy.

The financial crisis of the early 1930s brought unpleasant economic realities inescapably to the fore. The effects of the Wall Street crash of 1929 made themselves felt only gradually in France, never reaching the dramatic proportions they were to attain in Germany or America. Yet, by 1931, even Brasillach—an observer not specialized in economic analysis—was able to note the symptoms of the end of an era of prosperity: "Several fashionable bars have just closed . . . . Negro dancers have reached the end of their vogue . . . . The people who were doing business are doing it no longer. It is the end of an era." [4] These superficial signs accurately reflected the declining economic health of the country. By 1932 foreign trade had been adversely affected by the revaluation of other European currencies, bumper crops had led to deflated agricultural prices, and industrial production was falling off. These tendencies had a direct effect on the unemployment figures, which rose sharply from 12,000 at the end of 1930 to 465,000 in 1935 (some estimates place the actual total of unemployed at this time closer to 802,000).[5] Workers threatened with unemployment, as well as petits bourgeois attacked through their standard of living, began to express their fears and discontent by taking to the streets, and their plight became a highly visible sign of the times.

Newly interested in social issues, novelists no longer wanted to follow the models of individual introspection provided by their great predecessors, Gide and Proust, or of their numerous imitators. As Brasillach noted at the time, "divided over the most serious issues, today's young people understand each other better than the writers of that era [pre-1930] who seem the closest to them." [6] The preference shown by Proust and the earlier Gide for the problems of the isolated individual and their overwhelming concern with questions of literary technique found little echo in the new generation. Indeed, Gide himself was among the first to recognize the need for a change in focus from the individual and esthetic to the social and economic. The revelation of his new-found social consciousness and, particularly, his enthusiastic devotion to the Soviet Union, stunned the literary milieu when certain pages of his journal for 1931–32 were published in the 1932 *Nouvelle Revue Française*. Gide, however, found himself unable to produce a literature that would reflect his new concerns.

With this increasing focus on the "petites gens," the influence of Zola and the other naturalists once again began to make itself felt, although many writers still voiced reservations about Zola's pseudo-scientific theories and the condescending attitude they discerned in his portrayal of proletarian characters. Zola was, however, admired for his heroic defense of the persecuted Dreyfus and his extension of the novel to the lowest classes in society. Henri Barbusse announced a rebirth of interest in Zola as early as 1928: "The greatness of Zola is again recognized. I believe the time is not far off when a decisive movement will suddenly declare itself in favor of an art of synthesis—of which, despite his minor flaws, Zola remains the formidable example—against a literature of algebraic abstraction and exaggerated individual cases."[7] In his speech before the 1935 Congress of Writers in Defense of Culture, Aragon cited with approval Gide's statement that labelled Zola's discredit a "monstrous injustice" and himself reminded the congress of the radical protest expressed in the early years of naturalism, "all that was profoundly subversive to the reigning bourgeoisie."[8] The new appreciation of the naturalists, particularly among intellectuals of the Left, is suggested by the frequent recourse of Jean Renoir, one of the era's most prominent filmmakers, to adaptations of Zola (*Nana, La Bête humaine*) and Maupassant (*Partie de campagne*). In the novel, the influence of Zola's *Nana* is directly felt in Aragon's *Les Beaux Quartiers*,[9] and naturalism reveals itself in more diffuse form in much of the literary production of the era. Even Céline, who is kept busy denying literary influences, paid the naturalists a backhanded homage in his 1933 speech at Médan.[10]

Although the new interest in social issues cut across political lines, ideological differences were evident in the various theories and literary movements that advocated this change.

Populists and Proletarians: Theory and Practice

Even before the "people" had again forced themselves into the literary consciousness, various writers had proclaimed the need for this change in literary emphasis. Prominent among them was Barbusse, who had gained a wide audience through his war novel, *Le Feu*, and through his unremitting work for peace among nations. He had joined the French Communist party in 1923, not long after its formation, and by the late 1920s he was the only writer of any stature to have remained with it through its period of *ouvriérisme*, an exaltation of the worker that tended to discourage the participation of intellectuals. Indeed, the dominant Soviet doctrine of the time encouraged a literature written exclusively by worker-correspondents (called *rabcors*). Barbusse and other French Communist intellectuals had always been wary of placing any hopes in worker-written literature, perhaps because of the small number of Communist workers on which the French party could draw.[11] They had preferred, instead, to encourage elements they found positive in the mainstream literary production.[12]

In the years 1927–30 Barbusse responded to a call from the Soviet Writers' Union to encourage the worldwide development of a new "proletarian literature" and wrote a series of important articles in his own paper *Monde* (founded in 1928) and in the party daily, *L'Humanité*. In these writings, he constantly speaks of a "new" proletarian, revolutionary literature: "that which adapts itself, to depict, illuminate, and animate it, to the new society that is actively organizing itself in the USSR and is in a stage of latent formation in the capitalist societies."[13] Except for his specific denunciations of Proust, Gide, and Claudel, Barbusse is conservative in his evaluation of the existing French literary corpus. He does, however, trace elements of what he calls a "modern" style, appropriate to the needs of the new literature, which had developed since the war. An essential characteristic of this style is an abandonment of outdated verbal formulas and a new directness of language, a judgment that is perhaps not surprising coming from the author of *Le Feu*. The essential element of the new literature that Barbusse seeks to encourage is not stylistic, however, but ideological: commitment to a revolutionary stance. But beyond this ideological commitment Barbusse does not prescribe any specifically "proletarian" subject matter or class origin. Like his other political activities, such as the Amsterdam-Pleyel peace movement, Barbusse's vague literary pronouncements seem aimed at grouping together writers of all classes who shared revolutionary goals. But, for whatever reason, his theories, moderate as they were, did not produce a groundswell of followers, and, indeed, his own literary production of the period did not serve to initiate the new literature he had advocated.

The call for a literature of the people was heard again in 1929, this time from a completely different quarter. On August 27, 1929, a professor and minor novelist named Léon Lemonnier announced the formation of a new "populist" school of literature, declaring, "We want to go to the 'little people,' the mediocre people who compose the masses of society and whose life, too, has dramatic interest."[14] Lemonnier's views received loyal support from his friend and fellow novelist André Thérive, who held the influential post of literary critic on *Le Temps*, and Lemonnier himself soon backed it up with the publication of two book-length manifestos.[15]

Populism as a literary doctrine prescribed essentially that literature should take as its subject matter the "people," a vaguely defined notion not to be confused with the Communist concept of the proletariat. In this concern, the populists claimed descent from the naturalists, although both Thérive and Lemonnier personally preferred Maupassant and Huysmans to Zola. They loudly criticized Zola's pseudo-scientific concepts and the deformation of language that, they said, resulted from his attempts to include in his novels the specialized vocabulary and *argot* of the various trades.

Both Lemonnier and Thérive illustrated their doctrine in their own abundant, but unfortunately quite mediocre, literary production. Their novels did indeed minutely examine the problems of the working poor, which they saw as primarily of a spiritual nature. Such titles as Lemonnier's *La Femme sans péché* and Thérive's *Sans âme* suggest the type of moralizing perspective that they had in common. It is certain that neither their own novels nor their vague theories would have sufficed to make of populism the critical phenomenon it became. Some have unkindly suggested that the movement drew attention only because it was launched at a dead moment of the summer vacation season. A much more important factor, however, was the need felt by contemporary critics for a heading under which to classify the works of talented young novelists like Guilloux and Dabit, as well as the many other works of lesser stature that were quickly attached to the new doctrine either by the founders themselves or by subsequent critics. The reputation of the populists was already solidly established when in 1932 Antonine Coullet-Tessier, herself a minor novelist of the "people," established the Prix Populiste. The first award was astutely made to Dabit for his *Petit-Louis*, a novel that is an example of his best work.[16]

While "populism" continued to appropriate the rising tide of literary productions that met its broad criteria, an attack was launched upon it by Henry Poulaille, who went the populists one better by demanding that literature be written not only about the people but also by the people. "In order to speak about poverty, it is necessary to have known it."[17] This demand seemed to find its justification in Poulaille's concept of the novel as essentially a form of *témoignage*: "The novelist should take to heart the need to be an impartial witness to his time—or even a partial one."[18] This concept of the artist as a witness to his time was widely shared, explicitly or implicitly, by many writers of the 1930s.[19] Poulaille's insistence on defining a writer by the class from which he arose, however, did not fail to produce a number of hostile reactions, particularly among the eminently bourgeois "populists." Because of the nature of his demands and the very name he gave his school, *l'école prolétarienne*, Poulaille, as a former contributor to *Monde*, might have found a more sympathetic audience in the Communists; such was not, in fact, the case.[20] Thus the three doctrines that claimed to represent a "literature of the people" found themselves engaged in bitter intergroup rivalry.

The new literary current that Poulaille announced was to be found, of course, in his own novels, a series of semiautobiographical works covering the period 1906–21, with its labor struggles and problems connected with the Great War. Their titles themselves—*Le Pain quotidien*, *Les Damnés de la terre*, *Les Rescapés*—indicate a left-leaning political perspective, clearly lacking in the works of the founders of populism, and a concern with relating the characters' individual lives to the larger context of political and social history. These concerns were shared by Poulaille's colleague Tristan Rémy, whose fiction treated significant events of his own decade. But Poulaille went beyond those writers directly connected with his journal and claimed descent for his proletarian school in a current of French literature written by workers and peasants that had predated the Russian Revolution and that, he claimed, was finding ever wider illustration. His manifesto, *Nouvel Age littéraire* (1930), mentions the names of a large number of his contemporaries, including, of course, the much-sought-after Guilloux and Dabit.

Writers of the Working Class: Guilloux and Dabit

The work of Guilloux and Dabit exemplified much of what was advocated by the various theorists of a literature of the "people." In fact, they did so much more successfully than the actual members of these literary schools, a situation that critics were quick to recognize. Both writers were sons of working-class families: Guilloux's father was a cobbler and Dabit's had been a teamster before taking over the small hotel near the canal Saint Martin that had provided the setting of his novel, *L'Hôtel du Nord* (1929). In the early 1930s both writers wrote almost exclusively about lower-class characters, reflecting the milieu in which they had spent their childhood (Guilloux's great success, *Le Sang noir*, was, by concerning itself primarily with middle-class characters, an abrupt departure from his earlier work).[21]

As might be expected, their novels approach these working-class characters with a great deal of sympathy. Although both authors ordinarily use third-person narration, the point of view is often that of one of the characters or is not far removed from them. It is perhaps this lack of condescension on the part of the writer that the populists were seeking through their criticisms of naturalism and that Poulaille, in his own way, was trying to encourage by declaring that only the poor were qualified to write about poverty. Gabriel Marcel, a sensitive philosopher and literary critic not allied with any of the contentious literary movements, came closest to defining this essence of "populism" in his review of Guilloux's *Angélina*: "A novelist is populist to the extent that, taking his heroes from among the 'people,' he avoids treating them as a spectacle. . . . They become not only 'you' but 'we.'"[22]

The stylistic expression of this sympathetic attitude seems to be a certain simplicity of tone, a rejection of sentimentalism or emotional inflation, a quality that reviewers have often chosen to call *pudeur*. Camus, himself from a background of poverty, recognized this quality, which had attracted him to Guilloux's work as an adolescent: "And Guilloux, who idealizes nothing, who always uses the truest and least garish colors, never seeking bitterness for itself, has been able to give his style the modesty of his subject."[23]

Although their work seemed to respond to the demands of Barbusse, Poulaille, and the populists, and although they were the objects of urgent sollicitations, both Guilloux and Dabit politely refused to be identified with any of the three warring schools. In a review of Poulaille's manifesto, Guilloux gently defined the areas in which he differed from the "proletarian school," while maintaining his personal sympathy for Poulaille.[24] He had already, more bitingly, stated his views on Barbusse ("the style resembles catechism") and the populists ("in what prisons are they trying to lock us up?").[25] Dabit's *Journal Intime* reflects his efforts to avoid enrollment in the ranks of the Poulaille group,[26] and, in a speech prepared for the 1935

Congress of Writers in Defense of Culture, he expresses a concept of literature that clearly went beyond populism: "As far as I am concerned, I refuse to allow it to be used only to depict the customs of a single class."[27]

Thus, despite the common tendency of critics to view the work of Guilloux and Dabit as part of a literary movement, their views must be carefully distinguished from those of the literary manifestos. They must also be carefully distinguished from each other. To say that both Guilloux and Dabit emerged from working-class families and always expressed a proud fidelity to their class of origin is somewhat to blur the considerable differences between them and their relationship to the French literary heritage, differences that immediately manifest themselves in their novelistic style. Dabit comes close to being what the Soviets would have welcomed as a genuine *rabcor*, although in his adult life—after his period of apprenticeship and military service—he earned his living as an artist and writer. As he told the Soviet-sponsored journal, *La Littérature Internationale*, he had attended primary school only until the age of 13 and thus did not feel himself in a position to comment on "capitalist culture." "Impossible for me to talk about capitalist culture, because I haven't been where it's given out."[28] He discovered the great works of French literature only as an adult, when friends at his art school offered to lend him their books. As a result of this rather disorganized reading, Dabit developed an overwhelming admiration for Gide,[29] who returned the young man's friendship but, recognizing the great difference in their literary concerns, wisely referred him to his friend Martin du Gard for technical advice, which the latter gave liberally. He began by sending Dabit a dictionary and advising the younger writer to look up carefully all words of whose meanings he was unsure, an act that is revelatory of the state of Dabit's culture at this time.

Guilloux, on the other hand, had had access to an appreciable education, although, partly because of financial need and partly because of his deep resentment of the French educational establishment, he had failed to take advantage of the opportunities that would have opened the way to a university career, as they had for intellectuals of working-class background like Jean Guéhenno. During his time at the lycée, Guilloux had received an excellent exposure to philosophical concerns from the famous teacher Georges Palante and, primarily through his own voracious reading, had acquired a grounding in the French, Russian, and English literary tradition, evidence of which is apparent in his own novelistic production, in the long *Le Sang noir* as well as in his shorter, relatively simpler works that have been termed populist. Thus, in large part because of his wider culture, Guilloux constantly undertakes experiments in style and novelistic technique that are lacking in the work of Dabit.

Guilloux's first novel, *La Maison du peuple* (1927), because of its date of publication and its setting in the pre-World War I era, unfortunately falls outside the scope of this study. It had announced many elements of Guilloux's subsequent literary production: a firm grounding in the Breton milieu with which he was intimately acquainted and an acute sense of historicity that led him in *La Maison du peuple* to mingle the private lives of the characters with events of a more public nature—labor agitation, electoral politics, the outbreak of war. As in all Guilloux's work, these events are intimately related to the destinies of the characters and are filtered through the milieu of a small provincial city, which becomes a microcosm of the larger community. Thus, for example, the breakdown of a local electoral alliance of Socialists and Radicals reflects the divergent tendencies of these two groups in the France of the post-Dreyfus era.

The characters and setting of *La Maison du peuple* reappear in the short *Compagnons* (1931),[30] which shows the reaction of a group of three masons to the death of one of its members. As in Malraux's *La Condition humaine*, the struggle of Guilloux's central character ends in death, but this death becomes an affirmation of the deep fraternity that binds together the members of a group—and, by extension, an entire working class—whose very survival is dependent upon the unity of their effort. *Compagnons*, like *La Maison du peuple*, is a story about fraternity. Malraux, whose own work was just beginning to treat these themes, immediately recognized the centrality of the concept of working-class solidarity in Guilloux's early work: "The domain of *Compagnons* moves from egoism to solidarity, the most constraining vice and virtue of the life of the people."[31]

The story concerns a partnership of three masons, and the characters are based on men whom Guilloux had actually known. The unique contribution of each of them is essential to their economic survival. While Jean Kernevel, whose health has been damaged in the war, is not the strongest of the three, his activity as the group's business manager is at the root of their successful collaboration. The story takes place some time after the war—to which Kernevel's friend Le Brix refers with much resentment—and in the precise milieu of Saint-Brieuc, but no events external to the lives of the characters intervene to alter the course of the narrative. Unlike *La Maison du peuple*, in which the effects of public as well as private events had produced a rhythmic oscillation between hope and despair, *Compagnons* proceeds in an unbroken line through the illness and death of Kernevel. As Malraux noted, "*Compagnons* is destiny in its simplest form."[32]

The narration adopts the point of view of each of the limited number of characters. The dominant perspectives are those of Kernevel and Le Brix, but the other characters—Le Brix's wife, the third partner, Dagorne, and his wife, Angèle—also serve as reflectors. Much of the story, in fact, is told through dialogue, and Guilloux once again displays his ability to create a series of dramatic scenes. The dramatic qualities of Guilloux's fiction were recognized in the 1960s, when, in the midst of the critical recognition given to his play based on *Le Sang noir*, *Compagnons* was successfully adapted for television.[33]

In its composition *Compagnons* shows a direct influence of Tolstoy. Guilloux is only one of many writers of this era, including particularly Martin du Gard and Malraux, to have come under the sway of the Russian master. But it was not *War and Peace* that provided a model for Guilloux but rather what has become the best-known of Tolstoy's short stories, *The Death of Ivan Ilich*. Camus, in his introduction to the 1961 joint edition of *La Maison du peuple* and *Compagnons*, declares succinctly, "Ivan Ilich here has become a mason."[34] But, while Guilloux's work follows the same inexorable path of destiny, through illness and death, preceded by a final moment of coming to consciousness, the world of solidarity that Guilloux depicts stands in direct contrast to Tolstoy's.

Tolstoy's Ivan Ilich is a successful civil servant who has attained a satisfying level of prosperity when he has an accident that leads ultimately to his death. During the long months of suffering that follow the accident, when Ivan Ilich finds himself in the presence of death, he realizes the depth of his own isolation from other human beings. His wife and newly engaged daughter, involved in their busy social life, find his presence almost unseemly, as his former colleagues make plans to grab his job. Tolstoy depicts a world of competition and human indifference that is the very antithesis of Guilloux's. Ivan Ilich's suffering is made bearable by the presence of two characters whose humanity has not been corrupted—his adolescent son, who now seeks the love the father had always been too busy to give, and the cheerful servant Gerasim, who accepts the unpleasant task of caring for the dying man with the acceptance he accords to other aspects of life. While the bourgeois characters try to ignore the fact that Ivan Ilich is obviously dying in order to mask the fact of their own mortality, Tolstoy's peasants are closer to the realities of the human condition.

From the perspective of his mortal illness, Ivan Ilich comes to realize the meaninglessness of the activities and values that had governed his life. But Tolstoy grants him the opportunity of freeing himself from this past existence in a moment of heightened consciousness that resembles a Joycean epiphany. Shortly before his death, with his wife and son before him, Ivan Ilich experiences the possibility of redeeming his life through love and compassion. He is able to feel pity for his family's sorrow and asks their forgiveness for the suffering he has caused them. By this act he conquers his fear of death and dies with joy in his heart.

Guilloux's Kernevel, in contrast, lives in a world governed by a solidarity that the threat of death only serves to reinforce. Kernevel's illness makes the other partners intensely aware of their dependence on him, and, when he realizes he is dying, his primary concern is to explain the accounts to the young Dagorne. But they all know the partnership will be hard put to operate with only two of its members and that a man capable of replacing Kernevel will be hard to find. Dagorne's wife, Angèle, envisions her three children reduced to utter poverty if her husband is forced to go to work as a salaried laborer. In Tolstoy's bourgeois world, men are interchangable; in the working-class milieu portrayed by Guilloux each individual is viewed as irreplaceable.

Kernevel is comforted throughout his illness by the devoted attention of his two friends and partners, and his only fear is that he may be forced into the isolation of the hospital. His awareness of the solidarity of which he is a part attains a level of consciousness that resembles Ivan Ilich's epiphany. Awakening one rainy October evening, Kernevel realizes he is going to die and that death is necessarily a solitary affair. Yet he has a deep feeling of peace. Looking back at his life, he finds, in contrast to Ivan Ilich, that he has nothing to regret: "Il lui semblait posséder l'amitié de tous ceux qu'il avait aimés, comme ils possédaient la sienne. Le reste ne comptait pas" (p. 179).

He suddenly feels a bond with his parents, whose familiar belongings fill his room: "Il se mit à penser à son père comme à un camarade" (p. 179).[b] After this moment of reconciliation Kernevel can fall back into an untroubled sleep.

The epiphany that he experiences enables Kernevel, like Ivan Ilich, to find peace and even joy in the acceptance of his own mortality. But, while Ivan Ilich's epiphany constitutes a radical break with the life he has led before his illness, Kernevel's understanding stands in continuity with his life and, indeed, flows from it. In both cases, the epiphanies of the protagonists provide a means of transcending a human condition that is universally the same. But Guilloux devotes his skill to stressing the fraternity that animates the world of his characters, in contrast to Tolstoy's picture of alienated individualism.

The relative optimism that radiates from *Compagnons* is notably diminished by the time Guilloux writes *Angélina* (1934),[35] the short work that immediately preceded his bitterly accusatory *Le Sang noir*. *Angélina* is set in a period of roughly twenty years during the relatively peaceful time between the Franco-Prussian War and World War I. While this is an era that does not fall strictly within the limits of our study, the work merits some examination because of the light it sheds on the particular concerns of the 1930s.

Angélina was for Guilloux a stylistic experiment in the use of popular speech not only in dialogue, as in *La Maison du peuple* and *Compagnons*, but in the voice of the narrator itself. The narrating voice, although never specifically identified, is brought close to the characters by its use of their speech, thus, as Gabriel Marcel had remarked, clearly identifying itself with their perspective. In allowing popular language to invade all parts of the novel, Guilloux had been preceded by Céline. However, the language of *Angélina*, while sharing with Céline's some of the dislocated syntax of popular speech, is of a totally different form and is used to effect different ends. Guilloux's aim seems not to be the creation of a new poetic form but simply the reproduction of a language appropriate to the humble provincial characters. And, in Guilloux's work, the narrator's tone is that of a person telling a story rather than of a man spewing forth his hatred of the world. But, as in the case of Céline, the adoption of

[b] He had the feeling of possessing the friendship of those he had loved, as they possessed his. The rest didn't count. . . . He began to think about his father as he would a friend.

popular language by Guilloux's narrator has important implications for both mood and tone. In Guilloux's case, it leads to an identification of the narrator with the characters, since it is almost impossible to tell where narration ceases and reported speech begins, and to the establishment of a friendly, conversational relationship between narrator and reader, features appropriate to the desires of the theorists of the "literature of the people."

Like many of the "historical" studies of the 1930s, *Angélina* takes a glance at a not-far-distant past in order to learn a lesson for the present. The lesson is in some sense a personal one: *Angélina*, like Nizan's *Antoine Bloyé* or Drieu's *Rêveuse Bourgeoisie*, is an examination of the experience of the preceding generation. The destiny of Angélina, whose growth to womanhood covers the time span of the book, is that of Guilloux's own mother, and the cobbler whom she marries at the end is the same one who appears in *La Maison du peuple*, Guilloux's father. This desire to understand their historical situation fully by exploring their roots in the immediate past seems to have been a common concern with this group of writers.[36]

But Guilloux's interest in telling this story transcends the personal. Like other left-wing writers of his time, he is seeking in *Angélina* the ties that link the revolutionary aspirations of the 1930s to the French revolutionary tradition, whose spirit was incarnated in the Paris Commune of 1870. The Commune was the archetype of a spontaneous popular uprising—fittingly directed against a German invasion—to which the entire spectrum of the French Left could look for inspiration. The French did not need to imitate the Russians slavishly in the quest for social renewal: they had had their own revolution, albeit short-lived. The spirit of the Commune was alive in the minds of everyone during the 1930s, and the ceremonies at the *mur des fédérés* in the Père Lachaise cemetery, where the last communards had been killed by the troops of Thiers, were more fervent than ever. Aragon, among others, often evoked the spirit of the Commune in his speeches, and *Commune* was the title chosen by the Association des Ecrivains et des Artistes Révolutionnaires for its journal.[37]

The spirit of the Paris Commune animates the revolutionary aspirations of Angélina's father, Père Esprit. It appears very early in the book, in the scene of Angélina's christening, where the family evokes the story of Cousin Auguste, who had deserted from Thiers's army in 1870 in an attempt to join the communards. In the mind of Père Esprit, the Commune is an ephemeral realization of a deeply felt dream of revolution. Nourished on the works of Hugo, Père Esprit can give expression to the dream only in vague terms: "Je veux vivre avec dignité, qu'on me traite en homme, non en esclave. Ah! si nous pouvions tous nous entendre, les gueux, ne plus seulement nous aider les uns les autres à supporter notre misère, mais tous nous accorder pour nous en défaire une bonne fois et chasser nos maîtres" (p. 49).*c* Later in the book, a former communard, Camille Fouras, appears on the scene and preaches to the young men who work with him in the factory a more violent revolutionary doctrine: "La main qui saisit l'outil, il faudra aussi, sais-tu bien, qu'elle apprenne à saisir le fusil" (p. 137).*d* Both these visions, that of Père Esprit, inspired by Hugo, or even that of Fouras, are vague and even "lyrical," as the Communist Nizan condescendingly pointed out in his review.[38] But Nizan fails to take into account the effective suppression of all concrete efforts toward revolution in the era about which Guilloux is writing; indeed, the people Nizan describes in his own *Antoine Bloyé* remain oblivious even to the Commune.

In *Angélina* all movements of revolt are quickly and brutally suppressed. The repression to which the communards were subjected is well known. This repression is repeated in the case of Angélina's older brother Henry, who, for having merely listened to the stories of Camille Fouras, is thrown into prison. Although he is released after forty days, this imprisonment has a permanent effect on the family. Henry, embittered, leaves home to become a sailor (he is last heard from in Madagascar, thus repeating the flight of Rimbaud, which Aragon attributed to the bourgeois victory over the Commune), and his little sister Angélina is taunted by her schoolmates to the point where she willingly abandons her education to become apprenticed to a hatmaker.

The cry for revolution in *Angélina* arises from the situation of a particular historical period, with its accompanying economic conditions.[39] It is clearly the humiliating period that followed on the 1870 defeat, and the schoolmaster is already teaching his pupils military drills and inspiring them with the need to retake Alsace and Lorraine. While Père Esprit's sons respond readily, he himself is not to be duped. He already knows that wars benefit only the rich,

*c*I want to live with dignity, to be treated like a man and not a slave. Ah, if only all poor people could get together and not only help each other to bear our poverty but agree to get out of it once and for all and get rid of our exploiters!

*d*The hand that holds the tool, you know, will also have to learn to hold the rifle.

who manipulate the people by such patriotic propaganda, a thesis Guilloux demonstrates in *Le Sang noir*. Both novels reflect the pacifist spirit that dominated the Left in the early 1930s. Wars, in the view of Père Esprit, serve only to accentuate the gap between rich and poor: "Les milliardaires forment un bataillon, Monsieur de Rothschild en tête, et partent dans un wagon de troisième classe: bonne raison pour que nous partions aussi. Mais, les milliardaires reviennent, et il le faut bien, car si les milliardaires étaient tués, à qui profiteraient les guerres?" (p. 83).ᶠ

The period is also one in which small independent artisans are being put out of business by the development of mass production. Père Esprit, who is shown at the beginning of the novel happily plying his trade, is a case in point. He has always made an adequate living by making specialized equipment for the many small independent weavers who inhabit the region. But, as factories replace artisanal goods, his clients disappear, and Père Esprit is driven by necessity to attempt factory work, a form of slavery that he finds himself unable to tolerate.

In the portrait of Père Esprit, whose spirit dominates the novel as it holds the family together, Guilloux has paid a tribute not only to his maternal grandfather but to the entire class of independent artisans who have provided the heroes of his previous novels. In his lucidity and understanding of economic realities, his unquenchable spirit of revolt, and his patient pursuit of a humble but productive daily task, Père Esprit resembles others of Guilloux's protagonists, the cobbler in *La Maison du peuple*, the masons of *Compagnons*. This vision of the artisan as hero does not in any way resemble Giono's apocalyptic utopianism of the same era. In Guilloux's work, the artisan, while often associated with revolutionary aspirations, is not a wholly optimistic figure. In the mid-1930s, when Guilloux's optimism about history seems to have reached a high point, he proposes a young revolutionary as an incarnation of hope in *Le Sang noir*. In *Angélina*, the artisan, Père Esprit, is finally defeated by economic conditions, and it is the revolutionary spirit of Angélina's cobbler husband that offers hope at the end of the book. But in this portrait of the artisan, Guilloux, as Malraux would do in his study of the

ᶠthe millionaires form a battalion, with Rothschild leading it, and leave in a third-class railroad car: a good argument for our going too. But the millionaires come back, and they should, because if the millionaires were killed, who would profit from wars?

Spanish peasants, has furnished himself with the reserves on which he would be able to draw when the events of the end of the decade brought about the failure of revolutionary dreams.

The seven volumes of novels and short stories that Dabit published in the 1930s are all within the tradition of the "literature of the people." In the personal statement that follows the short stories in *Train de vies*, he expressed a desire to "bear witness to anonymous lives,"[40] an intention that could well be applied to all his work. He is here closely following the advice of Martin du Gard, who, after reading the manuscript of what was to become *Petit-Louis* (finally published, in much-revised form, in 1930), urged Dabit to make use of his observations of the people around him.[41] It was by following this suggestion that Dabit had produced his first-published and widely acclaimed novel, *L'Hôtel du Nord*, which was based on the lives of the residents in the working-class hotel run by his parents. All his works, in fact, were based on the lives of people whom he had been able to observe very closely—members of his own family,[42] inhabitants of the working-class districts of Paris where he continued to live, and even the fishermen of the Balearic Islands, where he spent summers in order to find the solitude necessary for his work.

Although there is no social distance separating Dabit from his characters, he does not idealize them. The existences recorded in *L'Hôtel du Nord* are empty, sordid, and almost unredeemed by examples of human dignity. These workers are far from possessing the revolutionary aspirations and proud independence of Guilloux's artisans. They seem totally crushed under the weight of their urban poverty, either because this weight is too heavy to bear or because they themselves lack the spiritual resources to combat it. It is not easy to tell which. As David O'Connell has noted, Dabit seems often to be saying, "If these people harbor little or no inner life and are almost all promiscuous, greedy, small-minded, and bored with life, it is no one's fault but their own."[43] To André Maurois, however, who came to visit him at the "hôtel du Nord," Dabit excused the emptiness of these lives by saying, "But, you know, for most of them, just living is such a problem."[44] In this portrayal of the poor districts of Paris, Dabit seems to present a world not far distant from Céline's, and it is significant that these two writers found they had much in common. Céline even came to visit Dabit at the "hôtel du Nord," and the warm, encouraging tone of the letters he wrote to his friend show none of the contemptuous attitude often associated with Céline's fictional persona,[45] despite the fact that Dabit was far from possessing a mastery of literary technique comparable to Céline's.

Dabit's somewhat negative view of humanity persists in *Villa Oasis* (1932)[46] and *Un Mort tout neuf* (1934).[47] The characters in *Villa Oasis* are concerned only with material success and, like those of *L'Hôtel du Nord*, are willing quite literally to prostitute themselves and their lives to attain it. The couple around whom the novel revolves, based on Dabit's uncle and aunt, have become prosperous through running a brothel behind the front lines during the war, the proceeds of which they have invested in a luxurious *hôtel de passe* near the Folies Bergères. They have thus been able to enter into the bourgeoisie: when they are not at the hotel, they live respectable lives in a comfortable apartment in a good district. If Dabit had not based this unusual situation directly on the lives of people in his own family, he might be suspected of having imagined it in order to imply, as Aragon quite intentionally does, that the bourgeois pursuit of material gain resembles prostitution. The association, however, remains.

The major sin of Irma and Julien, in Dabit's view, is not prostitution but betrayal. In order to succeed, they have abandoned their poverty-stricken families, who might have impeded their rise in fortune and class. This abandonment of family is illustrated by the episode that opens the novel, the arrival of Irma's daughter Helen, whom Irma had left as a baby in order to make her unimpeded way in the world. Helen reappears in Irma's life as a young woman, when she is orphaned of the father and stepmother who had raised her in Irma's stead. At first, the mother is amused by her new acquisition, but she finds it hard to understand this child from a world of poverty she has chosen to forget. And it is too late for understanding: Helen has developed tuberculosis and, by the time Irma and Julien are willing to face up to this unwelcome reminder of her lower-class background, is already past help. Unable to face the unpleasant reality of death, the mother once again rejects all ties with her daughter.

But the experience has weakened Irma's health, and the couple decides to sell their share in the hotel and retire to a villa in the Paris countryside, hoping to gain full acceptance into the lives of their leisured neighbors. As might be predicted, neither the people of the village nor the rich proprietors of neighboring villas will accept them on an equal basis. The couple is condemned to live in complete isolation in their carefully furnished house with its reflecting pool in the garden. Irma makes a cult of her dead daughter, and Julien returns more and more frequently to his old Paris neighborhood.

Their rejection of their own world is brought out by the visits of Julien's poor sister and brother-in-law, who run a lower-class café. Julien resents their presence because he has rejected his solidarity with the poor: "Il pensait aussi que la présence des Arenoud manquait de gaiété; avec eux, on ne parlait que de la cherté de la vie, du chômage, des guerres, des injustices sociales, et après tout il n'était pas sorti de cette mélasse pour y retomber, meme en pensée. Chacun pour soi" (p. 166).[f] In choosing a life of devotion to material gain over human values, Irma and Julien have condemned themselves to a sterile existence. Irma dies accidentally by drowning in the reflecting pool, and Julien, on the verge of returning to the *hôtel de passe*, the only milieu in which he can feel comfortable, dies of a heart attack. The novel is a clear, almost caricatural statement of Dabit's own fierce loyalty to the class of his origins.

Un Mort tout neuf treats the world of similar people (the dead man is based on another of Dabit's uncles) but this time the need for fraternity finds more positive expression. Taking up the idea of Jules Romains's short unanimist work, *Mort de quelqu'un*, Dabit shows how the death of one member of a family succeeds in momentarily uniting brothers and sisters long separated by different lives and divergent economic situations, as the death of a brother recalls them to the basic realities of life and death. They remember the shared poverty of their childhood years and realize that, once again, death will soon subject all of them to a common fate. Through the days they spend together arranging the dead man's affairs, they are pulled from their habitual solitude and forced to experience shared emotions. At the end of the book, as they return from the burial, they find that they form a group distinct from the rest of the world, "réunis par une même douleur, et, plus que leurs voisins, sensibles à leur condition d'homme" (p. 255).[g] But, as Dabit realizes, their unity is only ephemeral; already various family members are returning to their separate lives. And Dabit's narrator plaintively com-

[f] he also thought the presence of the Arenouds dampened the fun; with them, you talked only about the high cost of living, unemployment, wars, social injustice, and after all he hadn't gotten himself out of that mess just to fall back in, even in thought. Each man for himself.

[g] united by the same grief and, more than those around them, sensitive to their condition as men.

ments: "Chacun vit seul, et seul trouve sa voie. Mais on pourrait peut-être aller la main dans la main, tous les hommes? être liés fraternellement par la vie, puisqu'on est liés obligatoirement par la mort?" (p. 252).[h]

In some of the last works published during his lifetime, *Train de vies* (1936)[48] and *L'Ile* (1934),[49] Dabit begins to give his persistent vision of a possible fraternity a more positive expression. The short stories of *Train de vies*, which were probably written over a period of time, do not all paint a rosy picture of proletarian life. The characters clearly show the effects of the economic crisis, and, like the old newspaper vendor, are often quite isolated in their misery. However, one story, "Les Rois mages," shows the unemployed grouping together to begin to do something about their fate. The occasion is a Christmas celebration organized by the narrator's friend Mespaul, who, despite his physical weakness (he has been gassed in the war) inspires workers with jobs to collect toys and Christmas gifts for those who have none. In the process, the workers overcome both their own timidity and the hostility of the local merchants, and they succeed in organizing a successful Christmas celebration. The unemployed, too, finding themselves united, also begin to admit the possibility of taking some action: "Peu à peu des visages s'éclairaient, s'animaient, c'était comme tout à l'heure, quand on remettait son jouet à un gosse" (p. 147).[i] Mespaul encourages them to force the municipality to adopt social measures already being put into practice in other parts of the country. As isolated individuals, they have been helpless, but through solidarity they have a hope of transforming their destiny.[50]

Dabit is finally able to express a wholly affirmative vision of fraternity in *L'Ile*, which is a grouping of three novellas, loosely linked by the reappearance of certain characters and by a common setting. As the title indicates, however, this fraternity exists on a small island utterly isolated from events on the continent. The place in question is apparently one of the Spanish Balearic Islands, where Dabit regularly spent his summers. He had evidently become familiar with the lives of the local fishermen,so much so that the dismay he felt at the thought of these very islanders being involved in the violence of the

[h]Each person lives alone, and alone finds his way. But all men could perhaps walk hand in hand? Be fraternally united by life, since we are obligatorily united by death?

[i]Little by little faces lit up, became animated, just as when, a few moments ago, the kids were receiving their toys.

Spanish Civil War darkened the days preceding his death. The particularly Spanish nature of the setting, however, is not stressed. What is emphasized is the relative backwardness of the island's economy, compared with the rest of Europe. In the port city, men work either on the small fishing boats or in the equally small-scale shoe industry, while the inland farmers can barely scrape a living from the dry soil.

The shoemakers are skilled artisans, not subjected to the rhythms of an assembly line like the workers on the continent, but, even so, the protagonist of the third story, "Les Deux Maries," comes to prefer the life of a fisherman, with its greater freedom and contact with the natural world. The main character, Arguimbau, like many others of the island's residents, has lost his job at the shoe factory because of the Depression and is taken on by his uncle as part of the crew of his two small fishing boats. The story follows Arguimbau's discovery of the world of the sea and of the virile camaraderie of the crew, who share the proceeds of their catch on an equal basis. This form of economic cooperative, much like that of Guilloux's *Compagnons*, seems to represent a sort of moral and economic ideal for Dabit, but he indicates his awareness that modern industry has generally rendered it obsolete.

The second story, "Un Matin de pêche," portrays the crew of an even smaller three-man fishing boat, who are suddenly confronted with death when fumes from the motor almost asphyxiate one of the members. The theme of a group of men united in a common effort also dominates the first and longest of the three parts, "Les Compagnons de l'Andromède." Here the team works for the local capitalist Quintana, who, not content with holding a monopoly on the island's production of wheat, decides to break down an abandoned cargo ship for its scrap metal. Obviously, this long and arduous job can be profitable for him only if he hires at the lowest possible wages. But the men of the island, victimized by the crisis that has even devalued the price of their fish, are in no position to bargain. Even at such exploitive salaries, however, the men are proud to measure their youthful strength against a job to be done, and they discover a real comradeship in sharing a common goal.

The three different groups of men that Dabit describes in *L'Île* represent the positive summit of his vision of fraternity. It is significant that he was unable to write with similar optimism about the working-class districts of Paris that formed the customary setting of his work. Animated not by an economic doctrine but by a personal vision of fraternity within small groups, Dabit, by the time of his death, had not succeeded in reconciling it with the realities of life in a modern urban society.

Views from the Right

Much of the literature of the lower classes produced in the 1930s originated with writers of the Left, but this interest in the people transcended political differences. Even Brasillach, an author not known for his social concern, was drawn to fantasizing about the lives of the people who lived near him in the Paris district of Vaugirard (*L'Enfant de la nuit*, 1934) [51] and in the area around the Cité Universitaire (*Le Marchand d'oiseaux*, 1936).[52] In dealing with the "petites gens" he observed in the poorer districts where he lived in his student days, Brasillach was not primarily motivated by an intention to produce political or social propaganda. In fact, his brother-in-law Maurice Bardèche implies that he chose this particular subject matter only because it happened to be close at hand: "This poet of Paris has really explored nothing of Paris; he looked at the districts where he lived. He does no more to seek the atmosphere of his time." [53]

The particular perspective from which Brasillach viewed the "people" seems to have been suggested to him by the films of René Clair, which Brasillach, a passionate moviegoer, preferred to all the other productions of the time. Clair's great films of the 1930s, *Sous les toits de Paris* and *A nous la liberté*, created a fairy-tale Paris of singing and dancing in the streets. Dealing, like Brasillach, with "petites gens," Clair made their lives into a poetic fantasy that has more in common with ballet than with the world of the naturalistic novel.[54] Nizan, himself interested in portraying the people, was quick to condemn Brasillach's approach as a "réalisme magique." [55]

Brasillach's characters are a strange blend of improbable figures, some with overtones of fantasy and magic. The two central figures in *L'Enfant de la nuit* are a fortune-teller and a shoemaker-poet, but the main plot involves a sad story of an abused child who is encouraged to steal from her aunt's neighbor at the behest of a criminal boyfriend. She is narrowly saved from drowning herself in the Seine. Again, in *Le Marchand d'oiseaux*, the featured characters are the magical bird-peddler of the title, along with his occasional young companion, who, in deference to the films of Charlie Chaplin, is known as the "Kid." The plot, however, is essentially a sad one. Mme Lepetitcorps, a small shopkeeper whose life has been a series of deprivations, finally opens her heart and her life to two runaway boys, only to have them commit a robbery and murder. But Brasillach does not take these tragedies too seriously. Perhaps this is because the stories, in each novel, are told from the perspective of a character who, like Brasillach himself, is only marginally involved with these people, interested in them much as one would be in picturesque marionnettes. The narrator in *L'Enfant de la nuit*, Robert B., and the group of students who look on at the events in *Le Marchand d'oiseaux* serve to distance the reader from the characters who experience the events of the plot, a distancing that seems clearly intended by the author.

Brasillach obviously had no desire to speak of his characters as "nous autres," as Marcel had described the attitude of the writers loosely termed populist. Indeed, Brasillach's novels seem to be a direct reaction against that approach: in the copy of *L'Enfant de la nuit* that he dedicated to his fellow critic Ramon Fernandez, Brasillach in fact termed the work an "antipopulist novel." After reading the novel, Fernandez could only concur with this definition: "His characters . . . were those of a populist novel, but presented in a different light." Fernandez saw this changed perspective as a positive aspect of the work. In his view, the populist writers tended to dehumanize their characters, while Brasillach was able to go beyond the grimy surface of their lives to their "truth" and "poetry," "because he perceives under the frightful exterior the old poetic, provincial Vaugirard." [56]

While the "populist" novelist seeks to make the reader understand the conditions of poverty, Brasillach focuses his attention on the picturesque qualities of humble lives. He prefers to create characters who, like the shoemaker-poet of *L'Enfant de la nuit* or the title character of *Le Marchand d'oiseaux*, remain joyously oblivious to their poverty. Some of the characters Brasillach creates, like Anne of *L'Enfant de la nuit* and the two young brothers of *Le Marchand d'oiseaux*, have been irrevocably brutalized by a childhood of abject poverty. But Brasillach does not attribute their misfortunes to the effects of social injustice. On the contrary, there is a strong indication that social change would have no effect on their natures. Indeed, Anne has already been taken in by her loving aunt before she commits her crime, and the boys have been adopted by the widowed shopkeeper, who grants all their material needs, before they go out and brutally murder an old lady. They, like the mother who has gladly sold them to Mme Lepetitcorps, simply seem to be devoid of moral sense. Not all of the poor come in for such condemnation. In *Le Marchand d'oiseaux*, the student Laurent delights in relating anecdotes about inhabitants of the *zone* who, despite their impossible living conditions, manage to maintain lives of dignity, cleanliness, and even some poetry. This transcendance of poverty is embodied in the unemployed man who lives in an old truck with his wife and six well-groomed children, refusing to pawn his silver-necked violin, which he occasionally plays for good luck. Like Patrick and Catherine, the two children encountered by the protagonists of *Les Sept Couleurs*, Brasillach's favorite characters are able to transform what would otherwise be a dismal existence (in their case, being left alone all day by their working parents) into a magical game.

Such an attitude works in contradiction to doctrines of social reform. Brasillach's position is clearly spelled out at the end of *Le Marchand d'oiseaux*, whose moral lesson of calm acceptance of one's destiny is incarnated in the ambulant bird-seller himself: "L'important était d'accepter, de jouer son role mystérieux, d'entraîner à sa suite les enfants ou les oiseaux, et de faire calmement cette figure de destin pour laquelle on a été choisi. Heur ou malheur, tout ce qui vient doit être pris, et se composer avec la substance même de notre vie" (p. 478).[j] Bardèche tells us that Brasillach himself had a strong belief in the force of destiny[57] (which did not, however, prevent him from engaging in political activism).

Brasillach's characters are determined not by social conditions but by their individual responses to the situations in which they find themselves. Like a medieval theologian, Brasillach expects each person to work out his own salvation in his given station in life. And, as in medieval theology, a successful response is essentially a question of grace, in a nontheological sense.

Accepting one's personal destiny, in the context of Brasillach's novels, also implies an acceptance of class differences. In our present divided world, social reform (Laurent's companion ironically alludes to the Spanish Popular Front) or even charity becomes futile: "Le

---

[j]The important thing was to accept, to play your mysterious role, to collect around you children or birds, and calmly to act out the figure of destiny for which you were chosen. For better or worse, everything that comes along must be taken up and woven into the very substance of our lives.

monde d'aujourd'hui est ainsi fait que les classes sociales y sont bien séparées, et qu'il arrive malheur à qui veut franchir la barrière" (*Le Marchand d'oiseaux*, p. 472).[k] Such differences, in Brasillach's view, could be overcome only by an utterly transformed society that, as in the Middle Ages, would share common values, a common faith. While yearning for such a utopian transformation of society, Brasillach's view of action in the present is essentially pessimistic. Social action in his novels is shown to be useless and even dangerous.

Brasillach's characterization is thus intimately related to his political philosophy, and it becomes clear that the tragic stories of *L'Enfant de la nuit* and *Le Marchand d'oiseaux* reflect Brasillach's vision of social division and political disorder in the mid-1930s. In creating the poetic, fairy-tale world of his two novels of the "people," Brasillach was presenting an interpretation of social reality that stood in direct opposition to that put forth in the works of populist and socialist realist writers.

Brasillach was not the only right-wing novelist to treat the poorer districts of Paris, nor was he the only one to adopt a negative view of their inhabitants. Céline, in the second half of *Voyage au bout de la nuit*, brings Bardamu back from his travels to the environs of the place Clichy, his original point of departure. And, except for a brief excursion to Toulouse, this is where he will stay until the end of the book. Most critical treatments of *Voyage* give more attention to the first half of the novel, and many reviewers have frankly condemned the second section, one saying flatly that it was 200 pages too long.[58] It is true, as the critics have pointed out, that the pace of the story slows radically in the Paris section and that Bardamu himself is less and less the center of the action. But, in an important sense, the long part set in contemporary France is the focal point of the novel, an experience for which all of Bardamu's preceding adventures have served as a necessary preparation.

Céline's blackened vision of life in society, his denunciatory tone, his vulgar language, and his images of filth and decrepitude were received with some shock by his contemporaries. Yet such negative fictional treatment was not a completely new phenomenon with respect to the war; previous war novelists had, as I discussed in Chapter 2, prepared the ground. Neither was Céline's unflattering account

[k]Today's world is so constructed that the social classes are clearly separated and anyone who wants to cross the barrier ends up badly.

of life in the colonies totally new. Gide had launched the literary attack on the abuses of colonialism in his nonfiction tracts of the 1920s, *Voyage au Congo* and *Retour du Tchad*, books that led to a government inquiry and some correction of the abuses. Nizan's more recent *Aden-Arabie*, in a different vein, had also presented a negative view of colonial life. And while French readers might still feel twinges of chauvinism at criticism of their colonial policy, they felt none at all on reading the nightmarish descriptions of life in industrial America that had become commonplace in this era of American economic domination. Georges Duhamel's *Scènes de la vie future* was a well-known example. Thus the targets of Céline's vituperation in the first section of *Voyage* had become familiar to the reading public. The tone, the oppressive monochromatic atmosphere, the hallucinatory imagery were all new, but the message was an acceptable one. In the book's second section, however, Céline goes on to show that everyday life in contemporary Paris is an exact repetition of Bardamu's previous experiences in the war and in his travels to Africa and the United States, experiences that Céline had been careful to relate among themselves. The atmosphere of hostility, oppression and decay that Céline carefully builds up, image by image, throughout Bardamu's wanderings finds its ultimate expression in the familiar reality of the working-class suburbs of La Garenne-Rancy. Thus Céline, carefully constructing his network of horrifying imagery, is able to force his readers to see the world that surrounds them through Celinian eyes.

As its name indicates, La Garenne-Rancy offers a dual image of reality. The opening descriptive passage shows its residents fleeing as if in panic: "On dirait à les voir tous s'enfuir de ce côté-là, qu'il leur est arrivé une catastrophe du côté d'Argenteuil, que c'est leur pays qui brûle" (p. 305). They resemble the hunted rabbits who, as suggested by its name, must have inhabited their suburb before them.[59] But, as they hurry along the "boulevard Minotaure," it becomes clear that these people are running toward something, and Bardamu soon reveals that their own particular "minotaur" is their employer: "C'est pourtant qu'un patron qu'ils vont chercher dans Paris, celui qui vous sauve de crever de faim, ils ont énormément peur de le perdre, les lâches" (p. 305). They are fleeing their fear of unemployment, "la lente angoisse du renvoi sans musique" (p. 306), an anguish as deadly as the metaphorical hunters, minotaur, and fire: "ces mémoires vous étranglent un homme" (p. 306).[l] The anguish of economic survival, which Céline specifically refers to as a product of the "Crise," is everywhere in this environment, poisoning relationships between doctor and patient, parents and children. It is particularly intense in the pathetic case of the Henrouille couple, who have lived their whole lives in fear of not being able to make the payments on their small house. By the time they do succeed in paying off the mortgage, their country setting has been invaded by the encroaching industrial suburbs, whose humid smoke is in the process of rotting the house and its laboriously acquired furnishings. The family, too, has disintegrated. The son, who has gone into the feather business—one whose product suggests the lack of stability his parents fear—has been turned away by their terror of having to lend him money. Meanwhile, they are actively trying to kill the husband's mother in order to economize still further. The husband has been so driven by fear of not being able to acquit his debts that, by the time all the bills have been paid, he is, like the house, ready to disintegrate: he is free only to turn his full attention to the high blood pressure that will soon kill him.

Bardamu is much less active as a character in the second section of *Voyage*: now that he has brought him back to France, Céline is primarily interested in using him as an optic for observing various aspects of French life, and therefore his capacity for observation and analysis must be sharpened. Céline effects this transformation of Bardamu from the naïve victim of the first part of the novel to the cynical observer of the second by having him undertake medical studies rather late in life (as did Céline himself). His career choice provides him with a new approach to reality: "Les études ça vous change, ça fait l'orgueil d'un homme. Il faut bien passer par là pour entrer dans le fond de la vie. . . . Avec la médecine, moi, pas très doué, tout de même je m'étais bien rapproché des hommes, des bêtes, de tout" (p. 307).[m] The study and practice of medicine re-

---

[l] Seeing them all fleeing in that direction you'd think there must have been some catastrophe at Argenteuil, that the town was on fire. . . . Yet all they're going to Paris for is a boss, the man who saves you from starvation. The cowards, they're scared to death of losing him (p. 205). . . .The nagging dread of being fired without ceremony. . . . Such memories can strangle a man (p. 206).

[m] Study changes a man, puts pride into him. You need it to get to the bottom of life. . . . Medicine, even if I wasn't very gifted, had brought me a good deal closer to people, to animals, everything (p. 207).

inforce the lesson Bardamu has learned in the course of his travels: not to be duped by words or appearances but to penetrate directly to the underlying reality. This, in essence, is the task of a doctor, and it is a technique Bardamu consciously attempts to extend to all his experience. When he first meets the priest, for example, he tries to imagine him naked; by stripping people of their appearances, "on discerne tout de suite dans n'importe quel personnage sa réalité d'énorme et d'avide asticot" (p. 426)." The medical experience of Bardamu, as well as that of his creator, goes a long way toward explaining Céline's vision of a humanity reduced to an often disgusting physical existence (for example, men are "des enclos de tripes tièdes et mal pourries" [p. 427] °) and his constant references to blood, vomit, excrement, and odor.

If disgusting, however, Céline's medical vision is also completely lucid. To see clearly is to understand, and comprehension seems, in Céline's view, the only thing capable of lifting human beings above the viscous morass of the human condition. Bardamu has already had this insight during the war, as he reflected on the mute incomprehension of his companions: "La grande défaite, en tout, c'est d'oublier, et surtout ce qui vous a fait crever, et de crever sans comprendre jamais jusqu'à quel point les hommes sont vaches. Quand on sera au bord du trou . . . faudra raconter tout sans changer un mot, de ce qu'on a vu de plus vicieux chez les hommes et puis poser sa chique et puis descendre. Ca suffit comme boulot pour une vie tout entière" (p. 38)." Céline does not make Bardamu into a writer, as he does the Ferdinand of *Mort à crédit*, but already in this exhortation to understand and "raconter tout" is visible Céline's concept of his own task.

Bardamu's slow progress toward understanding is the one positive element in an otherwise increasingly negative experience of life. *Voyage* ends in the debacle of Robinson's death and leaves the numbed Bardamu working in a directorless insane asylum. Despite its evi-

---

"regardless of who it is, you will instantly discern the underlying reality, namely, an enormous, hungry maggot (p. 290)

°packages of tepid, half-rotted viscera (p. 291)

"The biggest defeat in every department of life is to forget, especially the things that have done you in, and to die without realizing how far people can go in the way of crumminess. When the grave lies open before us, let's . . . make it our business to record the worst of the human viciousness we've seen without changing one word. When that's done, we can curl up our toes and sink into the pit. That's work enough for a lifetime (p. 18).

dent pessimism, however, left-wing readers of 1932 were quick to see in the Céline of *Voyage* a kindred spirit who shared their condemnation of the capitalist system. Aragon and Elsa Triolet even translated the book into Russian, and Céline made a visit to the USSR in 1936 just to use up his Soviet royalties.[60] But at least one early commentator saw immediately that Céline did not really participate in the ideals of the Left. Nizan, in his review, recognized that *Voyage* was "une oeuvre considérable," but he warned against the wholesale adoption of the work by the Left: "Céline is not one of us: it is impossible to accept his deep-seated anarchy, his contempt, his generalized revulsion that makes no exception for the proletariat. . . . Missing from his work is the revolution, the real explanation of the deprivations he denounces, the cancers he lays bare, and the precise hope that carries us forward."[61] In an important article in the *Atlantic Monthly*, Leon Trotsky himself echoes this point of view. While recognizing the unquestionable literary merit of *Voyage* ("Céline has written a book that will survive," he astutely predicted), Trotsky saw that Céline's profound pessimism could only lead away from revolutionary change to a reactionary defense of the status quo. He equated the political stance of Céline's novel with the recent, cliché-ridden memoirs of the conservative politician Poincaré: "By rejecting not only the present but also what must take its place, the artist gives his support to what is. To that extent Céline, willy-nilly, is the ally of Poincaré."[62]

Céline does portray a society of exploiters and exploited that appears to have much in common with that found in the fiction of the Left. Unlike Brasillach, he recognizes the importance of economic factors in shaping human lives, and he does not seek to romanticize the difficult existence of the poor, of whom he seems to feel himself a part. Yet Nizan is right when he speaks of Céline's general revulsion that makes no exception for the proletariat. The people who move through his novel are an unsavory lot, rich or poor, but the workers who inhabit the rear courtyards of La Garenne-Rancy seem to be particularly lazy, violent, alcoholic, and filthy. They have no scruples about exploiting Bardamu as badly as he had previously been exploited by the rich. Céline's workers have neither the energy or the desire nor even the capacity for transforming the social structure. In this sense, Céline's work is not far from that of his friend Dabit, whose *Hôtel du Nord* had also painted a depressing picture of the workers.[63] Nonetheless, Dabit's work is animated by a vision of love and fraternity that is utterly lacking in Céline's world. Even in *L'Hôtel du Nord*, the hard-working and compassionate parents provide a locus of hope, and Dabit seems to attribute the hopeless lives of the other characters to their economic deprivation. But Céline, while recognizing the effects of poverty and exploitation, seems to see the root of the problem in a profoundly corrupted human nature. If the almost uniform egoism of the characters were not ample evidence of this fact, *Voyage* is filled with aphoristic commentaries that insist on such a conclusion: "Je ne peux m'empêcher de mettre en doute qu'il existe d'autres véritables réalisations de nos profonds tempéraments que la guerre et la maladie, ces deux infinis du cauchemar" (p. 525).[q]

Céline's characters are not all evil. Two notable exceptions illuminate Bardamu's own experience with others, the Detroit prostitute Molly and the colonial sergeant Alcide. Both these characters pursue their demeaning work in order to provide for a member of their family, Molly for her sister and Alcide for his orphaned niece, yet both have time to take in the disoriented Bardamu as well. Each of them possesses, as Bardamu says of Alcide, "assez de tendresse pour refaire un monde entier"—but, Céline adds immediately, "cela ne se voyait pas" (p. 208).[r] Molly and Alcide, and even Bardamu himself, who devotes himself to caring for the poor with very little remuneration, cannot make a difference in the people around them. Like Bardamu's tubercular patients, most people are glad to remain as they are. The examples of tenderness in Céline's world are rare, and their impact is limited to a few individuals. Most of his characters are too busy destroying others in their own egoistic struggle to survive. *Voyage* does depict a world of social injustice, but, no mere consequence of a poorly arranged economic order, the injustice here is the result of profound tendencies in human nature.

This conclusion is even clearer in Céline's second novel, *Mort à crédit*,[64] whose very title suggests the slow suffocation of the child Ferdinand and all the other inhabitants of his modern urban world. Céline's language and imagery in this novel depart even more radically from the accepted norms: punctuation is replaced by ellipsis, the vocabulary is so obscene that certain passages had to be sup-

---

[q] I can't help suspecting that the only true manifestations of our innermost being are war and insanity, those two absolute nightmares (p. 359).
[r] enough tenderness to make the whole world over, and he never showed it (p. 138)

pressed, and scenes of delirium, rare in *Voyage*, appear with great frequency.

Like *Voyage*, *Mort à crédit* is dominated by the viscous imagery of putrefaction and defecation. The point around which much of this imagery clusters is the "passage des Bérésinas" (really the still-existing passage Choiseul, where Céline himself had lived as a child). The enclosed, glass-roofed space of the *passage* sums up the salient characteristics of the Celinian world. Even its name is significant, referring to the famous Napoleonic "passage" of the river at Berezina during the retreat from Russia in 1812. Like this nineteenth-century passage, the "passage des Bérésinas" permits to its inhabitants a chance of survival in the midst of a general (economic) debacle. In his evocation of life in the *passage*, Céline seems almost to be writing a reply to Aragon, whose *Paysan de Paris* had transformed the grimy commercial reality of the recently demolished passage de l'Opéra into a magical, surrealistic fantasy world. As a resident, Ferdinand views his *passage* from a less mystified perspective. He can see beyond Aragon's fascinating window displays into the back rooms and airless apartments, whose inhabitants can eat only noodles for fear of contaminating the merchandise with cooking odors in the unventilated space.

But there are already plenty of odors in the *passage*, which the local doctor has termed a "pissotière sans issue" (p. 96).[5] This description is literally correct, since in the covered street the shops are urinated upon by passing dogs and even adults: "On avait beau répandre du soufre, c'était quand même un genre d'égout le Passage des Bérésinas. . . . Pissait qui voulait sur nous" (p. 60). The smell of urine, so much a part of Céline's urban landscapes, is magnified in the enclosed *passage*, where it contributes to the oppressive atmosphere. In addition, the state of being urinated upon comes to describe the situation of the struggling little shopkeepers, always at the mercy of their disdainful clients. Céline goes out of his way to make the connection explicit: "Souvent ça devenait des clients, les pisseurs, avec ou sans chien" (p. 60).[6]

As in La Garenne-Rancy, the imagery of defecation also plays an important role in the life of the *passage*: Ferdinand's father's most

---

[5] a urinal without doors or windows (p. 116)

[6] It was no use sprinkling sulphur, the fact is that the Passage des Bérésinas was a kind of sewer. . . . Anybody who felt like it pissed on us (pp. 74–75). . . . Often a pisser, with or without a dog, gets to be a customer (p. 75).

hated job is that of cleaning up the dog droppings in front of the shop. Ferdinand and his family seem to be the recipients of all the excrement of Paris, and the father is, literally and figuratively, an *emmerdé*, entrapped by the hopeless existence that restricts his freedom. Céline's imagery of urination and defecation is used, in the case of the *passage*, not only to create a generalized atmosphere of putrefaction but also, very concretely, to describe the economic situation of Ferdinand's entrapped parents.

It is somewhat ironic that the courageous and capable grandmother Caroline, who first calls the father an *emmerdé*, is herself struck down by death while attempting to clean her tenants' blocked toilets. Her entire life represents an extraordinary effort to combat this engulfment in viscous excrement, an effort that, in the world of *Mort à crédit*, seems doomed to failure. After her death, the buildings and their fixtures are left to fall apart, since the tenants have long ago ceased to battle against their filthy lot.

In addition to accumulating and intensifying the effects of garbage and excrement, the *passage* is, in every way, a restriction of freedom. It is a physical incarnation of the economic impasse faced by the three central figures. Ferdinand cannot find a decent job, his incessant search for employment and subsequent exploitation by employers forming much of the substance of the plot. His misadventures, supposedly set in the early 1900s, reflect an experience common in the Depression era. Céline, like Aragon, Guilloux, and other authors of this era, seems to be using a setting early in the century as a way of approaching conditions of his own time.

Ferdinand's mother, proprietor of a small lace shop, also leads a precarious economic existence, always on the verge of bankruptcy because of competition from the large department stores and an increasing disregard for fine handmade goods. As she constantly laments, "le goût des belles choses se perdaient" (p. 228)." The father, employed beneath his educational level in the office of an insurance company, is harrassed by his boss and prevented from moving up or out by competition from younger men with more modern skills, like the typing he unsuccessfully tries to learn. Ferdinand's parents thus represent the two faces of the petite bourgeoisie, the small-business owners and the white-collar employees. Both these categories had, of course, been severely injured by the Depression, which

"the taste for lovely things was dying out (p. 272).

they felt had forced them economically into the lower classes,[65] and Céline's evocation of his parents' problems had great contemporary resonance.

The increasingly restricted possibilities open to the characters in the economic sphere are reflected in the enclosed physical world of the *passage*. With the odors emanating from its human and animal inhabitants and its gas lighting system, it literally threatens to asphyxiate its residents. This suffocating effect of the *passage* explains the meaning of Céline's title, for life there is a slow death: "C'est fait pour qu'on crève, lentement mais à coup sûr, entre l'urine des petits clebs, la crotte, les flaviots, le gaz qui fuit. C'est plus infect qu'un dedans de prison" (p. 56).[v] Céline's preoccupation with asphyxiation seems to have been shared by other writers in this troubled era, like Guilloux, Malraux, and Martin du Gard. Nizan even uses the same setting, a commercial *passage*, to symbolize this suffocation in his *Le Cheval de Troie*.

The enclosed, prisonlike atmosphere of Céline's *passage* is accentuated by the fact that there are bars on the window of the one room in the family apartment that rises above its glassed roof. Nevertheless, it is to this room that the father retreats to work on his paintings of ships at sea. His love for ships and yearning for the sea, the residue of a happy childhood at Le Havre, communicate itself to his son, with whom he shares a rare period of understanding during the family's one seaside vacation.[66] This motif of escape on a ship, which is finally reduced to the mundane comings and goings of barges on the Seine, had also been visible in the recurrent ship imagery of *Voyage*. The father, however, never gets further out to sea than a ferryboat across the Channel, where the passengers engage in a surrealistic orgy of vomiting and where the family is forced to turn back by the drenching English rain and fog.

More successful than his father, Ferdinand is able to get free of the *passage*, through the efforts of his uncle Edouard, and completes the trip to England, where, despite the exceptionally viscous atmosphere and the disasters of Meanwell College, the improved air allows his body to develop. Later, after a violent attack on his father, he is permitted to live with his uncle in a Parisian apartment that over-

---

[v]It was made to kill you off, slowly but surely, what with the little mongrels' urine, the shit, the sputum, the leaky gas pipes. The stink was worse than the inside of a prison (p. 70).

looks gardens. Ferdinand immediately responds to his release from the physical and symbolic oppression of the *passage*, where his parents have brought to bear on him the economic pressures by which they themselves are being crushed: "Je me sentais plus du tout traqué au domicile de l'oncle Edouard! Je recommençais à respirer! " (p. 272)."

Ferdinand's mother, too, is a victim of the physical repression of the *passage*, which is, as Céline has earlier said of New York, "un abominable système de contraintes" (*Voyage*, p. 264).ˣ The vertical arrangement of the family apartment, consisting of single rooms piled one on top of the other and joined by narrow, winding staircases, exacerbates the condition of her bad leg, through the constant running up and down from shop to kitchen.[67] The leg forms an abscess that finally bursts in an outpouring of pus, a process typical of Céline's world, where anguish accumulates until it finds an outlet in a viscous outpouring (in Ferdinand's case, in nausea and diarrhea). The mother's leg is, of course, also the victim of her frantic attempts to keep her business afloat by carrying huge bundles of merchandise to sell at fairs and markets. She is crippled emotionally and physically by her total devotion to the small-shopkeeper ethic of work and freedom from debt, an ethic she constantly attempts to force on her resistant son, as she clothes him in tight shoes, oppressive woolen clothing, and stiff celluloid collars.

At one point, Ferdinand threatens to set fire to the world of the *passage*, and in the feverish state during which he relates the story of his childhood, he has an apocalyptic vision of a giant client who leads its inhabitants to their destruction. This vision, along with the opening hallucination of a burning Paris, as well as the later scene of a destructive crowd invading the Tuileries, seems to reflect the frequent mob violence of the 1930s, particularly the memorable antirepublican riots at the place de la Concorde in February 1934 (which did extend to the Tuileries). Ferdinand's hallucinations seem to reveal a deep desire to destroy the system, but Céline's analysis of the social situation does not provide an indication of the direction of change. While Ferdinand seems to reject the oppressive petit bourgeois ethic of his parents, he does not therefore espouse the ideals of another class. As in *Voyage*, the proletariat is portrayed as wallowing in its own violence and filth. Ferdinand's encounters with the ple-

---

ʷI didn't feel hunted at Uncle Edouard's place. I began to breathe again (p. 321).
ˣan abominable system of constraints (p. 177)

beian youths his parents warn him against inevitably lead to disaster, and, as is illustrated in the opening scene, his attempts as a doctor to minister to poor patients are discouraging. While Ferdinand expresses hostility to his parents' ethic of strict economy and self-deprivation, he seems to share their horror of people who—like his employer Courtial or the poor artisans who do repairs for his mother—throw away their money on alcohol, women, and horses.[68] During the Courtial episode, Ferdinand proves that he has absorbed his family's lesson of money management: it is only through his strict hold on the purse strings that Courtial's magazine *Genitron* is able to survive as long as it does.

Like his parents, too, Ferdinand is hard-working but constantly persecuted. As he tells his own story, it is clear that he considers his apparent failures to be really the fault of others. In this attitude, he is the image of his father, whose vituperations always blame others for his lack of success: "Il se voyait persécuté par un carnaval de monstres....Il déconnait à pleine bourre....Il en avait pour tous les goûts. Des juifs...des intrigants...les Arrivistes...Et puis surtout des Francs-Maçons" (p. 125).[y] This stance is also very much like that of Céline himself, whose growing antisemitism soon burst out in the series of political pamphlets he published in the years immediately following the publication of *Mort à crédit*. This type of response to life condemns in advance any practical efforts to bring about social change and supports the contention of left-wing critics that Céline's novels, for all their castigation of society, really tend to give support to the status quo.

However, two characters in the world of *Mort à crédit* seem to function as moral ideals: grandmother Caroline and uncle Edouard. They are competent and even moderately successful in their efforts to make their way in the world, and they work hard, responding to failures with renewed effort instead of the helpless accusations of Ferdinand's father. While they share the essentially petit bourgeois work ethic of Ferdinand's parents, they do not allow their struggles with a harsh economic reality to destroy their humanity. They are careful with their hard-earned money, but they give generously to members of their family who are in need: Caroline helps her daughter to set up shop in the *passage* and Edouard gives Ferdinand his

[y] He was being persecuted by a whole carnival of demons. . . He really turned on the gas. . . . He dragged everybody into it . . . Jews . . . schemers . . . social climbers. . . . And most of all the Freemasons (p. 152).

own share of the family inheritance to finance his stay in England. But Caroline and Edouard are able to give Ferdinand even more than money: they give him the affection and wordless understanding that he craves, instead of making him the scapegoat for their own unhappiness. Like Molly of *Voyage*, they are able to preserve their souls from the contamination of their environment and are even able to make life more bearable for a few people around them.[69] As embodied in these characters, then, Céline's moral ideal is somewhat like that of Brasillach, although his "decent poor" are not poetic inventions but real people of flesh and blood.

Céline, in his fiction, sees little possibility of massive social change, and most people (although, in Céline's case, not only the proletariat) are irredeemably condemned by their own corrupt nature. The only direction for positive action lies in the attempt of the individual to preserve decency and humanity as an individual in the face of a world ruled by egoism and entrenched injustice. This is not an ideal that leads to change on a social level, but it is not, therefore, one of total pessimism. As is shown by the figures of Caroline and Edouard, Céline feels it is possible to live a life of quiet dignity and refuse to be crushed by the outside world.

The "People" in the Countryside

Not all the literature of the 1930s concerns the people of Paris and its suburbs. Some attention is also paid to the people of the small country villages, the rural backbone of France. This vogue for the peasant existence was already well established in the 1920s, with the early work of André Chamson on the peasants of his native Cévennes region and the first poetic novels of Jean Giono, which celebrated the beauties of rural life on the rugged plateaux of his native Provence.

It may be speculated that this lyricism about rural life is not unrelated to the literature of evasion that overcame the novelists of the 1920s. Giono's 1931 antiwar novel, *Le Grand Troupeau*, which offers the life-creating values of the rural peasantry as an antidote to the death and destruction of war, suggests that this is the case. Chamson indicates that his own motivation was very similar, telling Frédéric Lefèvre that, after the historical turmoil of the war years, he had wanted to "set in opposition to the world of history, of events, a more stable world untouched by these events and the catastrophes they bring with them."[70]

The rural literature of the 1930s, however, is no longer a literature of escape from history. It, too, reflects the political and social concerns that invade the novels of this period. Giono, as we have seen, uses the values of the people of the land as the base for his vigorous pacificist campaign, which increasingly occupied his attention during the decade. His novels become less realistic (his memoirs, *Jean le bleu*, are an exception) and more prophetic and apocalyptic. In his mind, the rural society, the community of self-sufficient artisans, is the utopian vision that provides an alternative to the corruption of the modern urban world.[71] His novels no longer reflect the daily lives of the people—nor the very real economic problems from which they suffered in this decade—but a prophetic vision that gave birth to some of his best-known novels, such as *Que ma joie demeure*, but which had few links to actually existing conditions.

Chamson's work, too, turned increasingly toward the current political situation. Even when he writes about rural regions, as in *L'Année des vaincus* (1934), the idea of intemporality has been lost. He traces the changes that the reopening of the mines have made in the lives of people previously condemned to the meager existences furnished by the land. He spends time showing the children, the natives as well as the workers who have come from other regions, forming their relationships in the course of their mutual discovery of the mountains and streams. But, while the mines have given prosperity, they do not offer security: by the end of the novel, the company, presumably affected by the declining economic situation, is slowly closing down, throwing the peasants back once again on their meager existence, to which they now find themselves unable to return: "We won't find bread in stones."[72] Chamson is aware that the country people have been profoundly affected by the economic changes of the 1930s. Like Giono, however, he continues to see them as a source of basic values: the protagonist of his 1939 novel about French political polarization, *La Galère*, finds renewed hope in the end by returning to work with the peasants of his native region.

The special economic problems to which rural regions were subject, specifically the seizure of farms because of failure to meet mortgage payments, do not enter into the social novel of the 1930s, which seems to have been preoccupied with the more acute problems of urban unemployment. A scene of the forced sale of farms, much like that shown in Renoir's 1936 film, *La Vie est à nous*, does appear in one of Guilloux's stories that was serialized in the 1937 *Commune*.[73] "Episode au village" weaves together the lives of a number of Breton peasant characters, all of whom end tragically—an old man who has never regained an equilibrium shaken by the war, his runaway daughter, and two young men who have helped organize local resistance to farm foreclosures. Guilloux's story reflects the economic realities of the situation of the Breton farmers while registering a protest against a society that, much like that which he had already portrayed in *Le Sang noir*, offers little room for hope.

French rural society of the Depression era, in fact, suffered much less disruption than, for example, the American Midwest, and it remained for the conservative parties the seat of the traditional French way of life. Many writers of the 1930s, however, did not share this appreciation of the peasant mentality, and a number of novels of the period paint an unflattering picture of village life. Martin du Gard's *Vieille France*[74] was an early example.

Vieille France is, as the author himself described it, a collection of village sketches joined together by the presence of the central character, the postman Joigneau, whose name appropriately suggests his function. In this short work, for which he held a great affection even in his later years, Martin du Gard indulges in a bitterly satiric tone, totally foreign to the Thibault chronicle, and has a chance to employ bits of popular speech, which he never tired of observing.[75] Although Martin du Gard was not himself a peasant, *Vieille France* shows evidence of being based on careful observation.

The postman is called upon by his trade to visit all the houses in the village, but he is more involved in the life of the community than is immediately apparent from his friendly chatter. He spies on the mayor's political enemies and, by steaming open judiciously selected letters, maintains a rigid surveillance over the activities of each of his customers. His daily contacts also make him a useful intermediary in the petty negotiations that preoccupy the townspeople: he persuades an old woman to live out her days with the greedy café owners, arranges for a maid to care for another doddering old couple— all these charitable acts motivated by the promise of a share in the eventual inheritance. In the center of village life, Joigneau is "pareil à ces araignées velues qui vivent au grenier, tapies pendant des jours au centre de leur toile, immobiles, redoutables, prêtes à bondir au moindre tressaillement du piège tendu" (p. 90).[z]

If Joigneau's time seems to be taken up in great part with the affairs of old people, it is because Maupeyrou possesses them in abundance: M. des Navières, who can hardly afford the bread and milk that constitute the only food of himself and his blind cat; old Pâqueux, locked into an earthen-floored shed by his children; deaf old Mme Massart, who spends her days behind closed shutters knitting for the poor. The presence of all these senior citizens suggests that the title is to be taken literally.

But even the active working population of the community shows little evidence of animation. Martin du Gard's concentration on the aberrant sex lives of his characters (an English edition reportedly bore lurid pictures on the cover) places emphasis on their failure to procreate. Joigneau has refused to let his wife have children so that she will be completely free to run his post office. His friend Flamart is impotent, but nevertheless furious at being cuckolded. The three local war widows, for whom there remain no other men, have maintained an untroubled chastity, "la chasteté orgueilleuse qui détraque lentement leurs cerveaux après leur avoir déréglé le corps" (p. 111).[a] The chastity and sterility displayed in all corners of the town quite evidently provoke Martin du Gard's contempt. Many of the town's young women, whose possible husbands had been killed in the war, have become dried-up old maids who find friendship in the parish priest's old maid sister and exercise uncontested domination over the church. But the marriages available to these women are little better: the mayor's older daughter has, in desperation, married a man too old to give her children, and the younger thinks the celibate state highly preferable to the fate of her sister.

The war obviously has had much to do with Maupeyrou's sterility. Much of its youth has been killed off, and those who have returned are mutilated in body and spirit. The three pensioned war veterans are content to spend their time fishing (significantly, they do not marry), and they use their past glory to beg drinks or money from the others. A stranger case is that of the truck farmer Loutre. He has

---

[z] like those hairy spiders who live in the attic, lying in wait for days at the center of their web, immobile, formidable, ready to strike at the least trembling of the set trap

[a] The prideful chastity that slowly unhinges their brains after having done the same to their bodies.

returned from four years in a German prison to find his wife made prosperous and a mother by an energetic German prisoner of war who had been assigned to her to help with the farm work. Too broken in spirit to want anything beyond material comfort, he accepts becoming part of a strange ménage à trois of which the *fritz*, as he is called, provides the driving force. The men in *Vieille France* are characteristically ineffectual and must be sustained by the vital force of elements from outside the community. Such is the case, too, of the impotent Flamart, who is supported by the unfailing efforts of his good-looking Southern wife, who willingly prostitutes herself to insure her husband's future comfort.

Apart from the child of the German, the only children in the novel seem to be the fruit of incest: the Pâqueux brother and sister have evidently produced the child who follows them around, and the pretty teenage daughter of La Mauriçotte finds herself pregnant by her tubercular stepfather. But generally children are not valued by the townspeople. The sexually perverted middle-aged brothers who run the local bakery have evidently used the fires of their ovens to dispose of the fruit of their activity with their young maid. Joigneau prefers to let his wife express her maternal instincts by raising spaniel puppies: they can be sold at a profit.

Making money, in preference to living, is at the forefront of the thoughts of each of the townspeople. It is the basis of all their relationships with each other. Those who work are almost all merchants, and the retired immediately become the subject of plots to steal their few remaining possessions. For some of them their concern with money is a necessity of survival. In *Vieille France* Martin du Gard attentively examines the economic realities of those unable to work, anticipating the demand for social reforms at the time of the Popular Front. He sets forth the case of the three local war widows, with children to support, who are reduced to spending long hours each day sewing coarse sacks at starvation wages while their employers reap the profits. Another case is that of La Philiberte, a woman from another region whose husband's death has left her with two small daughters. Unable to work because of the children, she is reduced to gathering brushwood and satisfying Joigneau's unassuaged desires, under the threat of being evicted from her hut on municipal land. M. des Navières, who has been retired without a pension after thirty years as a cashier in a bank, is acutely aware of the importance of money. He is intrigued by vague stories he has heard of the Soviet experiment, which he imagines as having completely eliminated the need for money. But a nagging doubt remains: the state, which would then provide for all his needs, is made up of men like the local mayor.

The mayor is an unflattering caricature of the reigning French politician. When judged from his speech, he appears energetic, efficient, and dedicated to the highest ideals of the Republic. But, the mayor, seen through the sad eyes of the schoolteacher Ennberg, who is required by his function to act as his secretary, is a fraud: "Cette franchise militaire, ce loyalisme viril, camouflent en homme d'action un bavard hâbleur, sans méthode, sans doctrine, sans caractère, sans droiture" (p. 88). But the worst thing for Ennberg is that the mayor claims to represent the sacred ideals of liberty, equality, and fraternity that stand behind the lay Republic: "Ce qu'il ne pardonne pas à tous les Arnaldon de France, c'est d'être l'incarnation dérisoire d'un idéal politique pour lequel, demain, lui, Ennberg, se ferait stoïquement tuer sur les barricades d'une guerre civile" (p. 89).[b]

The few healthy young men in the village despair of their future and, like the younger generation in Guilloux's *Le Sang noir*, are preparing to flee as soon as they can: "On est jeune, on veut vivre, quoi!" (p. 137).[c] Joigneau is amazed at the young men's charge that the villagers are behind the times and points out, without irony, that 90 percent of the votes always go to the Left. The reader has already seen the result of that political will. Martin du Gard has furnished in his young men an accurate sketch of the rebellious younger generation of 1930 (see chapter 4), disgusted by the current political choices but eager for change and promising to bring about radical reforms when they come to political maturity. One of them tells Joigneau: "Vous direz pas que le monde tourne rond, et qu'on pourra jamais le faire tourner mieux. . . . Nous autres, si un jour on s'en mêle, de votre politique . . ." (p. 138).[d]

M. Ennberg, along with his schoolteacher sister, and the village priest, represent the two sources of spiritual energy available to

[b] That military openness, that virile loyalism, disguise as a man of action a talkative braggart, with no method, doctrine, character, or integrity. . . . What he cannot forgive all the Arnaldons of France for is that they are the derisory incarnation of a political ideal for which, he, Ennberg, would stoically give his life tomorrow on the barricades of a civil war.

[c] We're young, we want to live.

[d] You can't tell us that things are going well, that things could never be better arranged. . . . If we ever get involved one day in your politics. . . .

Maupeyrou—as, in this period, the secular school system and the Church were the two spiritual poles of the French countryside. Both the priest and the schoolteachers are potential sources of renewal for this dying world. But the priest, at least, has already given up, devoting his life-giving forces, in the spirit of Candide, to the cultivation of his garden, from which he derives enough income to distribute some small charities. But he has long ago lost the missionary zeal that had animated him on his arrival in the parish. In his attempt to introduce a spirit of Christian cooperation, he has been defeated by "la frigidité religieuse de ce vieux pays sclérosé, où chacun ne pense qu'à soi, à son petit commerce, à sa petite épargne, à sa petite sécurité" (p. 49).^{e} Retreating to his vegetable patch, he has allowed his church to be taken over by his sister's old maid friends, who jealously dispute its privileges. As Martin du Gard returns to the priest in the quiet of the evening, his anguished prayers are interspersed with the little clique's hate-ridden gossip, which rises up from the garden below. Taking up the theme that dominates the novel, he despairingly asks, "A qui la faute si rien ne germe dans cette terre stérile?" (p. 148). Yet he wonders, "Dans chacune de Vos créatures, mon Dieu, n'y a-t-il pas un reflet de Votre Divinité?" (p. 149).^{f}

The Ennbergs have not yet reached this state of discouragement, and they continue their work with the youngest, and therefore most promising, elements of the community. But their task is not facilitated by the indifference of both educational authorities and villagers alike. Mlle Ennberg has just had her most promising pupil, one who seemed to justify her seven years of sacrificial effort, removed from school by her parents, who feel she has already learned more than she needs to know. Her brother's life is being slowly smothered by the demands of his fat wife and untidy children, for whose support he slaves night and day. Mlle Ennberg's discouraged reflections provide the book's final note. Intuitively recognizing that the case of Maupeyrou is typical of villages all over France, she gives voice to a dilemma that also troubled Martin du Gard: is the problem one of social organization or human nature? But she concludes on a note of moderate hope: "Que vienne enfin le règne d'une Société nou-

---

^{e}The religious frigidity of this old, sclerotic country where each person thinks only of himself, his little business, his little savings, his little security

^{f}Whose fault is it if nothing germinates in this sterile earth?. . . In each of your creatures, my God, is there not a reflection of your Divinity?

velle,—mieux organisée, moins irrationnelle, moins injuste,—et l'on
verra peut-être enfin ce que l'Homme peut donner!" (p. 153).*ᵍ*
    Readers are tempted to identify Mlle Ennberg's perspective with
Martin du Gard's, and a letter he wrote to the *Nouvelle Revue Française* after the book's publication confirms that this is the case. In the
letter he repeats almost word for word the hope of his schoolteacher,
a hope based, however, not on the regeneration of the French peasantry but on the new masses of the cities: "What I should have made
clear is that, on the contrary, I hope for great things from the urban
working classes. There, yes, despite the defects, there are immense
possibilities of altruism, fraternity, spiritual impulses. If a society
comes about where the distribution of goods is less arbitrary, less
unjust, where all workers have some leisure, the luxury of a little joy,
the time to think of something other than where the next meal is
coming from—then, as my Maupeyrou schoolteacher believes, we
will probably see at last what the man of the people is capable of." [76]
    As Denis Boak has commented, in *Vieille France* Martin du Gard's
ideas were as close to Communism as they ever became. [77] It will be
remembered that Martin du Gard wrote *Vieille France* in a burst of
concentrated activity, at the moment when his coming to historical
consciousness had contributed to the crisis in *Les Thibault*. In this
context, the work appears as his disabused statement of the situation
of France in the postwar period, enfeebled by the war, clinging to
traditions as mediocre as M. des Navières's pitiful rat-eaten Bible and
the other worthless "antiques" that he hopes to pass off to the Mu-
sée Carnavalet, and unable to depart from its sterile pursuit of gain
to move toward renewal. The conservative critics found such a view
reprehensible: rural France served them as an ideal. Even Marcel
Arland, to whom Martin du Gard had addressed his letter, felt compelled to put in a good word for the moral qualities of the peasants.
    But Martin du Gard's attitude toward the country folk, the guard-
ians of the traditional way of life, was shared by men of the younger
generation and of different political views. Drieu la Rochelle had de-
plored in his political essays the avidity of the French that prevented
them from having the children needed to replace the soldiers lost in
the war. His Gilles, passing through almost deserted country villages
on his way to visit his guardian in Normandy, receives an impression

----

*ᵍ*Just wait until the coming of a new society—better organized, less irrational, less
unjust—and perhaps we'll finally see what man is capable of doing.

of the death of a civilization: "Les paysans qu'il rencontrait sem-
blaient l'arrière-garde hargneuse d'une armée en déroute. . . . Ames
en peine, âmes humiliées, destituées, découronnées, âmes rongées
par le doute et n'ayant plus d'autre recours qu'un lucre et un alcool
maniaques. . . . Ce n'était donc pas seulement l'hiver de la nature
que Gilles voyait; c'était un autre hiver et une autre mort, plus du-
rables, portant la menace, peut-être, de l'irrémédiable. Il s'agissait
de l'hiver de la Société et de l'Histoire, de l'hiver d'un peuple." [h][78]

Céline's brief evocation of life in the country in the Courtial episode of *Mort à crédit* is not dissimilar to Martin du Gard's. Ferdinand
arrives with Courtial and his wife in a deserted hamlet, much like
those described by Drieu. Blême-le-petit, whose name suggests its
deathly pallor, is, in fact, inhabited only by two old people, who refuse to emerge from their shelter and whose only activity consists in
urinating upon each other.

Ferdinand and Courtial soon discover the nearby village of Saligons-
le-Mesloir, whose name reflects the *saligaud* ("filthy pig") tendencies of its inhabitants. At first they welcome the Parisians, the maid
at the local café eagerly responding to Ferdinand's initiation to sexual perversion while the patrons absorb Courtial's tips on playing the
horses. As soon as things appear to be going badly for the outsiders,
however, the inhabitants turn upon them, attacking Courtial's wife
at the market and refusing to associate with them at the café (there
is no longer anything to be gained from them, since the local barber
has already taken over the betting business). Ferdinand's final scene
of contact with the locals shows him pounding on a locked door to
solicit the neighbors' help in moving Courtial's body off the roadway
of the bridge where he has committed suicide. Only when Ferdinand's shouting threatens to implicate them in the event do they
break their hostile silence long enough to let him have a handcart.

This image of the rural people, barricaded in their limited world
and insidiously destroying outsiders, is that which also dominates
Dabit's *La Zone verte*.[79] The setting of this novel is Boismont, a small
village in the throes of its transformation into a Paris suburb. The
building site of a new housing development, which promises the

[h]The peasants he met looked like the belligerent rear guard of a routed army. . . .
Tormented souls, humiliated, destitute, dethroned, souls eaten away by doubt and
having no other recourse but a mania for money and alcohol. . . . Thus it was not
only the winter of nature Gilles saw; it was another winter and another death, more
lasting, bearing the threat, perhaps, of the irremediable. It was the winter of society
and history, the winter of a people.

good life for all and which is financed by a company quaintly called "Le Grillon du Foyer," has already been the scene of hostility between local workers and those who have come from Paris to help in the construction.

The protagonist, Leguen, through whose eyes the reader discovers the rural milieu, is a Parisian worker, temporarily unemployed because of the Depression, who comes out to the nearby countryside to gather the traditional lily of the valley for sale on May Day. His life reflects the story of his generation. The woman he has loved has abandoned him while he was away fighting in the war. On his return, free of economic pressures, he has floated from job to job in the prosperity of the times. But this peace succumbs to a new form of hostility: "Insensiblement une nouvelle guerre avait commencé, silencieuse et blanche pour gagner sa croûte, dénicher une place, et cette fois on trouvait des ennemis dans tous les camps" (p. 17).[i]

When he first arrives in the country, Leguen is enchanted by the beauty of untouched nature, the freedom of the open spaces, the work of the fields, which still proceeds at a human pace: "Les paysans? Il les voit s'arrêter, souffler, regarder le ciel; ils ont des gestes lents, larges, libres, de vrais gestes d'homme. Ce n'est pas dans les usines de banlieue qu'on peut se permettre ça" (p. 78).[j] Yet he realizes that these men, too, have their economic problems: many work on the land of others, and the small proprietors must often sell their produce at unfair prices.

The May Day observance brings out hidden facets of the apparently peaceful existence. The local workers, who have not attained the level of social consciousness of the Parisians, resist the idea of not working on the French Labor Day, and the disputes between the workers awakens fear and suspicion among the villagers. They even accuse Leguen, whose arrival has coincided with the trouble, of being an instigator. In a café, surrounded by gossiping locals, Leguen is made aware of the disadvantages of country life. Although Dabit's villagers are far less lethal than Martin du Gard's or Céline's, they share many of the same qualities: "Ainsi leur dimanche, les loisirs que leur laissait un travail aride, ces gens les employaient à médire

[i] Imperceptibly a new war had begun, quiet, colorless, to earn his bread, find a job, and this time there were enemies on all sides.

[j] The peasants? He sees them stop, take a breather, look at the sky; they have slow, broad, free gestures, real men's gestures. You can't allow yourself that in the suburban factories.

les uns des autres, à se détester. Comme à Paris, c'était la même lutte d'homme à homme qui se poursuivait. Mais, ici, rien ne vous en détournait—il faut croire que le spectacle de la nature laisse le paysan indifférent? —et les propos se faisaient plus rusés, plus vivaces, plus haineux et destructeurs qu'à la ville" (p. 108).[k]

The issue of rural versus city life is later taken up among the workers, most of whom prefer the stifling urban life that Leguen had formerly been glad to leave behind. The two Bretons point out that life is even more difficult in their part of the country, where small farmers are being forced off their land by foreclosures, and others, those who work for the large landowners, earn barely enough to support their families. And a former peasant from central France makes it clear that farther away from Paris, things become even worse. He confesses that when he goes to spend time with his old parents, "au bout d'une semaine, j'étouffe" (p. 126).[l] Even the popular distractions of the cinemas and cafés begin to look desirable in comparison to the heavy silence of the country evenings. It is not surprising when, at the end, worn out by the petty jealousies of rival café owners, Leguen too finds himself glad to return to Paris. His friend Négrel has preceded him, carrying off with him his local girlfriend, eager to be free of her slavelike existence.

Returning to Boismont a year later, Leguen finds that the villagers have ultimately won their war of attrition with the imported Parisians. The housing development has gone bankrupt and the Parisian inn owner, for whom Leguen had worked, has committed suicide because of his debts. Although Leguen had disliked Bergès, he recognizes that his spirit was far more open and lively than that of the avaricious villagers: "Tas de croquants, cela ne vaut-il pas mieux que votre acharnement au gain? votre manque d'enthousiasme? vos petites manoeuvres: votre prévoyance de fourmi?" (p. 254).[m]

Yet Dabit's aim is not to denigrate the country to the advantage of the city. He recognizes that life in Paris, cut off from nature, is horrible, and the suburbs that lie between Boismont and the city come

[k] So these people use Sundays, the little leisure they get from a sterile work, to slander each other, detest each other. As in Paris, it was the same struggle between man and man that went on. But here nothing distracted you from it—you'd have to think the spectacle of nature leaves the peasant indifferent—and the remarks were more cunning, more lively, more hate-filled and destructive than in the city.

[l] at the end of a week, I start to suffocate

[m] Gang of yokels, isn't that better than your avidity for gain? Your lack of enthusiasm? Your little maneuvers: your ant-like stockpiling?

in for no better treatment. What, in Dabit's view, does make the urban worker superior to the peasant is that he has a clearer understanding of his economic condition and has learned to fight against it in united action, represented by the May Day observance. The peasants and villagers, with their hostility toward outsiders and their egoistic lives, have not yet reached this consciousness. The two worlds, nevertheless subject to the same economic exploitation, remain separate, but, like Martin du Gard, Leguen expresses the hope that the urban workers will end up by convincing the peasants that "tous les hommes doivent marcher la main dans la main" (p. 254)." But the peasants portrayed by Martin du Gard, Drieu, Céline, and Dabit do not seem about to absorb the lesson of solidarity. Unlike the imaginary utopian world of Giono, the real world of rural France in the 1930s, as it is portrayed by the writers in this study, does not seem to offer the hoped-for source of renewal for French life.

Socialist Realism: Aragon and Nizan

Communist writers, above all, might be expected to make the proletariat the major subject of their fiction. However, the writings of Aragon and Nizan, the two major French Communist novelists and literary critics of the 1930s, reveal that this is not necessarily the case. Their practice is in keeping with the theories of "revolutionary" literature that, as editorial board members of *Commune* (published by the Association des Ecrivains et des Artistes Révolutionnaires) and prolific writers of journalistic and critical pieces, they had ample opportunity to express. In these writings, both Communist novelists vehemently reject the "proletarian" school's exclusive emphasis on writers of working-class origin. Nizan, always ready to encourage worker-writers in their efforts,[80] is nevertheless realistic enough to realize that, at least under the existing capitalist regime, most good "revolutionary" writers would continue to be "rebellious sons of the bourgeoisie."[81] Nor does he feel writers should be limited to the proletariat in their choice of subject matter, as the "populist school" would demand.[82]

Neither Nizan nor Aragon limits himself to the portrayal of lower-class characters in his own fiction. In Aragon's novels, in fact, the ordinary life of the workers is barely mentioned. In *Les Beaux Quar-*

"All men must walk hand in hand

tiers stories of oppressed lives are told through the biographies of three women: the servant girl Angélique, who commits suicide in Sérianne; the laundress Yvonne with whom Armand Barbentane has an affair at boarding school; and Quesnel's mistress Carlotta, who has emerged from the slums of Sérianne to become a high-class prostitute. Like the Nizan of *Le Cheval de Troie*, Aragon describes the oppression of bourgeois society primarily through its effect on women, with whose struggle for equality he has identified himself in *Les Cloches de Bâle*, where three women also provide the framework of the story.

Aragon's focus on women is a unique feature of his work, and it has raised questions in the minds of readers. Susan Suleiman, for example, has remarked that the attention given to the portrayal of Carlotta in *Les Beaux Quartiers* seems to conflict with the overall thesis of the work.[83] In my view, the prominence given women is a central element in Aragon's analysis of capitalist society: in the condition of women can be seen an image of the fate of all people who are its victims. Aragon later explained his emphasis on female characters by saying, "I wanted the heroes of these books to be women because I thought women in our society, and even more so in 1933, find themselves in a unique situation, in which the contradictions of this society appear more clearly than in the case of men."[84] In Aragon's novels women's common experience of prostitution—i.e., the literal selling of their bodies—is not very different from the fate of all those who sell themselves for material goods. And, as men's lives are crushed through exploitation and war, women suffer from pregnancies, miscarriages, and abortions that result from the lust of rich employers, as in the case of Angélique, or from the policies that restrict access to contraception and legal abortion for the purpose of breeding additional soldiers, as in the case of Judith Romanet in *Les Cloches de Bâle* or Catherine in Nizan's *Le Cheval de Troie*. Both writers, like Céline, seem to use miscarriages and abortions as emblematic of life in the world of the oppressed. This perversion of the process of normal reproduction is related to the profound corruption of society. It is interesting that both Communist writers, especially Aragon, have chosen to focus more intensely on the condition of women than on the problems of the working class. Perhaps they found in situations involving the exploitation of women, which were familiar to all their bourgeois readers, a means by which they could more convincingly lay bare the oppressive structures of capitalist society.

When he does portray workers, Aragon rarely places them in their homes or places of work, preferring to show them during strikes, mass rallies, and street demonstrations, where their revolutionary spirit is in the forefront. Nizan, who also emphasizes this form of mass meeting, had in fact complained in his reviews that much of the new literature of the people tended to focus on private lives and individual dramas to the exclusion of the workers' participation in the life of the larger society.[85] In *Le Cheval de Troie* Nizan does take his central character Bloyé into the lives and homes of the Communist workers, in the Maillets' small grocery shop as well as the Cravois's housing project, where he closely observes the exhausting household labor of Catherine. But Nizan reiterates again and again that problems of the characters' "private" lives, such as the Cravois's inability to afford another child, do not in fact belong to a "private" domain cut off from politics, as Catherine's husband seems to think. The omniscient narrator tells us that the character himself, like others of his class, does not yet know this: "Comme il ne s'agissait après tout que de sexe, d'amour, de naissance, de son rapport privé avec une femme, il n'arrivait pas à appliquer à un cas solitaire des habitudes politiques de pensée qu'il n'avait pas encore eu le temps d'étendre à tous les objets" (p. 97).[*] The Cravois's particular dilemma is as much the result of social policy as the unemployment that has spread throughout the country in the Depression years, and it too can only be solved through revolutionary analysis and collective action. Nizan takes pains to portray the death of Catherine simultaneously with the workers' demonstration, which has itself been born of many such episodes of victimization. He goes on to contrast Catherine's absurd death from economic oppression to the demonstrators' consciously chosen death in revolutionary struggle.

In Nizan's view, the political and economic crisis of the 1930s, like the catastrophe of war, has the positive effect of making the French people aware of the interrelatedness of all aspects of their lives—local and international politics, "private" and public domains—overcoming the fragmentation that had long seemed to be a fact of

---

[*]Moreover, this was a matter concerning only sex, his personal relations with a woman, and it did not occur to him to apply to it that faculty of political thinking which he had not yet learned to extend to all spheres (p. 99).

existence. As Nizan had noted in his review of Martin du Gard's *L'Eté 1914*, "Since 1914, all life has become public."[86] In the novel the fusion of private and political domains in the consciousness of the workers is shown during the demonstration when Catherine's husband gives expression to his anger at her death and, later, when the police pursuing the retreating workers are bombarded with old household objects, which now participate in the political struggle: "Tout ce qui avait servi à la vie de tous les jours et aux gestes les plus distraits et les plus pacifiques entrait dans cet orage de violence, blessait comme des armes: avant de disparaître, les ustensiles des ménages prenaient une nouvelle dignité" (p. 215).[p] While the political aspirations of the proletariat play an important role in the fiction of Aragon and Nizan, these authors do not focus their attention exclusively on the lower classes, and when they do portray the lives of the workers, it is always to set them within a larger social and political context.

For Aragon and Nizan, the proletariat is essential to literature not as subject matter nor as a breeding ground for worker-authors but as the source of a writer's ideological perspective: "It [revolutionary literature] may describe any object at all, but from the proletarian point of view."[87] The "proletarian point of view," as far as Nizan is concerned, of course, is not just any attitude shared by members of the working class but specifically the Marxist perspective that had created a proletarian consciousness of class. Aragon first tries to define this perspective in his articulation of a French version of the newly proclaimed Soviet doctrine of socialist realism,[88] *Pour un réalisme socialiste*, which remains the major French statement on the issue. In this text, Aragon puts forth a call, much like Nizan's, for a revolutionary literature that would be the expression of the class rising to power, a class that, in the twentieth century, he sees to be the proletariat. In their writings both Communist critics advocate a "realistic" treatment of subject matter, a "realism" that in practice seems to mean a critical approach to the institutions of the existing society.[89] They also value a certain amount of *expérience vécue* in order to guarantee the authenticity of the social analysis.

But in their emphasis on the correct ideological approach, neither Aragon nor Nizan makes detailed recommendations about matters

[p] All sorts of things which had once been the commonplace ingredients of a pacific everyday routine—now contributed to this storm of violence. Employed as weapons, these familiar objects achieved a new dignity (p. 223).

of form, which they appear to subordinate to content. In *J'abats mon jeu*, his 1959 reexamination of socialist realism, Aragon makes clear that it involves less a "style" than a "conception of the world."[90] Nizan expresses vague hopes that "a formal revolution in the commonly understood sense will follow the real revolution in the content,"[91] but he, too, clearly subordinates literary form to animating ideology, sometimes coming forth with statements that seem to reduce the role of art to that of propaganda for the revolutionary transformation of society. At one point, for example, he writes, "Art for us is what makes propaganda effective."[92] While Nizan's own novelistic practice testifies to the fact that he himself was not indifferent to formal considerations, the type of attitude that expressed itself in the statement just cited was responsible for the few bad critical judgments that mar a record of amazing astuteness,[93] causing him, for example, to set Malraux's pro-Communist *Le Temps du mépris* (or at least its ideologically sound preface) above the artistically superior but less doctrinaire *La Condition humaine*.

One result of this nonprescriptiveness in matters of form was an openness on the part of Aragon and Nizan as critics to the work of the large number of Communists and *compagnons de route* of the mid-1930s. Both seemed to be working on the theory that a good novel that reflected pro-Communist convictions must, by definition, be a work of revolutionary literature, and they compensated for a lack of precision in their definition of socialist realism by bestowing the flattering label on each other's novels. It was, in fact, Aragon who first used the term to describe Nizan's *Antoine Bloyé* in 1933, calling it "the expression of this *socialist realism* . . . in which reality has its class aspect, in which the real is not an end in itself but a means to its own revolutionary transformation."[94] Nizan later returned the compliment by hailing Aragon's first realistic novel, *Les Cloches de Bâle*,[95] as "one of the first examples of what socialist realism might be in the French literary development."[96]

In fact, however, the demands that Nizan and Aragon placed upon "revolutionary literature" did have important consequences for their own novelistic form. In their criticism of the works of others, both insist on the necessity of a complete analysis of the historical and economic factors underlying the situation presented in a novel. Nizan, for example, criticizes Chamson in *L'Année des vaincus* for failing to perceive the "deep forces" that determine the world of his novel,[97] and he condemns Guilloux's *Angélina* as "an intemporal story"[98] despite the fact that, as I have noted, it is set in a precisely-defined historical period. What Nizan evidently finds lacking in these novels of non-Communist men of the Left is the type of Marxist historical analysis with which he and Aragon fill their own fiction.

In order to make such analyses, they both seem to find it imperative to move beyond the limitations of a proletarian milieu, where, as in Guilloux's *Angélina*, the workings of economic forces can be but dimly perceived. Aragon, in particular, often prefers to portray people actually in a position to determine the course of events. In his first two novels of the 1930s, *Les Cloches de Bâle* and *Les Beaux Quartiers*, this means an important focus on the world of the rich industrialists whose machinations have prepared the way for World War I. While Nizan's novels remain within a world of more modest economic dimensions (in fact, both *Antoine Bloyé* and *Le Cheval de Troie* do incorporate the experience of working-class life), he too feels the need to present some representatives of the centers of power.

Even so, the analysis of large-scale social and historical forces often involves the necessity of communicating to the reader facts or ideas that could not possibly be fully known to the characters who themselves experience the events of the novel. Nizan, for example, seems to expect a good novel to display an explicit vision of the nature of the proposed Communist revolution, even if the characters themselves could not possibly do so, because of the historical era in which they live or because of lack of political sophistication.[99] Such a demand clearly creates a need for an omniscient narrator capable of taking a broader view of events, as in Balzac, whom Nizan finds particularly praiseworthy in this regard. Thus both Communist novelists are quick to abandon the limited perspective that had characterized the great novels of the early twentieth century and continued to be favored by most other writers of the 1930s.

They often present a central character, generally a bourgeois (perhaps meant as a stand-in for the reader) from whose perspective the narration seems to flow. But such a character inevitably proves inadequate to the task of being used as a filter for the often complicated facts the authors want to convey. In attempting to present the complex developments of the Spanish Civil War efficiently, Malraux faces a similar narrative problem in *L'Espoir*, as I will point out. But he takes care to weave his omniscient narrating voice almost imperceptibly into the texture created by the movement between more limited points of view. Nizan and Aragon, however, seem to feel no compunction about using an omniscient narrator and are quite open about it. Aragon, in fact, flaunts the device by speaking in his own voice at the end of *Les Cloches de Bâle* and by making clever use of an ironic commentary furnished by his privileged knowledge of the future. He thus turns his solution of an ideological problem into a novelistic advantage.

Nizan's unanimist portrayal of the riot in *Le Cheval de Troie*, where each of the opposing social forces takes on the reality of a character in a drama, is another effective use of an omniscient perspective (see chapter 4). Yet, despite their inventiveness, neither Aragon nor Nizan is entirely successful in avoiding the traps of undigested abstractions and unsupported generalizations abundantly supplied by their omniscient narrators. Indeed, they seem prepared to put up with certain deficiencies in fictional technique rather than risk losing an opportunity to give the reader the correct ideological perspective.

Both Aragon and Nizan speak frequently of the desirability of creating social "types" à la Balzac and of the difficulty of doing so in the unstable modern world.[100] The characters in their novels are indeed designed to represent entire social groups. The three women of Aragon's *Les Cloches de Bâle*, for example, are each representative of a social class: Diane participates in the world of the oppressors, Clara symbolizes the emergent proletariat, and the bourgeois Catherine is described at a moment of passage from one world to the other. In *Les Beaux Quartiers* the two brothers each represent a different choice of class identification, while in *Les Voyageurs de l'impériale* Pierre Mercadier is the incarnation of the spirit of bourgeois individualism. Such typecasting reduces the upper-class characters to little more than caricatural figures, a fact that is true also in Nizan's *Le Cheval de Troie*. Yet this type of portrayal seems quite intentional. As Gerald Prince has pointed out, the narration of the "Diane" section of *Les Cloches de Bâle*, with its constant reproduction of the characters' cliché-ridden speech, is designed to stress superficial appearance and to prevent the reader from participating in their consciousness.[101] This technique is altered in the subsequent portrayal of Catherine, with whose dilemma Aragon wishes the reader to identify. Ironically, Aragon seems most successful in portraying such tormented representatives of the bourgeoisie. The working-class character he portrays in *Les Cloches de Bâle* is, on the other hand, so typical of his class and so ideologically sound in his observations that he lacks any contact with reality.

More interesting than the attempt to create social types is the use that both Aragon and Nizan make of architecture as a means of social analysis. In this they had certainly been influenced by Jules Romains's unanimist vision of the city,[102] which had found expression in his early prose works and, more recently in 1932, in the opening volume of his massive study of the prewar world, *Les Hommes de bonne volonté*. He had discovered the principle of unanimism in a moment of sudden vision in 1903, when, as André Cuisenier describes it, Romains suddenly had "the intuition of a vast and elementary being of which the street, vehicles, and passers-by formed the body and of which he, in this privileged instant, could call himself the consciousness."[103] Romains subsequently elevated this vision into a doctrine and made portrayals of this collective consciousness the center of his work. Such a sympathetic identification with a collective subject matter—one that was usually, by preference, the dynamic reality of the modern industrial city—could not but appeal to the Communists.

In Nizan's *Le Cheval de Troie*, unanimist techniques play an important role and reflect his early interest in Romains. The novel offers a panoramic vision of a provincial city,[104] most often seen from the perspective of the Communist group, to whom it presents a hostile façade. It is first seen from the mountaintop that has formed the goal of their Sunday outing in the country, and, viewed from this distance, the entire city offers an appearance of hardness, evoking a coral reef rising from the sea of the fields. Nizan's central character has earlier reflected on the contrast between the soft earth and the hard city pavement. The principal social institutions that dominate the city, visible in the factory chimneys, church steeples, and courthouse spire, are immediately perceived as enemies, an impression reiterated as the Communist group returns home that night to encounter at close range the "cathédrale insolente, habituée au commandement" (p. 43). Further on they see the abject slums of the Armenian immigrant workers, which are almost physically crushed by the mansions of the factory-owners with their feudal powers: "Au dessus de ce quartier venaient finir les grands jardins noirs des usiniers: leurs puissantes villas avec des cordons de brique sombre dominaient les termitières des arméniens comme les châteaux à tourelles dans les peintures des Livres d'Heures" (p. 56).[q] The city seems to surround the group with prisonlike walls, the walls of the lycée where Bloyé works hardly distinguishable from the "interminable walls" of the convents across the street. The lycée itself evokes an army barracks and is guarded by a concierge who is fittingly a former gendarme.

One of the most oppressive of all the structures is the workers' housing project, where Albert and Catherine live. It too is compared to an army barracks, and its lifeless architecture reflects the emptiness of the lives of poverty that go on inside it. Catherine, dying in her bedroom from an amateur abortion, feels herself stifled, crushed to death: "Catherine était écrasé contre son lit et elle ne connaissait plus rien du monde que cet écrasement; rien ne ressemblait moins à la lutte d'un moineau contre un aigle, c'était plutôt l'étouffement d'un oiseau par le vide sous la cloche d'une machine pneumatique" (p. 173). When her husband returns home to find her dead, he too feels imprisoned by the small apartment, which symbolizes the limitations of his life: "Il tournait dans la chambre, il était prisonnier" (p. 175).[r]

The atmosphere of the city is connected with lifelessness and active suppression of life. While scenes set in the country and the workers' demonstration take place during the day, many of the scenes where the city itself is observed occur at night; thus the city is constantly identified with deathlike darkness. In *Le Cheval de Troie* people in the middle-class districts put off the moment of going into their bedrooms, "les réduits funèbres de leurs chambres" (p. 45).[s] The factories, like the housing projects built for their workers, are a lifeless world: "Il ne poussait rien sur toutes ces pierres, ce mâ-

[q] a cathedral . . . insolent, accustomed to commanding (p. 41). . . . Beyond this quarter rose the large dark gardens of the factory owners whose imposing mansions, built of sombre brick, dominated the Armenian antheap like those towered castles in the illuminations of an old Book of Hours (p. 45).

[r] Catherine lay crushed against her bed and was aware of nothing but this weight. Nothing could remind you less of the struggles of a sparrow in the claws of an eagle. No, this was more a stifling by empty space, beneath the sound of the strokes, like a bell, of an air pump (pp. 177–78). . . . He turned about in the room. He was a prisoner (p. 180).

[s] the tombs that are their bedrooms (translation mine)

chefer: c'était une planète sur laquelle le travail planait comme un oiseau noir dont l'ombre étouffait les paroles" (p. 139).' Motifs of suffocation are everywhere, and Bloyé identifies the stifling physical atmosphere with the orientation toward death of contemporary philosophy: "L'idée de la mort . . . était comme un gaz essentiel dans l'air que tout le monde respirait, un air irrespirable à cause de tout cet azote de la mort" (p. 135)."

Nizan's identification of the bourgeois city with death recurs in all three of his published novels, where the city of the living and the city of the dead are seen as interchangeable. In *La Conspiration* the empty streets of the affluent districts are like a cemetery, and the petit bourgeois character, Pluvinage, literally grows up in a world of mortuaries. In *Antoine Bloyé* the cemetery in which Bloyé is buried is itself an image of the hierarchical organization of society that has determined his life. Bloyé, the worker who has risen into the ranks of the bourgeoisie, is laid to rest in the area that corresponds exactly to his chosen station in life: not in the main avenue whose stone pavilions shelter "des morts qui avaient été riches, bâtisseurs de domaines, d'entreprises et de tombeaux," nor in the common grave of those who cannot afford the upkeep of a tomb, but in the area reserved for the bourgeoisie, "le lieu des funérailles de l'aisance bourgeoise, le cimetière des gens qui avaient mené des vies qui ne trouvaient ni la grande richesse, ni l'inquiétude du lendemain" (pp. 27–28).ᵛ ¹⁰⁵

For Nizan the city is a tangible representation of the society that has produced it. Its constructions have been created by its inhabitants and thus express the form they have given their lives: "elle [la ville] avait grandi comme une colonie de zoophytes, chacun de ses habitants, de ses propriétaires laissait après sa mort sa coquille, l'alvéole minéral blanc et rose qu'il avait mis sa vie à secréter" (p. 30)." It goes

---

'Nothing grew here from all this stone and slag. It was a region of cement, brick and metal, above which toil hovered like some dark bird whose shadow stifled speech (p. 144).

"The idea of death was like an essential component of the air everyone breathed, air that was unbreathable because of all the nitrogen generated by death (translation mine).

ᵛthe wealthy dead, builders of fortunes, businesses, and tombs . . . the burial ground of bourgeois comfort, of people who lived lives troubled neither by great riches nor care for the morrow (pp. 28–29)

ʷIt [the town] had grown like a settlement of zoophytes, each of its inhabitants leaving his shell there, after his death: that white or pink mineral cell in which he had secreted his existence (p. 28).

without saying that this architecture is the work of only those inhabitants who have been in possession of the means of construction; thus the city reveals itself to Bloyé as a fitting reflection of capitalist society: "un merveilleux édifice de bassesse, de cruauté, de haine, d'histoire, de marchandages, de connivences et de délits" (p. 131).[x]

The particular world of the petite bourgeoisie is summed up in the description of the covered commercial *passage* where Bloyé's colleague Lange likes to stroll at night. Like the *passage* that Céline would later evoke in his *Mort à crédit* this enclosed space reiterates the motifs of suffocation and death that characterize Nizan's vision of the entire society. For Lange, the *passage*, with its black and white shopfronts, never fails to suggest thoughts of death. There is even a shop that sells tombstone decorations,[106] and the shopkeepers' families asleep in their bedrooms are compared with corpses in family vaults. The fragmentation of bourgeois life finds its expression in the shop signs, which feature segmented body parts (a severed hand) or disconnected items of symbolic bourgeois clothing (a detachable collar, a bowler hat). With its gas lamps and its opaque glass roof, the *passage* has developed a stifling hothouse atmosphere. Lange finds it particularly in tune with his own obsession with solitude and death, and the *passage*'s glass-enclosed space becomes a metaphor for his own metaphysical anguish: "La pensée se heurtait contre elle [l'angoisse], comme un insecte dans une cage de verre admirablement transparente: elle apercevait un monde où des êtres vivaient, elle s'élançait vers lui, la paroi invisible arrêtait le mouvement, la paroi qui était la mort; elle faisait des circuits de plus en plus étroits à l'intérieur de sa prison . . . et Lange sentait venir le temps où complètement épuisée, incapable d'affolement même, elle demeurerait absolument immobile" (p. 127).[y]

Both Lange and the oppressed workers attempt to break out of their imprisonment in the political confrontation that pits workers against fascists and forces a collision of the separate worlds. Always obsessed with death, Lange finds a new communion with the fascists when he pulls the trigger on his revolver, thus becoming one

[x] an extraordinary edifice of baseness, cruelty, chaffering, chicanery, and crime (p. 138)

[y] his mind beat against it [the pain] like an insect in a glass prison. His mind could see a world in which creatures live; it darted towards them, but that invisible partition arrested the movement—that barrier which was death. His mind revolved in ever lessening circles inside this prison . . . and Lange could foresee the day when it would become immobile, exhausted, incapable even of madness (pp. 131–32).

with the death-dealing forces of society. The workers also attempt to break out of their confinement in more positive ways. The local Communists go out at night, their joyous group forming a contrast with Lange's solitary nocturnal promenade in the *passage*. They transform the oppressive walls of the social institutions—the *préfecture*, the factory, and *monument aux morts*—into vehicles for revolutionary slogans. In the demonstration that follows, the movement of the entire crowd is depicted in terms of an aspiration toward open space. This is particularly true of Catherine's husband, who has left the enclosing walls of the apartment where she lies dead to look for his friends in the crowd. Finding himself in the front row, he is suddenly and irresistibly attracted by the empty space that separates the crowd from the police: "Il avait une sortie, il se faisait fureur" (p. 183).[z] He is, of course, arrested for resisting the police, but the demonstration has permitted him and the other workers to make the first positive gesture of revolt against the social oppression.

In *Le Cheval de Troie* Nizan presents no specific blueprint for the structure of a transformed French society, but the opening passage, where the group of workers spend a Sunday in the country, provides a poetic image of what life might be like in a world without oppression, a world that would be the exact opposite of their daily lives. Within the city itself, only the prefect has the opportunity to enjoy nature in his much-admired garden, which looks out upon the hills. The workers, however, spend their Sunday not in a walled garden but in nature itself, whose soft earth seems to welcome their tired bodies. After dinner, in an episode that becomes allegorical of their struggle for liberation, they climb to a plateau: "Ils montaient comme s'il s'était agi d'une délivrance, ou de leur vie, d'échapper à une inondation, à un feu, à l'angoisse qui saisit les enfants dans la nuit, les nageurs dans les herbes" (p. 27).[a] In order to get there they must break their own path through underbrush, in the process becoming separated from one another. The women, in particular, have difficulty making the climb, for reasons directly related to their oppressed feminine condition: the pregnant Catherine is forced to turn back immediately, and the other two women are constantly catching their dresses on brambles. Once on the plateau, however, they are

---

[z] Here was a way out. His anger mounted (p. 189).

[a] They persisted in their climb as though it were a question of escape, of their lives, of deliverance from some flood of fire, from the panic that seizes children in the night or swimmers caught in the reeds.

able to look down on the world of the city, just as the prefect and the factory owners have been able to look down on them from their hilltop mansions. In the city the upper classes have been able to dominate them (in both senses of the French verb) from the heights where they have a larger view of the situation; on the plateau, armed with the understanding afforded them by their political ideology, the workers' vision symbolically dominates the city. But in the novel, as in contemporary reality, this moment of liberated vision is brief: the workers must descend into the city streets to continue the slow struggle to achieve liberation in their daily lives.

Aragon had, in the 1920s, approached the portrayal of urban reality in a prose work whose subject was nothing other than the minute description of two districts of the French capital. His *Paysan de Paris*, along with Breton's *Nadja*, is enduring testimony to the success of the early surrealist effort to unmask the poetry hidden in the most mundane of surroundings. In his urban panoramas of the 1930s, however, Aragon's aim is to unmask not the poetry but the economic mechanisms hidden beneath the façades. The passage de l'Opéra, on which Aragon had fixed his attention in *Le Paysan de Paris*, recurs in his second realistic novel, *Les Beaux Quartiers*,[107] where it serves as one of the concealed exits of a gambling den around which the action revolves. The *Passage-Club*, in fact, comes to function as an important metaphor for the nature of capitalist society.[108] Located in the heart of Paris but hidden from sight, it is one of the concealed mechanisms that determine the direction of society. This luxurious gaming establishment serves as the meeting place of a heterogeneous mixture of the monied elements of French society: rich capitalists mingle with ominous underground figures, their *demi-mondaine* mistresses with respectable *mères de famille*, all carefully observed by gossip-vending policemen. These people are brought together by the lure of quick financial gain, like the more socially acceptable players on the nearby stock market, the history of whose deals forms the background of the individual adventures. As Aragon's narrator helpfully points out, "Les maisons de jeu sont les formes les plus élevées d'un système qui les condamne hypocritement, mais qui ne vit que de la Bourse" (p. 531).[b] In the larger world of finance, diverse interests are conspiring to bring about the catas-

---

[b]The gaming houses are the highest form of a system that hypocritically condemns them, but that itself lives off the Stock Market.

trophe of war, just as the same interests succeed in finally closing down the *Passage-Club*, a move that drives one character to the brink of madness and another to murder and suicide.

The *Passage-Club* lays bare the instability underlying the apparent tranquillity of the "beaux quartiers," upon which Aragon's attention is often focused, especially in the book that bears this title. In his opening panorama of Paris, Aragon has already defined these affluent districts as both a refuge from and a cause of the black world of factories on which they border: "Les beaux quartiers. . . Ils sont comme une échappée au mauvais rêve dans la pince noire de l'industrie. De tous côtés, ils confinent à ces régions implacables du travail dont les fumées déshonorent leurs perspectives" (p. 264).[c] The worldly Barbentane brother, Edmond, spends much of his time in his mistress's home in Neuilly, where gardens provide rustic settings for the Sunday dinners of the prosperous bourgeoisie. Later, he is summoned to the industrialist Quesnel's even grander residence overlooking the calm of the parc Monceau: "Ici la fortune apparaissait presque le bien de tous, comme le soleil. Quiétude française, paix profonde. . . On oubliait ces perpétuelles alarmes de la presse et du Parlement" (p. 571). The apparent tranquillity of the setting causes Quesnel himself to comment, "Je bénis le ciel . . . de vivre dans notre époque. Tout n'est peut-être pas encore à sa place mais enfin comme la sagesse des hommes domine la nature et la sauvagerie du grand nombre!" (p. 571).[d] Quesnel's remark, of course, becomes ironic[109] in the context in which Aragon has placed it: the omniscient narrator has already called the reader's attention to the war that is soon to destroy this deceptive tranquillity, a war that is already being prepared in the dealings of these very financiers.

In contrast to this world of "beaux quartiers," of richly-appointed interiors and luxury restaurants, is the universe that the reader enters in the company of Edmond's brother Armand, when he at first finds himself alone and penniless in Paris. As he wanders through the dark streets in search of a job, of money, or even a quiet corner in

[c]The rich districts. . . They are like an escape from a bad dream in the black vise of industry. On all sides, they border on those implacable regions of work whose smoke dishonors their views.

[d]Here money seemed almost the property of all, like the sun. French tranquillity, deep peace. . . . You forgot the perpetual alarms of the press and *Parlement*. . . . I thank heaven I am living in our time. Perhaps not everything is yet perfect, yet how the wisdom of man governs nature and the violence of the masses!

which to sleep, Armand discovers the existence of streetwalkers and *clochards* in their desperate struggle to maintain the basic functions of life in the face of relentless pursuit by the police. As Armand himself is transformed from a young, middle-class student into a dirty, unshaven bum, he comes to share in the humiliation of the old woman beggar whom the police kick in the head, and he discovers "ce mépris total de l'homme qui semblait habituel aux pavés de Paris" (p. 414).[e] He begins to see its victims, like the young worker whom the police haul off ignominiously, as similar to the butchered meat hanging in the meat markets of Les Halles. This image, of course, prefigures the war, as the young man becomes for Armand, "la voix anonyme de ces hécatombes en série" (p. 415).[f] Armand frequents the dark *quais* of the Seine, the nocturnal working world of Les Halles and the newspaper district, the darkened boulevards where prostitutes flee before police roundups. He spends his Sundays at Socialist demonstrations on the pré Saint-Gervais and so has an opportunity to observe the early manifestations of the *zone*, which, by the 1930s, had grown up along the old Paris fortifications (which still, at the time of the novel's setting in 1913, mark the limits of the city). From the pré Saint Gervais can be seen the symbol of the hostile world of the Parisian bourgeoisie in the form of the Sacré Coeur, whose whiteness variously evokes a nauseating cheese or the threatening brightness of clenched teeth. At the end of the novel Armand has settled down in the factory district of Levallois-Perret, near his job at the Wisner auto works. Here, he discovers, is to be found the true France.

*   *   *

The proletarian ideology of Nizan and Aragon inspired them to undertake in their fiction the analysis of as broad as possible a segment of French society, stressing the forces of economic determinism and the opposition of social classes. The need to place this analysis constantly in a Marxist perspective led both writers away from the use of the limited point of view that had become characteristic of twentieth-century narration and that was adopted, with some modifications, by the other writers in this study. Aragon and Nizan's use of omniscient narration, their attempt to create social types, and their tendency to present panoramic views of urban scenes reflect an as-

---

[e]that total contempt for man that seemed habitual on the streets of Paris
[f]the anonymous voice of those mass-produced hecatombs

surance that their ideology affords them a comprehensive means of understanding modern reality. Although they evidence an awareness of oppression central to the social vision of almost all the writers in this chapter (with the possible exception of Brasillach), the Communists' faith in a revolutionary future enabled them to draw somewhat more optimistic conclusions.

CHAPTER 4

Political Commitment and Polarization

Alors que le monde se scinde en deux et que deux barricades se dressent face à face, nous comprendrons que l'un des deux partis doivent nous rejeter et qu'il nous faille fatalement, obligatoirement, nous diriger vers l'autre. . . . Voici donc venus pour l'artiste, pour l'écrivain, les jours de la responsabilité.[a]

JEAN CASSOU, *Commune*

In the 1930s the political opinions of intellectuals took on an importance they had not known in France since the Dreyfus Affair. Once again, the country was divided into two opposing camps of Right and Left, and the division was driven deeper by the urgency of the European situation, which, as became increasingly evident, threatened to repeat the holocaust of the Great War. Under the pressure of events, political battle lines began to form, and by the mid-1930s most French intellectuals had clearly aligned themselves with one side or the other.

The political divisions that existed by mid-decade, however, were radically different from those of 1930. At the beginning of the decade, the split was not primarily a political opposition between Right and Left; rather, it was a generation gap, which pitted those who yearned to recapture the prewar *belle époque*, in which they themselves had reached maturity, against a younger generation who wished only to speed the collapse of the existing French social order. As Denis de Rougemont expressed it in 1932, "There are two sides:

[a] when the world divides itself in two and when two barricades are set up against each other, we will understand that one of the two sides must reject us and that we must fatally, obligatorily move toward the other. . . . Now have arrived for the artist and writer the days of responsibility.

those who want to get out of it—and those who would be willing to go on, since they have certain interests in the matter." [1]

The rebellion of youth against the repressive family had, of course, long been a characteristic of the prewar Gidean novels. Such works as *Les Nourritures terrestres* had gained Gide a continuing audience among the young, and the Lafcadio of *Les Caves du Vatican* had even been admired by the generally disdainful surrealists. In the 1920s, however, this attitude of youthful rebellion began to take on a political content, a phenomenon that certainly had its origins in the disruptive experience of World War I. [2] It is thus no accident that fiction of the 1930s that deals with that period—for example, Martin du Gard's Thibault chronicle, Guilloux's *Le Sang noir*—tends to emphasize the differential attitudes and experience of conflicting generations (see chapter 2). The political position articulated by the young protagonist of Drieu la Rochelle's *La Comédie de Charleroi* could be taken as the slogan of an entire generation: "I am against the older generation."

The attitude of young political rebels in the early 1930s can be seen in the *Cahier de Revendications* issue published in the respectable *Nouvelle Revue Française* in December 1932. This issue grouped together statements from a number of radical young intellectuals, ranging from Thierry Maulnier, who wrote for the *Action Française*, on the Right to the Communist Paul Nizan on the Left. It was Nizan who best articulated the attitude of revolt against a crumbling society that united all the contributors, transcending the limitations of specific political affiliations. In his statement entitled, "Les Conséquences du refus," Nizan declared: "The joke has gone on long enough, confidence has gone on long enough, and patience and respect. Everything is swept away in the permanent scandal of the civilization we are in, the general ruin into which men are sinking. A refusal, a denunciation will be published everywhere, despite all the police and all the conspiracies, so total, so radical that even the deafest will hear them." [3]

So characteristic was the attitude expressed by Nizan that certain French political scientists have identified it as the "spirit of 1930." [4] Jean Loubet del Bayle's study of a number of small groups of intellectuals clustered around periodicals like *Ordre Nouveau* and *Esprit* provides one of the most complete definitions of this spirit, which, in its most important aspects, extended far beyond the specific groups with which he is concerned. [5] An impression of witnessing the death throes of a social order, a feeling inspired by the war, had gained currency with the young at the turn of the decade, as the Wall Street crash dealt an apparently fatal blow to the capitalist economy, and governmental instability proved the inherent failings of the parliamentary regime. In response to this specter of continuing disintegration, there was a widely felt need for radical social transformation, a transformation commonly referred to in the vocabulary of the era as a revolution, with or without the capital *R*. The introduction to the *Nouvelle Revue Française Cahier de Revendications* suggests that the groups contacted represent "the first forces of a new French revolution,"[6] and, indeed, talk of revolution was commonplace not only among Communist and extreme right-wing intellectuals but even among Socialists and moderates.

In the years around 1930 this spirit of rejection of a moribund world and the concomitant call for radical change formed a bond among young intellectuals who would later take up positions at various points on the political spectrum. Their attitude might best be defined as one of fundamental anarchism, a term that was, in fact, used in self-description by thinkers as different as Brasillach and Malraux.[7] In this era Malraux, who would later emerge as the spokesman of the Left, found he had much in common with a Drieu la Rochelle who had not yet discovered fascism; it was Drieu who had recognized that Malraux, in his early novels, had created a "new man" strikingly in tune with the spirit of a new time.[8] Slightly earlier, a common perception of reality had formed a close bond between Drieu and Aragon. The bond was broken primarily because of Aragon's increasing commitment to Communism, a political solution that, despite its intermittent fascination, ultimately repelled the latent fascist.[9] Before his own adherence to Communism, Nizan had temporarily sought an outlet for his rejection of the status quo by joining Georges Valois's Faisceau, an ephemeral early fascist group. And a spirit of shared youthful rebellion made the young Brasillach, who himself never wavered from his allegiance to right-wing groups, consider Communist fellow students as kindred souls.[10]

The spirit of 1930 thus united much of the intellectual youth in the early part of the decade, but this situation was not destined to endure. By the mid-1930s, as Jean Cassou had noted, the pressure of events had forced French writers and intellectuals to choose positions on either side of a line that clearly separated Right and Left. As the Communists became willing to join with other leftists in a com-

mon front against fascism and as right-wing groups began to pro-
liferate under the impetus of fascist success in neighboring countries, French opinion polarized into two major blocs: Communists
and their sympathizers on the one hand, fascists on the other. By
1936 the young rebels, along with most other politically conscious
Frenchmen, had chosen their political camp.

For some—like Guilloux, Dabit, and Brasillach—this polarization
was merely the necessity of acting on a preexisting political fidelity.
For others, however, it was the result of a lengthy search for the appropriate political form. Aragon and Nizan, the two major Communist writers of the era, had made their commitment to the party by
1930, but this decision had been the outcome of years of searching
and experimentation. Throughout the 1920s Aragon had participated in the surrealist movement's uncertain flirtation with political
commitment, and Nizan had experimented with fascism and flight
to colonial Aden before deciding on the necessity of joining the
Communist party. On the other hand, Nizan's contemporary and
close friend Sartre, who shared Nizan's leftist sympathies, did not
feel the same need for active participation in politics; it was not until
he found himself in a German prison camp that he was to understand his friend's theory of a committed literature.[11]

If Sartre and Nizan continued to exemplify the contrasting roles
of observer and participant, many other writers were to exchange
one for the other. While trying to maintain his distance from the
political arena, Martin du Gard found himself more and more out-
spoken in his opposition to war. Even Céline, who was never a
"joiner," was finally drawn out of the politically ambiguous position
he had staked out for himself in 1932 with *Voyage au bout de la nuit*, a
novel at first hailed by both Left and Right for its depiction of a decaying social order. His vitriolic condemnation of the Soviet Union
on his return from a visit there in 1936 did much to set the record
straight, but it was not until his publication of two hate-filled antisemitic pamphlets in the late 1930s that the extent of his identification with the ideals of the Right became clear. These pamphlets,
whose hysteria was inspired in part by Céline's terror of the approaching war, were his major gesture of political commitment, and
it was primarily because of them, rather than for any overt political
activity, that he was pursued by French justice in the postwar years.

It was not uncommon for writers to change their political position
altogether. Drieu la Rochelle, for example, whose 1930 novel, *Une*

Femme à sa fenêtre, testified to a certain fascination with Communism, had by 1934 identified his political philosophy as fascist. In 1936 he entered the political arena as the intellectual spokesman for the Parti populaire français, whose leader, Jacques Doriot, had himself recently made the transition from Communism to fascism. As his friend Drieu moved toward fascism, Malraux translated his own fascination with revolutionary action, which had been embodied in the protagonist of his 1927 novel *Les Conquérants*, into a close identification with the Communist cause. If *La Condition humaine* could be accused of Trotskyism in 1933, Malraux's next novel, *Le Temps du mépris*, was criticized in 1935 for too slavish adherence to the party line. Increasingly drawn into the struggle against fascism in the mid-1930s, Malraux quickly moved into a position of prominence on the speakers' platforms of the antifascist meetings. His importance in this role reached its height with his personal participation in the Spanish Civil War.

The Impact of European Fascism

The events that drove French writers and intellectuals into making a political commitment were numerous. Most important, of course, was the accumulating evidence of Nazi oppression in Germany and aggression on the international scene. Soon after Hitler's acquisition of power, French intellectuals were roused by stories of the fate of many of their German colleagues and by Hitler's relentless persecution of all political opponents. In 1933 Malraux and Gide were sent to Berlin as personal representatives of French antifascist intellectuals to work for the release of Dimitrov, the Bulgarian Communist leader imprisoned after the Reichstag fire. It was Hitler's suppression of intellectual as well as political freedom that enabled the Communist-inspired Association des Ecrivains et des Artistes Révolutionnaires to gather together a wide range of leftist intellectuals under the slogan "Defense of Culture." [12]

Mussolini's attack on Ethiopia and Hitler's remilitarization of the Rhineland seemed to pose a threat, if a distant one, to international peace. But it was only the attempted fascist overthrow in 1936 of a legitimate democratic government in neighboring Spain, an attack liberally subsidized by fascist Italy and Germany, that forced many Frenchmen to see how close the danger lay to home. The closing years of the decade, which saw the annexation of Austria, the Munich agreement, and Hitler's march into Poland, were years of anxiety and intellectual mobilization for or against the inevitable European war.

The growing strength of the Nazis begins to be reflected in the French fiction of the middle of the decade, particularly in Malraux's *Le Temps du mépris* (1935). Brasillach's *Les Sept Couleurs* (1939), written at the end of the period, incorporates the reactions he had articulated in 1936. The authors of these works reveal their apprehension in the face of the Nazi rise to power, an apprehension accompanied by fascination or open hostility, depending on the political point of view. Fictional treatments of Nazi activity in Germany seem to have been supplanted in the later years of the decade by the more visible atrocities of the Spanish Civil War, which gave rise to an important literature of its own (see chapter 5).

Malraux's novel *Le Temps du mépris*[13] was the only piece of fiction he wrote between the Goncourt-winning *La Condition humaine* in 1933 and his Spanish Civil War novel of 1937, *L'Espoir*. It can be argued that in *Le Temps du mépris* he fully carries out the intention, proclaimed in the preface, of writing a modern "tragedy" that would focus exclusively on "man and his sense of life." In contrast to the long and extremely diffuse *L'Espoir*, this classically austere novel centers its attention on the protagonist, Kassner, and his struggle to survive his imprisonment. The other characters are almost without substance, and the central episode of the story, covering four of the book's eight parts, concerns Kassner alone in his cell.

In the years following the publication of *La Condition humaine*, Malraux had become active in the antifascist movement, and it is certainly in this involvement that *Le Temps du mépris* had its roots, a fact that illustrates once again the intimate relationship between Malraux's life and his art.[14] The story, which concerns the brief incarceration and ultimate release of a Communist leader in Nazi Germany, was, as Malraux states in his dedication, inspired by the experiences of real German antifascists. It is certainly related to Malraux's own role in working for the liberation of Dimitrov and in the continuing struggle to obtain the release of Thaelmann, the imprisoned leader of the German Communist party,[15] a cause that received much public attention in the early days of the Popular Front. Inspired by its author's own political *engagement*, *Le Temps du mépris* presents a strong argument for the involvement of the artist in the political struggle.

Despite the care taken by Malraux in the preface to distinguish between works inspired by "passion" and those that fall victim to "the will to prove," *Le Temps du mépris* has long suffered from the judgments of critics who place it in the second category. Indeed, Malraux himself did not wish to include it in his collected novels, allegedly referring to it as a failure (*navet*).[16] It is unclear whether his subsequent distaste for this work stemmed from purely artistic dissatisfaction or disaffection with its political perspective. Such an attitude on the part of the later Malraux would not be surprising because *Le Temps du mépris*, more than any other of his novels, seems to advocate a wholehearted acceptance of the Communist position.[17] Indeed, it was the only one of Malraux's works allowed to circulate freely in the Soviet Union.[18]

The situation of imprisonment described in the novella reflects a historical reality that had only very recently come to occupy an important place in the European consciousness, although it may have found its most lasting expression in the seventeenth century in Pascal's famous *pensée* about men imprisoned in a dungeon, which came to haunt the French writers of the 1930s and 40s.[19] *Le Temps du mépris* is thus an early example of the "concentrationary poetry" that dominates French literature during and after the war.[20]

In his treatment of an issue of burning contemporaneity, Malraux makes use of the methods that had recently been developed for portraying the "stream of consciousness" of a literary character,[21] transcribing the confused wanderings of Kassner's mind as he struggles with insanity. Malraux's use of this technique is not innovative from a technical point of view: he rarely departs from the use of the third-person pronoun, using *style indirect libre* rather than direct discourse, and the context of each of the images presented to Kassner's mind can be readily determined by the reader. Nevertheless, Malraux does evoke the confusion of a mind cut off from the normal external stimuli of light and human contact and produces a mélange of images from Kassner's past, which are connected apparently only by the process of free association. Thomas J. Kline points out the importance of the water images Malraux uses to suggest the reality of a mind set adrift.[22] But if the mind of the character is sometimes without direction, the mind of the author is not. The images that seem to float through Kassner's consciousness are, in fact, linked by more than the associative process of a disoriented mind. In these scenes of Kassner's solitary confinement, Malraux uses his character's physical and psychological experiences to evoke the positive relationship be-

tween the individual and the collectivity he stresses in the preface.
There, citing the phrase he had used in *La Voie royale*, "Il est difficile
d'être un homme," Malraux goes on to add, "Mais pas plus de le
devenir en approfondissant sa communion qu'en cultivant sa différ-
ence,—et la première nourrit avec autant de force au moins que la
seconde ce par quoi l'homme est homme, ce par quoi il se dépasse,
crée, invente ou se conçoit" (pp. 12–13).[b]

This communion is one that exists not only in space but also in
time, time that had in the 1930s, as Malraux himself was to note,
assumed its full historical dimension. Alone in his dark, underground cell, Kassner's mind can find stimulus only in his past experience, and Malraux has furnished him with a biography that, quite
plausibly, coincides with a number of significant twentieth-century
events. The son of a miner who is also a political militant, Kassner
has engaged in leftist activity before being taken prisoner by the
Russians in World War I and thus being in a position to participate in
the Soviet Revolution. His party activity has also gained him famil-
iarity with Asian revolutionary movements and with the developing
Soviet Union (here Malraux can draw on his own experience) before
involving him in the underground opposition to Hitler in his native
Germany.

Even in the first flood of images, activated by his memories of music, the linked scenes proceed with great speed but also with a
chronological rigor that makes them comprehensible to the reader.
This first flow of images is like a musical overture, presenting an
overview of the themes that will later be developed in greater detail.
Realizing that this uncontrolled flow of consciousness leads only to
madness—one that is dangerous because of the possibility of his revealing secret information—Kassner makes an effort to regain control over the production of his memories: "non pas être emporté:
recréer" (p. 70).[c] He decides to focus intently on a scene in Russia
during the Revolution, which was originally evoked by the memory
of a German shop glimpsed just before his imprisonment. However,
the fortuitous similarity of the elements that lead Kassner from one

[b]It is difficult to be a man. But it is not more difficult to become one by enriching
one's fellowship with other men than by cultivating one's individual peculiarities. The
former nourishes with at least as much force as the latter that which makes man
human, which enables him to surpass himself, to create, invent or realize himself
(pp. 7–8).
[c]not be carried away: recreate (p. 62).

moment in time to another signal for the reader a deeper link between past oppression in czarist Russia and the present in Nazi Germany. Kassner's fight against the White Russian army is clearly in continuity with his present struggle to hold out against his Nazi jailers.

As Kassner makes even further progress in getting his mind under control, he begins to articulate his memories in the form of language, delivering an imaginary speech to the comrades he envisions all over Europe. The speech itself focuses on the scene of his father's death in a mine explosion. When all rescue efforts fail, the mine must be walled up to prevent the spread of the fire, making certain the asphyxiation of the trapped miners. This physical suffocation is, however, only the culmination of a long process that has trapped his father in the solitude, humiliation, and meaninglessness of a life shared by many workers. Kassner now realizes the similarity between his father's suffocation, which exemplifies the "time of contempt" of the French title, and his own figuratively underground activity and literally underground imprisonment. Speaking of himself and his fellow antifascists, he concludes, "Nous sommes ensemble dans la mine fermée" (p. 112).[d]

Intermingled with these major moments of Kassner's past experience are memories of the workers' movement in Germany: a meeting in Hamburg, a demonstration during which the inhabitants of an entire street had spontaneously sheltered leftists being pursued by the police, the scene of tortured workers at Essen shot while singing the *Internationale*. What emerges from the increasingly ordered pattern of Kassner's reminiscences is a history of European revolutionary struggle, from its origins in the oppressed proletariat to its apparent realization in Russia to the current struggle against fascism in Germany. Kassner's imprisonment is not represented as a rupture with his past activity—as is, for example, the imprisonment of Sartre's Pablo in "Le Mur" or of Camus's Stranger—but as an act of continuity with the effort that has always formed his life project. Thus, although Kassner has lost the consciousness of passing time during his imprisonment, he is able to reconstruct for himself a history that endows his personal battle against the absurd with a more general significance.

"Non pas être emporté: recréer": the effort Kassner undertakes in

[d]We are together in the sealed mine (p. 103).

his prison is the same one that he has long been accustomed to making with respect to history, for Kassner is a writer, and the aim of his writing has been precisely that of reconstructing in language the revolutionary action in which he has taken part. His role as chronicler of the Revolution is, Malraux tells us, his most important function: "Tous ceux de la défaite aimaient en lui, à la fois, le compagnon (sa fonction était importante, mais non capitale), et le chroniqueur futur de leurs jours accablés" (p. 29).*

Kassner is the only one of Malraux's protagonists, at least before the young Berger of *Les Noyers de l'Altenburg,* who is at the same time both man of action and writer. Even the intellectuals of *L'Espoir* do not find time in the midst of their military action to take on the additional role of chronicler that Malraux himself would assume in the Spanish Civil War. But the ethnologist Garcia at least takes the time to assert, in a context that has not really prepared the ground for his remark, that the highest human function is "transformer en conscience une expérience aussi large que possible."*ᶠ* This formulation is not far from the definition of the highest human capacity with which Malraux ends the preface of *Le Temps du mépris:* "ce par quoi l'homme est homme, ce par quoi il se dépasse, crée, invente ou se conçoit" (p. 13).*ᵍ* It is significant that, in these statements, artistic reconstruction is closely linked with, in the one case, experience and, in the other, communal action with other men. Like Kassner himself, Malraux at this point seems to envision a close link between action—and, in Kassner's case, specifically political action—and artistic creation. Far from conflicting with each other, Malraux is saying, each activity nourishes the other: political action provides the living experience on which the art is based, while the creative activity of the writer submits this chaotic series of isolated events to the ordering function of the human mind, transforming it into a coherent structure of meaning. This is the nature of Kassner's effort in his cell as well as in his chronicles of the Revolution. And it is also the nature of Malraux's own effort in *Le Temps du mépris,* where he creates a context of meaning for the events that constitute the object of his current political commitment.

ᵉall the defeated treasured in him both the companion (his rôle was an important, but not a crucial one) and the future chronicler of their oppression (p. 22).
ᶠto convert as wide a range of experience as possible into conscious thought (p. 396)
ᵍthat which makes man human, which enables him to surpass himself, to create, invent or realize himself (p. 8).

While he is creating a historical context for Kassner's suffering, Malraux is also creating a community in which his solitary struggle can take its place. The existence of this community is evidenced, to some extent, by the prison itself, whose walls bear the inscriptions and transmit the tapping of fellow prisoners. The very content of these communications is one of fraternity: Kassner writes as his own inscription, "We are with you," and an unknown prisoner tirelessly transmits the word "comrade." Kassner's memories also remind him that he is part of a wider community, one of revolutionary workers that extends beyond the boundaries of his own country. The prison noises that blend into the episodes of his waking dream serve to underline the similarity of experience between past and present: the remembered cries of tortured Russian peasants mingle with the real screams of neighboring prisoners. And Kassner feels the fraternity that binds him not only to the other Germans who participate in the clandestine struggle but also to the meetings in Paris and later in Prague that proclaim their solidarity with the underground fighters (this reference to a recent Paris antifascist rally is, of course, an overt plea for support for Malraux's cause). Thus Malraux places Kassner's solitary struggle with madness in the context of the revolutionary community that gives it its meaning. As Kassner himself is able to reconstruct this community, his isolation becomes bearable.

The experience of Kassner, whose destiny seems controlled by hostile and incomprehensible forces, is not without parallel to that of a well-known twentieth-century literary predecessor, the protagonist of Kafka's *Trial*. Even the initial K that begins his name evokes Kafka's protagonists, and, like Kafka himself, Kassner is a German-speaking resident of Prague. In the prison he frequently sees himself as reduced to an insectlike existence,[23] and the vaguely outlined guards who come to beat him or to carry him off resemble, in their very anonymity, the men who take Joseph K. to his execution. Malraux was almost certainly familiar with Kafka, whose work had a great impact on the literature of the 1930s, and he seems to have been conscious of Kafka's strange prefiguration of the Nazi terror (which, of course, took place only well after his death). The immediate physical backdrop against which Kassner is placed is not far different from that of Kafka's Joseph K.—inconclusive interrogations, apparently unmotivated behavior on the part of others, a distant and unknown judgment. But, unlike Joseph K., Kassner has within himself the ability to order his experience in meaningful form, an ability that enables him to sustain the fight against madness and the hovering vulture of the absurd.[24] If the world of the prison itself—that of the Nazi Reich—attempts to deny human meaning, in *Le Temps du mépris* there can be posited, in opposition to it, a meaningful community of human struggle. *Le Temps du mépris* is thus an "anti-*Trial*," a fact that is underscored by Kassner's ultimate release and reintegration with the human community, a fate that contrasts with Joseph K.'s solitary execution.

Malraux stresses the role of the writer—the man who can give communicable form to the isolated workings of his mind—in the establishment of this human community. In the prison the effort to establish communication is represented in the episode of Kassner's laborious decoding of the other prisoner's tapping. Once Kassner discovers the language through which to express his fraternal presence and to receive the fraternal message of the other, a community is created that overcomes the barrier of prison walls. When the other prisoner is beaten into silence, Kassner invents a speech, designed to reach out to an imagined community of sympathizers, just as he himself has presumably used his rhetorical skills to create a community of European support for his underground movement. And the artist Malraux is using Kassner's speech, like the many speeches he himself made in this period, to forge the community of antifascist unity that forms the object of his efforts in the mid-1930s.

The community of revolutionary struggle in which Kassner finds his meaning is enlarged in the concluding sections of the novella to encompass the epic battle of man against the earth. This is the confrontation that Malraux, in his London speech of 1936, had called the real subject of leftist art.[25] The anticlimactic scene of the plane ride through the storm, which follows Kassner's release from prison, is surely a reflection of Malraux's desire to link this specific political struggle with the larger battle of man against the elements. As he reflects on this effort as revealed in the cultivated fields around Prague, Kassner even envisions the apple trees—"les grands pommiers droits au centre de leur anneau de pommes mortes" (p. 152) [h]—a replica of which would figure so prominently in a scene with similar function at the conclusion of *L'Espoir*.[26]

The optimism about historical action evidenced by Malraux in *Le Temps du mépris* is not found to the same degree in another Malru-

[h] the tall straight apple trees in the center of their rings of dead apples (p. 144).

cian novel. Not only does the protagonist live on at the end, a distinct departure from Malraux's three preceding novels, but the values that move him are never seriously thrown into question, a factor that separates it from Malraux's later work. Goldmann notes this when he describes *Le Temps du mépris* as "the narrative of the non-problematic relationship of the individual, Kassner, with the non-problematic community of revolutionary combatants."[27] Yet there is also in this politically committed work a reflection on the centrality of the role of the artist that will continue to dominate Malraux's thought and that will provide a locus of meaning when purely historical values appear to have failed. In addition, there is in the figure of Kassner an effort to link the creative function of the artist to a man of the "people," a link unprecedented in Malraux's work. The role of the common man, of whom Kassner is both the descendant and the spokesman, will also grow in importance in Malraux's work.

For Brasillach, like Malraux, the political situation of the 1930s offered the possibility of tragic action. As the heroine of *Les Sept Couleurs*[28] reflects at the end, the chaotic political confrontations of the era had given even the most humble of actors access to a tragic destiny: "Les métallos de Belleville, les bourgeois, les prolétaires, ils entrecroisent leur destin sentimental et un grand destin qui les dépasse, bien orgueilleusement. Ces hommes d'aujourd'hui, ils jouent la tragédie à tous les coins de rue" (p. 246).[i] And again like Malraux, Brasillach saw a modern tragic form as the fitting literary expression of this action.

The form he adopts in *Les Sept Couleurs* is a striking departure from his earlier works, which were not remarkable for their technical innovations. In his last novel of the decade, however, no doubt inspired by the example of Joyce's *Ulysses*, he chooses to experiment with a variety of narrative devices, which he compares with the seven colors of the spectrum available to the painter. The book is divided into seven sections of varying length, each of which uses a different narrative technique appropriate to the content: third-person narration, letters, a journal, personal reflections, dialogue, documents, and first-person monologue.

This modern, innovative form, however, is inscribed within the framework of one of the greatest of French classics, Corneille's trag-

[i]Belleville metal workers, bourgeois, proletarians—they very proudly mingle their sentimental destiny with a great destiny far beyond them. These men of today participate in tragic action on every street corner.

edy of Christian martyrdom, *Polyeucte*. The plot of Brasillach's novel, set in the 1930s, mirrors as nearly as possible the triangular situation of a heroine torn between husband and lover that provides the drama of *Polyeucte*; to reinforce the comparison, Brasillach opens each section with a relevant quotation from the play. But in *Les Sept Couleurs* the faith that animates Polyeucte/François and ultimately wins over both Pauline/Catherine and Sévère/Patrice is not Christianity but fascism, the faith of a new era.

As an important literary critic of his time, Brasillach was fully aware of current literary developments. Furthermore, he had recently published a full-length study of Corneille, an author much in vogue with the Right because of his emphasis on heroic action and civic virtue.[29] But the combination of twentieth-century technique and classical tragedy in *Les Sept Couleurs* is no mere reflection of Brasillach's literary interests of the moment. This inscription of the modern in the framework of the classical is the principle that also governs his vision of the fascist movements he describes in Italy, Germany, and Spain.

For *Les Sept Couleurs*, in addition to being the story of Catherine, Patrice and François, is also the drama of Europe in the period between the two world wars. Like Malraux and Nizan, who are at the same time writing a new history of the European Left, Brasillach is constructing the history of the new fascist Right. This movement begins with Mussolini's Italy, where Brasillach's young protagonist Patrice finds himself in 1928 (Brasillach himself did not visit Italy until 1937) as a French tutor in a Florentine family. His letters to Catherine attempt to convey the atmosphere of youthful exuberance that forms the essence of his impression of Italian fascism: "tout un peuple s'amuse" (p. 65). His dream, he tells Catherine, is that she too might get to know "ce petit peuple gracieux qui veut devenir fort. . . . Vous aurez une nuée d'enfants abattus autour de vous comme des pigeons, et vous pencherez la tête, et vous chanterez" (p. 74).[j] But this new spirit is set against the background of the city of Florence, the embodiment of Italian Renaissance culture. It is with a shoemaker near the Piazza della Signoria that Patrice discusses the new architectural constructions of the fascist regime, and he sees in the new Italians themselves a continuity with the graceful

---

[j] an entire people enjoys itself . . . this small, gracious people that wants to become strong. You will have a crowd of children at your feet like pigeons, and you will nod your head and you will sing.

beauty of the past: "Je vois naître cette Italie nouvelle dont on nous fait, en France, un épouvantail. Je suis sûr qu'elle vous plairait, parce qu'elle reste gracieuse" (p. 65).[k]

Patrice's stay in Germany seven years later is set in another historic city, Nuremberg, where he has become head of the French Chamber of Commerce. His journal, which fills in the background of his five-year enlistment in the French Foreign Legion, goes on to describe the Nazi party Congress that is held every year in that city. The journal form is well adapted to include the accounts that Brasillach himself had written of his visit to the Nuremberg congress of 1937.[30] The journalistic material is integrated into the text of the novel through the legion flashback, which describes Patrice's friendship with a fellow legionnaire, the disillusioned young German Siegfried Kast. After watching the process of Siegfried's "resurrection" through Nazism, Patrice and the reader are prepared to understand the significance of the celebration of the high cult of the Nazi party at the annual Nuremberg congress.

As the new fascist regime had found itself in harmony with Florence, a cultural high point of Italy's past, the Nazi emblems are set against medieval Nuremberg, the embodiment of a past moment of German greatness: "Dans les petites rues pavées de Nuremberg et de Bamberg au long des rivières et des canaux, auprès des cathédrales et des admirables statues de pierre, c'est l'ancienne Allemagne du Saint-Empire qui se marie avec le IIIe Reich" (p. 110).[l] The Nazi flags displayed everywhere seem to ally themselves with the baroque sculptures and the ancient dwellings, a significant mixture of past and present that was certainly not absent from Hitler's mind when he chose Nuremberg as the site of the party congresses.

Many of the characteristics of German Nazism repeat those Patrice had earlier noticed in Italian fascism. There is a similar atmosphere of joyful exuberance and youthful singing: "On s'amuse en Allemagne, beaucoup plus que ne le croient les antifascistes de mon pays" (p. 105).[m] There is also in Germany, however, a seriousness that Brasillach can only describe in the language of the sacred. The

[k]I am witnessing the birth of the new Italy that they're trying to scare us with in France. I'm sure you'll like it, because it remains gracious.

[l]In the little paved streets of Nuremberg and Bamberg along the rivers and canals, near the cathedrals and the admirable stone statues, the ancient Germany of the Holy Empire is being married with the Third Reich.

[m]They enjoy themselves in Germany, much more than the antifascists in my country think.

descriptions of the ceremonies of the Congress are filled with religious terms. Brasillach at first describes the rites as "l'office hitlérien" and "la messe du travail" (p. 111), as later the ceremony of the consecration of the party flags through contact with the flag of the failed Munich *putsch* is described as a "transfusion mystique" (p. 124),[n] to be compared with the Eucharist. Attention is focused on the appearance of Hitler amid thousands of spotlights trained on the sky, an effect known as the "cathedral of light," which becomes for the observer "le lieu sacré du mystère national" (p. 113).[o] There are frequent references to the "martyrs" who form the subject of the *Horst Wessel Lied* and who transmit their "benediction" through the "flag of blood." Finally, Hitler himself—at first disarmingly described as sad, tired, almost childlike, and nice—is portrayed as a man whose mission it is to lead Germany toward its "devouring destiny," even at the price of great sacrifices (p. 123). In short, this "sad vegetarian civil servant" harbors the soul of a great religious leader, a phenomenon that does not fail to trouble Patrice, who wonders if it does not go beyond the bounds of the permissible. He is especially uneasy because he realizes that Germany, because of its "eternal nature" (p. 103), will inevitably go to war again with France, a France that he sees as weakened by the excesses of the recently-elected Popular Front.

The feeling of the sacred transmitted to Brasillach by the Nuremberg ceremonies was, of course, not foreign to the intentions of Hitler himself, as witnessed by Leni Riefenstahl's officially commissioned film of a Nuremberg Congress, *Triumph of the Will*. In the context of *Les Sept Couleurs*, however, repeated evocations of religious reality are especially significant. If Brasillach's modern Polyeucte is to become a martyr for a cause, the cause itself must attain the status of the religious faith that animated Corneille's hero. Thus the modern cult of fascism must be set firmly within the framework of traditional religious belief.

Similar themes are taken up in the third example of modern fascism, that of Franco's Spain. Since the Spanish section is set during the Civil War, however, the typical fascist exuberance is somewhat toned down. This section consists of "documents," supposedly accumulated by François Courtet, who has gone off to fight with the

[n] the Hitlerian service, the mass of labor . . . mystical transfusion
[o] the sacred place of the national mystery

Spanish fascists when he mistakenly believes his wife Catherine has run off with her old boyfriend Patrice. The "documents" are, in reality, a mélange of Brasillach's nonfictional writings on the Civil War, excerpts from newspaper articles[31] or selections from the *Histoire de la guerre d'Espagne*,[32] which he wrote in collaboration with Maurice Bardèche.

Brasillach seems intuitively to realize the weakness of this section when, in his preface, he feels it necessary to present a special argument that "a series of documents placed end to end . . . can pass as another form of this art [of the novel]." Despite the possible merit of his case, the particular documents of the Spanish section remain stubbornly outside the scope of his novel. The background of the Nuremberg sequence had been prepared through the story of Siegfried Kast, but there is no such development of a Spanish character. Furthermore, the character of François, whose experience in Spain supposedly unifies the collection of documents, has remained almost unknown to the reader. While the strong presence of Patrice had convincingly carried over into the voice who described the Nazi congress, the distant figure of François is incapable of bringing together the varied documents. The Spanish section of *Les Sept Couleurs* can thus hardly qualify as a "fictional" treatment of the Civil War.

Nevertheless, the view of Spanish fascism that emerges from it is in harmony with the rest of the novel, to which it provides a fitting conclusion. In the context of the *Polyeucte* parallel, it provides a plausible occasion for the "martyrdom" of Polyeucte/François—although François is apparently only wounded and not killed. Furthermore, as is spelled out in one of the articles quoted, the Civil War in Spain represents the culmination of the fascist movement that has begun in Italy and Germany and spread to all parts of Europe. This movement finally receives its consecration in the Spanish "war of ideas," a war that is for Brasillach, as for many of his contemporaries, a playing out of the more general European conflict between fascism and antifascism.

This "spiritual war" attains its full religious dimensions in the atmosphere of Catholic Spain. Brasillach seems to find the sacred aspects of the "crusade" in Spain more in tune with the French Catholic tradition: none of the "documents" records the impression of strangeness that had given a menacing overtone to the descriptions of Hitler's Germany. The history of Spain is itself a religious history, and it is against this background that its fascist movement must be placed: "Le double idéal de la 'Sainte Tradition,' comme chantent les carlistes, et de l' 'aube' nouvelle, du 'printemps' qui vient rire sur l'Espagne, comme chante la Phalange, il est visible à chaque pas que nous faisons sur cette terre admirable de l'exaltation et de la foi" (p. 231). As Malraux had already done from a different political perspective, Brasillach sets the modern legend of the Toledo Alcazar (the fascist version, of course, about which he had already written in his nonfictional study, *Les Cadets de l'Alcazar* in 1936) against the war ruins of the ancient city. The war itself is described as a new Reconquest, an effort to recapture the glory of the Spanish past: "Il faudrait plaindre ceux qui ne découvriraient pas dans l'Espagne nouvelle la naissance ou plutôt la renaissance d'un grand destin. C'est que la nation, oublieuse des erreurs libérales du XIXe siècle, est en train de redevenir ce qu'elle a été au siècle d'or" (p. 232).[p]

Thus, in *Les Sept Couleurs*, Brasillach is presenting his vision of modern European fascism, a movement that he envisions as a reincarnation of the spirit of the most glorious moments of each nation's past, as it is animated by a spiritual force like that of the traditional European religions. By placing his own history of twentieth-century fascism within the framework of a classical French tragedy, Brasillach offers an indication of his hope that these sources of spiritual renewal will permit his own country to recapture the glory of its pre-Revolutionary past.

A Political Turning Point: The Riots of February 1934

The rise of fascism in Italy and Germany was significant for the French not only because of its threat to European peace but also because of its influence on the political situation in France. By the early 1930s the optimistic illusions of the 1920s were fading away. The old leaders—Poincaré, Clemenceau and Briand—who had maintained a precarious equilibrium in the postwar period, were dying off, and their successors were already proving incapable of

---

[p]The double ideal of the "Holy Tradition" that the Carlists sing of, and of the new "dawn," the "spring" that comes to smile on Spain, that the Falangists sing of, is visible at each step we take in this admirable land of exaltation and faith. . . . You have to be sorry for those who cannot see in the new Spain the birth, or rather the rebirth, of a great destiny. The nation, forgetful of the liberal errors of the nineteenth century, is in the processs of becoming again what it was in its greatest age.

adapting their policies to meet unprecedented crises in the economy and foreign affairs. Alienation from the political regime, current among the young intellectuals of 1930, became increasingly widespread as various segments of society began to feel the effects of the economic slowdown, and criticism of government policies came from both Left and Right. French politics became a microcosm of the ideological conflicts of Europe as a whole, from which French thinkers could not remain isolated. A visit to the 1935 Nuremberg congress, for example, forcibly made Drieu la Rochelle aware of the inevitability of French involvement: "It is more and more clear to me that the future will not stay calm, in one way or another. In any case, it is impossible for France to continue to remain immobile next to such a Europe."[33]

Intellectuals of the Left looked to the rapidly developing Soviet Union as a model for social change, and a long list of French writers, including almost all the figures featured in this study, made tours of the USSR during the mid-1930s. Céline, Malraux, Guilloux, Dabit, and Drieu la Rochelle each traveled to the Soviet Union on at least one occasion; as members of the party, Aragon and Nizan spent considerably more time there. Right-wing movements naturally looked to Italy and Germany as sources of renewal, and many intellectuals, like Brasillach, were seduced by these countries' relative economic prosperity and youthful energy, phenomena that formed a striking contrast to the declining situation in France.

To the influence of Italy and Germany—and in many cases to their outright subsidies as well—can be ascribed the proliferation of French fascist movements, many of which adopted the paramilitary tactics that had proven so successful elsewhere. Followers of both Left and Right took their case to the streets more and more frequently, the Right emphasizing marches and military maneuvers, the Left utilizing mass rallies and the traditional strikes, which became more common from 1933 on in the face of increasing economic instability.

These street demonstrations reached a point of crisis in the "days of February" in 1934. A riot of right-wing groups on the Place de la Concorde on February 6 was followed by massive left-wing demonstrations on February 9 and 12, events that radically altered the course of French politics.[34] Prior to February 6, the right-wing leagues—and, indeed, much of French public opinion—had been agitated by the revelations in the Stavisky case, yet another financial scandal involving figures in the corrupt Radical regime. Further en-flamed by a new government's dismissal of Chiappe, the right-wing Paris prefect of police, the veterans' organizations of the Right as-sembled their followers on February 6 in the region of the place de la Concorde. They were joined, strangely enough, by the equally anti-parliamentarian Communist veterans' organization. These crowds made repeated assaults on the police guarding the bridge that led across the Seine to the Palais Bourbon, where the Chamber of Deputies had just given its approval to the new cabinet headed by the Radical Edouard Daladier, supported in part by the Socialists. The demonstrators did not succeed in entering the Chamber—al-though only the strange hesitation of Colonel de La Rocque pre-vented his Croix-de-Feu, who surrounded the Palais Bourbon on the Left Bank, from effecting an easy takeover. But the mêlée at the Concorde resulted in the deaths of fifteen to twenty people,[35] who were immediately acclaimed as rightist martyrs, and the resulting outrage against the government of "assassins" forced Daladier to re-sign. He was replaced by a seemingly innocuous former president of the Republic, Gaston Doumergue, whose policies were much fur-ther to the Right. As one historian notes, the Daladier government was the first since 1848 to be overthrown by revolt in the streets.[36]

While the fascists seemed to have won the battle, the Left was to profit from the Concorde riots in the long run. The magnitude of the fascist threat demanded a similar show of strength from the opposi-tion, and a demonstration called by the Communists on February 9 drew forth large numbers of supporters that extended far beyond the membership of the party alone. Although this demonstration near the place de la République posed no danger to the Chamber, there were confrontations with the police and several demonstrators were killed, incidents that provided the Left with martyrs of its own. Ara-gon, in his article for that month's *Commune*, was already putting these victims in the context of past and present revolution: "What we hail in the dead who are carried off is the heroism of the Parisian proletariat who already at the time of the Commune, in the striking words of Marx, stormed the heavens."[37] All this culminated on Feb-ruary 12 in the march down the cours de Vincennes, when the sepa-rate columns of Communists and Socialists merged into one at the place de la Nation. This spontaneous union at the base paved the way for the formal political union of the Left, which was ratified by the agreement signed by Communists and Socialists on July 27 of the same year. Thus the most tangible result of the nearly successful fascist attempt on the regime was, ironically, the formation of the Popular Front, which would triumph in the elections of 1936.

The days of February had a galvanizing effect on both political camps, making each aware of the possibilities of direct collective action. This was their effect on Drieu la Rochelle, whose description of the riots at the place de la Concorde, which occurs at the conclusion of his autobiographical novel *Gilles*, is certainly the best known. The February riots and the subsequent direct confrontations between Left and Right that took place over the following two years were also important as a catalyst in a process of rapid political polarization, forcing many Frenchmen into a public admission of hitherto private political views. This process is illustrated by the evolution of Drieu's protagonist in *Gilles* and by the protagonist in Brasillach's posthumously published work, *Les Captifs*. While Drieu and Brasillach focus on the personal reactions of their protagonists, Nizan in *Le Cheval de Troie* analyzes the dynamics of mass action in a reenactment of the Parisian confrontation in a typical provincial city. The Communist Nizan is in accord with the fascists Drieu and Brasillach in viewing this event in the context of a historical struggle and a portent of revolutionary upheaval to come.

It is interesting that the 1934 riots claim the attention of writers at the end of the decade; by this time, many of them were able to see in this moment of crisis an episode that had shaped French destiny. Certain moderates of the Left, like André Chamson, saw in the Concorde riots a threatening attempt by right-wing forces to gain power, as they had in other countries, through cleverly manipulated mob violence. On the Right, however, writers tended to see the demonstrations as a spontaneous outburst of popular sentiment. To them, this expression of the people's will promised to overcome the traditional political barriers between Right and Left, and they attributed its failure to effect the promised social transformation to lack of direction and poor leadership. Writing about the 1934 riots from the perspective of the end of the decade, Brasillach shares many elements of their more famous treatment by Drieu (of course, he had presumably had the benefit of reading Drieu's *Gilles* just prior to the composition of his own work). Brasillach's unfinished novel, *Les Captifs*,[38] was, as its title suggests, written in a German prison camp just after the French defeat. It was never put in final form, and it was not published during Brasillach's lifetime.

According to the existing manuscript and Brasillach's outlines of the completed work, *Les Captifs* was designed to trace the political evolution in France during the 1930s just as *Les Sept Couleurs* had traced the growth of fascism in other parts of Europe. Brasillach tells this story by focusing on the destiny of Gilbert Caillé, who, according to Maurice Bardèche, combines traits of both the author and himself.[39] Born, symbolically, on August 1, 1914, Gilbert is a young man whose life sums up the experience of Brasillach's generation; as one of the manuscript fragments states, he is "un garçon arrivé à l'âge d'homme vers 1933, où le siècle a pris définitivement son tournant" (p. 658).[q] According to Brasillach's outline, Gilbert's story is to be told during the imprisonment of the narrator, Robert B., in various German prison camps, a fate reflecting that of the author. Thus Brasillach's aim is to place the destiny of Gilbert firmly within the context of defeat and captivity, which had formed the conclusion of what he could now look back on as "the prewar era." What Drieu, writing in 1939, could only project into the future, Brasillach in 1940 knew as hard reality.

A central event in the development of Gilbert Caillé is the night of February 6, 1934. He sees this revolt as flowing from a shared popular resentment that unifies the nation, and at the place de la Concorde he notes with approval the presence of the Communists at the side of the right-wing leagues: "Il semblait qu'au dessus des divisions un vaste rassemblement national et social commençait de s'opérer" (p. 540).[r] But, despite their promising beginning, Gilbert realizes that the leaderless demonstrations have no chance of changing the direction of the nation.

While they cannot bring about change in a larger sense, the riots have a lasting effect on Gilbert's individual existence, teaching him two important lessons that will govern the rest of his life. The revolt is for Gilbert "a sort of baptism," fulfilling a yearning for the action denied to the young man born too late to participate in World War I. Having heard the whistle of bullets around him for the first time, Gilbert feels he has been initiated into the reality of combat through the mystic force of spilled blood: "Le néophyte a besoin de la cérémonie populaire, et du liquide plus mystérieux que l'eau, du liquide

---

[q] a boy who reached manhood around 1933, when the century definitively declared its direction

[r] It seemed as if, beyond the divisions, a vast national and social movement was beginning to organize.

tiède, gluant et rouge, du fleuve sacré entre tous . . .—le liquide du sang" (p. 550).[s] The riots also provide him with the foundation of a political position by revealing to him, as if in a religious vision, "the form of the nation" (p. 549). Gilbert feels he has now found a direction, however vague, for his future activity: "Parmi eux, ou à côté d'eux, il y avait bien quelque combat à mener, quelque place à tenir" (p. 548). Returning home, he gives expression to his hopes by writing, "*6 février 1934—An I de la Révolution nationale*" (p. 551).[t] And, in the last glimpse of him afforded by the existing manuscript, Gilbert is in Spain in 1938, still hoping that France will have its own "national revolution" so that it can become the "natural ally" of Germany. The scene says much about Brasillach's attitude at the time.

While sharing many of Brasillach's impressions of the Concorde riots, Drieu la Rochelle is far from sharing the long-term optimism of Brasillach's young protagonist. The description of the riots that forms the conclusion of Drieu's long, autobiographical novel, *Gilles*[40] is by far the best-known literary treatment of the event. Often quoted in historical accounts is Drieu's evocation of "le couple divin revenu, la Peur et le Courage, qui préside à la guerre" (pp 595–96).[u][41] Brasillach make a similar connection with war; naturally, the two right-wing writers see this as a positive element.

Gilles's rediscovery of the experience of combat in the riots of February 6 concludes the main body of a novel that begins during World War I when the young soldier returns to Paris on leave from the front. In the over 500 pages that intervene between these two events, Gilles experiences the decadence of postwar French society in its various manifestations. Because it promises to break free of this decadence, the popular élan of February 6 appears to Gilles as the last sign of hope for his generation. When he sees that it has been allowed to collapse without leadership, he knows the crucial battle of the decade has been lost for France.

Drieu's description of the events of February 6 is set in the context of Gilles's relationship with his wife, Pauline, whose fate is linked with that of France itself. Attracted by Pauline's love for life, Gilles had hoped to break out of his personal and political stagnation by

[s]The neophyte needs the mass ceremony and the liquid more mysterious than water, the warm liquid, sticky and red, the river sacred above all . . . the liquid of blood.
[t]among them, or alongside them, there was surely some fight to lead, some place to occupy. . . . *February 6 1934— Year I of the National Revolution*.
[u]the return of the divine couple, Fear and Courage, who preside over war

marrying her and engendering a child. This decision parallels and comments upon his attempt to initiate a new political movement through the intervention of his politician friend Clérences.[42] But the old men who dominate the party congress at which Clérences takes his stand are obviously incapable of overcoming their sterility. To Gilles, the convention reveals that France has grown old and thereby lost its creative power: "Les Français avaient fait des églises et ils ne pouvaient plus les refaire ni rien de semblable. . . . Ce peuple avait vieilli" (p. 561).[v] Clérences's speech itself is in fact portrayed as a failed sexual encounter:[43] "Au lieu d'une saine et féconde rencontre sexuelle, on voyait deux onanismes s'approcher, s'effleurer puis se dérober l'un à l'autre" (p. 556).[w]

The impossibility of regeneration in the public sphere is echoed in the private when Pauline's doctor discovers a cancer that necessitates the sacrifice of the baby and renders her permanently sterile. But the operation cannot totally eradicate the disease, which has attacked the core of her being. As if to express this internal decay in the form of her life, Pauline begins to spend her time with Clérences's wife and, under the influence of the young bourgeoise, gradually loses her own natural spontaneity. In the disease that destroys her both physically and morally, Pauline comes to embody Drieu's conception of France between the wars, a France mortally attacked by a decadence that Drieu proclaimed in his preface to be the major subject of his fiction.[44]

In equating Pauline's sterility and fatal cancer with the destiny of France, Drieu is repeating a metaphor that seems to have permeated the writing of the decade. Few children are born in the novels of the 1930s (Martin du Gard's Jean-Paul is, of course, an exception, but a point is made of his failure to continue the Thibault name, thus bringing about the family's extinction). Miscarriage and abortion are frequent, as in Céline's *Voyage au bout de la nuit*, Nizan's *Le Cheval de Troie*, and Aragon's *Les Cloches de Bâle*. Also, it is not uncommon for characters, especially women, to be attacked by diseases that eat away at their internal organs: the tuberculosis of Catherine in *Les Cloches de Bâle*, the many illnesses treated by Céline's Dr. Bardamu, the corrosive lung condition of Antoine Thibault. The repe-

---

[v]The French had created churches and they could no longer recreate them or anything of the sort. . . . This people had grown old.
[w]Instead of a healthy and fruitful sexual encounter, you saw two onanisms approach each other, brush past, and then move away.

tition of such situations in the fiction of the 1930s suggests that all these writers are mirroring in their characters their impressions of French society as a whole, victim of a fatal decay and incapable of regeneration.[45]

In *Gilles*, as the Concorde riots prepare themselves, Pauline has reached her last days, a situation that coincides with Gilles's vision of France itself. The "beaux quartiers" in which Gilles is now visiting his new mistress are described as "ces derniers coins où le Paris d'autrefois, plein de verdure et de silence, agonise sous le progrès inexorable de la petrification" (p. 584).[x] And as Gilles walks past the Palais Bourbon on the night of the riot, he reflects on "la vieille bande radicale qui tient la France et qui sera encore là à son chevet dans l'heure de son agonie" (p. 591).[y] But, even in this atmosphere of decay and death, Gilles remains aware of the remnants of a past beauty, like that of a woman, in the sight of the Louvre lying in the curve of the river.

When Gilles arrives at the place de la Concorde itself, he implicitly compares it with the internal destruction wrought by Pauline's illness; he sees it as "ce grand vide qui s'étend soudain au milieu des cités malades" (p. 591). The emptiness of the perspective, not yet invaded by the crowd, is a graphic representation of the void at the core of French life and the emptiness of a time when no movement is possible: "La police et le peuple, rencognés dans les angles, renonçaient à occuper la scène. Ainsi finit l'Histoire" (p. 595).[z]

When the action finally begins, it evokes for Gilles numerous and repeated references to the war. The pure world of virile combat had always formed the implicit contrast to the decadent world of Paris that Gilles had reentered in the beginning of the novel, and its return at this moment is of great significance. Gilles at first doubts that anything important will happen, as he had doubted the possibility of war in 1914. Later, in his movement against the crowd, he recaptures moments on the battlefields of Champagne and Verdun. But, as in the combat scenes Drieu had portrayed in *La Comédie de Charleroi*, the experience of exaltation lasts only for a moment, leaving the

[x]these last corners where the old Paris, green and silent, is slowly dying under the inexorable progress of petrification
[y]the old radical gang that holds France in its power and will still be there at her bedside at the hour of her death
[z]the great void that suddenly opens in the middle of sick cities. . . . The police and the people, huddled in the corners, no longer wanted to take the stage. Thus ends history.

original emptiness: "Gilles courait partout aux points de plénitude qui lui apparaissaient dans la nuit et dans les lueurs et, quand il arrivait essoufflé, il trouvait un carré de bitume déserté qu'un corps couché ne comblait pas" (p. 596).[a]

Nevertheless, Gilles sees in the brief popular élan of the Concorde a new promise of life: "Ce peuple n'est pas mort" (p. 596), he announces, and he adds, "C'est la première fois que je vis depuis vingt ans" (p. 597). He begs Clérences to take over the direction of this new energy: "Les barrières seront à jamais rompues entre la droite et la gauche, et des flots de vie se précipiteront en tout sens. . . . Le flot est là devant nous: on peut le lancer dans la direction qu'on veut, mais il faut le lancer tout de suite, à tout prix" (p. 599).[b46] Gilles is conscious only of the affirmation of life over death, action over immobility, unity over fragmentation, plenitude over emptiness; the content and direction of this new force are of minor importance. But as he delivers his tirade in front of Clérences and his followers, they instinctively realize the nature of Gilles's political position: he is a fascist.

As he pleads vainly with Clérences, Gilles begins to realize that the forces revealed at the Concorde have little hope of surviving. They will be destroyed by the sterility of the traditional political leaders, embodied in the men whom he faces: "La source de vie derrière ces yeux était absolument tarie. Et la bouche ironisait faiblement dans un semi-aveu d'impuissance. Un coup d'oeil autour de lui fit voir des visages de vingt ans figés dans les expressions vieillottes de faible méfiance, de tâtillonne irrésolution" (p. 598).[47] None of the political leaders—from the right-wing leagues to the young Radicals like Clérences to the Communists on the Left—is capable of prolonging this life-giving movement. As Gilles returns home to the dying Pauline, he realizes again the intimate connection between his relationships with his wife and his country: "Les ponts qu'il avait lancés dans sa vie vers les femmes, vers l'action, ç'avait été de folles volées, insoucieuses de trouver leurs piliers. Il n'avait pas eu d'é-

---

[a]Gilles ran everywhere to the points of plenitude that appeared to him in the night and the glimmers, and when he arrived, breathless, he found a deserted square of asphalt that a fallen body was not able to fill.

[b]This people is not dead. . . . I'm living for the first time in twenty years. . . . The barriers will be broken forever between the Right and Left, and floods of life will rush in all directions . . . . The flood is there before us: we can direct it where we want, but we must set it in motion right away, at all costs.

pouse et il n'avait pas eu de patrie. Il avait laissé sa patrie s'en aller à vau-l'eau" (p. 604).^{c} In *La Comédie de Charleroi* Drieu had linked sexual union with the action of combat; here he equates the failure of both in the ultimate sterility of a marriage and a nation.

Pauline dies, appropriately enough on the eve of the Communist counterdemonstration: "La révolte communiste, guettée et circonvenue comme la révolte nationaliste, échouait au milieu d'une France sans gouvernement, acéphale, mais qui de toute sa masse intestinale, noyée de graisse, étouffait son coeur" (p. 606).^{d} Gilles sees the confirmation of the failure of the Communist revolt on February 12, when Communists and Socialists join forces in what would become the Popular Front. In Gilles's view, this is the final stage in the mortal illness of the French nation.

Interestingly, Drieu does not place the blame for this failure solely on forces external to his protagonist. Gilles realizes he has shared in the moral deficiences that have led to French sterility, and he is finally convinced of the impossibility of action by accepting the truth of Clérences's accusation: "Il n'y a rien à faire dans ce pays parce qu'il n'y a rien à faire avec nous: tu le sais aussi bien que moi" (p. 603).^{e} Gilles knows the sterility of the nation has manifested itself first in his own life: his relationships with women have reflected his inability to give of himself and to create new life.[48] He has betrayed the dying Pauline with another woman, as he feels he has betrayed France itself. But the failing that seems most to haunt him is the loveless marriage he had contracted with his rich first wife, Myriam. In this case Gilles reproaches himself with avarice, the very sin that, on a larger scale, has been, in his view, responsible for France's low birth rate, a literal manifestation of the country's failure to regenerate itself. In examining the failures of his time, Gilles/Drieu is able

^{c}The source of life behind the eyes was absolutely dried up. And the mouth spoke ironically and weakly in what was almost an admission of impotence. A glance around him showed the faces of twenty-year-olds frozen into old-looking expressions of weak contempt, of finicky irresolution. . . . The bridges he had tried to build in his life to women, to action, had been mad flights, careless of finding their supports. He had had no wife and he had had no country. He had let his country go to rack and ruin.

^{d}The Communist revolt, watched and circumvented like the nationalist revolt, was failing in the middle of a France without a government, without a brain, a France that, however, with its whole intestinal mass, drowned in fat, was stifling its heart.

^{e}There is nothing to be done in this country because there is nothing to be done with us: you know it as well as I.

to recognize his own participation in that failure. Drieu's retrospective analysis of his own life is thus not merely an exercise in introspection but a document about his entire generation.

Like Drieu, Nizan juxtaposes the death of a woman and a confrontation of demonstrators with the police, but the purpose of the juxtaposition is totally different. For Nizan, the workers' demonstration that he describes in *Le Cheval de Troie* is not the last spasm of a dying France but rather a first movement of revolt against hitherto passively accepted deaths from social oppression, which are reflected in the fate of the character of Catherine. *Le Cheval de Troie* is divided into two parts, the second of which is devoted entirely to the description of a confrontation between Right and Left—or, rather, between left-wing demonstrators and the police—which mirrors the events of February 9, 1934, and its multiple reenactments in the provinces. The scenario presented by Nizan is a close approximation of events that actually took place during the years 1934–35 in such provincial cities as Grenoble, Toulouse, Toulon and Brest.[49] One reviewer found the confrontations described in the novel so typical that Nizan's analysis could be applied to incidents that occurred even after the novel's publication.[50] Nizan could not have gone further in fulfilling his "passion for the present."

The street demonstration is the major event in the novel, and the entire first part is designed merely to set it in its proper context. First, Nizan must present the social configuration of the city, the local industrial and administrative elite, and the lycée professor Lange, whose philosophy of solitude and death is the intellectual expression of bourgeois society. Most important, he must analyze the origins of the long-suppressed anger that bursts forth in the workers' demonstration. The character of Paul, an unemployed union militant from another region, represents the fate of millions of unemployed throughout the country. Unable to find a regular job because of his past activism, he is thrown back on the work relief program of the municipality, which, appropriately, involves him in digging up corpses in the cemetery (it is apparently the only work that this dying society is capable of providing). And through the marriage of Catherine and Albert Cravois, Nizan introduces the reader to the suffocating life of the working poor (see chapter 3).

In the first section of the novel, attention is focused on the six or seven characters who make up the core of the Communist group. The novel seems generally to follow the activities of the Communist professor Bloyé, obviously the stand-in for Nizan himself.[51] Although Bloyé is the figure whose point of view predominates, he is not the novel's central character: the protagonist of *Le Cheval de Troie* is this entire small Communist group, and most of the important scenes involve group actions and reactions. Nizan abandons his focus on this group only long enough to examine the consciousness of the solitary Lange and, through his intermediary, to present the views of the local power structure.

In the second half, which takes place on the day of the riot, the perspective broadens considerably. The point of view is no longer that of an individual nor even that of a small group whose individual members are identified. It is, rather, that of a series of social categories: the apathetic local bourgeoisie; the left-wing crowd that gathers to demonstrate; the young fascists; and the police. Only after the action is over does the focus return to the original group, some of whose members are now dead or in prison.

The scene of the riot opens on the perspective of the local bourgeoisie, who go about their normal Sunday activities, finally settling down in the local cafés to combine their apéritif with speculation about the day's political meeting. The views of these "café luminaries" are presented through the use of direct or indirect discourse, always attributed to an undifferentiated "they," and the entire passage employs a conversational tone. The voice of the author does intrude itself from time to time, however, to emphasize a vision of the workers that, because it is not really part of their consciousness, these people cannot believably express (for example: "Ils avaient perdu l'habitude de regarder les gens des usines comme des combatants" [p. 150]*). This is the voice of the apathetic "silent majority": these spectators welcome the arrival of the *gardes mobiles* to maintain order, but they themselves are not planning to participate in the fascist meeting.

After a brief glance at the arrival of the young out-of-town fascist leaguers, the focus switches to the left-wing crowd gathering on the place du Théâtre. The influence of Romains's unanimism is evident in Nizan's treatment of this crowd as a single entity with a life of its own. He traces its growth from a collection of isolated groups to a dense mass that eats away at the empty borders of the square until it

---

*They had long ceased to look on the factory workers as potential combatants (p. 154).

finally succeeds in filling the entire space. "Une foule n'aime pas s'amasser au centre d'une étendue vide, elle n'aime pas se sentir menacée par une bordure déchiquetée, incertaine, elle veut se sentir à peine contenue par des parois résistantes qui la façonnent sur ses frontières et la contraignent à combler toutes ses lacunes, à occuper le moindre espace intérieur" (p. 156).[g]

The narrative technique adopted by Nizan in this passage emphasizes the communion that, for him, distinguishes the Communists and that is here extended to the entire Left, in the spirit of the Popular Front. He portrays the crowd as displaying a single emotion: "Elle [la foule] chanta quand elle vit le drapeau socialiste et le drapeau communiste monter. Elle s'étonnait d'en être là" (p. 156).[h] Despite the new spirit of unity, however, Nizan cannot seem to resist a few jibes at the unfortunate Socialists, at one point describing them as "pintades poussiéreuses" (p. 163).[i]

The dynamic of this crowd is consistently described in terms of force and expansion, usually in an analogy with fire ("il [le chant] jaillissait comme un feu qui s'allume sur plusieurs points" [p. 157]) or water ("quand il eut empli complètement la place, il déborda de ce cirque sonore, il coula par l'écluse du boulevard" [p. 157]). It is this dynamic, rather than any prearranged plan, that accounts for much of the crowd's activity. Nizan wants to present the demonstration as the spontaneous action of a collective mass, moved by long-contained anger and frustration. When the crowd sees the fascists emerging from their meeting and marching through the streets, it is irresistibly attracted, as if drawn by a vacuum pump: "Elle [la foule] était tournée vers l'ouverture du boulevard, elle supportait avec impatience la ceinture des maisons, des murailles; elle ne voulait plus que se déverser par ce canal desséché du boulevard Wilson.[52] Le barrage des gendarmes n'était pas épais: derrière eux, ils sentaient le vide qui les aspirait, sur lequel ils ne pouvaient pas s'appuyer" (p. 164).[j]

[g] Crowds never like to gather in the middle of an empty space, with only a loose, indecisive margin of people. They like to be so potent that they are barely held together by resistant walls which compel them to press closer, closing all gaps (p. 160).

[h] They [the crowd] began to sing when they saw the Socialist and Communist flags comning up together. They marvelled happily at being there together, that day (p. 161)

[i] dusty guinea pigs (p. 168)

[j] It [the song] spurted sporadically, like a prairie fire which is kindled at scattered points (p. 161) Once it had filled the square, it began to flow out of that sonorous

In order to avoid the danger of abstraction, Nizan presents the workers' feelings through the concrete experience of a single individual, whose actions repeat the dynamic of the crowd. This individual is Albert Cravois, whose wife has just died from the effects of an amateur abortion, crushed by the weight of her oppressive existence. Albert too yearns to break free of this restraint, and he finally instigates the workers' attack against the *gardes*, who are protecting the fascist march.

From the left-wing crowd Nizan's focus switches to the fascist side of the barricade, a movement made by the reader in the company of Lange, who has attended the left-wing rally but has consciously resisted being swept along with its current. The fascist meeting itself has earlier been described from a collective point of view, that of the young leaguers, with whom Nizan, perhaps remembering his own experience in the Faisceau, seems to show some sympathy. The fascists have felt ill at ease in the dark grotto of the movie theater (which, of course, contrasts with the sun and air of the Left's outdoor rally). The movie theater's bizarre décor resembles that of an underwater cave, and when they emerge into the air the fascists themselves resemble seaweed: "Une salle étalée au grand air ternit et se racornit comme une algue arrachée à ses roches marines" (p. 161).[k]

The dynamic of the fascists, however, in contrast to that of the workers, is one of disintegration. Through his descriptive terms, Nizan sets the Communist ethic of solidarity against bourgeois individualism. The townspeople who have attended the right-wing meeting quickly disperse, and the marching leaguers are soon forced to run in all directions under the pressure of the advancing workers. Coming upon the fleeing fascists, Lange recognizes their difference from the crowd he has just left: "Il était soudain dans un groupe dont la loi n'était pas la cohésion mais l'éparpillement" (p. 196).[153]

---

enclosure along the sluices of the boulevard (p. 161). . . . The crowd had turned away from the theatre steps and was now facing the entrance to the boulevard. It was impatient of the girdle of walls and houses and longed to flow out through the channel of the Boulevard Wilson. The gendarmes formed only a thin line and the empty space behind them offered them poor support (p. 164).

[k] A crowd from an indoor meeting fades and shrivels in the open air, like seaweed torn from its rock (p. 165).

[l] Now he suddenly found himself part of a group whose motive tendency was dispersion (p. 203).

In his narration of the fascists' actions, Nizan discontinues the use of a collective point of view; the entire event is told from the perspective of the isolated individual Lange, a change in narrative technique that coincides with Nizan's political vision. Awaiting the arrival of the crowd of workers, Lange feels as if suspended in a void they threaten to overwhelm. By firing the revolver he has found in the street, Lange is finally able to escape from the empty world of solitude and death where he has always lived and to participate in a collective action. But this collective action is portrayed as different from that of the workers. Lange finds himself participating not in a living force but in "a machine" (p. 201); he fires not out of brotherhood but out of hatred for the workers; and he acts not to protest against death but to administer it, thus revealing his fundamental solidarity with the bourgeois merchants and industrialists, from whom, as an intellectual, he had always considered himself apart.

Nizan now switches the narrative focus to the brutal cleaning up operation of the police and *gardes*, who are consistently portrayed as inhuman brutes: "Ils avaient moins l'apparence d'une troupe humaine qu'une machine. . . . C'étaient des animaux bien nourris et il paraissait impossible de leur crier: frères" (p. 207).[m] They are shown beating to death helpless fallen rioters, impassively watching them die under their blows, until finally the square that had earlier been filled by the mass of the workers is again empty, "cette place qui était vraiment en ordre après tout et nettoyée" (p. 212).[n] The workers, however, have their moment of vengeance when they retreat to the less hostile atmosphere of their own district and receive the active support of the inhabitants, who drive off the police by throwing things from their windows. The workers thus are able to end their day as a united force: "Les ouvriers marchaient en rangs. Ce n'était pas une dispersion, mais une colonne. Ils nàvaient plus leurs drapeaux, mais ils chantaient" (p. 216).[o]

After the mass action of the demonstration, Nizan turns his attention back to the small group of Communists in order to analyze the meaning of the event. He is here adopting the device of alternating

[m] They resembled a machine rather than a body of men. . . . They were well-nourished animals, and it seemed useless to call out to them, "You are our brothers!" (p. 205).

[n] this square which was at last cleared and orderly (p. 220)

[o] The workers marched in regular order and with measured step. This was a parade, not a retreat. They hadn't their flags with them, it is true, but they were singing (p. 224).

action and analysis that Malraux would use to great effect in por-traying the Spanish Civil War. This narrative strategy is fully in ac-cord with Nizan's political outlook, for, in seeking to gain an overall perspective on the confusing series of episodes that each member of the group has seen only from the limited viewpoint of a single indi-vidual, the Communists are undertaking a historical analysis in the Marxist tradition: "Ainsi continuaient-ils à composer un tableau du jour de combat pour qu'il se disposât entièrement devant eux avec toute son étendue, son poids et ses leçons" (p. 222). "Ils commen-çaient à composer l'histoire de ce jour" (p. 219).[p] The group is, in fact, performing the task that Nizan himself has undertaken for the reader of *Le Cheval de Troie*, the task that justifies his own commit-ment to writing about contemporary events.

The most evident lesson that they draw is simply that their hopes have finally taken the form of action and that they have shown themselves capable of affirming their human dignity in a common act: "Le sens politique de la journée c'était peut-être simplement que des milliers d'hommes avaient été capables de colère, après tout" (p. 220).[q] This analysis on the part of Nizan is not, after all, very different from that of the fascists Brasillach and Drieu. All three writers are sensitive, above all, to the force of the crowd's passion, one they see as a thrust toward the future. However, the mass move-ment that Nizan describes, despite its spontaneity, is not leaderless and without direction, as the crowds of the Concorde had been. In Nizan's fictional universe, the Communist group is there to provide both leadership and direction, a fact underlined by the change in narrative focus in the aftermath of the riot.

Nizan also attempts to place the events of the day in a larger spa-tial and temporal context of revolutionary action. The experience of the old militant Maillard provides a point of contact with the history of the French working-class movement, previously discussed by the group on its Sunday outing. The aspirations toward the future of the younger characters, Bloyé and Marie-Louise, place it in the context of a future revolutionary struggle in France, itself related to the great

[p] Now they began again to build up piece by piece that picture of the struggle, until it should be complete, in all its variety, richness, and significance (p. 230). They began to patch together the history of the day (p. 227).

[q] And, after all, the chief political significance of this day—was it not simply that thousands of men who had hitherto submitted and been silent had now moved unit-edly and in anger? (p. 228)

revolutionary battles of recent history, "comme au temps de la Commune de Paris, de la Commune de Vienne, de la Commune d'Oviedo, de la Commune de Canton, comme au temps de la guerre civile dans l'Oural, au temps des incendies" (pp. 238–39).[r]

The group's mood of celebration is broken by the arrival of a colleague who announces the death of Paul, who has been one of the anonymous bodies beaten to death by the police. With this new consciousness of police brutality, the group is suddenly reminded of their participation in the world's political oppression, of which they recite the litany. The news of Paul's death also forces them to meditate on the meaning of this death in the larger context of human mortality itself. Death, in this larger sense, preoccupies the character Bloyé in the novel as much as it does Lange, and it was a major source of anxiety for Nizan himself, as witnessed both by his fiction and by the testimony of his friends.[54] In *Le Cheval de Troie* Nizan is able to contrast the death of Paul, which takes on meaning from his effort to affirm his dignity, with the meaninglessness of passive deaths like Catherine's. Bloyé sums up their view in the judgment "Accepter la mort quand elle offre la dernière chance d'être un homme" (p. 242).[s] The words of Nizan's fictional persona provide a fitting commentary on his own death at Dunkerque in the early days of the German invasion. Unlike Drieu la Rochelle, Nizan was ultimately to die the death he had chosen in his fiction.

A Political Education

The political polarization that occurred around the time of the February riots was a process that came to define the nature of the 1930s in France. Near the end of the decade, in particular, writers began to look back on this process and to analyze the personal and political evolution that had led some to fascism and others to Communism. Nizan's last novel, *La Conspiration* (1938),[55] a semi-autobiographical study of a group of students at the turn of the decade, records the first steps in the movement of a young intellectual toward the Communist party. *La Conspiration* is considered by many critics to be Nizan's best novel. It indicates, observes W. D. Redfern, just how much was lost to literature through his tragic death in the

[r] as in the days of the Commune of Paris, the Commune of Vienna, of Oviedo or Canton, and as in the days of civil war in the Urals (p. 246).
[s] We must accept death when it offers us the last chance of being men (p. 249).

1940 defeat.[56] Based in large part on memories of his own experiences as a student at the Ecole Normale Supérieure and as a marginal member of the group of young Marxists who gathered around the review *Philosophies*, *La Conspiration* gives an impression of life that is often lacking to the more schematic *Le Cheval de Troie*.

The descriptions of the quartier latin of the late 1920s, which still showed vestiges of rural life, and the evocation of the feeling of a precise and ephemeral historical moment find their rival only in Brasillach's memoirs, *Notre Avant-guerre*. Nizan, however, is far from sharing Brasillach's obvious nostalgia for his youth. In the first lines of *Aden-Arabie*, he had expressed his attitude in no uncertain terms: "I was twenty. I won't let anyone say it's the best time of life." [57] Sartre has characterized his friend's perspective by calling him "the man who is unable to forgive his youth." [58] Yet, without wallowing in nostalgia, the author of *La Conspiration* displays a sense of what Sartre was later to call "historicity," a sense of the irreversibility of time within a context of rapid change.

The precise historical period evoked is that of the years 1928–30, a period of calm before the storm that is intimately related to the directionless freedom experienced by Nizan's five students before their entry into the adult world. Between the "lyricism" of the electoral victory of the Left in 1924 (which had prompted the transfer of Jaurès's ashes to the Pantheon, a ceremony that forms a central scene in the novel) and the economic crisis of the 1930s, there stretched years of prosperity and tranquillity for the French. Older people are happily reminded of the stability of the period preceding the Great War, but the young men are appalled by the apparent breakdown in the process of history, which seems to condemn them to repeat the dull, bourgeois lives of their parents. They are thus delighted when history, in the form of the Wall Street crash, provides them with the decisive event, the complete rupture with the status quo, that they seek vainly in their own lives. Nizan's students, like his own statements of that period, are typical expressions of the "spirit of 1930."

These young men, like Sartre's Orestes, desperately seek the liberating act that will free them from their existence of "larves en nourrice en attendant d'être de brillants insectes de cinquante ans" (p. 26).[f] As Sartre notes in his perceptive review, their state is grounded

[f]larvae out to nurse while waiting to become brilliant insects of fifty

not only in history but also in their class situation.[59] The problems with which they struggle—smothering families, the need for commitment—are particular to their status as young, middle-class students momentarily relieved of the necessity of facing the real responsibilities of life.

Like Barrès's *Les Déracinés*, with which it was inevitably compared, Nizan's novel is centered on a group of five students, only three of whom (Rosenthal, Laforgue, and Pluvinage) take a major part in the action. A fourth, named Bloyé, forms a nominal link with Nizan's two other novels, but he is a minor presence in *La Conspiration*. A central role is instead assigned to Rosenthal, absorbed in his rebellion against his upper-class Jewish family, and a strong minor part is given to the pathetic, lower-middle-class Pluvinage. Although he is not at the center of any of the plot lines, the character who, in the end, will learn from these developments is Laforgue.

Nizan's students are clustered together around a small philosophical review defiantly called *La Guerre civile*, which displays certain affinities with the actual Marxist *Philosophies* group, with which Nizan himself had been marginally associated. Former members of this group were quick to recognize these affinities and did not always find them flattering.[60] The three individual attempts to act that form the substance of each of the novel's three parts end in failure. The students' conspiracy to steal military secrets almost comes to a tragic end when their drafted friend Simon is caught reading secret documents. He manages, however, to convince the authorities he was collecting material for a novel; nothing these middle-class students can do can force others to take them seriously. Rosenthal's love affair with his sister-in-law Catherine, which he had undertaken as a statement of his independence from his family, ends with a reassertion of familial authority that leads the young man to a pitiful suicide. In the third part, Pluvinage confesses to Laforgue the steps that had led him to betrayal, which Nizan calls another form of suicide, in his effort to prove his superiority to his rich and self-assured friends.

While each of the individual stories ends in failure, a fact that has caused some critics to see *La Conspiration* as a fundamentally pessimistic novel,[61] it nevertheless ends on a positive note with the "resurrection" of Laforgue from a near-fatal illness. Nizan makes it clear that this confrontation with death has served as a rite de passage, a formal transition from youth to manhood: "Tout était consumé, son enfance, son adolescence, il existait, il avait commencé à exister pour la première fois à la seconde même où il s'était réveillé dans la nuit de la clinique sous la lumière bleue" (p. 307). For Nizan, in opposition to Brasillach, this coming to manhood is a wholly positive step. His students, like the young Nizan himself, are frustrated by their inability to perform any but inconsequential acts. But after his confrontation with death, Laforgue discovers a new intensity and seriousness in life: "Le grand jeu des tentatives avortées avait pris fin, puisqu'on peut réellement mourir" (p. 307)."

Clearly, Laforgue's new readiness for meaningful action must eventually be given a precise direction, and, from the hints not too subtly scattered throughout the novel, it is evident that the path Nizan is laying out for him leads toward the Communist party, the course Nizan himself had followed and a course to which he was still firmly committed when he wrote *La Conspiration*.[62] However, Laforgue's story stops short of this political commitment. From Nizan's letters to his wife during the *drôle de guerre*, we know that he had planned to make the continuation of Laforgue's story the subject of his subsequent novel, *La Soirée à Somosierra*. In this work his young protagonist was apparently to realize the possibility of real commitment in both love and politics.[63] Unfortunately, this manuscript, which a comrade-in-arms buried in a field after Nizan's death in combat at Dunkerque, has never been recovered. Yet it does not seem untrue to Nizan's intention in *La Conspiration* to say that at least one of his characters is moving toward political commitment and to view the novel, in the present context, as an incomplete movement in this direction. This is the way in which it was seen by Emmanuel Berl, who asserted: "*La Conspiration* is a pre-communist book. Its heroes are not sure about communism, but they are sure that life is not worth very much outside it."[64]

Authorial hints that Communism would represent the only positive direction for the students' obviously misguided energies are inserted throughout the novel. Laforgue observes at one point that the students would do more good putting up posters with a Communist cell group than publishing their ineffective review. Nizan even hints at the existence of a Communist future for which the experiences

---

"It was all finished, his childhood, his adolescence. He existed; he had begun to exist for the first time at the very moment when he had awakened in the blue-lit hospital night. . . . The great game of failed attempts had come to an end, since it is really possible to die.

described are only preparatory stages. From this perspective, the real value to be derived from their publication, for example, is the contact it affords them with the printing workers. And the Communist demonstration they watch with pleasure in 1924 is useful in providing them with "reserves" to carry them through their troubled youth: "Les fausses manoeuvres où se disperse la vie difficile des adolescents empêchèrent longtemps Laforgue et ses amis de tirer de ces violents souvenirs du 24 et du 25 novembre toutes les suites pratiques qu'ils devaient comporter" (p. 57).ᵛ

Nizan's need to present at least one positive example of Communist commitment seems to account for the presence in the novel of two representatives of a slightly older generation, the poet Régnier and the Communist militant Carré. The character Régnier is presented through a visit the student group makes to his house and through his diary, which occupies an entire section of the novel. This material, which seems out of place in what is essentially the story of the student group, seems to be Nizan's attempt to project the students' attitude of purely intellectual revolt onto an older man. Régnier, who is nearing 40, is dissatisfied with his life and work and cannot seem to find a direction for his efforts. In contrast, his old wartime friend Carré, whose portrait is probably based on Nizan's admired colleague Vaillant-Couturier,⁶⁵ spends a visit trying to convince Régnier of the need for a positive commitment and for the reconciliation of thought and action, individual and society, which is possible only within the context of the party. Naturally, after two weeks of this, the message begins to come across: "Régnier commençait à se faire une idée d'un monde dur et enviable où il ne lui semblait toujours pas possible d'entrer" (p. 213).ʷ Carré's appearance in the text, however, is very brief. It serves merely to indicate the existence of an alternative to the negative world described in the rest of the novel.⁶⁶

The direction of future commitment is more subtly pointed out by Nizan's orchestration of the motifs of life and death that dominate the novel. The bourgeois world of the students' parents—the world of business and parliamentary government—is constantly identified

---

ᵛThe meaningless activities into which the adolescent's difficult life disperses itself prevented Laforgue and his friends for a long time from drawing from these violent memories of November 24 and 25 all the practical consequences they were to entail.

ʷRégnier began to picture a hard and enviable world that it did not yet seem possible to enter.

with death. In an analysis reminiscent of Guilloux's *Le Sang noir*, Nizan's Rosenthal at one point theorizes, "Si les gens sont à l'agonie, c'est qu'ils étouffent sous des coquilles de mensonge" (p. 63).[x] Rosenthal's family lives in a quarter whose streets evoke cemeteries: "le long de rues nettes comme des allées de cimetières à concessions perpétuelles" (p. 16).[y] When Rosenthal looks at his much hated father he sees first of all his own decomposition and death: "Il ne savait plus si c'était son père qu'il détestait, ou lui-même, sous sa forme future; son père était comme un présage de ce que le temps lui révélerait après une terrible métamorphose" (p. 135).[z]

While the prosperous Rosenthals, who work in the Stock Exchange, embody the qualities of a coldly materialistic and sterile upper bourgeoisie, the petit bourgeois background of Pluvinage is immersed in an atmosphere of rotting corpses. His father had been a civil servant in charge of municipal burials, and as a child Pluvinage had often visited his office, grotesquely decorated with pictures of cemeteries, and had amused himself cutting out pictures of tombs and coffins from the illustrated mortuary catalogues. In his confession to Laforgue, Pluvinage describes himself as having lived in a world that had revolved around death and decay: "J'ai grandi dans le monde qui se voue à l'élimination des déchets urbains et à l'enregistrement des catastrophes privées" (p. 269). And he adds, relating this description to the real targets of Nizan's condemnation, "c'est le sort des ouvriers des choses impures, des espions, des policiers, des fonctionnaires de la mort et de l'agonie" (p. 269).[a] While Rosenthal's family represents the elegant and antiseptic death of the world of the Stock Exchange, the milieu of Pluvinage is its unsavory underside, like that of an overturned rock. He sees himself returning to it, "dans quelque destinée humide et noire d'insecte de la pourriture et du bois" (p. 279).[b]

Nizan unequivocally connects this world with the clandestine activity of the police, represented by the ominous Pluvinage family

[x] If people are dying, it's because they are suffocating under shells of lies.
[y] along streets neat as the paths in perpetual-care cemeteries
[z] he didn't know if it was his father he detested, or himself in his future shape; his father was like a forewarning of what time would reveal to him after a terrible metamorphosis.
[a] I grew up in a world dedicated to the elimination of urban refuse and the recording of private catastrophes. . . . It is the fate of workers in impure things, spies, policemen, clerks of death and dying.
[b] in some humid, black destiny of an insect of rot and wood

friend, Inspector Massart. Here Nizan rejoins a conception of police activity common to many of the anti-Establishment novels of the 1930s, including Drieu's *Gilles*, Aragon's *Les Beaux Quartiers*, and Chamson's *La Galère*. During a conversation with Pluvinage, Massart sets forth an entire theory of police influence on events. At the root of this theory, based on the power of political blackmail that always belongs to those who possess complete dossiers on public figures, is the idea that "de petites chances et de petits hommes fabriquent les grands événements" (p. 259).[c] Massart obligingly does Nizan's job for him by pointing out that, of course, this type of action is only a form of consolation for the powerless.

Thus the police are one of the "conspiracies" that reflect the title of the novel. In fact, the world of the novel is filled with such conspiracies, the least effective of which is the absurd Dostoevskian spy plot initiated by Rosenthal and his friends. Their efforts predictably amount to nothing: not willing to risk himself, Rosenthal acts only through intermediaries and then, absorbed in a love affair with his sister-in-law, forgets to pass the information on, probably through lack of any interested party.

But the conspiracies in the world that surrounds the young men are much more lethal, although masked by a surface appearance of softness and passivity. Here Nizan's imagery joins Sartre's in his application of the category of the viscous to the entire world of bourgeois activity: "Ils [les étudiants] ne savaient pas comme c'est lourd et mou le monde, comme il ressemble peu à un mur qu'on flanque par terre pour en monter un autre beaucoup plus beau, mais plutôt à un amas sans queue ni tête de gélatine, à une espèce de grande méduse avec des organes bien cachés" (p. 30).[d] This world passively resists the young men's open attacks on it by absorbing their blows without a trace. Their review appears but fails to incite to revolution.

Like Catherine, life refuses to respond to their advances by making any substantial change. Rosenthal's affair with his elegant sister-in-law is, as even he realizes, more an attack on the sanctity of his family than a great passion. He rejoices when they are discovered, a discovery in which he seems to have played an active role, and arrives

[c]little strokes of luck and little men make great events
[d]They [the students] did not know how heavy and soft the world is, what little resemblance it bears to a wall you tear down to build another, much more beautiful one; rather it is like a shapeless mass of gelatin, a sort of great jellyfish with its organs well hidden

at the subsequent family council expecting the long-awaited confrontation. But the family acts in more subtle ways, absorbing the blow. Their real action takes place beneath the surface in hidden but nevertheless effective reactions: "Comme c'est puissant et inflexible, une famille! C'est tranquille comme un corps, comme un organe qui bouge à peine, qui respire rêveusement jusqu'au moment des périls, mais c'est plein de secrets, de ripostes latentes, d'une fureur et d'une rapidité biologiques, comme une anémone de mer au fond d'un pli de granit, tranquille, nonchalante, inconsciente comme une fleur, qui laisse flotter ses tentacules gorge de pigeon, en attendant de les refermer sur un crabe, une crevette, une coquille qui coule" (p. 229).ᶠ Still hoping to provoke the desired resistance, to turn the "drame bourgeois" into a "tragédie," Rosenthal swallows a lethal dose of sleeping pills. But even this final act cannot penetrate the family solidarity, and they deflect its attack by placing the blame on the evil influence of their son's friends.

The really powerful conspiracies in Nizan's novel are the moving forces of society, but because they are true conspiracies their tentacles are well hidden beneath an innocuous surface like that of the sea anemone, just as the subterranean action of the police hides itself beneath the appealing myth of societal protection. In this world of inverted values, real conspirators are quick to place the blame for the destruction they have wrought on the conspiracies they claim to find among their attackers. Thus Rosenthal's family blames his friends for his death, and the government, in order to stifle criticism, creates the scare story of a Communist conspiracy to overthrow the state. As Aragon had already shown in *Les Cloches de Bâle*, this technique is useful as a way of taking people's minds off the real sources of responsibility for social problems. In reality, Rosenthal's friends had provided him with the only sense of companionship he had known, and similarly, the Communist party cell gives Pluvinage his only real feeling of belonging to a human community. Perhaps because they embody authentic values, which could show up the hypocrisy of the dominant ethos, the Communist party and the stu-

---

ᶠHow powerful and inflexible a family is! It is calm like a body, like an organ that hardly moves, that breathes dreamily until the moment of danger, but it is full of secrets, latent riposts with a biological furor and rapidity, like a sea anemone at the bottom of a granite crevice, calm, nonchalant, unconscious as a flower, that lets its pigeon-breast-colored tentacles float until it closes them on a crab, a shrimp, a shellfish.

dent group must be denounced by the lethal hidden conspiracies that dominate the bourgeois world.

The identification of the world of the societal establishment with the forces of death is summed up in the significant scene of the transfer of Jaurès's ashes to the Pantheon in 1924. This scene, which forms the subject of a flashback, is an episode of crucial significance in the students' lives and in the structure of the novel. The students have had the honor of being invited, along with the dignitaries of the regime, to keep watch over the ashes on the night preceding their transfer to the Pantheon. The ceremony significantly takes place in the Palais Bourbon, the parliamentary heart of the French government, which has been hung with violet gauze and transformed for the occasion into a mortuary chamber, a use that Nizan seems to find appropriate. The guests have adopted funereal expressions suitable to the occasion, a mode in which they too are singularly at ease. The students are introduced, in particular, to Léon Blum (when Nizan was writing *La Conspiration*, the Popular Front had breathed its last), who gives little evidence of humanity and resembles a bird or mechanical toy. Connected with this aura of death is again the impression of a conspiracy: "Laforgue et ses amis avaient lìmpression d'être les complices silencieux de politiques habiles qui avaient adroitement escamoté cette bière héroique et cette poussière d'homme assassiné, qui devaient être les pièces importantes d'un jeu dont les autres pions étaient sans doute des monuments, des hommes, des conversations, des votes, des promesses, des médailles et des affaires d'argent" (pp. 49–50).[f] The Jaurès funeral watch is thus only another aspect, and an extremely revelatory one, of the entire deadly parliamentary game.

In contrast with the world of death and conspiracy in the Palais Bourbon is another world that waits on the streets outside. The students are conscious of it at first through the muffled shouts that, like the noise of the sea, succeed in penetrating the walls: "Il devait exister dans la nuit une espèce de vaste mer qui se brisait avec de la rage et de la tendresse contre les falaises aveugles de la Chambre"

---

[f]Laforgue and his friends had the impression of being the silent accomplices of clever political maneuvers that had adroitly made off with this heroic casket and the dust of the assassinated man, which were to be the important playing pieces in a game whose other pawns were probably monuments, men, conversations, votes, promises, medals and money matters.

(p. 50).[g] This source of life emanating from the crowds in the street will reappear in greater force in the following day's procession to the Pantheon. As the young men await the procession on a gray November day, the boulevard is empty, "comme un lit de rivière à sec" (p. 53). It is hardly animated by the cortège of dignitaries that follows, "un mince ruban d'hommes en deuil" who march past the immobile crowds, "le long de ce torrent pétrifié" (p. 53).[h]

Suddenly a second cortège arrives, the people from the working-class districts who have come to venerate Jaurès and to protest his appropriation by the establishment.[67] They fill the boulevard and render it its life, renewing the water metaphors they had suggested in the night: "Le fleuve finalement s'était mis à couler"[68] (p. 54). As the parliamentary dignitaries are slyly linked with the corrupt underground world of police intrigues ("On se disait que les députés socialistes venaient de voter les fonds secrets de l'Intérieur") the strength of the people is identified with blood and with the renewal of life: "On ne pouvait penser qu'à des puissances drues, à la sève, à un fleuve, au cours du sang." Renewing a metaphor whose power had been lost through repetition, Nizan observes, "Le boulevard méritait soudain son nom d'artère" (p. 55). The contrast between the life exhibited by the popular throngs and the mortuary world of the status quo, between their open enthusiasm and the secret machinations of the politicians, is not lost on the students, nor, Nizan seems to hope, on the reader: "Il n'y a pas de question. On sait avec qui il faut être" (p. 56).[i]

Portraits of the Fascist as a Young Man

The newer phenomenon in the France of the 1930s was not Communism but fascism, and it is this political attitude that claims the center of literary attention. While the philosophical basis of Communism and even the party's current doctrines at any given moment were relatively easy to identify, the concepts of fascism were not.

---

[g]There must have existed in the night a sort of vast sea that broke with rage and tenderness against the blind cliffs of the chamber.

[h]like a dry streambed . . . a thin stream of men in mourning; along the petrified torrent

[i]The river finally began to flow. . . . People said the Socialist deputies had just voted for the secret funds for the Interior Ministry. . . . You could only think of dense forces, of sap, of a river, of the flow of blood. . . . The boulevard suddenly deserved its designation as an artery. . . . There is no doubt. You know with whom you must be.

Tarmo Kunnas's study of the three well-known French novelists of the Right—Brasillach, Céline, and Drieu la Rochelle—compares their attitudes on fifteen beliefs generally associated with fascism.[69] Rather surprisingly, he finds that the ideas of the three "fascists" do not coincide on a single item, or, if they do, it is only under the common influence of larger fascist groups that became more vocal near the end of the decade. Kunnas concludes that the eccentric Céline manifests attitudes that are not easily reconciled with the mainstream of fascist thought. Brasillach's ideas, Kunnas finds, were only marginal to the main movement, while Drieu emerges as the most typical. In the case of Céline, this finding is in line with his unwillingness to participate in any political group. Drieu, however, despite his abortive efforts to become involved in a fascist political party, was an isolated figure on the French political scene. Of the three, only Brasillach was able to find groups, albeit small, who shared his political outlook—the intellectuals clustered around Annie Jamet's *rive gauche* lecture series (whose only association with the Left was its location with respect to the Seine) and, later, the "team" at the newspaper *Je suis partout*.

While it is extremely difficult to analyze these writers' "fascism" in a larger sense, both Drieu and Brasillach at the end of the decade wrote analyses of the movement toward fascism of a fictional character, who, in each case, bears a strong resemblance to the author. It is in these works, Drieu's *Gilles* and Brasillach's *Les Sept Couleurs*, that their fictional representation of fascism must be sought. As if to comment upon their presentations, two vehemently antifascist writers also created fictional portraits of fascist characters designed to reveal the inadequacy and inauthenticity of their response to life. Nizan's professor Lange in *Le Cheval de Troie* and Sartre's Lucien Fleurier in "L'Enfance d'un chef" are both, in a sense, caricatures of the attitudes presented by Drieu and Brasillach.

Drieu's *Gilles* is, as Frédéric Grover has called it, "the self-portrait of a fascist."[70] Like *La Conspiration*, *Gilles* is a bildungsroman in which the protagonist receives an essentially negative education. But, unlike Nizan's students, Gilles finally does discover the true object of his political allegiance in fascism, a discovery Drieu sets in 1934.

The novel begins with Gilles's return to Paris, "the land of women," from the virile world of the front. Although he makes a brilliant marriage to the wealthy sister of a wartime friend, Gilles is quickly dissatisfied with the emptiness of this materialistic and hypocritical world. Casting about for a new source of value, he becomes involved with a group called Révolte (a barely-disguised portrait of the surrealists) headed by a pretentious prophet named Cael (Breton) and his weak lieutenant Galant (Aragon). Drieu himself had at one time been very close to the surrealists, although he never participated fully in their group, and his public break with them in 1925 seemed to be a result of their alliance with the Communists.[71] He had been particularly close to Aragon, who was himself one of the group's most politically committed, and the bitterness of their personal rupture is still visible in Drieu's vicious treatment of the character Galant in the 1939 novel. Although Drieu trivializes the reasons for Galant's adherence to Communism (having him join the party in response to a failed love affair, whereas Aragon himself was drawn to this commitment through his relationship with Elsa Triolet), he continues to express admiration for the Communists' revolutionary spirit even at the end of the novel.

Indeed, the charges leveled at the Révolte group in *Gilles* are not political but moral: they come to incarnate for Gilles the very spiritual decadence they claim to be trying to destroy. Gilles's old tutor Carentan, an intellectual who has isolated himself from the society's corrupting influence, is disgusted by the group's antics at a testimonial dinner for the poet Boniface St. Boniface. And Gilles himself is appalled by their callous manipulation of their young follower Paul Morel, the rebellious son of the president of the Republic. Morel is lured into a homosexual club by Galant (Drieu makes repeated hints that Galant is a concealed homosexual), a situation that is subsequently used by the powerful police intelligence network to blackmail both the Révolte group and Paul's father. The incident ultimately results in Paul's suicide, which Gilles sees as evidence that the Révolte group inevitably leads to death and destruction rather than the regeneration he seeks for himself and France.

Gilles now turns his attention to politics, this time of his own choosing. He undertakes the publication of his own political newspaper, *L'Apocalypse*,[72] and attempts to bring about a renewal of the French political structure through his politician friend Clérences. Although his ideas fail to come to fruition, through his instinctive response to the riots of February 6, Gilles does discover his true political identity in fascism. Since this discovery coincides with the failure of his personal and political commitments in France, he is free to devote himself totally to the cause. In the Epilogue we see him two years later in Spain as the agent of a mysterious organization of international fascism.

While Drieu is clear about the political label he wishes to attach to his protagonist—and to himself—he is notoriously imprecise about its meaning.[73] His imprecision may be related to his disillusionment with the specific fascist movement that he had chosen as the vehicle of his own political action. This period of Drieu's life is noticeably absent from *Gilles*, which ends in 1934 (except for the short and almost entirely fictitious Spanish Civil War segment). Drieu himself, like Gilles, had proclaimed himself a fascist on the morrow of the February riots, but not until two years later did he feel he had found the right political expression of his ideas in the movement led by the former Communist Jacques Doriot. Mayor of Saint-Denis and fervently admired by its working-class population, Doriot had split with the Communist party in 1934 when they had rejected his idea of joining with the Socialists to form a widely based union of the Left. The idea was so timely that the Communists themselves finally came around to the same position a few months later, but by that time Doriot had been excluded and was seeking another framework for the popular movement he envisioned. Making a rapid swing from Left to Right on the political spectrum (a change of allegiance not unusual for the time, as evidenced by the cases of Pierre Laval and Marcel Déat in France and Robert Moseley in England), Doriot founded his own French fascist party, the Parti populaire français (PPF) in July 1936. Drieu was one of its most enthusiastic supporters and devoted much of his time to writing weekly editorials for its paper, *L'Emancipation nationale*. After the revelation of Doriot's dependence on funds from Mussolini, however, Drieu's fervor began to cool, and by January 1938 he had finally broken with the party— and with any attempt to play an active part in French politics. It was during this period of disillusionment that he was composing *Gilles*.[74]

In Drieu's novel, the action Gilles proposes to his friend Clérences on the morrow of the February riots is almost without political content. Organize "combat sections," he tells him, to do "anything at all" (p. 599). While the emphasis on action for the sake of action and the use of a paramilitary form have clear fascist overtones, Gilles obviously has no defined political program, and the program of the mysterious organization of which he later becomes an agent is similarly undefined.

While Drieu purports to hold as an ideal the union of intellect and action, his protagonists seem to find themselves most satisfied when they are engaged in action unencumbered by ideological considerations. The appeal of fascism for Gilles is not very different from the appeal of Communism for the protagonist of Drieu's 1930 novel, *Une Femme à sa fenêtre*. For Boutros, clearly indifferent to Marxist-Leninist doctrine, Communism is merely an opportunity for living to the full: "J'aime la vie, je vais où est la vie. . . . Cela durera ce que cela durera. Mais je me serai donné à ce qu'il y avait de plus fort dans le monde, de mon temps" (p. 144).[j][75]

Gilles seems to find release from his solitude and anguish only in the violent action of combat, which forms his true spiritual home. He had discovered this realm of virile purity in the war and glimpsed it again briefly during the Concorde riots. When he rediscovers it in the Spanish Civil War he finally realizes that this is his only possibility of regeneration, a regeneration that Drieu sees as possible only through destruction and death. This paradoxical idea is appropriately expressed in religious language:[76] "Dieu qui crée, qui souffre dans sa création, qui meurt et qui renaît. . . . Rien ne se fait que dans le sang. Il faut sans cesse mourir pour sans cesse renaître" (p. 687).[k] Drieu appears to be saying that his protagonist must be washed of his own participation in decadence by the purifying force of blood, just as the old, corrupt society must be destroyed in order for a new one to be built. Many commentators, however, have seen in this ending an expression of the desire for self-destruction that Drieu had long known, a desire that was finally to realize itself in his 1945 suicide.[77]

Fascism, at least as it functions in *Gilles*, is not really a political doctrine. It is a concept called forth by the novel itself, with its oppositions of life and death, purity and corruption, unity and fragmentation, war and peace, male and female, creation and destruction. Its realization is possible only in a situation far removed from any reality, in the paradoxical vision of the creator God who dies to be reborn. In the end, Drieu's politics are a poetic ideal that, at this point in his life, as he may have recognized, find their most appropriate expression in a world re-created by the imagination.

---

[j]I love life, I go where life is. . . . It will last as long as it lasts. But I will have given myself to the strongest thing in the world, in my time.

[k]God who creates, who suffers in his creation, who dies and is reborn. Nothing is created without blood. You must constantly die to be constantly reborn.

In the character of the philosophy professor Lange in *Le Cheval de Troie* Nizan offers his version of the development of a fascist. Nizan's portrait of Lange, not unexpectedly painted in the blackest of terms, is in many ways a caricature based on real men of his era. It is also a condemnation of the type of person portrayed in *Gilles.*

Lange is not meant to represent the masses of Frenchmen who were at this time attracted to various fascist movements. Nizan clearly differentiates him from, for example, the young members of fascist leagues who come to attend the local right-wing meeting (this type of person would receive the attention of Brasillach and Sartre). Neither is Lange one of the powerful capitalists who form the most frequent object of Aragon's irony. He is primarily an intellectual; in fact, as a graduate of the prestigious Ecole Normale Supérieure (like Sartre and Nizan himself), he is a member of the French intellectual elite. One of the best of France's young intellectuals, he is intended to represent the furthest development of a philosophy that grows from what Nizan portrays as a dying and death-oriented culture: "Il était à l'extrême limite où la culture rejoint l'épuisement dans une terre frontière de la solitude et de la mort" (p. 58).[1]

For Lange, each human being is irremediably isolated from others, and human life is ultimately rendered meaningless by death. He sees existence itself as a scandal that makes human activity absurd, especially political activity that, like Bloyé's, aims to change the world. Although Lange himself is an alienated individual, Nizan shows that his philosophy of solitude and death embodies the central characteristics of bourgeois society, incarnated in the commercial *passage* where Lange takes his nocturnal walks, a world in which he is strangely at home.

The philosophy attributed to Lange, with its emphasis on the scandal of existence, seems to have much in common with the Sartrean vision expressed in *La Nausée,* a book on which Sartre was working by the time of the composition of *Le Cheval de Troie.*[78] In fact, the book Lange thinks of writing himself sounds suspiciously like *La Nausée*: "Il imaginait un livre qui décrivait uniquement les rapports d'un homme avec une ville où les hommes ne seraient que des éléments du décor, qui parlerait d'un homme seul, vraiment seul,

[1] He dwelt at that far boundary where culture merges with enervation in a frontier territory of solitude and death (p. 58).

semblable à un îlot désert" (p. 121).[m] Sartre and de Beauvoir themselves were forced to recognize that, to some extent, Nizan had used his friend as a model for this most unpleasant character.[79]

Is Nizan, then, accusing Sartre of being a latent fascist, a man likely to pick up a gun and aim it at a young worker? That Nizan and Sartre were able to discuss the book together at all seems to point to the conclusion that such was not the case. Certainly, some of the German thinkers whose work Sartre had studied during his year in Berlin found it possible to cooperate with the Nazi regime. But Nizan does not really seem to be making specific charges of fascism against the Sartrean side of Lange. Rather, he is presenting a sort of warning. The primary danger Bloyé sees in Lange's philosophy of the absurd is its incitement not to violent action but to apathy. For Bloyé, Lange's attitude condemns a priori any effort to change the present situation. An attitude that sees existence itself as a scandal, Bloyé tells Lange, "te permet d'accepter le scandale de ce monde. C'est ainsi qu'on s'arrange" (pp. 59−60)."[80] Nizan also accuses Lange of being a spectator, unwilling to join the living current of collective action, a charge he illustrates by Lange's desperate struggle to extricate himself from the left-wing crowd. This is an attitude that coincides exactly with Simone de Beauvoir's characterization of the reaction of Sartre and herself at this period; writing about their attendance at the 1935 Bastille Day celebration, she says: "Up to a certain point we shared this enthusiasm, but we had no inclination to march in procession, or sing, and shout with the rest. This more or less represented our attitude at the time: events could arouse strong emotions in us, whether anger, fear, or joy, but we did not participate in them. We remained spectators."[81]

Many of Lange's characteristics, however, particularly the attraction to violence mentioned in his first appearance in the novel, do not reflect attitudes of Sartre. They are more similar to the character portrayed by Drieu in *Gilles*, a character that, as we have seen, is not very different from Drieu himself. Such a reference to Drieu would not be surprising, because at the time Nizan began work on *Le*

---

[m] He always imagined one [a book] which would describe only the relations of a man with a town where other men were only minutiae of the background—a book about a man alone, really alone, as upon a desert island (p. 125).

[n] permits you to condone all the shame of the present order. That's how people adapt themselves to things (p. 59).

Cheval de Troie, Drieu had just publicly announced his conversion to fascism.

Lange most resembles Drieu's *Gilles* in his welcoming of action, any action, that promised to free him from a world he recognized intellectually as dominated by immobility and death. In the still moment before he aims his revolver at a member of the left-wing crowd, Lange goes through an experience very similar to that of Gilles at the place de la Concorde. Like Gilles, Lange feels history has stopped: "Les secondes défilaient l'une derrière l'autre,—égales, décharnées, et elles mesuraient un monde immobile qui ne progressait pas, ne se transformait pas, mais qui se répétait" (p. 198). And his subsequent action expresses a need to break out of this impasse, even at the cost of a cataclysm: "Quand l'attente fut véritablement comme une douleur . . . le coup éclata dans la tête de Lange comme une mine capable de faire sauter le monde, et justement le monde paralytique se remit à marcher" (p. 201).[82] In this action Lange, like Drieu's protagonist, is finally freed from the painful need to think: "Il ne contemplait plus, il connaissait la passion" (p. 201).[o] He also feels "a sexual satisfaction" (p. 202) which is not without analogy to Drieu's characteristic literary metaphor for participation in violence.

Nizan, writing in 1934–35, did not, of course, have before him the model of *Gilles*, which was published four years later. But he was well acquainted with the public figure of Drieu himself, who had already put into his fiction the multiple facets of his personality, his immersion in decadence as well as his fascination with violent action. Furthermore, Drieu had made numerous public statements of his own political views, not only in his essay *Socialisme fasciste*, but in the articles he wrote for various periodicals, particularly the widely read *Nouvelle Revue Française*, where he offered his views on important issues of the times. Especially well known were his reactions to the February riots, which he rushed to articulate in the *Nouvelle Revue Française* of March 1934. He expressed, in particular, his admiration for the violence of the event: "They were men who with a single spontaneous and generous gesture offered their blood and took that

---

[o]The seconds followed each other, uniform and naked, measuring a still world which neither progressed nor altered but extended itself (p. 206). . . . When waiting had actually become an agony, . . . the sound burst in Lange's head like that of a mine capable of shattering the world. And, at that moment, the world began to move. . . . He no longer meditated, he knew passion (p. 209).

of others. One does not go without the other—it is a question of proving love."[83] Drieu had given his attitudes such publicity that in 1935 Nizan felt compelled to write an article condemning his views for the liberal weekly *Vendredi*. Many of the characteristics he attributes to Drieu in that article are those also identified with the character Lange. Nizan cites in particular Drieu's tendency to confuse the political and the erotic and his "dispersion," a characteristic attributed to the fascist group as a whole in the novel. He also cites Drieu's constant donning of masques and pursuit of women; and he writes of Lange: "Il jouait son propre personnage, il se donnait la comédie. Cette comédie trompait parfois des femmes" (p. 59).[*] Most important, he sees Drieu as irremediably alone and accurately predicts his lonely suicide: "He will die alone. As he has always suspected . . . He is already alone under a sky extraordinarily haunted by literary ghosts."[84] Drieu is thus clearly the model for a large portion of the character Lange.

Through this portrait, Nizan attempts to reveal in fiction, as Simone de Beauvoir would later do in philosophical terms (using Drieu as an example),[85] the intimate relationship between philosophical nihilism and political fascism. Nizan's character brings out in concrete human terms the mechanics of this process. What de Beauvoir describes as an effort on the part of the nihilist to refuse his own existence by destroying the others who confirm his presence in the world, Nizan shows through the attitude of Lange toward the young worker at whom he fires. The worker—young, happy, and enjoying a warm relationship with the girl at his side—is all that Lange is not, a fact that his presence forces Lange to recognize. In fact, he recalls to Lange scenes from his childhood in which other workers had inflicted similar humiliations. By attempting to annihilate this worker, Lange is also attempting to obliterate a disturbing image of himself, a process that could obviously lead to endless violence. Lange's effort is, of course, condemned to ineffectiveness: just as his bullet is unable to reach its target, Lange can never succeed in eradicating all those who would confirm his humiliating self-image.

By placing Lange's action in the larger context of his novel, Nizan is able to impress the reader with its brutality and danger. Although this intellectual is incapable of acting effectively himself, the shot he fires touches off the violence of the police, who are themselves ex-

---

[*] He played his own character, he put on a play for himself. This act sometimes fooled women.

tremely efficient. The scenes of police brutality and the subsequent revelation that Paul has been one of their victims are the concrete results of Lange's incitement to action. Nizan offers them as a judgment on the activity of intellectuals who, like Gilles, gleefully urge others to violence.

The most complete sympathetic account of the evolution of a fascist in the 1930s is provided not by any fiction but by Brasillach's memoirs, *Notre Avant-guerre*. A good deal of this autobiographical material, however, is woven into the text of *Les Sept Couleurs*. This novel is thus not only a history of European fascism but also a story of growth, maturation and personal commitment. The commitment in the novel is that of Catherine, who renounces her adolescent fantasies, embodied in the character Patrice, to accept fully the reality of her adult life with her husband François. Catherine's choice of reality over fantasy, of maturity over youth, of serious action over play is echoed in the lives of Patrice and François as well.

It is also, the reader feels, a personal statement on the part of the author himself. The identification of Brasillach with his characters is especially evident in the section entitled "Réflexions," which presents the musings of a man (apparently Patrice) who has reached the age of 30, an age the speaker identifies with adulthood. In 1939, as he wrote this novel, Brasillach himself had turned 30, and, like the voice in his novel, he knew that his generation was about to have its first personal experience of war. The fictional narrator sees the age of 30 as marking the end of youth, an age for which he manifests an evident predilection: "Il n'est dans la vie qu'une jeunesse, et l'on passe le reste de ses jours à la regretter" (p. 145). Compensating (only somewhat, one feels) for this loss is a newly acquired lucidity that enables the individual to evaluate his situation in the world and to choose an appropriate path of action: "Pour nous, notre seul mérite dans tous les domaines, est de nous être acceptés et d'avoir *choisi*" (p. 158).[q]

The path chosen by this anonymous narrator, as by Brasillach himself, is identified with fascism. In an era crushed between two wars, the men of his generation, he says, have seen the rise of a new human phenomenon, "fascist man." The narrator gives several characteristics of this new creed—nationalism, antiliberalism, an ideal of

[q] In life there is only one youth, and you spend the rest of your days regretting that it's gone. . . . For us, our only merit in all domains is having accepted ourselves and having *chosen*.

racial purity, a belief in justice born of force—but most important is joy, a youthful joy best expressed in singing. It is this joy that Brasillach sees as the striking new reality of his era: "Je ne sais pas si, comme l'a dit Mussolini, *'le vingtième siècle sera le siècle du fascisme,'* mais je sais que rien n'empêchera la joie du fasciste d'avoir été, et d'avoir tendu les esprits par le sentiment et par la raison" (p. 158)."
The section ends with the narrator preparing to take up the responsibilities of adulthood handed down to him by his parents. At the same time, for some unexplained reason, he evokes the fate of those who do not live long beyond their youth: "Vous avez connu de ces apparitions un peu exaltantes, un peu mystérieuses. Elles brûlent leur propre vie, parfois celle d'autrui, mais elles donnent la flamme, l'avenir" (p. 160).' In this passage Brasillach, who was to be condemned to die at the age of 36 for his activities as a Nazi collaborator, seems strangely to prefigure his own fate, or at least the image of his life that would be piously preserved by his family and friends. This passage seems almost to express a secret yearning not to outlive his youthful energy; if this is so, he was, like Nizan, to die the death he had wished.

The characters of *Les Sept Couleurs* do not die, however, but accept the passage into adulthood. This passage is represented by the choice Catherine is forced to make between Patrice, the lover of her bohemian youth, and François, the husband of her womanhood. She articulates the reasons for her decision in the interior monologue, somewhat reminiscent of that of Molly Bloom in *Ulysses*, with which Brasillach concludes the novel. Patrice is described in terms of insubstantiality, of indecision, of dream and play, while François is connected with motifs of weight, hardness, and concrete reality. As she herself realizes, the two men are essentially different aspects, different moments, of the same being: "Je ne m'étais pas aperçue à quel point le premier n'était que la préparation, l'esquisse de l'autre" (p. 245).' And she sees that Patrice, who has married his German sweetheart, is now entering on the course of commitment to a fascist ideal as François had already done by risking his life in the

---

'I don't know if, as Mussolini has said, "the twentieth century will be the century of fascism," but I do know that nothing will prevent fascist joy from having existed, from having stretched minds by feeling and reason.
'You have known these slightly exalting, slightly mysterious apparitions. They burn up their own life, sometimes that of others, but they show the flame, the future.
'I had not perceived to what extent the first was only the preparation, the outline of the other.

Spanish Civil War. The choice made by Catherine in *Les Sept Couleurs* is symbolic of a choice that, Brasillach is saying, would soon have to be made by all members of his generation under the increasing pressure of war.

While the novel seems overtly to affirm the values of maturity and serious commitment, the spirit that most forcefully impresses itself on the reader is one of youthful joy. It is this spirit that constitutes the essence of foreign fascism for Patrice, as we have seen, and that even seems to survive in war-torn Spain. As William R. Tucker has observed in his "political biography," Brasillach never articulates a detailed political program; he seems rather to be expressing "a response to the movement of time, a style, and a feeling of exhilaration." [86] It is this spirit that provides the unique emotional climate of *Les Sept Couleurs*, one of joy tinged with sadness at the prospect of the hard realities of aging and war. What attracts Brasillach's characters is not a political program but an atmosphere. As Brasillach himself was to say, "fascism for us was not, however, a political doctrine. . . . Fascism is a spirit." [87] In his testament written for a young man of the future, "Lettre à un soldat de la classe 60," [88] Brasillach sums up the content of his fascism in the very images he has presented in *Les Sept Couleurs*: "this exaltation of millions of men, the youth camps, the glory of the past, the parades, the cathedrals of light, the heroes struck down in combat, the friendship among the youth of all awakened nations, José Antonio, fascism immense and red." He describes it to the imagined young man as a youthful passion, "our *mal du siècle*," and concludes, "it was a form of poetry— the poetry of the twentieth century." *Les Sept Couleurs* must thus be seen as an attempt to give expression to the lyrical images that had formed Brasillach's youth. It is not a political statement but a poetic one, and it is not an acceptance of adulthood but an attempt to preserve the fugitive moments of his youth.

Like Brasillach's characters in *Les Sept Couleurs*, Sartre's Lucien Fleurier, the protagonist of "L'Enfance d'un chef," [89] moves from youthful adventure to what he sees as a mature commitment to fascism. Although the stages of his development, especially his flirtation with surrealism, show parallels with the itinerary of Drieu's Gilles, Lucien is a different sort of person. He is attracted to the right-wing group that he joins at the end of the story only partly because of the violence of its activities. Much more important is its camaraderie and spirit of youthful exuberance; like Brasillach's Pa-

trice, Lucien had always been "galvanized" by the feeling of participation in a collective emotion.[90] Such a group spirit can exist only by
a process of exclusion, and Sartre exposes its destructive consequences for those against whom the group asserts its identity, in this
case, Jews and foreigners. The antisemitism that is the most visible
trait of Lucien's new fascist personality was also a factor in the fascist
movements evoked in *Les Sept Couleurs*, although it is hardly alluded
to in the descriptions of the stirring beauty of Hitler's Nuremberg
congress or, in *Notre Avant-guerre*, of Brasillach's own happy times on
the notoriously antisemitic *Je suis partout*.

Dissatisfied with his adolescent existence, Lucien yearns, through
his participation in a larger group, to take on the qualities of weight,
hardness, and seriousness that he associates with adulthood. Although they are happier with their youth, Brasillach's characters,
too, seek to acquire these characteristics. In "L'Enfance d'un chef,"
however, Sartre's ironic analysis of Lucien's evolution exposes the
vanity of his pretentions. While Brasillach seeks to integrate his characters into a world shaped by the eternal values of their national past,
Sartre consciously undermines the entire notion of self-justification
through values external to the individual.

"L'Enfance d'un chef" was published as the last story in Sartre's
1939 collection *Le Mur*. Even more than the title story itself, it is the
reflection of events of the era. It could as well have been entitled
"The Childhood of a Fascist," for the word *chef* is intended in its
most politically loaded sense and is to be identified with the concepts of *duce* and *fuhrer* so dear to the fascists of other countries. In
this story, which imitates and parodies the traditional *roman d'ap-
prentissage*,[91] Sartre traces the development of Lucien from his earliest childhood memories to his definitive acceptance of a ready-made
social and political role. Lucien is a slightly younger contemporary
of Sartre himself: a mere child at the time of the outbreak of World
War I, he reaches university age in the 1920s. In his search for identity he is attracted to the major intellectual modes of the era—
Freudianism, surrealism, even homosexuality—before finding a
spiritual home in the Camelots du roi, the youth organization connected with the right-wing Action française.

Geneviève Idt, in her insightful study of *Le Mur*, dates the concluding section of "L'Enfance d'un chef" in the years 1924–25,[92] the
years when Sartre himself, like his character Lucien, was preparing
the entrance exams to a *grande école* (unlike the business-oriented

Lucien, Sartre was preparing for the Ecole Normale Supérieure). While the various arguments for dating the story rest finally on internal evidence concerning the chronology of Lucien's academic progress,[93] there is a strong case to be made that Sartre had in mind the years of the mid-1920s, when the fascist leagues had a brief period of great activity; Idt points out, for example, that *L'Action Française du Dimanche*, the Sunday newspaper Lucien is described as selling outside the Neuilly church, ceased publication in 1925. This was also a time when public attention was focused on the political figures mentioned by name in the story, the Radical leader Herriot, the Socialist Léon Blum. These mid-decade years represented a brief period of crisis in economic and international affairs, a situation that contrasted with the relative tranquillity of the rest of the decade.

The years 1924–25 thus had much in common with the agitated period of 1935–36, and Idt argues convincingly that "L'Enfance d'un chef" intends to superimpose the two periods. The fascist leagues, for example, showed a recrudescence of activity in the years 1932–36, and right-wing xenophobia and antisemitism were at a particularly high pitch during the period when the Jewish Léon Blum had assumed the leadership of the Popular Front. Even the surrealists, most active during the 1920s, received new notoriety for their 1938 Surrealist Exposition, and Idt points out that the description of the apartment of Sartre's character Bergère reads like a catalogue of that exposition. Thus Sartre, like the novelists who had written about World War I earlier in the decade, has set his story in the recent past only in order to speak more freely about the events of his own time.

The world Lucien perceives is portrayed in terms strikingly similar to those used by other politically sensitive writers of the era. As a child, Lucien has the impression that he and all the people around him are playing roles: "C'était amusant parce que tout le monde jouait. Papa et maman jouaient à être papa et maman; . . . Et Lucien jouait aussi, mais il finit par ne plus très bien savoir à quoi" (p. 160).[u] Later, in a period of Cartesian doubt, he conceives of the world as a "play without actors" (p. 181). This vision of the world as an absurd *comédie* is similar to that which dominates Drieu la Rochelle's fiction, as in *La Comédie de Charleroi* (see chapter 2). Drieu's protagonists are able to attain a moment of authentic being only in the brief moment

---

[u]It was amusing because everybody was playing, Papa and mama were playing papa and mama;. . . And Lucien was playing too, but finally he didn't know at what (p. 87).

of physical combat. Lucien also attains what he believes to be his true self after an act of violence, but Sartre alerts the reader to the fact that Lucien has simply assumed another role, one that goes along with his new "props," a cane (used by the right-wing gangs to beat up their opponents) and, at the end of the story, a mustache. He has always wanted people to take him seriously, and he achieves this in his new identity as young fascist. In Sartre's view, of course, he has fallen into "the spirit of seriousness," the false belief that this role or any of the various other roles with which he experiments could provide a sufficient justification of his existence. Ironically, his initial childhood impression of existence overflowing the limits of social roles is, in Sartre's view, a much more accurate reading of reality.

When, as a child, Lucien ventures out of the protected garden that limits the world controlled by his parents' values, he confronts dog droppings buzzing with flies and nettles that begin to ooze a white substance when he hits them with his cane. There is also a strong odor of decomposition, and the effect of the entire scene sends him running terrified back into the house. While Lucien is frightened by the viscosity of reality, he is also attracted by his power to assert his own being against its soft, unresisting existence, thus lessening the risk of being engulfed. The scene where he hits the nettles with his cane prefigures later ones where he will use the cane of a *camelot* to attack soft, defenseless human beings. This type of behavior is also prefigured by his childish torture of a grasshopper, from whose belly emerges a viscous yellow cream.

Lucien often sees his own being as a vague and amorphous substance, not so different from the objects around him. As an adolescent, he feels overwhelmed by the uncontrolled existence of his body: "Il avait toujours l'impression que ce corps était en train d'exister de tous les côtés à la fois, sans lui demander son avis" (p. 174). He begins to perceive others as large, soft masses of flesh. Spying through a keyhole, he watches his mother washing herself: "Elle *était* cette grosse masse rose, ce corps volumineux qui s'affalait sur la faience du bidet" (p. 175). And when he tries to envision the thoughts in his head, he becomes lost in images of fog and mist: "Il n'était plus qu'une chaleur blanche et humide qui sentait le linge" (p. 179).[v]

---

[v]No matter what he did, he felt this body existing on all sides at once, without consulting him (p. 96). . . . She *was* this gross pink mass, this voluminous body

A search for identity has always instinctively dominated Lucien's confrontations with the world outside himself, and as an adolescent, he finally succeeds in articulating the question, Who am I? Shortly after becoming aware of his problem, Lucien is attracted to a school-mate named Berliac, who seems to have absorbed all of the avant-garde clichés of the era. Berliac laments being part of "a sacrificed generation," uses the technique of automatic writing to produce poems full of stereotyped surrealist images, and, most important of all, introduces Lucien to the ideas of Freud.[94] Freudianism proposes an answer to Lucien's identity crisis by telling him that his true self lies forever lost in the unconscious, the concept that Sartre himself found most objectionable in Freudian thought. But Lucien finds himself increasingly put off by Berliac's supposed passion for his mother, who is disfigured by warts, and by his own disgusting habit of rubbing saliva over his numerous adolescent pimples—all evidence of an invasion of the viscous.

The next self-definition is proposed by a surrealist poet appropri-ately named Bergère, an older man who has befriended Berliac. Bergère begins by terming Lucien's problem one of *désarroi*, a word that itself seems to have clarity and even a metallic precision: "Dé-sarroi: le mot avait commencé tendre et blanc comme un clair de lune, mais le 'oi' final avait l'éclat cuivré d'un cor" (p. 194).[w] The poet surrounds himself with a décor that is a veritable museum of typical surrealist objects, but the one he selects to display to Lucien, a perfect imitation of an excrement, suggests disquieting parallels with the earlier visions of nettles and dog droppings.

The real menace in Bergère's influence is not his surrealism, how-ever, but his homosexuality, which is the hidden motive for his kind-ness to his young followers (in this, he is a cruel caricature of Coc-teau and Gide). Lucien's single homosexual experience with Bergère is dominated by unpleasant viscous imagery. Bergère's physical pres-ence disgusts him ("Une bouche tiède et molle se colla contre la si-enne, on aurait dit un bifteck cru" [p. 208][x]), and the experience

---

hanging over the porcelain *bidet* (p. 96). . . . He was no more than a damp white warmth which smelled of linen (p. 99).

[w] Disorder [désarroi]: the word had begun as tender and white as moonlight, but the final syllable [oi] had the brassy blare of a horn (translation mine).

[x] A warm, soft mouth, like a piece of raw beefsteak, was thrust against his own (p. 117).

reduces Lucien himself to a soft mass ("Il était lourd et mou comme une éponge mouillée" [p. 206] [y]), finally disintegrating him into diarrhea.

Finding that the experiences of Freudianism and surrealism only mire him deeper in the viscous substance of existence without giving him the clearly defined identity he seeks, Lucien is only too happy to return to the bosom of his family. It is there that he finds some signs of the qualities he seeks. Against the decadence and putrefaction of the world, they offer "the moral health of the Fleuriers," to which Lucien attributes his preservation from the corruption of his avant-garde friends. And Lucien begins to see his resemblance to his father, who is described in terms of solidity and hardness: "M. Fleurier était carré d'épaules, il avait les gestes lourds et lents d'un paysan, avec quelque chose de racé et les yeux gris, métalliques et froids d'un chef" (p. 214). [z]

But after his surrealist fiasco, Lucien's world seems to return to its former softness. When he spends the summer in his family's provincial home in Férolles, he feels uncomfortable in the countryside: "La campagne était extraordinairement tranquille et molle, inhumaine" (p. 217). [a] He is surrounded by dying crickets, which he later clearly recognizes as images of himself.

But into Lucien's amorphous world comes a new classmate. Lemordant is both physically solid and ideologically firm, impermeable to corrupting forces. Lucien suddenly recognizes the perfect being: "Voilà comme je devrais être: un roc" (p. 224). [b] And through watching Lemordant, Lucien learns how he himself can develop these qualities by practicing antisemitism. Lemordant also completes Lucien's education by lending him a copy of Barrès's novel *Les Déracinés*, a book that provides him with an instant new self-definition and, in fact, transforms his vision of the world. As Idt points out, the post-Barresian Lucien has an entirely different vision of the soft countryside at Férolles: "Il devait retourner à Férolles, y vivre: il le [l'inconscient décrit par Barrès] trouverait à ses pieds, inoffensif et fertile,

---

[y]He was heavy and soft as a wet sponge (p. 115).

[z]M. Fleurier had square shoulders and the slow heavy gestures of a peasant with something racial in them and his grey boss's eyes, metallic and cold (p. 120).

[a]The countryside was extraordinarily calm and soft about Lucien, inhuman (p. 123).

[b]That's how I should be; a rock (p. 127).

étendu à travers la campagne férollienne, mêlé aux bois, aux sources, à l'herbe, comme un humus nourrissant où Lucien puiserait enfin la force de devenir un chef" (p. 232).[c][95]

Lemordant introduces Lucien to his merry "band" of right-wing leaguers (Sartre takes a swipe at the foundations of their ideology by pointing out that they hold their *assises* at the brasserie *Polder*, which refers to a marshland). Swept up in the merry fun of the *camelots*, Lucien still has moments of depression, when he sees himself as a "little gelatinous transparency." But, more often, he recognizes that he is being taken seriously by others: his parents treat him with consideration because of his new political commitment, and he acquires a reputation among his new friends as an unbeatable Jew-hater, an identity confirmed by his participation in the gang's gratuitous beating of a dark-skinned immigrant they come across who happens to be reading *L'Humanité*. In this attack Lucien realizes his childhood ambition of affirming himself against another being, as his blow reduces the man to an inert mass. He reaffirms his new identity as an antisemite by publicly refusing to shake the hand of a Jewish guest at a friend's party.

When his friend's admiring reaction confirms the image he has adopted, Lucien feels he has finally attained the pure, hard existence of a metal (a steel wedge or steel blade), the ordered, meaningful existence of a mechanical object (a chronometer, a monstrous clock). In the café around him, he sees the other people as "cette foule molle," a crowd that metamorphoses into soft underwater creatures: "Tous ces métèques flottaient dans une eau sombre et lourde dont les remous ébranlaient leurs chairs molles, . . . ils n'étaient guère plus que des méduses" (pp. 246–47). He rejoices in his abandonment of his fruitless introspection, itself identified with the viscous: "En fouillant ainsi dans cette intimité muqueuse, que pouvait-on découvrir, sinon la tristesse de la chair, l'ignoble mensonge de l'égalité, le désordre?" (p. 249).[d] He sees now that the only way to attain an identity is to seek it in the eyes of others, in the

---

[c] Or, simply return to Férolles and live there: he would find it harmless and fertile at his feet, stretched across the countryside, mixed in the woods, the springs, and the grass like nourishing humus from which Lucien could at last draw the strength to become a leader (p. 132).

[d] All the dagos were floating in dark, heavy water whose eddies jolted their flabby flesh . . . they were hardly more than jellyfish (p. 141). . . . What could one discover searching in this mucous intimacy if not the sorrow of flesh, the ignoble lie of equality and disorder? (p. 142)

admiration of his fascist friends and the awed respect of the workers in his father's factory. Like the consciously constructed objects he sees as reflecting his new being—a clock and even a cathedral—he comes to see his existence not as inexplicable and amorphous but as defined and justified by his fulfillment of a necessary role in the social structure.

Sartre tells the story from Lucien's point of view, but he furnishes the reader—most readers, at least [96]—with the possibility of another judgment. The ending he provides is clearly an ironic commentary on the entire text. As Lucien emerges from the café where he has imagined himself a "chef," he expects to see reflected back at him from a shop window an "impermeable" face like Lemordant's. But what he sees is "une jolie petite figure butée, qui n'était pas encore assez terrible" (p. 252),[e] a situation he decides to remedy by growing a mustache.

But even more damning is Sartre's depiction of the *camelots*. In his own descriptions, Lucien emphasizes their gaiety and lack of seriousness: "Mais c'était leur bonne humeur qui séduisait surtout Lucien: rien de pédant ni d'austère; peu de conversations politiques. On riait, et on chantait, voilà tout . . ." (p. 233).[f] The terms he uses are strikingly similar to those used by Brasillach in describing foreign fascism in *Les Sept Couleurs* or his own participation in a fascist gang, as he terms it, in *Notre Avant-guerre*. Sartre, however, takes pains to contrast this air of insouciant merriment with detailed accounts of the band's cruel and brutal actions, particularly their vicious beating of the foreigner. Like Nizan, Sartre is very much aware of the very real human suffering that results from this boyish camaraderie.

In Sartre's view, Lucien's adoption of an identity that provides a justification for his existence is clearly a flight from the truth, an attitude Sartre refers to elsewhere as bad faith. The particular form of *mauvaise foi* on which Sartre focuses his attention in "L'Enfance d'un chef" is a political ideology, which it had not been in the case of the *salauds* of *La Nausée*. Idt notes, for example, the specifically fascist overtones of the idea of the right to exist that Lucien finally asserts, and she says that "L'Enfance d'un chef" emphasizes the sociological significance of a concept that had been explored in its metaphysical

[e] a pretty, headstrong little face that was not yet terrible (p. 144).
[f] But it was their good humor which especially captured Lucien: nothing pedantic or austere; little talk of politics. They laughed and sang, that was all (p. 132).

dimensions in *La Nausée*.[97] The viscous, putrefying world that Lucien perceives is not, in the Sartrean ethic, a temporary state of affairs occasioned by historical change, as Drieu la Rochelle would appear to believe. Rather, for Sartre, this situation is characteristic of the human condition as a whole. Although in "L'Enfance d'un chef" he does not indicate a successful way of coping with it, he vigorously condemns all attempts to deny its reality.

Thus the characteristics of decadence and corruption, which had seemed to be the symptoms of social collapse, had become for a younger writer like Sartre a metaphysical reality, transcending time and place. Such a reality was not susceptible to elimination by a mere political doctrine. Perhaps it was because of his ability to confront this situation, without illusions about its miraculous transformation by a mythical "revolution," that Sartre was able so rapidly to regain his equilibrium after the collapse of France in 1940. Unlike many of the other writers in this study, he had never really placed his faith in political action or historical change. The use he makes of a historically situated reality in both "L'Enfance d'un chef" and, as I will illustrate, in "Le Mur" reveals that, although he is intensely aware of the events of his time and, in fact, has staked out a clear political position, his true concern is not with these events themselves but with their potential for revealing the nature of a timeless human condition. Without historical illusions and accustomed to dealing with a world with no inherent values, Sartre had already prepared himself, at least in his fiction, to live with the total collapse of traditional values that many Frenchmen were forced to confront for the first time in 1940.

CHAPTER 5

The Fiction of the Spanish Civil War

L'Espagne ainsi achevait de transformer en combat spirituel et matériel à la fois, en croisade véritable, la longue opposition qui couvait dans le monde moderne. Ses brigades internationales, des deux côtés, scellaient dans le sang les alliances. Par toute la planète, des hommes ressentaient comme leur propre guerre, comme leurs propres victoires et leurs propres défaites, le siège de Tolède, le siège d'Oviedo, la bataille de Teruel, Guadalajara, Madrid et Valence.[a]

ROBERT BRASILLACH
Les Sept Couleurs

The outbreak of the Spanish Civil War in July 1936 was an event that left few of the French indifferent. Even Simone de Beauvoir, who had not before felt touched by the decade's political controversies, wrote of the war in Spain, "It was an overwhelming epic event with which we felt ourselves directly concerned. . . . We knew the Spanish war brought into play our own future."[1] The election of the Spanish Popular Front, preceding that of its French counterpart by only three months, soon produced a reaction on the part of a hostile Right that plunged the country into civil war. The analogies between the events in Spain and the French political situation, already polarized into hostile blocs of Left and Right, were too striking to be ignored. Frenchmen could not help but project onto their perception of the Spanish conflict their hopes and fears for their own country, and emotions already inflamed by the political unrest in France ran high.

The entire French Left, from the premier, Léon Blum, down to the humblest militant, rallied to the support of the Spanish Republican

---

[a] Spain thus succeeded in transforming the long opposition that was fermenting in the modern world into a combat both spiritual and material, a veritable crusade. Its international brigades on both sides sealed alliances in blood. All over the planet, men saw as their own war, their own victories and defeats, the siege of Toledo, the siege of Oviedo, the battle of Teruel, Guadalajara, Madrid and Valencia.

government, menaced by an uprising of right-wing generals. Blum, through his air minister, Pierre Cot, immediately responded to the Spanish president's appeal for arms, while various left-wing groups as well as individuals like Malraux began to organize their own support efforts. Blum's Popular Front government, however, had not counted on the vehemently hostile reaction of the French Right, nor on the attitude of the Conservative government of Great Britain, which informed Blum that any French intervention in Spain would pose a threat to Anglo-French treaty arrangements. Under great pressure at home and abroad, Blum at first offered to resign and then reluctantly agreed to pursue a policy of nonintervention. A treaty to that effect was signed in August by France and the other world powers—which, however, did not all feel bound to respect its provisions. The Popular Front government's failure to engage itself directly in the struggle against fascism disappointed many of its supporters and exacerbated tensions already existing between the government parties (Socialists and Radicals) and the Communists, who felt free to pursue their own policies with respect to Spain.

At first, the Spanish Republican[2] government seemed to be holding its own against the superior military strength of the rebellious generals headed by Francisco Franco. While much of southern Spain, with the exception of Malaga, immediately fell to the military uprising, the important cities of Madrid, Barcelona, and Valencia, as well as the entire Basque region, resisted the military coup. Especially in the early days of the Civil War, when emotions were running understandably high, there were numerous episodes of vengeance, murder, and sometimes even mass execution perpetrated by both Left and Right, accounts of which served to add fuel to the fire of French public opinion. A noted victim of one of these summary executions by the Falangists was the young Spanish poet and dramatist Federico Garcia Lorca.

During the fall of 1936, a Falangist column drove north to Madrid but was stopped at the gates of the city by the determined population, supported by the regrouped Republican army and the newly arrived International Brigades. The brigades, which organized the volunteer combatants from all over the world, included particularly large contingents from France. As the price of holding the Falangists to a standoff, the population of Madrid was subjected to severe shelling and even aerial bombardment. The bombing of helpless civilians by modern aviation, which was liberally supplied by Nazi Germany and Falangist Italy, continued to play a part in Franco's military strategy throughout the war and was an important factor in turning world opinion against his forces. Particularly shocking was the complete destruction, in April 1937, of the ancient Basque capital of Guernica, an episode that gave rise to Picasso's famous painting, exhibited at the 1937 Paris Exposition, and that inspired protest poems from such writers as Paul Eluard.

At the time of the Republicans' successful defense of Madrid, reinforced by victories on the Jarama River and at Guadalajara, the strength of the Spanish Left had reached its peak. From then on, it began to disintegrate, both politically and militarily. Bloody power struggles between the newly dominant Communists and their ideological rivals, Trotskyites and anarchists,[3] combined with military setbacks to slow the Republican momentum. After the loss of the Basque country and the definitive Falangist victory in the long battle of Teruel (February 1938), it was only a question of time until the eventual fall of Barcelona and Madrid. The collapse of Republican Spain in 1939 was followed by the pathetic flight of thousands of refugees over the mountains to France; the great Spanish poet Antonio Machado was only one of those who died from the effects of this mass exodus.

The war in Spain, which played out the political oppositions of Europe, immediately caught the imagination of writers and intellectuals. Spain became in their eyes, as Jean Duvignaud has described it, "a symbolic place where contemporary problems are transporting themselves."[4] The Spanish Civil War quickly became the most literary of wars. Spanish writers and artists, including those, like Miguel de Unamuno, who had wished to remain neutral, were immediately forced to take sides. The list of foreign writers who visited, wrote about, and even fought in the war (in most cases, on the Republican side) is almost unending. Ernest Hemingway worked in Spain as a reporter, wrote several works of fiction, including his great novel, *For Whom the Bell Tolls*, and participated in the making of a film, *The Spanish Earth*, which remains one of the most important documents on the war. Another American novelist, John Dos Passos, visited Spain briefly before writing his *Adventures of a Young Man*. George Orwell fought near Barcelona with the anti-Stalinist Partido Obrero de Unificación Marxista and witnessed its bloody suppression in May 1937, an experience that informed his *Homage to Catalonia*. Arthur Koestler, as a newspaper reporter and agent for the

Comintern, saw various fronts of the war and survived imprisonment at the hands of the Falangists before writing *Spanish Testament*. The young English poet John Cornford, as well as Virginia Woolf's nephew Julian Bell, died in combat, while Stephen Spender filled British periodicals with long propaganda poems. The Chilean Pablo Neruda, serving in Madrid as a diplomat, produced a memorable collection of poems, which soon appeared in French with a preface by Aragon.

The involvement of French intellectuals and writers was particularly widespread. The war in Spain served to shake some out of their former apathy or indecision—this was notably the case with Sartre, de Beauvoir, Eluard, and Tristan Tzara—and called for new effort from those who had already entered the political arena. Almost all the writers who have already figured in this study actively participated in some aspect of the Spanish support effort. Nizan, who had already written journalistic studies of Spanish Popular Front politics before the outbreak of hostilities (which he had accurately predicted) returned to Spain again as a reporter.[5] His last, unfinished novel, *La Soirée à Somosierra*, as its title indicates, was to have taken the Spanish war as one of its settings. Aragon also participated actively in the various manifestations of French Communist support for the Spanish Republicans, traveling around Spain in a truck outfitted by the Association des Ecrivains et des Artistes Révolutionnaires[6] and taking a major role in organizing the Congrès International des Ecrivains Antifascistes held in Madrid and Valencia in 1937. The French delegation included Malraux, Tzara, André Chamson, and Julien Benda. Guilloux, as a *responsable* of the left-wing Secours rouge, led local efforts to aid numerous refugees who had arrived in his native Brittany, an experience he later wrote about in *Le Jeu de patience* (1949) and *Salido* (1976).

Brasillach, representing an opposing political viewpoint, wrote a number of articles and essays during the course of the war, and in 1939, with his brother-in-law Maurice Bardèche, compiled one of the first historical studies of the war as a whole.[7] Imbued with enthusiasm for the Falangist effort, Brasillach had visited the front in 1938 and returned to the country of a victorious Franco in 1939. The notes from these visits that appear in his autobiographical *Notre Avant-guerre* play a role in his novel, *Les Sept Couleurs* (see chapter 4).

Many great Catholic writers of the era, whose fictional work had remained immune to politics, became involved in the polemic. The novelist François Mauriac, shocked by the Falangist massacres at Badajoz, publicly expressed his condemnation of Franco's tactics,[8] without, however, throwing his support to either side in the conflict. He was soon joined in this protest against Falangist atrocities by his fellow novelist Georges Bernanos, whose *Les Grands Cimetières sous la lune* (1938) recounted the horrors of the Falangist regime on the island of Mallorca, where he had previously taken up residence. Many noted Catholic intellectuals, such as Jacques Maritain and Gabriel Marcel, and the Catholic periodicals *Esprit* and *Sept* shared this attitude, despite the support of the French Catholic hierarchy for the Franquist "Crusade." The poet Paul Claudel was a notable exception to this group of liberal Catholic intellectuals; his poem "Aux martyrs espagnols" was a vigorous condemnation of the Spanish Republicans for their attacks on the Church.

The amount of French fiction inspired by the Spanish Civil War would certainly have been greater if the Nazi invasion of France only four years later had not given writers other, more immediate concerns. Nevertheless, a great deal of literature was generated by this event in the 1930s.[9] Some of it was merely polemical, like the sagas of nuns turned prostitute who slit priests' throats with their fingernails. At least three fictional works of real significance were inspired by the war: Sartre's short story "Le Mur"; the Epilogue of Drieu la Rochelle's *Gilles*; and Malraux's *L'Espoir*, quite possibly the greatest Spanish Civil War novel in any language.

L'Espoir

Of all the foreign intellectuals who came to Spain, Malraux may well lay claim to having performed the most valuable service. In his previous novels about revolutions—*Les Conquérants* (1927) and *La Condition humaine* (1933)—the exploits of his characters had far surpassed his own peripheral involvement in Asian politics; in *L'Espoir* the actions he attributes to the aviation leader Magnin seem to be a fundamentally accurate record of his own. Perhaps for the first time, the Malraux legend is firmly grounded in fact. Although neither Magnin's biography nor physiology correspond to Malraux's (he has hidden himself behind glasses and a mustache),[10] his role is that which Malraux himself played as organizer and leader of the volunteer squadron of international aviation, as it is called in the novel, or the Escuadra André Malraux, as it was, in reality, baptized by its own men.[11] After the squadron's demise in the first year of the war and its replacement by more modern Russian planes, Malraux continued his efforts on behalf of the Spanish Republic by making a successful fund-raising tour in the United States and, most important, by writing *L'Espoir*. He had the novel ready for serialization in Aragon's paper *Ce Soir* by the beginning of November 1937 (excerpts also appeared in *Vendredi* and the *Nouvelle Revue Française*). In 1938 he returned to Spain to make a filmed version of his novel, with the support of the Spanish government, but only part of the projected scenario was completed before the company was forced to flee during the fall of Barcelona. The film that finally emerged, variously known as *Sierra de Teruel* and *Espoir*, is centered on episodes in the last section of the novel and ends with the scene of the descent from the mountain.

Because of his participation in the Republican air operations, Malraux was well placed to gain an understanding of the war, in both its details and its larger reality. Unlike many writer-combatants who were confined to a limited section of the front, he was able, because of the nature of his flights, to move easily around Spain, and at the end of the day's missions he was free to frequent the Madrid cafés and absorb the experience of other combatants and observers.[12] These included the many excellent foreign correspondents, like the *New York Times*'s Herbert Matthews and *Paris Soir*'s Louis Delaprée, both of whom may stand behind the reporter Shade in *L'Espoir*. Malraux's novelistic descriptions of the war have been verified in almost all significant details by the major non-Spanish historians. In fact, the reader who seeks to compare their accounts with Malraux's is frequently confounded by their use of his work as a source.[13]

The history of the war, from the generals' uprising on July 18, 1936, to the Republican victory at Guadalajara, seems to have determined the structure of the novel Malraux was to write. *L'Espoir* closely follows the movement of the war itself—of course, from the Republican perspective. It begins with the enthusiasm of the spontaneous popular resistance to the Falangist coup, shares in the pessimism of the Republican disarray that accompanies the rapid Falangist advance to Toledo, and gathers new hope from the successful defense of Madrid and the victory at Guadalajara. The major divisions of the work reflect moments in the military situation and are not very different from those adopted by historians. The first and by far the longest of the novel's three major parts, "L'Illusion lyrique," shows the first days of the war in the two major Republican cities of Madrid and Barcelona and the organization of Magnin's international aviation squadron. The second half of this part takes place entirely in and around Toledo, covering several episodes of the long siege of the now legendary Alcazar, the ultimate collapse of the city, and the last moments of its defenders. The concluding chapters of this part fall at the novel's midpoint, and they represent a moment of despair in the novel, as in the Republican struggle.

The second of the three major parts is devoted to what has become known as the Battle of Madrid. After showing the desperate regrouping of land and air forces in preparation for the last-ditch defense of the city, the first section ends on a note of optimism with the repulsion of the Falangist attack. The second division of the Madrid section goes on to show the martyrdom of the city under siege, its people subjected to one of history's first large-scale bombings. The third part, which bears the same title as the novel itself, concerns the Battle of Guadalajara and some of the events preceding it. Guadalajara, however, does not serve as a unifying framework for this part, as Toledo or Madrid had done for the earlier sections. Although the battle is appropriate to Malraux's apparent desire to end the novel on a note of victory, the last section is really a slow-paced meditation on the larger meaning of the war and is thus the only part of the novel whose content is not imposed upon it by the force of history.

In addition to supplying the plot and determining much of the structure of the novel, history contributes many of the characters and, to a great extent, assigns them their roles. Many of the them are based on real-life models.[14] Each character represents a point of view on the war, which is often determinative of his fate in the novel. The progress of the war had, for example, diminished the importance of the Spanish anarchists and strengthened the power of the Communists, from whose ranks emerged many of Spain's leading military figures. Thus Malraux's anarchist characters, Puig and the Negus, featured in the early scenes in Barcelona, are soon killed off, while Manuel, the young Communist sound engineer, goes on to become an important commander in the Battle of Guadalajara. This is consistent with the fate of the characters' real-life counterparts.[15]

Malraux's treatment of the historical events themselves is impressively comprehensive. He does, of course, exercise the novelist's right of selection, but those events he has chosen to emphasize—the siege of the Toledo Alcazar, the defense of Madrid—are the ones historians themselves have come to see as central. Malraux rejects the comparative facility of the solution adopted by Hemingway in *For Whom the Bell Tolls*, that of equating the entire Civil War with the destiny of his protagonist. This was essentially the technique Malraux himself had used in his earlier novels, with its consequence of making the political events appear as mere backdrops to the tragedy of his heroes. In *L'Espoir* the situation is reversed: as critics have noted, the protagonist of *L'Espoir* is the Civil War itself.[16] Therefore, Malraux has set himself the task of making novelistic sense of a war fought on various fronts and for a wide variety of ideological reasons.

The conflicting political ideologies emphasized—Communist, Catholic, anarchist, and left-wing liberal—are those that also concern Malraux's French readers. Others, like the Basque and Catalan separatist movements, are left entirely out of the novel. The Spanish Civil War was thus above all, for Malraux, a playing out of the struggle between Left and Right taking place on its own terms in his own country. In no novel before his last, *Les Noyers de l'Altenburg*, does he write directly about events in France. But in *L'Espoir*, despite its Spanish setting, the reader can see not only the result of Malraux's experience in the Civil War but also the reflection of the years of political militancy in France that had preceded it: his effort to regroup the forces of the French Left in a common struggle against fascism and also his ongoing, often contentious relationship with the Communist party.

Despite his unusual fidelity to the historical reality of the Spanish Civil War, at certain moments Malraux clearly demonstrates his willingness to adjust events to suit his artistic needs. A clear example is his structuring of the section that describes the siege of the Toledo Alcazar. In that section, Malraux allows his liberal Republican officer, Captain Hernandez, to perform a noble but strategically inefficient act: to transmit letters from the entrapped Falangist commander, Colonel Moscardo, to his wife in a Madrid clinic.[17] In the novel Hernandez is roundly criticized by the Communist characters and Garcia, who imply that he would have done well to refuse to carry the letters—and even to use Moscardo's wife as a means of obtaining the release of the Republican hostages. Not only do historians make no mention of this episode, but they give credence to a

Falangist legend that is the exact opposite of Malraux's. This story, which may be read in a number of languages by any visitor to the Alcazar, tells how Moscardo bravely rejected a Republican threat to execute his son Luis if he refused to surrender.[18] Apparently, in reality, the Republicans were not above using the very tactics Malraux seems to recommend.

Malraux's insertion of an anecdote that so directly flies in the face of the contemporary Falangist legend, of which he certainly must have been aware, invites speculation. At this point in his novel, historically the moment when the Republicans came nearest to total collapse in the first year of the war, Malraux needs an example of inefficient nobility. It is in Toledo, in the famous conversation in the Santa Cruz Museum, that Hernandez and the Negus, the two characters who have chosen noble purity over compromise, make their finest statements, displaying attitudes that will lead them straight to catastrophic defeat. The anarchist Negus has just been given an opportunity to prove his selfless courage in a scene where he turns a Falangist flamethrower back against its owners, who have penetrated into the city through an underground tunnel. Now, according to at least one historian, there was no such underground tunnel:[19] the episode, as Malraux tells it, would have been impossible. Thus the noble gestures of both doomed characters appear to represent something of a departure from the truth of history, a transformation effected by Malraux because it reinforced the theme he intended to treat in this Toledo sequence. The solitary death of Hernandez, at the end of the section, occurs almost exactly at the halfway point in the novel, and it marks the low point on the parabola that moves from victory through defeat to renewed victory, from fraternity through isolation to renewed unity. Malraux's concern for novelistic theme and structure have dictated the treatment of characters and events at Toledo, even if he has had to adjust minor historical anecdotes to suit his purposes. In the same way, as Walter Langlois has shown,[20] he combines the episode of a bombing raid guided by a peasant with a subsequent mountain plane crash and inserts them both in the prelude to the battle of Guadalajara, thus providing reiterated examples of the fraternity he wishes to stress at this culminating point in the novel.

The simple matter of rendering the multiple aspects of the Spanish Civil War posed unprecedented problems for a novelist. The best fiction of World War I had adopted the viewpoint of a single character or group of soldiers, which, like Stendhal's famous treatment of the Battle of Waterloo, conveyed a vivid impression of the confusion and horror of war but made no sense whatsoever of military strategy, let alone political issues. An important work that appeared in the same year as *L'Espoir* did try to permit some understanding of the political intricacies of World War I, and it is interesting that Martin du Gard in *L'Eté 1914* adopted the very method of analyzing political problems that Malraux chose in *L'Espoir*: continual dialogues between various characters who represent different points of view. But Martin du Gard did not feel called upon to treat the actual fighting of the war in addition to all this discussion. The unique texture of *L'Espoir* results from its combination of these two methods: scenes of action alternate in an irregular pattern with the dialogues that permit a deeper appreciation of their meaning.

This is the technique Malraux had used in his previous novel of revolution and civil war, *La Condition humaine*. But in *L'Espoir* the task is even more complex. In the earlier novel, Malraux had used a situation (the abortive Communist uprising in Shanghai in 1927) that involved relatively simple political positions, a limited number of characters, and a single city. He could follow the destinies of his two protagonists, Kyo and Katow, from the moment of the first uprising to their deaths at the hands of the Kuomintang: their story is that of the Revolution. In *L'Espoir* the complicated military and political maneuvers, involving large numbers of characters, take place over an eight-month period all over the map of Spain.

Despite the hopping from place to place, from character to character, Malraux's novel does not disintegrate into an incoherent mass of battles. This is due to the author's unremitting effort to subordinate such elements as physical description and character development to his central concerns and to create devices that link the various scenes. Scenes of discussion comment on the action that has gone before and prepare the way for what is to follow: thus the conversation at the Santa Cruz Museum puts into a single context of meaning the noble gestures of Hernandez and the Negus. At the same time, it analyzes the forthcoming deaths of both the liberal officer and the anarchist.

Scenes involving completely different characters and settings are often juxtaposed to emphasize a common theme: the fighting at both Barcelona and Madrid reveals the unified will of the Spanish people; the scene of disarray in the international aviation squadron is placed next to the description of the despairing militiamen who have fled from Toledo; a scene of communion between peasants and airmen in Malaga precedes the long passage treating the same theme in the descent from the mountain.

Malraux provides continuity between scenes often hundreds of pages apart by the reiteration of common elements. Thus Garcia's definition of the Republican cause as a refusal of hierarchy recalls to Manuel, from a much earlier scene, Barca's similar definition of fraternity. Scali thinks back on the words of old Alvear as he discusses Unamuno with Garcia, and Garcia remembers the conflicts of Hernandez. Images are repeated in different contexts to underline the common experiences linking different characters in different situations.[21] Ximénès, for example, evokes the pigeons that had appeared again and again in the early fighting in Barcelona and turns them into a symbol that reveals their meaning. The major themes—fraternity, political unity, the dialectical relationship of thought and action—are taken up repeatedly in different contexts, functioning like musical motifs to unify the work.

The various scenes in *L'Espoir* are generally narrated from the point of view of a single person, although in some cases, as in some World War I novels, the perspective is that of a small combat group. The reader observes not precisely through the eyes of the characters but often from a point slightly behind them, so that they, too, are part of the picture.[22] Malraux uses the point of view device with great freedom, perhaps because it had not yet become a commonplace of French critical doctrine.[23] He does not hesitate to change the point of view within a scene and often uses an omniscient narrator to provide necessary information in the most efficient way, particularly in the case of military actions. So much material has been included in the novel that Malraux could not hope to dramatize every event, and such shortcuts seem both necessary and effective.

The "reflectors," the characters whose point of view Malraux uses, are relatively numerous. Jean Carduner has counted 58 characters in *L'Espoir* (as opposed to 16 in *La Condition humaine*),[24] and many of them are used as reflectors. These include soldiers of the International Brigades, large numbers of international aviators, several anarchists, and various Spanish writers and artists. The constant change in reflectors, especially in the early scenes, makes no small contribution to the reader's confusion. Malraux must constantly deal with the problem of finding appropriate reflectors for the scenes he wishes to dramatize, and his principal ones are chosen for their ability to participate in important aspects of the war, as well as for their embodiment of important political perspectives. The American correspondent Shade is particularly useful as a reflector because he is free to travel to the points of greatest interest. In addition, as the citizen of a neutral country, himself rather indifferent to politics, he can come to feel the impossibility of remaining uncommitted in the face of this struggle, an attitude he expresses clearly in the articles he sends out from a flaming Madrid. Manuel serves as the reflector for virtually all the scenes of infantry combat, except for those crucial battles in which Spanish forces do not take part. In addition, Manuel's perspective allows the reader to follow the evolution of a young professional man of Communist sympathies as he becomes a Republican military commander.

Another important reflector, the ethnologist-turned-intelligence-chief Garcia, has, like Shade, a certain freedom of movement and, in addition, a privileged understanding of the pertinent facts. His lucid comments illuminate many of the dialogues; like Gisors in *La Condition humaine*, he is a character with whom many of the others feel drawn to talk. Unlike almost all of the other characters, Garcia seems to have lacked a model in reality; his place in the novel seems due to literary rather than historical necessity. Garcia's perspective often seems to reflect Malraux's own, and critics have been quick to attribute to the writer himself such statements as Garcia's well-known definition of the most important human activity, "transformer en conscience une expérience aussi large que possible" (p. 397).[b][25] Although in the end Magnin casts doubt on the infallibility of Garcia's seeming wisdom, the economy of the novel nevertheless gives great weight to his statements.

The perspective of Magnin, the character whose activity parallels Malraux's, also occupies a central position. His point of view grows more and more important in the final section of the book, where it dominates the culminating scene of the descent from the mountain. And it is again Magnin who, flying over the battle of Guadalajara in his old plane, is able to interpret both military and political developments. The penultimate scene, where the three principal reflec-

---

[b]converting as wide a range of experience as possible into conscious thought (p. 396)

tors—Garcia, Manuel, and Magnin—are brought together for the first time in the book, is also dominated by the perspective of Magnin. That Magnin defines his political position as "socialist,—the revolutionary left," a situation not unlike Malraux's own at this time, must be kept in mind by those who would see the experience of the Communist Manuel as fully expressing the lesson of the novel. Manuel is accorded the brief last scene, as he was given the first: he thus provides the novel with a certain structural symmetry and, at the same time, stresses that the struggle is one of the Spanish people, not merely of the foreign volunteers. Manuel dominates many important scenes and participates in a number of significant dialogues, particularly his ongoing discussions on the Church with the Catholic Ximénès, with whom he is linked by a mysterious bond of affection. But his point of view is not the only one, nor is it even incontestably dominant. Although his views are often supported by Garcia's greater intellectual depth, Manuel's domination of the novel is strongly contested by the emphasis given to Magnin.

The interplay of Malraux's reflectors has important implications for the thematic development. If Manuel alone were the central character, the message of the novel might well be, as many readers have thought, that the spontaneous revolutionary sentiments of the Spanish people must be organized into an efficient army under the direction of the Communists. This is certainly the object lesson of the various situations in which Manuel finds himself, and at the end of the novel, he has emerged as commander of a brigade that plays a central role in the Republican victory at Guadalajara.[26]

The story of Manuel's military apprenticeship, which proceeds in harmony with the events of the war, provides the plot of *L'Espoir*. He is the only character who undergoes a decisive evolution and who appears with great regularity in the novel from beginning to end. Thus it is tempting to equate Manuel's position in *L'Espoir* with that of Kyo in *La Condition humaine* and to conclude that, therefore, his experience must sum up Malraux's central novelistic statement. This interpretation finds support in the fact that the more intellectually gifted Garcia constantly gives verbal reinforcement to the thesis that Manuel illustrates in action. In the face of Magnin's objections to the exaltation of technical matters over revolutionary fervor, Garcia insists on the necessity of "organizing the Apocalypse." At the Santa Cruz Museum, it is again Garcia who defends this position against the attacks of Hernandez and the Negus. His function in the novel seems, at many points, to be that of transforming Manuel's experience into classic Malrucian prose.

The thrust of the combined arguments presented by Garcia and Manuel would be that the army must replace the scattered militias, that revolutionary ideals must be sacrificed to military efficiency, and that salvation lies with the Communists. This would indeed be a partisan conclusion; it is nevertheless the way _L'Espoir_ was interpreted by a number of commentators at the time of its appearance. Drieu la Rochelle, for example, felt called upon to answer this argument with an entire article designed to illustrate the Communists' very lack of efficiency.[27] This view of _L'Espoir_ as an expression of support for the Communist position is repeated by later critics as well; Lucien Goldmann, for example, terms it "a book written from a Stalinist perspective."[28]

Certainly, Malraux perceptively observed in Spain a process of centralization and organization among the Republican forces. This process has since been traced in a similar, although perhaps less admiring fashion by historians, who, unlike Malraux, are no longer able to believe that such a process could have led to a Republican victory.[29] Malraux in 1937 seems to think victory possible, and, for that reason, he is ready to praise the Communists for their skill in military organization and for the Soviet military aid to the Republicans.

But the novel clearly does not give universal approval to the Communists in Spain. "Ils ont toutes les vertus de l'action—et celles-là seules," (p. 498)[c] says a disillusioned Garcia, quoting a pacifist friend, after Guadalajara. With the exception of Manuel, Communist characters in the novel are not sympathetically portrayed. Moreover, within the ongoing novelistic debate, a number of significant objections are raised to the thesis of Communist organization. The most important confrontations occur at Toledo in the positions represented by the Negus and Hernandez. The Negus, who had been introduced in the early scenes in Barcelona, is a character of great fascination. He embodies qualities of ethical purity and personal heroism, as illustrated by the flamethrower episode. Like Malraux's other Republicans, he is fighting for human dignity, but, in opposition to the Communists, he feels that economic and social reforms

[c]They have all the virtues of action and no others (p. 504).

designed to increase individual liberty must be asserted immediately, rather than being postponed until military victory is achieved. Now Malraux has made it clear that the anarchists, with their ideological rejection of organization, have contributed mightily to the military disarray that Toledo epitomizes. The Negus, identified with the mutilated crucifix behind him in the bullet-riddled Santa Cruz Museum, admits that military victory is not the only anarchist priority: "Si nous sommes écrasés ici et à Madrid, les hommes auront un jour vécu avec le coeur" (p. 202).[d] In Malraux's portrayal, it is evident that, even at best, the anarchists are content to die nobly: they cannot win.

Captain Hernandez, in his noble gesture to the Falangist commander, expresses another version of the same argument for purity of means over ends, a version that, coming from a liberal, can have deeper resonance for Malraux's French readers. A Spanish career officer, he shares the Republican affirmation of human dignity. Garcia equates Hernandez's ethically noble act with the gesture of the militiamen, who have distributed cigarettes and razor blades to the besieged Falangists during the brief truce at the Alcazar.[30] They display a need to affirm their individual dignity and the dignity of their cause: "prouver à ceux de là-haut qu'ils n'ont pas le droit de les mépriser" (p. 209).[e] Hernandez's respect for the liberty of others, however, leads him to pass by opportunities of crushing the Alcazar and of establishing a disciplined command over the rebellious militias. Although he does not share the anarchists' fascination with suicidally heroic acts, his ethic inevitably leads him to the same fate. He is overcome at his machine gun in the Toledo arena, while covering the escape of his trapped comrades.

As Frohock notes, the fate of Hernandez evokes the destinies of Kyo and Katow in *La Condition humaine*:[31] unable to accept the calculating political maneuverings of the Communist party, they had gone to their deaths in all the purity of their revolutionary ideals. But the deaths of Kyo and Katow enable them to attain an almost mystical fraternity that transcends even the absurd condition of human mortality. Although Hernandez, too, states repeatedly that he does not want to die alone, he is accorded no such transcendent experience. He has sacrificed himself for his comrades but is not

[d] Even if we're beaten here and at Madrid, . . . at least the men will have given their hearts a few days' run (p. 200).
[e] prove to the men up there that they've no right to despise them (p. 206).

allowed to share their death, and his imprisonment and execution are haunted by a consciousness of the absurd. He has earlier confided to Garcia that suicide would provide the only possible solution to his internal contradictions. As he is being led off to his execution, too tired to go on, he refuses to share his companion's desperate attempt to escape. The scene of the execution of Hernandez, unlike that of Katow, is designed to stress absurdity rather than meaning: because of an optical illusion, the victims, positioned in ever-renewed groups of three, seem to jump backwards into their graves even before the shots are fired. Despite the presence of the streetcar conductor who raises his fist to destiny, the execution scene in *L'Espoir* forms a contrast to that in *La Condition humaine*, a contrast that underlines the difference in outlook between Malraux's two major novels. In the second he is more interested in revolutionary victory than tragic failure. Revolutionary action, although difficult, is not necessarily fatal in the Spanish Civil War novel, and transcendent fraternity is to be found among those who live to fight on.

There is, as Garcia sadly points out, an inevitable tension between ideals and the realities of action: "Pour un homme qui pense, la révolution est tragique. Mais pour un tel homme, la vie aussi est tragique" (p. 399).[f] He thus articulates one of Malraux's major themes, which takes on its full significance only in the middle sections of the novel. The conflicts created by the confrontation of thought and action under the pressure of war provide the drama of Malraux's central characters. In some cases, as with the Negus and Hernandez, the tension becomes unbearable. Others, like Manuel and Garcia, learn to accept a painful reality, even if they must in the process sacrifice certain deeply held values. Manuel, who had been drawn to Communism because of concern for the people, laments, "Il n'est pas un des échelons que j'ai gravis dans le sens meilleur, qui ne m'écarte davantage des hommes" (p. 411). Even Garcia, the ethnologist who had earlier enjoyed a close relationship with the peasants of the Sierra, confides bitterly to Magnin, "Plus vous vous battez, plus vous vous enfoncez dans l'Espagne; moi, plus je travaille, plus je m'en écarte" (p. 496).[g] The Spanish Civil War provided for

[f] For a thinker, the revolution's a tragedy. But for such a man, life, too, is tragic (p. 397).

[g] every step I've taken towards greater efficiency, towards becoming a better officer, has estranged me more and more from my fellow men (p. 407). . . . The longer you fight, the nearer you get to the real heart of Spain. . . . But in my case, the harder I work, the further away I get (p. 502).

Malraux a privileged opportunity to observe the interplay of ideas and action, which had formed the two poles of his own life, and it is this conflict that he has chosen as the subject of *L'Espoir*. Indeed, this problem, that of the *engagement* of the intellectual, was brought home to many writers of this era by the Spanish Civil War.[32] If this question is seen as a major subject of *L'Espoir*, Malraux has rightly given the fate of Hernandez equal attention with the evolution of Manuel: they share the same conflict but adopt different solutions. If Malraux's intent had merely been to prove the Communists right, he would have had no need to provide such strong statements of the alternative position as those of the Negus and Hernandez. If Communist propaganda had been his sole aim, then his artistic sense has often led him into conflict. The artistic unity of *L'Espoir*, however, becomes apparent once its true concerns are located.

The intellectual, the man who thinks, inevitably suffers from the contradictions between thought and action, but in Malraux's ethic, he cannot therefore refrain from acting. This question of the role the intellectual is called upon to play in the Civil War is analyzed in depth in Garcia's reflections on the death of Miguel de Unamuno and again in the important dialogue between old Alvear and the art historian Scali, a member of Magnin's squadron, on the eve of what seems to be the collapse of Madrid. Like old Gisors in *La Condition humaine*, Alvear expresses a deep pessimism about the possibility of social change: politics are inevitably corrupt, revolutions can only create new forms of oppression rather than increased liberty, and change must first occur within the individual rather than on the level of society. Alvear's life has been devoted to preserving Spain's cultural heritage, and he is prepared to die among his books and paintings when the Falangists enter Madrid, as he is convinced they soon will. Reflecting a lifetime of meditation on art and culture, Alvear's position must obviously be taken seriously in the context of a Malraux novel.

But even as the old man speaks, Malraux indicates—through setting, action, and the reflections of the equally intellectual Scali— just how futile is his attempt to remain aloof from the war. Indeed, he has already been rendered vulnerable through the blinding of his aviator son Jaime, which, Scali reflects, accounts for much of his present despair. Through the carefully closed shutters of Alvear's apartment, where he has walled himself in with his books and cognac, come the noises of military preparations, reminders of which constantly interrupt the dialogue. And when the attack comes, in the next section, the gutted apartments of a bombed Madrid prove that such walls provide no protection against the realities of modern history. Ironically, the bombs also threaten to destroy the Spanish cultural heritage (the Prado Museum, the National Library) that Alvear had thought to preserve through his refusal to become involved. Many of Alvear's pessimistic prophecies are, in fact, proven false: Madrid does not fall, and his son Jaime eventually regains his sight, as predicted by the doctors (this event provides an appropriate beginning to the final section, titled "L'Espoir").

It is Scali himself, a respected Italian art historian, who provides the clearest articulation of a value capable of compensating the intellectual for the torment of action. He is another character like Hernandez and the Negus, torn apart by his effort to reconcile his ideals with the unpleasant realities of war. Although he is capable of holding his own in the confrontation with old Alvear, he does not emerge from it unscathed, and he later echoes some of Alvear's words in his own conversation with Garcia. He never fully resolves his conflicts before being put out of the picture by a serious injury received in the mountain plane crash. But in his conversation with Alvear, Scali describes what has been for him the positive dimension of the war: "Les hommes unis à la fois par l'espoir et par l'action accèdent, comme les hommes unis par l'amour, à des domaines auxquels ils n'accéderaient pas seuls, . . . l'essentiel de l'homme, si vous voulez, est, à mes yeux, en de tels domaines" (pp. 322–23).[h] He thus sums up a second major theme of the novel, the dominant Malrucian theme of "virile fraternity."

The aspiration toward fraternity is the motivating force not only of the intellectual Scali but also of the old peasant Barca, wounded in the early battles in the Sierra, who must weigh his ideals against the reality of the pain in his injured leg. Even though he admits, "Ma jambe me fait plus mal que d'être vexé par un fasciste" (p. 99), he nevertheless finds a reason for going on in the hope of ending humiliation for all: "Le contraire de ça, l'humiliation, comme il dit, c'est

---

[h]men who are joined together in a common hope, a common quest, have, like men whom love unites, access to regions they could never reach left to themselves. . . . I find it's just such circumstances bring out what is—how shall I put it?—most fundamental in men (p. 324).

pas l'égalité. . . . Le contraire d'être vexé, c'est la fraternité" (p. 100).[i] In *La Condition humaine* Kyo had fought against humiliation in the name of human dignity and had thereby discovered the meaning of fraternity. In *L'Espoir* Barca's statement shows that the two themes have become fused.

Yet the conflicting forces in the Santa Cruz Museum conversation make apparent the great paradox of the war: while the spontaneous fraternity and popular enthusiasm of the beginning of the war must be organized into an effective army, this fraternity itself must be preserved. Organization alone, as exemplified by the cold and efficient Communists, cannot move men to give their lives; fraternity alone, as exemplified by the Negus and Hernandez, leads to defeat. It is the delicate equilibrium between these often opposing forces that is finally attained in the novel at the moment of the defense of Madrid.

The fraternity in question in *L'Espoir* is not merely a comradeship on the level of individuals. It is also, and more importantly, a union of the disparate forces of the Spanish Left in a desperate struggle against fascism. This fragile union of antifascist elements was a historical reality of the opening days of the Civil War, and it was a factor on which Malraux, as an organizer of antifascist forces in France, wished to place great stress. In Barcelona the anarchist Puig and his old enemy, the civil guard Ximénès, can face each other at last on a basis of mutual understanding and respect. In Madrid, Manuel revels in the companionship of the first night of the war, as socialists, Communists and anarchists work together to man the improvised barricades, their unity summed up in their common use of the greeting *Salud*: "Le salud obsédant, abandonné, repris, scandé, perdu, unissait la nuit et les hommes dans une fraternité d'armistice" (p. 54).[j] Jaime Alvear realizes the force of a common will as he takes his place among the men wielding a primitive battering ram that beats down the gates of the Falangist Montana barracks in Madrid: "Pour Jaime . . . le Front populaire, c'était cette fraternité dans la vie et dans la mort" (p. 45).[k] But the spontaneous fraternal action of the

[i]my leg bothers me more than these fascist questions (p. 94). . . . The opposite of that—humiliation, as he calls it—isn't equality. . . . that's just what 'fraternity' means: the opposite of being badgered (p. 95).

[j]sounded incessantly the cries of *Salud*, fading away and roaring up again, rapped out in measured beats and dying away. Men and darkness seemed united in a fraternal pact (p. 50).

[k]To Jaime . . . the Popular Front meant fraternity in life and death (p. 38).

people, while capable of winning the early battles, is not able by it-self to bring about victory in a modern mechanized war. As Man-uel's experience illustrates, military technique must be mastered and the various popular militias brought under a unified control.

Manuel is responsible for the first realization of this equilibrium between fraternity and efficiency as he gathers the scattered rem-nants of the Toledo militia together at Aranjuez. Even though he has drawn certain lessons from the Communist commander, Manuel does not act with a ruthless and inhuman efficiency. His first con-cern is with sheltering and feeding the men, and they in turn re-spond by spontaneously organizing themselves into small working groups: as he returns to his command post, he is surprised to be greeted by a sentinel, "la première garde spontanée de la guerre d'Espagne" (p. 274).[l] The regroupment at Aranjuez is the result not of a rigid application of party discipline, but of "une fraternité qui prenait la forme de l'action" (p. 273).[m] Less obviously fraternal acts will be necessary as well and will threaten the fragile balance. When the effectiveness of the newly reconstituted force is menaced by Falangist infiltrators and deserters, Manuel is forced to resort to exe-cutions and must turn a deaf ear to appeals for mercy. But he finds some compensation in the fraternal understanding he sees in the fa-miliar faces of the men under his command; he realizes it is pre-cisely his responsibility for the lives entrusted to him that has made him order the executions.

Fraternity is also an essential motivating force within Magnin's air squadron. The almost physical solidarity of the fliers is stressed when, on several occasions, they await the return of crippled planes; Scali has given expression to a feeling that all seem to share. But even this solidarity threatens to break down under the pressures of imminent defeat. Like the militiamen who have abandoned their guns at Toledo, the pilot Leclerc turns back without dropping his bombs when faced with apparently overwhelming enemy fire, an incident that threatens to tear the squadron apart. Magnin imme-diately takes steps to reorganize his group, in an action that parallels Manuel's regroupment at Aranjuez. Mercenaries like Leclerc are eliminated, to be replaced by more volunteers from the International

[l] the first self-appointed guard of the Spanish war (p. 273).
[m] a fraternity that expressed itself in action (p. 272)

Brigades. Here, too, the forces of fraternity are stressed, and the fliers rediscover their troubled unity.

In the closing section of the novel, the reconstituted squadron becomes the source of a still-wider fraternity, which links the international volunteers to the struggle of the Spanish peasants. With the striking exception of the old peasant Barca—and perhaps this is one reason he is so often cited—almost all the characters who have previously expressed their points of view are of bourgeois background; many are admittedly intellectuals. The much-discussed "people," for whom and by whom this war is being fought, are largely relegated to crowd scenes, of which there are many, most often reported through the observing eyes of the journalist Shade. The Spanish peasants are given a few speaking parts at certain moments: Shade hears their comments in Toledo, and Manuel and Ximénès listen at length to their denunciation of the Church. In these scenes, however, the speakers remain faceless, their features obliterated by the Spanish night. Only in the brief third part do the peasant characters emerge into the light and begin to express themselves, a change of emphasis that has important implications for the evolution of Malraux's thought.

First, the crew of a bomber that has crashed while slowing the Falangist pursuit of the refugees from Malaga is rescued by the efforts of local militiamen, who manage to transport the wounded to a hospital in the midst of the chaos of the Republican exodus. The strong bond between peasants and airmen is vividly expressed in the linked hands of the flier Pol and an old peasant who has hitched a ride on the running board of their car.

The succeeding scene, the one that forms a major portion of the film *Sierra de Teruel*, reemphasizes this point. A peasant who has learned of the existence of a clandestine Falangist airfield is brought to Magnin's squadron to guide the bombers. The planes must take off at night from an airfield lit only by the headlights of cars lent by the local peasant villages at great cost to themselves. Once in the air, the peasant, totally befuddled by his first airplane flight, is incapable of recognizing even his own village; the pilots must fly at treetop level until he can find the airfield. But this man from a premodern world and the twentieth-century warriors who transport him can all share in the triumph of the attack, as all share a common struggle against fascism.

This scene leads directly into the descent from the mountain sequence. On its return from this mission, one of the three bombers is crippled by enemy fighters and crashes into a snow-covered mountainside. The nearby villagers hurriedly construct improvised stretchers and a coffin, and all share the burden of carrying the injured bomber crew down the steep mountainside. Magnin, who has hurried to meet the procession, observes it at length against the background of an austere and seemingly eternal mountain landscape, within which each element of the scene seems to take on deeper significance. An isolated apple tree surrounded by its ring of fallen apples becomes a symbol of the renewal of the earth itself: "Cet anneau pourrissant et plein de germes semblait être, au delà de la vie et de la mort des hommes, le rhythme de la vie et de la mort de la terre" (p. 478)." The peasants and fliers, too, share in this eternity, moving beyond their individual realities to evoke a more fundamental human nature. Through the tenderness of her gestures, a peasant woman following the stretchers becomes an emblem of "l'éternelle maternité" (p. 476)." Physical suffering transforms the individual faces of the fliers, and the noseless face of Gardet becomes "l'image même que, depuis des siècles, les paysans se faisaient de la guerre" (p. 480)." Like the apple tree, the peasants have maintained their simple lives in an ever-renewed struggle with the barren and forbidding mountains, just as the fliers have continued to struggle with the hostile elements. The procession that joins the proud devotion of the peasants with the courage of the volunteer fliers comes to sum up for Magnin "la volonté des hommes" (p. 479)," which he sees as strong and enduring enough to set itself against the nonhuman universe: "Tout cela était aussi impérieux que ces rocs blafards qui tombaient du ciel lourd, que l'éternité des pommes éparses sur la terre" (pp. 478–79)." This defiant human will is embodied in the repeated gesture of the clenched fist, which recalls the gesture of the condemned streetcar conductor in the earlier execution scene. Magnin's feeling of "austere triumph" when he glimpses the distant flames of

---

"the ring of decaying fruit seemed to typify the passage from life to death that not only was the doom of men but was an immutable law of the universe (p. 482).

"the imperishably maternal instinct (p. 480)

"the visible incarnation of the peasants' immemorial conception of war (p. 485).

"triumphant human will (p. 484)

"[It] had something as compelling about it as the pale rocks that merged into the lowering sky, something as fundamental as the apples scattered on the ground (p. 483).

the burning Falangist airfields relates not merely to the momentary military success but to the accomplishments of all united human effort.

In the last section of the novel, Malraux has lifted the Spanish Civil War above the contentions of warring political factions to view it as one aspect of the eternal "combat of man against the earth."³³ *L'Espoir*, then, has as its subject the same conflict that had animated Malraux's precedinq novels: the confrontation of man with destiny. This struggle against destiny is, in Malraux's view, a fundamental human reality, which links the Spanish peasants and the foreign pilots, as it unites the various political factions that fight to affirm human dignity. Magnin's lyrical vision of human fraternity on the steep mountain path is confirmed by the united action of the Republican forces at Guadalajara. The battle thus expresses in a single military event the vision of fraternal human effort that forms the true subject of the concluding section.

The first two parts of the novel are filled with conflict, expressed in dialogues that set one character against another. In the conclusion, Malraux attempts to provide some resolution to the various conflicting themes. The problem is set forth through Scali's words in its opening pages: "Voilà vingt ans que Scali entendait parler de 'notion de l'homme.' Et se cassait la tête dessus. C'était du joli, la notion de l'homme, en face de l'homme engagé sur la vie et la mort. Scali ne savait décidément plus où il en était. Il y avait le courage, la générosité—et il y avait la physiologie. Il y avait les révolutionnaires—et il y avait les masses. Il y avait la politique et il y avait la morale" (p. 430).⁵ Many of the oppositions cited by Scali, the very conflicts that have governed the movement of the novel, are brought together in the scene of the descent from the mountain, where, through Magnin, Malraux approaches a definition of a general notion of man. Like the transcendent experience of Kyo and Katow in *La Condition humaine*, Magnin's vision of man is capable of surviving the objections raised by mere political defeat. It is not a pessimistic vision, and Malraux in *L'Espoir* chooses to confirm it with a military

⁵For twenty years now Scali had been hearing talk about 'the human ideal' and had puzzled over it. Metaphysics! Now they were up against the spectacle of men engaged in a life-and-death struggle, a fine show it was making! Scali was completely unable to sort out his ideas. There was courage, generosity—and there was the physiological side. There were the revolutionaries—and there were the masses. There was politcs—and ethics (p. 429).

victory. But Guadalajara was to be the last significant victory for the antifascist forces in Spain—and, for many years, in Europe as a whole. In the dark years that followed *L'Espoir*, Malraux was to return to and deepen this understanding.

The Epilogue of Gilles

Drieu la Rochelle received the Spanish Civil War novel of his friend Malraux with little enthusiasm, finding it, according to Dominique Desanti, not only biased but "journalistic, too close to an anecdotal present."[34] He must certainly have found in it the reflection of some of his own deepest concerns, particularly the problems of the intellectual and action that had been the subject of his own 1934 play, *Le Chef*. But he could not share Malraux's support for a Spanish Republican government he saw, as he wrote to Victoria Ocampo, as entirely run from Moscow.[35] At the very moment Malraux had plunged into action on behalf of the Spanish Republic, Drieu himself had entered the arena of French politics, but on the opposite side of the fence. Although Drieu's disappointment with Jacques Doriot is noticeably absent from *Gilles*, which jumps directly from the Paris of February 1934 to the Spain of 1936–37, the Epilogue reflects Drieu's increasing disillusionment with political action in the real world.

The break in the novel between the February riots and the Epilogue is all the more disorienting because of the abrupt disappearance of the protagonist, Gilles. In his place, the reader finds an inexplicably nervous man named Walter, who wanders through Barcelona in an atmosphere reminiscent of the numerous spy films of the period. Only well into the segment, in the moment of truth that results from his murder of a Dutch companion, is Walter finally identified as Gilles. The Barcelona section of the Epilogue is fabricated solely of suspense and adventure; the political realities of the Civil War are barely mentioned, except as they contribute to the confused situation within which the one-dimensional characters move. Although earlier parts of *Gilles* have closely followed incidents in Drieu's own life, he is here constructing a destiny of pure fantasy for his persona. Where Malraux's Spanish Civil War fiction had been firmly based in reality, Drieu's begins by inventing an imaginary world of international espionage and adventure.

In fact, the entire role in which Gilles/Walter is cast in the Epilogue is based on fantasy, Drieu's fantasy of the ideal political movement. As Walter reveals later to a group of companions, he is an undercover agent for a strange worldwide fascist conspiracy: "J'appartiens à un nouvel ordre militaire et religieux qui s'est fondé quelque part dans le monde et poursuit, envers et contre tout, la conciliation de l'Eglise et du fascisme et leur double triomphe sur l'Europe" (pp. 674–75).[1] The mystery with which Drieu surrounds this "new order"—it has no name, it has been founded "somewhere in the world"; Walter may or may not be one of its leaders—all these factors indicate that such an organization is a pure product of Drieu's imagination. In fact, at the end of the decade, the organization Gilles describes could only exist in an imaginary world. The organization's supranational political outlook certainly conforms to what Drieu would have liked ("Je me suis retiré d'entre les nations," [p. 674] Walter claims), and Walter reiterates a major theme of all Drieu's political writings when he says, "Le triomphe du Fascisme ne peut pas se confondre avec le triomphe d'une nation sur les autres nations" (p. 675).[a] But by the time Drieu wrote these words, there were few left who shared this faith, and certainly no political party, undercover or not. In a manner that is revelatory of his entire manner of relating to reality, Drieu has given his alter ego an outlet in purely imaginary action and a political affiliation that flies in the face of the actual political developments.

From Barcelona, Gilles/Walter moves on to the Balearic Islands, where a plane crash lands him in the middle of the Falangist invasion of Ibiza. For all his disdain of Malraux's "journalistic" treatment of the Spanish Civil War , Drieu's handling of this segment of the Epilogue is not dissimilar to the technique used in *L'Espoir*: scenes portraying various forms of action are followed by conversation that brings out their wider significance. The subjects of the action scenes themselves—combat, a plane crash, crowds in the streets, interrogations, and executions—are quite similar to those of *L'Espoir*; Drieu's treatment of them, however, is very different.

Since Gilles moves back and forth between the Republican and Falangist lines on the small island, Drieu finds it necessary to portray

---

[1] I belong to a new military and religious order that has been founded somewhere in the world and pursues, against all obstacles, the conciliation of the Church and fascism and their double triumph over Europe.

[a] I have withdrawn myself from nations. . . . The triumph of Fascism must not be confused with the triumph of one nation over the others.

both sides of the conflict (as Malraux does not) in a fashion that makes his own point of view apparent. The Falangists with whom Gilles fights are young, masculine, ardent, and severe, while the "Reds" with whom he is repeatedly forced to associate are repulsive. The Dutchman he kills (a Communist agent) is fat, sweaty, and flashily dressed. A left-wing companion on the menaced plane is also sweaty, and cowardly to boot. And the Communist agent with whom he has to deal on Ibiza is a wily Jew. The crowd he observes in the section of the island under Republican control embodies for Gilles the decadence he has come to hate in postwar Paris: "Cent maladies faisaient cette immense maladie dont mourait ce peuple, dont il avait manqué mourir. Les drogues, les hommes caressant les hommes, la peinture de Picasso. . . les music-halls, les casinos sur les plages. . . . Il se rappelait tout le grouillement de son cauchemar de vingt ans. Et tout cela, ce soir, reparaissait dans cette foule" (pp. 646–47).[v] There is no evidence in the novel that the people he sees have, in fact, been involved in any of these "decadent" activities, and, at any rate, Gilles/Walter has himself just arrived on the island. But it is immediately clear that neither Drieu nor his protagonist is really interested in what is happening in Spain, except as it crystallizes the confrontation of political ideologies taking place all over Europe. The left-wing crowds in Ibiza manifest the symptoms of Parisian decadence for the same reason that the Falangist soldiers Gilles later sees in Extremadura resemble the popular assemblies, presumably fascist, into which he has "plunged" himself in Hungary, Poland, and Yugoslavia: "Ils étaient faits de cette race éternellement primitive qui remplit encore les profondeurs de l'Europe et d'où sort maintenant tout ce grand mouvement irrésistible qui étonne les esprits délicats dans les villes d'Occident" (p. 677).[w] Both crowds are elements in a political allegory rather than real persons, popular entities into which Gilles/Drieu may read the conclusions of his two decades of political reflection.

Drieu makes it clear to his reader that his discussion of the Spanish situation is only a pretext for speculating on the situation in

[v] A hundred diseases contributed to this immense disease from which this people was dying or had almost died. Drugs, men caressing men, Picasso's painting . . . music halls, casinos on the beaches . . . . He remembered all the swarming activity of his twenty-year nightmare. And all that, that night, reappeared in this crowd.

[w] They were made up of the eternally primitive race that still fills the depths of Europe and from which is now emerging the great, irresistible movement that astonishes delicate spirits in the cities of the West.

France. With a young Falangist officer in Extremadura, Gilles forecasts his own fate after the inevitable outbreak of war in France: "Il reviendrait se battre et, tôt ou tard, il serait retiré des premières lignes, brûlé par les revolvers communistes, à l'instigation de quelques juifs" (p. 678).[x] Earlier, he had proven his ability to maintain an attitude of complete philosophical detachment while walking through an Ibiza newly reconquered by the Falangists, with corpses still littering the sidewalk and men being dragged away from their screaming wives before his very eyes. Undistracted by all this, Gilles reflects calmly on the universality of the situation: "Il y avait une immense lutte dans le monde, ici éclatante, latente là. Une énorme bagarre se poursuivaient partout, avec des moyens divers, à des degrés différents et changeants. . . . Dans les pays apparemment plus calmes, les adversaires ne faisaient encore que se tâter, s'épier" (p. 667).[y]

The extent to which Drieu's rendering of this type of scene reduces it to the status of a mere stage setting for his politico-philosophical reflections becomes clear when *Gilles* is compared with Bernanos's *Les Grands Cimetières sous la lune*, a nonfictional treatment of similar events on the nearby Balearic island of Mallorca. Bernanos's deep concern for the individuals involved in the executions is clear, and the political conclusions seem to grow out of the experiences described—as they, in fact, did in Bernanos's case.[36] Drieu, on the other hand, uses the Spanish situation as a framework within which to express conclusions worked out in a totally different context.

The conversation that serves to comment on the action on Ibiza is also uniquely preoccupied with the political situation in Europe as a whole. The participants are a group of international volunteers with whom Gilles has found himself associated in combat, and their conversation cannot help but evoke the discussions of the international aviators in *L'Espoir*. Drieu's Irishman, Pole, and Frenchman discuss not the Spanish combat they have just seen but the possibilities of a fascist victory over all of Europe. The problems evoked include the very immediate one of the stand to be taken in the case of a war between the fascist powers and their own countries (answer: fight

---

[x]He would go back to fight and, sooner or later, he would be pulled out of the front lines, finished off by Communist revolvers, at the instigation of a few Jews.

[y]There was an immense struggle going on in the world, bursting out here, latent there. An enormous fight was going on everywhere, with various means, to different and changing degrees. . . . In apparently calmer countries the adversaries were only feeling each other out, looking each other over.

for your own country, even if it means putting off the ultimate fascist victory) and what the role of a victorious Germany should be (answer: "Il faudra que naisse un esprit de patriotisme européen. Cet esprit ne naîtra que si l'Allemagne a d'avance donné une pleine garantie morale à l'intégrité des patries, de toutes les patries d'Europe" [p. 675][z]). The optimism here expressed by Gilles, perhaps never more than a pious hope on the part of Drieu, nevertheless points to the reasons for Drieu's early collaboration with the Nazi authorities in France. His misreading of the reality of Hitler seems, like the activity of his protagonist, to fly in the face of evidence.

But the frequent optimism of Gilles's words is tempered by a deep undercurrent of pessimism that runs throughout the entire Epilogue, sometimes directly contradicting its profascist fervor. This pessimism, which clearly stems from a deep disgust with the European political situation, points beyond the period of collaboration to Drieu's suicide in 1945, a death he engineers for his protagonist far earlier and in a far more ideal setting. While Gilles describes himself as devoted to the cause of fascism and satisfied by his austere new existence, he does not seem to participate with enthusiasm in the Spanish conflict. He seems happy for a moment when he wields a machine gun in a brief attack on the Ibiza harbor, but he does not find joy in the Falangist victory he has helped to bring about.

Always present underneath the surface is the suspicion that all the killing has accomplished nothing, that the two sides of the conflict are interchangeable, that nothing can act on the inert masses of the crowd. While observing the evening walkers in the Republican-held part of Ibiza, Gilles has reflected on the crowd's ability to remain untouched by the revolution: "cette foule où l'on avait tué déjà beaucoup dans les deux sens et en vain et qui se promenait, idiote, inquiète et oublieuse de son inquiétude" (p. 647).[a] And when he returns to the same town after the successful Falangist invasion, he finds that little has changed. Blue Shirts have replaced the Communists and Socialists at the very table before which he had previously been questioned. The prisoners now being judged are no different from those who guard them, "confondus avec leurs gardes, difficiles

---

[z]A spirit of European patriotism must be born. This spirit will come to be only if Germany has given in advance a full moral guaranty of the integrity of individual nations, all the nations of Europe.

[a]this crowd where many on both sides had already been killed in vain, this crowd that walked around like idiots, anxious and forgetful of its anxiety.

à distinguer d'eux" (p. 665).[b] Even the crowd itself has not changed: "A peine déchirée par l'éclair du combat, l'âme obscure de la masse se refermait sur la pauvre énigme de son inertie, de son effroi" (p. 666).[c] One wonders what differentiates this inert Falangist crowd from the "eternally primitive" peasant-soldiers whom he later envisions as giving birth to great events.

Seemingly penetrated by this profoundly pessimistic outlook on the struggle, Gilles/Walter often comports himself as if he were fighting for a lost cause and as if he himself were inescapably condemned. After participating in the successful Falangist invasion of Ibiza, the Irishman O'Connor unexpectedly points out to his two companions, "Nous nous battons tous les trois pour une cause perdue" (p. 670).[d] Walter has earlier described Barcelona as "ce monde qui marchait d'un pas terriblement sûr vers un dénouement atroce" (p. 615)[e]—although one wonders what the fascist Drieu found so terrible about the dénouement of the Spanish Civil War . It is somewhat ironic that, while Malraux wrote with optimism about a war where victory for his cause was doubtful at best, Drieu writes pessimistically about a war that, he knew, had been won by the side he supported. Yet, in this victorious war, of the three situations in which Drieu places his protagonist, only one is a Falangist victory, and Gilles finds even that far from satisfying. The closing segment, which takes place somewhere on the Extremadura front in December 1937 (it was at this time that Drieu himself spent two weeks in Falangist Spain as a reporter)[37] concerns a successful Republican attack—a phenomenon relatively rare in the course of the war and extremely rare in later 1937, when the tide had definitively turned in favor of Franco's forces. The nature of the military situation in which Gilles finds himself—cut off in a bullring menaced by Republican heavy artillery and as many as seven or eight Republican planes—is hard to find credible at an era when the Falangists had a superiority in arms and aviation and when what little resources the Republicans had were concentrated at Teruel, on the other side of the country.

What Drieu appears to have done, however, is to reconstruct for

[b] mingled with their guards, hard to distinguish from them.
[c] Hardly torn by the lightning of combat, the obscure soul of the masses closed itself in on the miserable riddle of its inertia, its terror.
[d] All three of us are fighting for a lost cause.
[e] this world that walked with a terribly certain step toward an atrocious outcome

his protagonist the exact situation of the doomed Hernandez in the Toledo debacle of *L'Espoir*. Like Hernandez, Gilles is trapped in a bullring about to be taken over or destroyed by superior enemy forces. Like Hernandez, Gilles refuses to take advantage of the repeatedly offered opportunity to escape from the doomed arena; instead he takes up a gun and joyfully begins to shoot. Hernandez chooses this suicidal stance because he is torn apart by internal contradictions that can be resolved only by death, and, despite Gilles's stated contentment with the path he has chosen in his mysterious clandestine organization, he nevertheless seems to share in this mentality. His reasons seem more related to the situation of the author than to that of the character, whose motivations are obscure at best. Very early in the Epilogue Gilles/Walter manifests a strange fatalism in risk: "Il était tenté par la mort" (p. 615).[f] When he imagines the approaching European war, he can only picture himself as being killed and sees France itself as inescapably doomed (this, despite his optimistic vision of independent countries in a Europe under German hegemony). In the end he submits to a mad fascination with death.

There is one source of positive value in *Gilles* capable of providing relief from the protagonist's unrelievedly negative vision of life. This value is to be found not in the fascist movement to which he belongs but in the "pure" experience of combat, to which he had been initiated in World War I. The novel had begun exactly twenty years earlier on a winter evening in 1917, showing Gilles as a soldier on leave who is suddenly confronted with the world of civilian life, which appears effeminate and decadent in comparison with the pure virility of the front. His initial sensation of disgust and disillusionment persists through the entire novel—until the moment when he recaptures the joy of combat in Spain: "Vingt ans étaient passés comme un éclair et il se retrouvait à son point de départ. Le lourd, le solide joug physique du danger, l'implacable barre sur tous les frémissements de l'individu et, en même temps, cette paix de l'âme" (p. 659). But, as in *La Comédie de Charleroi*, this feeling is destined to be fleeting. Gilles finds himself on the evening following the attack on Ibiza disgusted by the fruits of his victory, an attitude that becomes a reaction to all modern warfare—and to life in general: "C'est cela, mon époque. Et c'est cela, la vie de l'humanité, toujours. C'est ce massacre

---

[f]He was tempted by death.

sordide, ce soir, et ce pur combat, ce matin" (p. 668). Like all mystical experiences, the state of perfection cannot endure. Drieu's description of combat includes a sort of "virile fraternity" quite similar to Malraux's, which, however, seems incapable of possessing any meaning beyond the mere fact of its momentary existence: "On savoure en commun le sacrifice à quelque chose qui, à mesure que le risque se prolonge, s'avère de plus en plus intime au coeur de chacun, tout en étant sensible à tous. C'est le miracle de pouvoir enfin s'aimer dans les autres et de pouvoir aimer les autres en soi-même" (p. 670). Matured by the twenty years that have separated his two combat experiences, Gilles has learned from Ibiza (as Drieu himself had learned from his reflection on Charleroi) that only death can preserve the purity of the moment: "Miracle si fragile et si fascinant que bientôt la mort seule paraît pouvoir en sceller la certitude" (p. 670).[9] Thus Drieu constructs for his persona an ending to which he seemed to aspire in his own life, his eventual suicide being only a less satisfactory substitute. Through writing *Gilles*, he seems to have understood the solution to his personal problems as he has, on another level, worked out an ideal solution to the political problems of his era; he finds in the Spanish Civil War a setting capable of bringing them together. Thus for Drieu the war in Spain is what Malraux's Garcia warns Hernandez it is not in reality: an occasion to work out his own deep contradictions. The Spain of the Epilogue is not so much, one feels, that country Drieu saw as a reporter as an imaginary realm, perhaps first encountered in the work of Malraux and Bernanos, that he now appropriates for his own use.

"Le Mur"

If Drieu uses the war in Spain as an appropriate dénouement for his character's life and as a vantage point from which to analyze the European political situation, Jean-Paul Sartre uses it to illustrate the

---

[9] Twenty years had passed in a flash and he found himself back at his starting point. The heavy, solid physical yoke of danger, the implacable power over all the quiverings of the individual, and, at the same time, this peace of mind. . . . That's my time. And that's human life, always. The sordid massacre tonight, and the pure combat this morning. . . . You savor together the sacrifice to something that, as the risk is prolonged, becomes closer and closer to the heart of each person, felt by all at the same time. It is the miracle of finally being able to love yourself in others and others in yourself. . . . Miracle so fragile and so fascinating that soon only death seems to be able to seal its certitude.

metaphysical absurdity of the human condition. The first written and the first published (in the *Nouvelle Revue Française* of July 1937) of the three works discussed in this chapter, "Le Mur"[38] nevertheless reveals a more pessimistic outlook about life and politics than the work of either Malraux or Drieu. Sartre had uncannily anticipated the sense of despair that was to attack all of these writers by the end of the decade. In "Le Mur," in opposition to *L'Espoir*, the reality of the Spanish Civil War does not play a major role in determining characters or plot. Even more so than in *Gilles*, the Spanish setting of "Le Mur" serves as a pretext for the evocation of more universal philosophical problems.

The story reveals, nevertheless, a clear political position. As Sartre later explained, at the time of the composition of "Le Mur," he was "simply in a state of total revolt against the fact of Spanish fascism."[39] Simone de Beauvoir has recorded that the Spanish Civil War was the first political event of the 1930s that succeeded in shaking Sartre and herself from their intellectual isolation: "For the first time in our lives, because the fate of Spain concerned us so deeply, indignation per se was no longer a sufficient outlet for us: our political impotence, far from furnishing us with an alibi, left us feeling hopeless and desolate."[40] Although many of their closest friends, Paul Nizan being a prime example, were actively engaged in the great political battles of the time, Sartre and de Beauvoir had been content to let the left-wing ideals that they shared impose themselves on reality without their own active help. The success of the Falangist generals in Spain provided one of the first real challenges to the validity of their stance of passive onlookers. While de Beauvoir seems to have maintained an early optimism, Sartre, by his own account, had foreseen the Falangist victory in Spain almost from the first. This political pessimism informs his story, as he was later to admit: "Since at that time we were operating in the context of the Spanish defeat ["Le Mur" was written in late 1936 or in early 1937 at the latest] I found myself much more sensitive to the absurdity of these deaths than to the positive elements that might emerge from a struggle against fascism, etc."[41]

There is a certain political protest in the story of three men condemned to death after a summary interrogation by a Falangist committee. The questioning of the prisoners takes place in the opening pages and is so brief that it comes as a shock when the guard informs them afterwards, "C'était le jugement" (p. 12).[h] The few bits of information exchanged seem to bear no relationship to the death sentences later read out in the cell. Two of the three men have, at least, been fighting on the Republican side: Tom Steinbock is an Irish volunteer in the International Brigades, and the narrator, Pablo Ibbieta, is an anarchist militant. The youngest of the three, however, is totally innocent. His only "crime" is in being the brother of a known anarchist. Nevertheless he is condemned to be shot with the others, a fate that he finds impossible to accept. While Tom and Pablo maintain a façade of stoic resignation, Juan protests, sobs, bites the hand of the doctor, and finally, in a state of total nervous collapse, he must be carried out to his execution by the guards. Although the narrator resists any temptation to sentimentalize over Juan, this cold-blooded execution of an innocent teenage boy cannot help but represent a severe indictment of fascist policy and thus takes up a privileged theme of the antifascist work of Malraux, Bernanos, and others. When "Le Mur" was turned into a film in 1967, Sartre saw this theme—"the horror of death inflicted on man by man"[42]—as the aspect of the story with the greatest continuing political relevance.

The fate of young Juan is also the anecdotal point of departure for the story. Sartre had been asked by a former student who had experienced some problems in his personal life (de Beauvoir identifies him as Jacques-Laurent Bost)[43] to arrange with Malraux for his passage to Spain as a volunteer. Although Malraux ultimately resolved the situation with great good sense by convincing the young man that he would be less than useless to the Spanish army until he learned how to handle a weapon, Sartre had found himself torn between his commitment to the Spanish Republican cause and his fear for the student's fate: "I was very disturbed because, on the one hand, I felt he didn't have sufficient military or even biological preparation to survive the bad times and, on the other hand, I couldn't deny a man the right to fight."[44] Sartre's meditation on the possible reactions to the situations the young man might have to confront gave birth to "Le Mur," which, Sartre claims, is not at all the philosophical study of the absurd that many readers have seen in it but simply a meditation on death.

Whichever of these definitions of the main theme the reader finds

[h] You have been sentenced (translation mine).

more appropriate, it is obvious that Sartre's central concern goes far beyond the Spanish Civil War, which serves as its point of departure. Sartre's first works of fiction, like those of the writers who share his existentialist outlook (for example, Malraux's *Les Conquérants* and *La Voie royale*, Camus's *L'Etranger*), begin by confronting the fundamental problem of human mortality. Only when human life is measured against the fact of its inevitable finitude can its real meaning be considered. Such a confrontation with death can take place only in a situation where the protagonist finds himself condemned—by illness (Garine in *Les Conquérants*), by a mortal wound (Perken in *La Voie royale*) or by a death sentence imposed by other men (Meursault in *L'Etranger* and Pablo in "Le Mur"). The progressive dissolution of all those elements that have seemed to provide life's meaning is in "Le Mur," as in Sartre's previous fictional work, *La Nausée*, an introduction to the absurd.

During the night on which Pablo awaits his execution, he devotes every mental faculty to the effort of understanding the idea of death, but it remains beyond his grasp. As his companion Tom says: "On a tout le temps l'impression que ça y est, qu'on va comprendre et puis ça glisse, ça vous échappe et ça retombe. Je me dis: après, il n'y aura plus rien. Mais je ne comprends pas ce que ça veut dire" (p. 23).[i] A consciousness cannot imagine its ceasing to be conscious.

In the course of the night Pablo becomes alienated from his physical body, which, he realizes, is separate from his consciousness of it: "Il suait et tremblait tout seul, et je ne le reconnaissais plus. J'étais obligé de le toucher et de le regarder pour savoir ce qu'il devenait, comme si ç'avait été le corps d'un autre" (p. 29).[j] In a characteristically Sartrean image, he sees himself as attached to a "vermine énorme" (p. 30).[k] As he is alienated from his own physical reality, he is even further removed from the physical presence of the others who share his cell, none of whom he finds particularly sympathetic. He is, however, forced to recognize the extent to which the other bodies—described in terms of excretory odors, sweat, and soft flab—

---

[i] you always have the impression that it's all right, that you're going to understand and then it slips, it escapes you and fades away. I tell myself there will be nothing afterwards. But I don't understand what it means (p. 8).

[j] it sweated and trembled by itself and I didn't recognize it any more. I had to touch it and look at it to find out what was happening, as if it were the body of someone else (p. 12).

[k] an enormous vermin (p. 12)

nevertheless resemble his own, and he sees that his own anguish is experienced in similar fashion by his companion: "Nous étions pareils et pires que des miroirs l'un pour l'autre" (p. 21).¹ This realization of a shared human condition does not therefore create a Malrucian fraternity; it simply makes Tom's presence even more intolerable and increases Pablo's feeling of solitude.

The confrontation with death forces Pablo to regard his past life in a new light. He marvels at his ability to have taken his activities seriously, but he did so because he lived as though he were eternal; now that he has definitively lost this illusion of eternity, nothing retains its former importance. He becomes progressively indifferent to his happy memories, to his love for his mistress, Concha, to his political ideals, and even to his friendship with Ramon Gris—in order to protect whom he is nevertheless about to die. Even his spontaneous emotions of resentment toward the Belgian doctor, who provides a graphic illustration of the hostile presence of the Other, are submerged by an overwhelming feeling of indifference.

The story ends with a clever Sartrean twist, which seems to underline the notion of the fundamental meaninglessness of life. After his two companions have been taken off to be shot, Pablo is once again questioned about the whereabouts of his friend Ramon. In the light of his newfound perception of the absurdity of existence, the seriousness with which his captors take their political activity appears ridiculous: "Leurs petites activités me paraissaient choquantes et burlesques; je n'arrivais plus à me mettre à leur place, il me semblait qu'ils étaient fous" (p. 34).ᵐ He can only imagine them as future corpses: "Ces deux types chamarrés avec leurs cravaches et leurs bottes, c'étaient tout de même des hommes qui allaient mourir. Un peu plus tard que moi, mais pas beaucoup plus" (p. 33). He even tells one of the Falangists to shave off his mustache: "Je trouvais drôle qu'il laissât de son vivant les poils envahir sa figure" (p. 35).ⁿ Overcome by the feeling that all this is a giant farce, Pablo cannot resist making fun of the overly serious Falangists by sending them off on a wild goose chase to a cemetery he knows is far from his friend's

---

¹We were alike and worse than mirrors of each other (p. 7).

ᵐTheir little activities seemed shocking and burlesque to me; I couldn't put myself in their place, I thought they were insane (p. 15).

ⁿThese men dolled up with their riding crops and boots were still going to die. A little later than I, but not too much. . . . I thought it funny that he would let hair invade his face while he was still alive (p. 15).

actual whereabouts. As chance would have it, Ramon Gris has, in the meantime, changed his hiding place, and he is shot by the Falangists in precisely the spot Pablo had indicated.

While many readers have interpreted this ending as a striking evidence of the absurdity of life, Sartre—at least the Sartre of thirty years later—sees Pablo's act and its consequences quite differently: "He tries to react by an individual action because he thinks it's a farce. It is because he tries to play with forces he does not understand that he lets loose against himself the forces of the absurd. It is not the result of an absurd 'destiny' that drags men along. . . . It is the result of inadequate knowledge . . . about the real actions to take. He has obtained this result through a childish act." [45] Whether or not the conclusion is a new revelation of the absurd, it fails to add a positive dimension to Pablo's experience. Since the story is a first-person narrative written in the past tense (the *passé simple*), it is clear that the narrator has continued to live. Sartre does not feel called upon to explain how he has managed to construct a life on the basis of the devastating philosophical conclusions to which the experience described has led him.

Strangely enough, Malraux creates a strikingly similar situation in *L'Espoir*,[46] featuring a minor character named Moreno, who is a friend of the doomed liberal, Hernandez. Almost on the eve of the Toledo debacle, Moreno and Hernandez spend an evening together in a Toledo café. Moreno, a Marxist army officer who had been captured and condemned to death by the Falangists in the first days of the war, has just managed to escape. Like Sartre's Pablo, he finds his experience has profoundly altered his outlook on life, totally obliterating his former ideals: " 'Je ne crois plus à rien de ce à quoi j'ai cru,' dit Moreno, 'à rien' " (p. 226).[o] His long imprisonment under sentence of death has taught him about the finality of death. Hernandez later reiterates this understanding in classic Malrucian terminology, in a phrase that Sartre, too, would take to quoting: "La tragédie de la mort est en ceci qu'elle transforme la vie en destin, qu'à partir d'elle rien ne peut plus être compensé" (p. 251).[p] The image that Moreno retains from his imprisonment is the sound of clinking pennies ("sous"), which had echoed through his prison, as

[o]"I no longer believe in all I used to believe," Moreno said. "I believe in nothing now" (pp. 223–24).
[p]The tragedy of death is that it transforms life into destiny, that from then on nothing can be compensated for (translation mine).

each prisoner had wagered on his chances of survival. The coins evidence the arbitrary nature of human existence and point to the vanity of human effort, which can at any moment be annihilated by death. Thus, like Pablo on his liberation, Moreno sees the frenetic activity of the Toledo soldiers as a vain *comédie*.

Hernandez, however, as disillusioned as he has become, cannot accept this nihilistic vision. Although human progress has proven itself to be slow and painful, he feels there are still some positive results: "On attend tout de la liberté, tout de suite, et il faut beaucoup de morts pour faire avancer l'homme d'un centimètre. . . . Et quand même le monde a changé depuis Charles Quint. Parce que les hommes ont voulu qu'il change, malgré les sous—peut-être en n'ignorant pas que les sous existent quelque part" (p. 230).[q] Hernandez sets in opposition to Moreno's vision of meaninglessness the meaning inherent in the fraternal effort of the Toledo militias. His statements take on deeper resonance as they are borne out by the scenes in the final section of the novel, where the long, painful struggle of the Spanish peasants sums up the efforts of "triumphant human will." Malraux in *L'Espoir* cannot allow Moreno's nihilism to remain unchallenged.

When Hernandez himself is about to be executed, he thinks of Moreno's experience, and he, too, feels a sensation of absurdity before his Falangist interrogators, a sensation quite similar to that felt by Pablo: "Que les vivants employaient leur temps à des choses absurdes" (p. 252).[r] Like Pablo, he begins to see everyone around him as a future corpse: "Quand l'homme serait mort, le cou serait plus long. Et il mourrait tout comme un autre" (p. 251).[s] Also like Pablo, he must witness the condemnation of an innocent man who struggles against his fate, in this case a streetcar conductor whose jacket, worn shiny at the shoulder by the strap of his money pouch, leads the Falangists to believe that he has been carrying a rifle. Unlike Sartre's Juan, however, Malraux's conductor dies bravely, raising his fist in the Republican salute as he is about to be executed and inspir-

[q] one expects everything all at once from 'freedom,' but for man to progress a bare half inch a great many men must die. . . . Yet the world has moved on since then [the time of Charles the Fifth]. Because men wanted it to move on, despite the pennies—perhaps even with full awareness that those pennies were waiting for them in the background (p. 228).
[r] How living people waste time over futilities! (p. 252)
[s] the long neck which would look still longer when the man was dead. And he'd die the usual sort of death (p. 255).

ing others to do the same. The execution scene, which Hernandez at first perceives as absurd, takes on a new seriousness as the humble little man with his raised fist defies his executioners and comes to embody the force of humanity defying its destiny: "Il est enfoncé dans son innocence comme un pieu dans la terre, il les regarde avec une haine pesante et absolue qui est déjà de l'autre monde" (p. 258).ᶦ

Moreno, too, survives his despair and goes on to find a new meaning in life. Reappearing in a Madrid café in the midst of the bombing, he sums up the hopeless determination of the soldiers and people of Madrid, who pursue their effort in the face of death and defeat. Like the aviator Scali, he has discovered the fraternity of men who have accepted the fact of their death in combat: "Il y a une fraternité qui ne se trouve que de l'autre côté de la mort" (p. 370).ᵘ Moving beyond solitude and beyond the absurdity of the human condition, he has found that new values can emerge from despair.

In "Le Mur," Sartre's Pablo does not go beyond his vivid perception of life's absurdity in the way that the characters in Malraux's later novels are almost all able to do. Surprisingly, however, when in 1940 he was faced with an experience of defeat and imprisonment in his own life, Sartre himself was immediately able to rise to the occasion. As a prisoner of war, he had his first experience with the direct communication of the theater when he wrote an optimistic Christmas play for his fellow prisoners. And he soon returned to Paris full of determination to participate in the Resistance—at a time when most Frenchmen were still despairing over the invasion. In an exchange of roles impossible to predict on the basis of their 1937 Spanish Civil War fiction, an enthusiastic Sartre was in 1941 trying to convince a recalcitrant Malraux of the necessity of creating a writers' resistance network.[47] The lesson Sartre had learned from his own experience in a fascist prison was formulated by the protagonist of his Resistance play "Les Mouches": "La vie humaine commence de l'autre côté du désespoir." ᵛ[48] It comes very close to the last statement of Malraux's Moreno. The Spanish Civil War confronted Malraux and Sartre in different ways and at different mo-

---

ᶦThe little man gazed at them, stolid in his innocence as a stake rooted in the soil, and gave them a look of undying, elemental hatred that had already something of the other world in its intensity (p. 259).

ᵘThere's a fraternity which is only to be found—beyond the grave (p. 370).

ᵛHuman life begins on the far side of despair.

ments in their personal trajectories. Thus despite the evident similarity of their concerns, they tend to draw different philosophical conclusions from it.

*   *   *

The profound meditations inspired by the Spanish war in three of the most important French authors of the 1930s testifies to the deep significance it held for Frenchmen of the time. For Drieu and Sartre, the war is an incitement to work out in fiction some of their own meditations on life and death in a setting only slightly removed from their own. For Malraux, of course, the war was much more a reality in its own right. Yet his Spanish Civil War novel attempts to explore many of the problems that had long preoccupied him: the conflict between thought and action, the meaning of human fraternity, and the fundamental nature of man. The techniques used vary widely and reflect the individual style of each writer. Yet each in his own way had been prompted to move beyond the superficial agitation of contemporary politics to confront the "limit situations" of life and death that, as each was intuitively aware, were not far removed from their own lives and those of their compatriots.

CHAPTER 6

On the Far Side of Despair

Plus tard, on ne comprendra peut-être pas tout à fait l'état d'esprit de ceux qui ont passé à côté de la guerre dans leur enfance, qui ont grandi dans une Europe pleine d'illusions . . . et qui, soudain, pendant plusieurs années, ont attendu la guerre pour le printemps ou pour l'automne. . . . Et ils ont beau faire bon visage à la destinée, ils connaissent une forme assez tranquille de non-espoir. [a]

ROBERT BRASILLACH
Notre Avant-guerre

By the last years of the decade, French involvement in another major European war seemed imminent. There were many who, like Brasillach, were sensitive to "that insinuating plot of destiny that does everything to persuade us, from one day to the next, one hour to the next, that war is inevitable."[1] Some writers made desperate efforts to ward off the threatening conflict, and, for them, fiction no longer seemed adequate to the urgency of the task. Like the pacifist Giono, Céline abandoned the structured fictional forms he had previously used in order to express his emotional opposition to war directly in two pamphlets, *Bagatelles pour un massacre* and *L'Ecole des cadavres*. Here the hostile social forces that had oppressed Ferdinand Bardamu in *Voyage au bout de la nuit* and *Mort à crédit* become coalesced into the figure of the Jew, whom Céline sees as pushing France into an unwarranted conflict with Hitler. Other writers of pacifist leanings, like Martin du Gard, gradually abandoned their antiwar stance as Hitler's new aggressions made it clear that France could not long hope to remain immune.

The French Left was particularly hard hit by the events of the late

[a] Later, perhaps people will not completely understand the state of mind of those who just missed the war in their childhood, who grew up in a Europe full of illusions . . . and who, suddenly, for several years, expected war in the spring or the fall. . . . And no matter how they put on a show of acceptance of their fate, they know a rather calm form of "non-hope."

1930s, which had defeated their aspirations on every front. The first casualty had been the Popular Front, the alliance of Radicals, Socialists, and Communists that had been forged in the aftermath of the riots of February 1934. It had come to power in a burst of popular enthusiasm in June 1936, but the euphoria was short-lived. The new government, headed by Léon Blum, faced its first crisis even before taking office, when workers in every French industry spontaneously launched a wave of factory occupations. Blum's cautious response to these unprecedented strikes alienated some of the more radical elements of the Left,[2] while this expression of workers' power frightened French employers, who hurriedly granted some of the demands in the Matignon Accords of June. But while workers were happily leaving on their first paid vacations in August 1936, French industrialists and financiers were already putting into effect the economic measures, primarily the flight of capital, that were ultimately to bring down the Blum government and, eventually, to defeat the entire Popular Front coalition. The Spanish Civil War had a similar effect on the French political scene, alienating the more radical elements of the Left from the government because of its noninterventionist policy, while increasing the hostility of the Right, which could claim that Blum's sympathy with the Spanish Republicans threatened to involve France in a foreign war. With all these pressures massed against it, little more than a year after taking office, Blum's government was forced to resign; despite efforts to continue the same regime, the Popular Front finally breathed its last in 1938, with the downfall of a short-lived second Blum ministry.

The Left was also profoundly affected by the victory of the fascists in Spain, and they watched in horror as the lines of refugees struggled across the border after the fall of Barcelona in 1939. Malraux had been in Barcelona making the film based on his Spanish Civil War novel, and he was forced to flee with the others, barely saving a camera and an essential prop.[3] Guilloux, too, had a deep personal involvement in the fate of the Spanish Republicans. He had spent the closing years of the decade working with Spanish refugees in Brittany and writing articles on their behalf for foreign publications.[4] By the fall of 1939, he was desperately attempting to help the Spanish exiles leave a France that was itself about to be invaded by a fascist power.[5] Following the publication of *Le Sang noir* in 1935, and despite his announcement at that time of a projected sequel, Guilloux published no other fiction of any length during the second half of the decade. He later attributed this gap in his literary production to the events of 1936 and 1937.[6] The despair that he felt over the various events of this time—which included, in addition to the defeat in Spain, the increased power of the Nazis in Germany, and the effects of the economic crisis on the Breton peasants—later found expression in his 1967 novel, *Les Batailles perdues*, whose title is an accurate summary of its themes.

Another cause of Guilloux's uncharacteristic silence during these years was his increasing disaffection from the Communists, a phenomenon that, extended to other left-wing intellectuals, contributed to the gradual dissolution of the French Left. One reason for Guilloux's abandonment of the projected sequel to *Le Sang noir* was that he had intended to use as its protagonist the young character who had last been seen going off to fight in the Russian Revolution; when that character later does reappear in Guilloux's fictional work, however, he has been disillusioned with politics. Guilloux's own disillusionment with French politics, and specifically with the policies of the Communist party, seems related to the controversies that followed the defection from the party of its most illustrious fellow traveler of the 1930s, André Gide. On his return from a visit to the Soviet Union in 1936, Gide had issued a denunciation of the Stalinist regime, one of the earliest in a long series of such denunciations from left-wing intellectuals. Guilloux, who had gone along on the same trip without sharing Gide's specific reactions, now found himself under pressure from his Communist colleagues on *Ce Soir* to refute Gide's allegations, a task he had no wish to undertake. Attempting to maintain his independence of thought as a non-Communist man of the Left, he was forced into a confrontation with Aragon and Jean-Richard Bloch, who eventually fired him from his job at *Ce Soir*, an event that precipitated Guilloux's retreat to his home in Brittany.[7] Dabit, who had also been part of Gide's group in Russia, would almost certainly have found himself in a similar position had he not died in the course of the trip of a sudden attack of scarlet fever. As it was, his death was exploited by certain anti-Communist leftists, who claimed the Russians had disposed of him to prevent him from supporting Gide's statements, a charge that seems to have little basis in fact.[8]

The Communists, too, gave evidence of impatience with the group of liberal intellectuals they had worked so assiduously to attract in the Popular Front era. Aragon later claimed his *Les Voyageurs de l'im-*

périale, written in 1938–39, was aimed primarily at a condemnation of bourgeois individualism, like that manifested by his erstwhile friends among left-wing liberals: "*Les voyageurs de l'impériale* was in 1936 an enterprise of liquidation of individualism, that shaggy monster I encountered then (I am thinking of the Committee of Antifascist Intellectuals) that is, in the Popular Front years, as the stubborn adversary, the unconscious roadblock."[9]

The disintegration of the French Left was consummated by the signing in 1939 of the Germano-Soviet nonaggression pact, which flew in the face of five years of Communist antifascist propaganda. The pact dealt the fatal blow to the Association des Ecrivains et des Artistes Révolutionnaires, once the meeting place of Communist and non-Communist intellectuals of the Left, and put an end to any hopes that non-Communist opponents of fascism had placed in the Soviet Union. Simone de Beauvoir speaks for herself and Sartre—and, quite probably, for many others—when she writes of her reactions to the pact, "Through the dark gathering clouds one great gleam of hope had shown until now; but the morning's news had extinguished it. Night was falling over the earth, and entering our very bones.[10] Of the writers in this study, most deeply affected by the news was Nizan, who immediately resigned his party membership. He condemned not the Soviet Union, which, he felt, had acted in the interests of self-preservation, but the French Communist party, which had failed to separate its position from that of the Soviets.[11] Although Nizan seems not to have wavered from his fundamental commitment to the Communist cause, he did not live long enough to consider returning to the party when, under the pressure of Hitler's attack on Russia, it launched its own Resistance network. After the war, Nizan was treated as a traitor by his former colleagues, who sought to bury his work and reputation as thoroughly as a fellow soldier had buried the manuscripts he had been working on at the time of his death. Only the continuing support of his friend Sartre and Nizan's appeal to a new generation of young radicals in the 1960s would save his work from oblivion. Of the left-wing writers in this study, Aragon alone remained unshaken in his Communist loyalty, calmly turning out his editorial for *Ce Soir* on the day he received word of the pact and continuing his work on *Les Voyageurs de l'impériale* while hiding in the Chilean embassy from French patriots who condemned the Soviet action.[12]

The French Right had not experienced the same defeats as the

Left, yet right-wing writers seemed to share in the pessimistic attitudes of their left-wing colleagues. The era of Popular Front domination of the French political scene had only strengthened their
original belief in French decadence. The Right was, of course, particularly critical of the Popular Front's foreign policy, which, they con-
tended, had alienated potential fascist allies and had, at the same
time, reduced French military and industrial readiness for war. But,
above all, the Right was discouraged by its own inability to create a
powerful, unified movement capable of assuming leadership of the
nation. Drieu la Rochelle and other intellectuals were already dropping out of Doriot's Parti populaire français, which had once promised to effect right-wing unification, and the Right as a whole, like
the Left, was beginning to disintegrate as a political force. This was
due, in particular, to the increasing threat of war with Germany: traditional right-wing groups, like the Action française, insisted on
maintaining their long-standing anti-German stance, while the
newer, fascist movements, like Brasillach's team on *Je suis partout*,
showed a more sympathetic attitude toward the Nazis.

Of the writers who continued their writing of fiction in the decade's last years—as we have seen, this category excludes Céline,
Guilloux, Malraux, and, of course, Dabit—many evidenced a feeling
of having reached the end of an era. Unable to project their characters toward a future about which they no longer wanted to specu-
late, they characteristically turned back to look at the process that
had led them to their present position. In 1937 and 1939 Drieu la
Rochelle published two novels whose length far exceeded any of his
earlier works. In their pages he undertook an extensive analysis of
his own personal past: his parental background in *Rêveuse Bourgeoisie* and his own postwar experience in *Gilles*. Aragon too went
back into his familial past for the subject of *Les Voyageurs de l'impériale*,
whose protagonist is a fictional incarnation of his maternal grandfather. As we have seen, both Nizan and Brasillach, in novels that
spanned the interwar years, began to retrace the steps that had led to
their own political commitments. Brasillach continued this reflection during his military service and even during his subsequent captivity; even as the Germans prepared their invasion of France, he
was finishing his memoirs of what he now knew was a closed historical period, an understanding conveyed by his title, *Notre Avant-
guerre*.

Many of the novels produced in this end-of-the-decade period end in catastrophe—war or, at least, the death of the protagonist. In 1939 Aragon finally brings his novelistic cycle, *Le Monde Réel*, up to the actual outbreak of a war that had only threatened during the first two volumes. As early as 1937 Martin du Gard had brought his own series up to the first moments of World War I and had, at the same time, killed off Jacques Thibault; in his 1940 *Epilogue* he records the last moments of Jacques's older brother, Antoine. In the Epilogue he attaches to *Gilles*, Drieu in 1939 creates an improbable catastrophic situation for his protagonist, so that he too can finish his life in a burst of violence.

Many writers sensed that the world they had known was about to disappear forever. Aragon later described the feeling of haste that had spurred the composition of *Les Voyageurs de l'impériale* as "this testimony to a universe that was going to become completely incomprehensible and, as I well knew, would soon be submerged." [13] Brasillach, finishing his memoirs in February 1940, speaks of the between-war years as "already far away, buried." [14] With the defeat of France itself, there was a widespread impression that all traditional meaning and value had suddenly disappeared from the universe, leaving a world that had to be discovered anew. De Beauvoir records a feeling of this sort: "Then, suddenly, History burst over me, and I dissolved into fragments. . . . All my ideas and values were turned upside down; even the pursuit of happiness lost its importance. . . . I was obliged to rediscover my links with a universe the very face of which I had forgotten." [15]

The complete political and moral breakdown of their own generation led certain writers, like Drieu la Rochelle, to despair. But it caused others to look beyond the present moment for some deeper validation of human endeavor. The preoccupation with contemporary events so characteristic of the literature of the 1930s gives way at the outbreak of war to less time-bound philosophical speculation. Only the two writers at the opposite extremes of the political spectrum, apparently sustained by the transhistorical values of their respective political creeds, seemed able immediately to take a long view of the event and to retain some confidence in the future vindication of their beliefs. Aragon continued to urge the necessity of political commitment in the conclusion of *Les Voyageurs de l'impériale*, although, in the reality of the French defeat, he returned to poetic forms of expression. Brasillach in *Les Sept Couleurs* and the un-finished *Les Captifs* calmly envisaged a fascist future, troubled only by the prospect of his own aging.

Sartre had already begun to develop resources capable of dealing with this collapse of values, which was, after all, a historical valida-tion of his fundamental perception of the inherent meaninglessness of the world. Values, he had argued, are not "in the world" but spring from each individual act of choice. In his metaphysical speculation, Sartre had already faced a world devoid of traditional concepts of value, and in the short stories he published in 1939, as has been dis-cussed, he had even related this understanding to contemporary po-litical reality. In addition, he had begun to establish the basis of a future ethical stance, one that recognized the limitations of the hu-man condition and condemned bad faith efforts at self-justification.

Two others of the writers included in this study also attempted to come to terms with a world suddenly bereft of any historically based reasons for hope, a world they both portrayed in terms of the almost inevitable asphyxiation of human life. In the *Epilogue* of his Thibault chronicle, Martin du Gard follows the evolution of a man suddenly forced to come to terms with both the fact of his own mor-tality and the irrationality of the forces governing the historical pro-cess. Malraux, for whom the absurdity of the human condition had been a point of departure, took longer to work out in fictional terms his response to the failure of his effort to combat this absurdity through participation in revolutionary action. Only in 1941, as he composed *Les Noyers de l'Altenburg*, does he, like Martin du Gard, begin to work out in fiction an ethic of human continuity capable of transcending historical defeat.

Epilogue

Epilogue,[16] the last volume of Martin du Gard's Thibault series, could serve as an appropriate epilogue to the entire decade. The novel is dominated by images of asphyxiation and incurable illness, appropriate to the state of the last of the Thibaults, who is slowly dying in a clinic for victims of poison gas. But the moribund situa-tion of Antoine Thibault in 1918 is also the source of sinister allu-sions to the fate of Europe in 1938–39, the period of the novel's composition. Ironically, its publication was delayed until January 1940, so that this meditation on the armistice of World War I appeared after the outbreak of hostilities between France and Germany in World War II.

Critics who saluted its appearance in the dark days of 1940 variously interpreted *Epilogue* as an invitation to keep hope alive or a statement of resignation to the general despair.[17] Certainly, this story of a man facing a slow but inevitable death is the most deeply pessimistic volume of *Les Thibault*. That this pessimism accorded with the state of mind of Martin du Gard himself at this period in his life is suggested by his correspondence of the early 1940s, which Schalk characterizes as "in a uniformly apocalyptic vein,"[18] and his inability to bring to fruition any subsequent literary project. His colleague Jean Paulhan, who saw much of Martin du Gard at the *Nouvelle Revue Française*, saw in *Epilogue* "despair without recourse . . . an absolute pessimism."[19]

Such despair was also implied by Martin du Gard's complete withdrawal from public life. By September 1939 he had had to abandon the faint hopes inspired by his fervent pacifism and to resign himself to the inevitability of another war with Germany. The mild hope he had expressed in his 1937 Nobel Prize acceptance speech, that Europe might yet be able to benefit from "the pathetic lesson of the past," had subsequently given way to a more despairing rhetoric. He repeats in his own correspondence of 1938 the desperate phrase his Jacques Thibault had uttered on the eve of war in *L'Eté 1914*, "anything rather than war." And in a pacifist declaration he wrote for the Rassemblement universel pour la paix in 1938, he uses the terminology he was at the same time putting into the mouth of a disillusioned Antoine: war is irredeemably "monstrous." As Martin du Gard points out in his own manifesto, the monstrosity of war is not limited to the bombing of innocent civilian populations: "What is monstrous is war itself." These words are echoed verbatim by Antoine in *Epilogue*. But more monstrous still, in Martin du Gard's view, was the failure of the peoples of Europe to create against the war "that vast movement of defense and fraternal cooperation that alone can assure the salvation of all."[20] But this statement, printed on July 30, 1938, was to be his last public utterance of this belief.

Only a year later even this desperate pacifism had ceased, and Martin du Gard was telling young people who sought his advice not to regard Jacques Thibault's conscientious objection as a model. He described his feelings of that era to Jacques Brenner in 1951: "There, I thought, that is my influence on the young. Alas! the war for some time had seemed to me to be inevitable, and I hoped that Nazi Germany would be defeated as rapidly as possible."[21]

Antoine in *Epilogue* is condemned to watch the slow process of his own asphyxiation, as the residual effects of poison gas manifest themselves in his damaged lungs. Martin du Gard describes the multiple symptoms of Antoine's physical degeneration in the same exhaustive detail he had previously used in narrating the death of his father, and Antoine's gradual decline is the novel's governing structural principle. As the work progresses, Antoine's sphere of activity becomes more and more limited. At first, he suffers only from loss of voice and attacks of coughing, but gradually he loses his former strength, as his lungs become increasingly infected and his heart begins to fail.

The progress of the disease is reflected in the narration. *Epilogue* begins with a third-person account of Antoine's trip to Paris to attend the funeral of his old housekeeper and to visit his remaining relatives and friends. Antoine's discussions with the diplomat Rumelles, his old teacher Dr. Philip, and the members of the Fontanin family give Martin du Gard an opportunity to bring out and discuss the events of the four years that have intervened since the ending of *L'Eté 1914*. Somewhat reminiscent of those that had proliferated in the preceding volume, these discussions are subdued in tone and greatly restricted in length and scope: in length because Antoine's condition prohibits him from sustaining a long conversation, and in scope because Antoine and Martin du Gard seem interested not in the minutiae of the battlefield events but only in the general pattern they form and its implications for the future. As Antoine returns to his clinic, bringing with him the sudden recognition that his case is hopeless, *Epilogue* for a time engages in the more restricted dialogue of an epistolary novel before narrowing still further into the monologue of Antoine's journal. The journal itself becomes fragmentary, the style more telegraphic, as Antoine's strength slowly fails him.

The fading capacities of Antoine's scarred lungs and the increasing confinement of his personal world are reflected in his repeated use of images of suffocation to describe the European political situation. This imagery is an intensification of the themes of asphyxiation that have run through the literature of the decade. Antoine compares the Wilsonian proposals for international cooperation to the oxygen pumped in to save miners trapped in a collapsed mineshaft, an image appropriate to the men still underground in the wartime trenches. A temptation to view men as essentially destructive brutes, a pessimistic vision that the war has suggested, must be rejected because it provides no breathable atmosphere: "Ca mène à des bas-fonds où l'air n'est plus respirable" (p. 367). And even long afterward, like the poison gas that lingers in the trenches, the consequences of the war will pollute the atmosphere; Antoine warns his young nephew, "Il faudra des poumons solides pour respirer cet air vicié" (p. 397).[b] When the world situation is viewed from Antoine's vantage point of 1918, these images of release from potential suffocation seem to suggest that the European world, long buried in the hopeless darkness of the war, is about to emerge into a future that, if troubled, at least holds forth great possibilities.

But Martin du Gard uses the imagery of asphyxiation ironically. In Antoine's personal case, both he and the reader are aware that the process is irreversible: soon no oxygen will be absorbed by his damaged lungs. And the reader knows that this is also true of the historical situation. In *Epilogue*, much more than in *L'Eté 1914*, there is clearly an ironic double perspective on history. While Antoine in 1918 tries to imagine the postwar era, both author and reader, by the end of the 1930s, are well aware of what has really happened. Although Martin du Gard does not adopt Aragon's device of making direct allusions to events subsequent to the narrative, he actively invites the reader's recognition of historical irony by allowing Antoine to make manifestly false predictions about the future. At one point, for example, he imagines that his nephew Jean-Paul, in the "pacific" reconstructed Europe of 1940, will be incapable of understanding the attitudes of the young men who went off to war in 1914. And he envisions the Germany of the 1930s as republican, patriachal, hard-working, and pacific, one of the most solid guarantees of European unity.

In fact, all Antoine's hopes for the future are doomed to failure, as author and reader well know. By allowing him to indulge in these evidently naïve speculations, Martin du Gard is, even more overtly than in *L'Eté 1914*, using a historical setting to analyze the events of his own time. Like his character, who can see all the facts of his case in their true light only after having diagnosed it as incurable, Martin

---

[b]Such thoughts drag a man down into an abyss whence there is no escaping (p. 958). . . . Lungs of steel will be need to cope with that polluted atmosphere (p. 979).

du Gard can now look back at the interwar years to see how events had once again resulted in war. Both medical and historical cases are hopeless, but, like Antoine, who keeps a record of his symptoms in the hope it may be helpful to medical science in the future, Martin du Gard still seems to find some value in the task of seeing what had gone wrong, even though the lesson can no longer be of any immediate benefit. He has apparently adopted the attitude toward history stated by the wisely skeptical Philip: "La seule attitude raisonnable . . . c'est *la recherche* de l'erreur, et non pas la recherche de la vérité" (p. 290).[c]

Martin du Gard's analysis of the postwar period, as it appears through the speculations of Antoine, is quite simple. Wilsonian ideals, which alone offered a possibility of peace, had been betrayed by the victorious European powers, with their residues of chauvinism and imperialism. Martin du Gard is clearly aware of German imperialistic tendencies and their threat to a European equilibrium. Yet he feels that enlightened postwar policies on the part of the Allies could have prevented the reemergence of this dangerous force. While the onus for aggression must, in his view, be borne by Germany, Martin du Gard blames France for having lost the peace after winning the war: "Il dépend de nous, si nous sommes vainqueurs . . . que cette Allemagne malfaisante disparaisse" (p. 391).[d] Like Antoine reviewing his failure to take the proper precautions immediately after his exposure to the poison gas, Martin du Gard sees what measures could have been taken only after the damage has been done.

Martin du Gard's views of political action are much more negative in *Epilogue* than in *L'Eté 1914*. In 1914 Jacques had been able to find some inspiration in the intelligent and courageous leadership of a Jaurès and in the fraternal spirit of the demonstrations for peace. These hopes were, of course, treated ironically: Jaurès was assassinated, and the peace marchers soon marched off to war with equal willingness. Nevertheless, Jacques's experience left some room for a positive view of political involvement, which reflected Martin du Gard's own fascination with politics in the early 1930s. By the time of *Epilogue*, however, such temptations are firmly rejected. At

[c]The only rational method . . . is the tracking down of error, *not* the search for truth (p. 901).
[d]It depends on us, if we win this war . . . whether this maleficent spirit is or is not to persist in post-war Germany (p. 975).

the Fontanins', Antoine condemns Jenny's uncritical parroting of Jacques's socialist doctrines, which he puts on a level with her mother's mindless chauvinism. And as for the Russian Revolution, he sees it as an incomprehensible chaos. Antoine realizes that the sacrifice of independent thought is always dangerous, whatever the reasons, and that political doctrines offer only an illusory comfort for the weak-minded. He warns Jean-Paul specifically, "Ne te laisse pas affilier," (p. 398),ᵉ words that sum up the sad conclusion Martin du Gard had drawn from the political agitation of the 1930s.

An even less flattering view is given of establishment politics through Antoine's old patient, the diplomat Rumelles. Previously an apparently well-meaning statesman of limited vision, Rumelles assumes more sinister dimensions as he sits across from the dying Antoine in Maxim's, complacently reviewing the catastrophe he has helped to orchestrate. He reveals that even the great leaders like Clemenceau have had no real control over events, a fact that has not prevented them from effectively manipulating public opinion, as they had quite shamelessly done during the crises of 1917. Rumelles's cynical presentation of the realities of government serves to render even more illusory Jacques's—and, apparently at one time, Martin du Gard's—faith in the pacifist action of the masses. Even those who have access to the facts cannot seem to direct history as they wish, and the people are denied even that advantage.

Rejecting the possibility of political involvement, Antoine attempts to construct a model of moral action on the level of the individual that would be adapted to the newly understood reality of the modern world. A secular model, deprived even of the "mystical" faith of the revolutionary, it is epitomized by the figure of the doctor. Camus, who brought forth a strikingly similar doctor-hero from the chaos of World War II, recognized the significance of such a figure in the world of Martin du Gard: "Of Martin du Gard's two major characters, the priest and the doctor, the first has practically disappeared. *Les Thibault* ends on the death of a doctor among other doctors."²² Again and again throughout his journal, Antoine refers to his profession and offers the attitude and activity of the medical practitioner as a general model for his nephew. His profession has instilled in him the habit of taking into account only knowledge verified by practical experience and of regarding each situation before

ᵉRefuse to become a "party man"! (p. 980)

him with fresh eyes: "Toute maladie—et, pareillement, toute crise sociale—se présente comme un cas premier, sans précédent identique, comme un cas *exceptionnel*, pour lequel une thérapeutique nouvelle est toujours à inventer" (p. 399).[f] His scientific lucidity can recognize the limits of his own knowledge and the limit of human efforts in death. Yet the doctor continues to strive, daunted neither by the certainty of ultimate failure nor the absence of an overarching cosmic plan within which human moral efforts might be inscribed.

Antoine's distaste for his father's religious authoritarianism, combined with his own inability to give credence to realities beyond human experience, have led him to reject the traditional Christian concept of the universe. His secular convictions are so firmly rooted in his being that, unlike Martin du Gard's troubled prewar protagonist, Jean Barois, he is not tempted to make a deathbed conversion. For this generation, the loss of the Christian promise of immortality is no longer tragic but merely a fact. Like Camus's Stranger, of whom he is surely a precursor, Antoine sends away the hospital chaplain and finds momentary solace in contemplating the indifferent vastness of the night sky. And the image he proposes of human activity is as ultimately purposeless as that of Camus's Sisyphus. He compares humanity's efforts with the games of children he has seen playing in a hospital recreation room. During the play period, the children use multicolored blocks to build structures that vary according to their differing abilities; when they leave, the blocks are left scattered over the floor. Yet, despite this ultimate defeat of his aspirations in death, Antoine feels that each person is called upon to put forth his best creative efforts: "Les plus doués cherchent à faire de leur vie une construction compliquée, une véritable oeuvre d'art. Il faut tâcher d'être parmi ceux-là, pour que la récréation soit aussi amusante que possible" (pp. 407–408).[g] This vision of mankind holds forth a certain ideal of absurd courage. Taken by itself, however, it would seem to provide little incentive for human moral endeavor.

But this cyclical vision of purposeless creation and destruction, corresponding to the finite lives of individuals, is modified by An-

---

[f] Each illness—and similarly, each social crisis—presents itself as a first case without identical precedent, as an *exceptional* case for which a new therapy has to be invented (translation mine).

[g] The most gifted try to make of their lives a complicated edifice, a real work of art. One should try to be among the gifted, for it is they who get the most fun out of the game (p. 987).

toine's discovery of a deeper reason for hope in the continuity of mankind as a whole and, especially, of the peculiarly human moral consciousness. Antoine first begins to suspect the presence of this moral consciousness at work in his own life: it has been the force behind his self-sacrificing efforts to alleviate the sufferings of others, which fly in the face of his intellectual denial of the traditional justifications for morality. This contradiction between his own acts and his intellectual theories has given rise to his perennial question, "In the name of what?" A representative fictional hero of the 1930s, he has always preferred action to theorizing—"Principe: renoncer aux 'pourquoi,' se contenter des 'comment'" (p. 374) [h]—but now, as his strength fails, he can do nothing but contemplate the sum of his acts. And, despite his intellectual admission that, logically, "all is permitted," his own acts form a pattern of altruistic behavior that Antoine is at a loss to explain. His intuitive morality and that which he observes in other men can only be attributed to some innate moral sensitivity that has survived or developed through the unbroken chain of generations that have led to his existence. This insight does not imply that moral progress is inevitable or instantaneous. Dr. Philip thinks it may take several generations to bring about a European equilibrium, and Antoine, in a particularly despairing moment, thinks it may well be thousands of years before man can justify hope. Yet he is buoyed by his biological vision of a world where all forms of life tend toward improvement: "*Foi dans une accession universelle à des états supérieurs*" (p. 376).[i] In the face of his own personal dissolution and the political disaster of World War I, Antoine still manages to maintain hope for the future, through a completely secular belief in the continuity of mankind's moral endeavors.

Les Noyers de l'Altenburg

Les Noyers de l'Altenburg,[23] the final work of Malraux's career as a novelist, stands in relation to his earlier work much as *Epilogue* stands in relation to *Les Thibault*. Like *Epilogue*, it is more a meditation than a novel of characters and events. In *Les Noyers* Malraux engages in the same sort of speculation as Martin du Gard and reaches a strikingly similar conclusion. Faced with the apparent failure of his

[h] The wise man dispenses with the whys, contents himself with the hows (p. 963).
[i] I believe in a universal movement toward ever-higher planes (p. 965).

political causes—first, defeat in the Spanish Civil War, and then the fall of France itself—Malraux, like Martin du Gard, seems to feel compelled to look back at his past life and work in order to see which of his former values remain. And, like Martin du Gard, he finally affirms a notion of human continuity that surpasses narrow limitations of time and space. In 1940, with the momentary defeat of efforts to act in history, the preoccupation with the here and now that had characterized the 1930s gives place to values capable of rising above a humiliating present.

Les Noyers de l'Altenburg imposes itself as a rare exception to the original restriction of this study to works of the 1930s. Written in the aftermath of defeat in 1941 and not published until 1943 in Switzerland, Malraux's last novel nevertheless takes its rightful place in the literature that marks the close of the interwar period. Like *Epilogue*, *Les Noyers* looks back to World War I as it attempts to absorb the more recent shock of a new military confrontation. And Malraux must face additional knowledge, which had been hidden from Martin du Gard in 1939, of the invasion and collapse of his own country.

The narrator of *Les Noyers* is an Alsatian named Berger, prophetically the name Malraux himself was later to assume as commander of the Alsace-Lorraine Brigade in the Resistance. The fictional Berger has fought as a tank commander in the brief war and is, in 1940, in a German prison camp, along with thousands of other defeated Frenchmen. Like the many retrospective narrators of the war novels with which this study began, he looks back to the battlefields of World War I. The experience he remembers, however, is not his own but his father's, which had been preserved for him in notes and memoirs. The single scene of combat, the most vividly narrated section in the novel, takes place during an experimental gas attack by the Germans on the Russian front. Vincent Berger, the narrator's father (who was, as an Alsatian, then fighting on the German side), is present as an intelligence officer accompanying the inventor of this new variant of poison gas, one that destroys vegetation as well as killing men.

The recurrence of the theme of poison gas in both *Epilogue* and *Les Noyers de l'Altenburg* invites speculation. The characteristic war scenes in novels written earlier in the decade had shown men wandering in trenches or trapped in shell holes. The use of poison gas was sometimes mentioned with horror, but it was not depicted as representative or even symbolic of the war experience. Yet, at the end of the 1930s, begin to appear important fictional heroes like Antoine Thibault and Vincent Berger who succumb to poison gas. It is an image more related to the images of asphyxiation that appear in much literature of the 1930s. Malraux points to a possible reason for his concentration on poison gas: it is a weapon that renders men completely helpless. The inventor complacently explains this advantage of his weapon to one of Vincent Berger's colleagues: "Si je crois que j'ai ma chance, même infinie, je suis courageux, mais si je sais du fond du coeur que je ne l'ai pas, il n'y a plus de courage qui tienne. Rien à faire" (p. 179).[j] Thus the effects of poison gas are appropriate to express the sense of helplessness felt by men like Martin du Gard and Malraux who, despite all their efforts, found themselves trapped in a hopeless historical impasse. This feeling of entrapment is also reflected in the incident of the tank trap at the novel's conclusion; here, however, Malraux has already begun to work out his personal response, and the men in the tank trap are able to escape.

As a weapon, gas is even more inhuman than the other modern engines of destruction. In *Les Noyers*, the gas, seeming to advance independently of human agency, removes all trace of life from the landscape, reducing nature to a gooey black substance strewn with tiny corpses of animals and birds, horses and men. This inhumanity, too, seems to correspond to a pessimistic vision of history as a series of events that, like Hitler's tanks, move relentlessly on, crushing the best efforts of human beings. The narrator of *Les Noyers* comes to identify war with the medieval plague, and, indeed, poison gas shares several characteristics of the plague, which would emerge in the work of Camus as the major fictional image of World War II.

The poison gas in Malraux's novel gives birth not only to a sense of individual helplessness but also to an experience of fraternity not unlike the last moments of the revolutionaries in *La Condition humaine* and the descent from the mountain in *L'Espoir*, the latter a scene that seems to lead directly into *Les Noyers*. After the release of the gas, Vincent Berger is amazed to see that the German soldiers, forgetting their orders to attack, are retreating toward their own lines, each bearing on his back a gassed Russian. This affirmation of

---

[j] If I think I have a chance, even if it is infinitely small, I am brave, but if I know in my heart that I have none, there's nothing courage can do. Nothing to be done.

a common humanity extending beyond national borders recalls to him a colloquium he had recently attended at the Altenburg priory, where the speaker had questioned the possibility of identifying a human continuity that could transcend the specifics of time and place.

Modeled after the conferences at Pontigny that had been frequented by intellectuals like Gide and Martin du Gard in the 1920s, the colloquium at the Altenburg is organized in the novel by Vincent Berger's uncle, a noted historian. He has included his nephew among the famous guests because the young man has made a name for himself as a lecturer on Nietzsche at Constantinople University and, more importantly, as an adviser to Enver Pasha, the flamboyant young Turkish military leader. Drawing on his wide experience in the Islamic world, Berger can offer the gathered intellectuals some theories of art that can be identified with Malraux's own thought. Art, he says, is man's way of confronting destiny: "L'homme sait que le monde n'est pas à l'échelle humaine; et il voudrait qu'il le fût. . . . Notre art me paraît une rectification du monde, un moyen d'échapper à la condition d'homme" (p. 128).[k] This validation of art is a theme that Malraux was to take up in the postwar period, when meditation on art replaced the writing of fiction as the center of his creative activity. In *Les Noyers*, this statement serves to comment on the effort of the narrator, an effort parallel to that of Malraux himself. The young Berger is admittedly writing his narrative as a way of dealing with an apparently hopeless human condition: "Ici, écrire est le seul moyen de continuer à vivre" (p. 30).[l] By discovering and re-creating for himself and the reader a vision of human continuity that transcends the immediately apparent Pascalian vision of men condemned to death, the narrator is effecting a "rectification" of the world, restructuring it in purely human terms.

At the Altenburg colloquium, however, the words of Berger and of all the others are momentarily negated by the presentation of the German ethnologist Mollberg.[24] A world expert on African culture, Mollberg has just abandoned a major work on the continuity of human civilization and now feels convinced of an absence of such continuity and thus the absurdity of any permanent idea of man. When

---

[k] Man knows the world is not made to his measure; and he wishes it were. . . . Our art seems to be a rectification of the world, a way of escaping from the condition of man.

[l] Here writing is the only way of continuing to live.

asked whether even the common men of different epochs are separated by unbridgeable chasms, Mollberg answers contemptuously. Clearly, he is primarily concerned with artistic and intellectual elites: "Moins les hommes participent de leur civilisation et plus ils se ressemblent, d'accord! . . . On peut concevoir une permanence de l'homme, mais c'est une permanence dans le néant" (p. 145)." As he rejects the idea of the continuity of man, Mollberg similarly dismisses the suggestion that there is, symbolically, any link between the sculptures in the priory library, two Gothic statues and a more modern ship's figurehead, all made of walnut. In Mollberg's view, there is no "fundamental" walnut, only logs—just as there is no "fundamental man."

In his important Unesco speech of 1947, in which he begins to sketch out the theories of artistic creation that preoccupy him in the postwar years, Malraux refers to the type of argument presented by Mollberg. Here he terms it one specific to the Germans, one that has been designed to combat traditional judgments of German inferiority in the plastic arts.[25] Rieuneau points out that Spengler's theories, on which Mollberg's are based, had a profound influence on Hitler's *Mein Kampf*.[26] Thus, as Malraux answers Mollberg's contentions in 1941 in *Les Noyers de l'Altenburg*, he is also reaffirming traditional European concepts of cultural continuity against denials that originated in Germany.

At the Altenburg, as he listens to Mollberg's discourse, Vincent Berger watches the activity of the woodcutters outside the window, who repeat gestures unchanged since the Middle Ages. And as he strolls outside at the close of the afternoon session, he is struck by the appearance of two walnut trees, which recall to him Mollberg's denial of a "fundamental walnut." In front of the walnut trees, Berger has a lyrical vision that seems to crystallize his unarticulated opposition to Mollberg's theories: "La plénitude des arbres séculaires émanait de leur masse, mais l'effort par quoi sortaient de leurs énormes troncs les branches tordues, l'épanouissement en feuilles sombres de ce bois, si vieux et si lourd qu'il semblait s'enfoncer dans la terre et non s'en arracher, imposaient à la fois l'idée d'une volonté et d'une métamorphose sans fin" (p. 151)." Seeing the Strasbourg

---

"The less men participate in their civilization, the more they are alike, right . . . . One can conceive of a permanence in man, but it is a permanence in nothingness.

"The plenitude of the ancient trees emanated from their mass, but the effort by which the twisted branches emerged from their enormous trunks, the spreading

cathedral in the distance, he realizes that even this great monument of human effort is merely the backdrop ("un décor") for the walnut trees themselves. The vision of the walnuts is the answer given by Vincent Berger to the questions raised by Mollberg, and the title chosen for the published novel indicates that it was also the answer given by Malraux himself.

The walnut trees reappear at the scene of the gas attack, where they function to link this concrete experience of human fraternity with the previous year's discussion at the priory. This relationship on the level of symbol only serves to make evident the conceptual link between the two scenes. The lyrical insight of the walnut trees is validated by the actions of the German enlisted men, to whose banal conversations Vincent Berger has listened at great length while awaiting the release of the gas. These men, clearly meant to represent the "common man," affirm a basic human fraternity in the face of the inhuman world created by the all-destroying gas.

The father's vision is validated by the experience of the son. The opening and closing sections of *Les Noyers de l'Altenburg*, which form a frame for the three parts dealing with Vincent Berger, take place in May and June 1940. In the opening pages, the narrator lies with other wounded prisoners in the nave of Chartres Cathedral (this is not as improbable as it might at first appear: Malraux himself was a prisoner in the cathedral town of Sens; he has merely replaced one cathedral with another). All conspires to make the narrator aware of the links between the men of the present and their medieval ancestors. The absence of the great stained glass windows, which have been removed for their own protection, makes him feel he is in a cathedral under construction; the voices of the German interpreters giving instructions evoke the cries of the medieval beggars flanking the great doors. Most importantly, the faces of the men around him, with their unshaven beards, are rapidly beginning to resemble those of Gothic sculpture. Their pathetic persistence in attempting to communicate with their families, their peasant wisdom on planting and harvesting, their reversion to life in primitive shelters—all underline their basic identity with men of the distant past. These parallels recur in the closing section, where the narrator recalls the men of his

---

forth in dark leaves of this wood, so old and heavy it seemed to sink into the earth and not tear itself from it, imposed at the same time the idea of a will and an unending metamorphosis.

tank crew, again representatives of various types of "common man," and the ordeal they have undergone together in a German tank trap, from which they have succeeded in escaping. The novel closes the following morning with a resurgence of life and an affirmation of human continuity communicated through the face of an old peasant woman.

As W. M. Frohock has noted, *Les Noyers de l'Altenburg* is almost transparently Malraux's contemplation of his own life and work.[27] The narrator is a writer in a prisoner of war camp, the situation in which Malraux found himself at the same period. Vincent Berger, the father, is an adventurer (in the Middle East rather than the Far East, but the effect is the same), an observer/participant in combat, and at least a dabbler in art history. He thus shows affinities both with Malraux's fictional heroes and with Malraux himself. In *Les Noyers de l'Altenburg*, then, Malraux, much like Martin du Gard a few years earlier, is attempting to distill from his fifteen years of active involvement in the fast-moving events of his time those values that retain some meaning in the face of the present catastrophe. He is thus much like the prisoner mentioned at the Altenburg, who finds that only three works of literature(*Don Quixote, Robinson Crusoe,* and *The Idiot*) can stand up to the experience of imprisonment. While, in both Berger *père* and *fils*, Malraux retains his familiar character of the adventurer-hero, this figure is redefined by the new context in which he is placed. The idea of humanity in *Les Noyers* and at the very end of *L'Espoir* has been enlarged to include the common man. As in the descent from the mountain, the central characters are surrounded by and become blended with the mass of ordinary peasants and workers. Malraux's world is no longer one where larger-than-life figures carry on anguished dialogues on an empty stage or before a dimly-lit chorus. In *Les Noyers de l'Altenburg* the many elements of the chorus have begun to step forward to assume separate identities, to speak in their own voices. The intellectual dialogues continue, but they are subject to criticism if they move too far from concrete reality: the narrator has intervened in the Altenburg discussions to point out that "une idée y naissait jamais d'un fait: toujours d'une autre idée" (p. 114).° The pointless conversations of the German soldiers, the words of the French peasants, are given equal attention with the words of the intellectuals.

° An idea was never engendered by a fact: always by another idea

This new emphasis on the common man represents, as Frohock notes, a major shift in attitude.[28] At the end of *La Condition humaine*, Malraux had tried to provide a counterweight to the deaths of his individual heroes by showing that the ideals for which they had fought and died lived on in the anonymous laboring masses, while the projects of the capitalist Ferral were torn to pieces by the self-interested Parisian bankers. But this assertion of continuity lacked emotional force, and the real argument had been made in the lyrical description of the deaths of Kyo and Katow. Now in 1941, faced with the apparent defeat of the causes for which he himself had fought, Malraux seeks once again in the mass of men a promise of continuity. In the "poem of the walnuts" he affirms that the ideal of human dignity can continue to realize itself in history despite momentary setbacks. Man's civilizations are not obliterated but continue to transmit their fundamental values through the plagues and wars of history. The French defeat in 1940 seems to have forced Malraux to call into question the importance of specific political doctrines—Communism, for example, which had played such an important role in *Le Temps du mépris* and *L'Espoir*, is conspicuously absent from *Les Noyers de l'Altenburg*.[29] But the collapse of some values has brought into focus a deeper commitment to a human fraternity based not on political ideals but on a shared participation in the fundamental effort to assert human will against a hostile universe.

A Literary Summation

Both *Epilogue* and *Les Noyers de l'Altenburg* offer an intensification and, in many ways, a summation of what have emerged as the major images and themes of the works of fiction I have examined. Both these novels, for example, are dominated by the images of suffocation and entrapment that have appeared throughout the fiction of the decade. The plight of Drieu's soldiers, pinned down in a shell hole of World War I, is not very different from that of Malraux's, stuck in a tank trap of World War II. Martin du Gard's Antoine is in the final stages of a process of asphyxiation that had begun in the oppressive commercial *passage* of *Mort à crédit*, the life-denying society of *Le Sang noir*, the crushing poverty of *Le Cheval de Troie*, the sealed mine of *Le Temps du mépris*. The societal forces that had crushed the characters of the early part of the decade are in *Epilogue* and *Les Noyers de l'Altenburg* transformed into poison gas, a weapon of the war that is destined to complete the process of destruction.

The idea of slow but inevitable death and dissolution is also suggested by the viscous substances that threaten to engulf the characters of Céline, Drieu and Sartre, before reappearing in the war scene portrayed by Malraux in *Les Noyers de l'Altenburg*. It also appears in the fatal illnesses—the sickness of an entire society reflected in the health of the individual—that attack a large number of fictional characters—Drieu's Pauline in *Gilles*, Bardamu's doomed patients, Dabit's tubercular Helen, Aragon's paralyzed Pierre Mercadier, and, finally, Martin du Gard's Antoine Thibault. Perhaps because of their belief in the promise of their doctrine, the Communist writers allow some of their protagonists to survive: Aragon lets his tubercular Catherine recover, and Nizan resurrects the student Laforgue in *La Conspiration*. Omnipresent images of death and sterility reflect an almost unanimous condemnation of the existing society on the part of these writers. They dominate the rural society of Martin du Gard's *Vieille France* as well as his extinguished Thibault family, the bourgeois world portrayed by Nizan and Aragon as well as that of Drieu. The numerous suicides that occur in the work of Aragon, Nizan, Guilloux, Dabit, Drieu, and Céline, and the frequent miscarriages and abortions that threaten women's lives in the fiction of Aragon, Céline, Drieu, and Nizan—all testify to a world whose energies are bent toward destruction rather than creation. These images of death find their culmination at the end of the decade in the renewed experience of war.

The violence of war itself is a central theme for those who treat World War I—Céline, Guilloux, Drieu, Aragon, Dabit, and Martin du Gard, who are now joined by Malraux. The war in Spain attracts the literary attention of Malraux, Drieu, Brasillach, and Sartre; and even Nizan, who does not write directly about war in any of his published works, describes scenes of physical violence on French streets in *Le Cheval de Troie*, as does Sartre in "L'Enfance d'un chef." War was for some writers of the 1930s a theater of action, a form of action particularly privileged in the work of Drieu. For most of the others, with the notable exception of Martin du Gard, violent action was attractive only as part of a revolutionary movement, where it was the expression of an ideology; such was the case with Malraux, Brasillach, Nizan, Aragon, and even the pacific Guilloux. The avowed aim of most of these writers was to conciliate the demands of action and thought, participation and observation, politics and art. This was a central theme of all Malraux's novels of the 1930s, and it was he who coined the phrase that best summed up the ideal: "transformer en conscience une expérience aussi large que possible." [p] The intellectual's participation in action was urged by Drieu as well as by Nizan and Aragon, and the issue was seriously debated by Martin du Gard. Even the nonviolent Guilloux condemned the passive intellectual and elevated the figure of the revolutionary. But beside the figures of warriors and revolutionaries, which are highly visible in the fiction of the 1930s, other models of action begin to emerge, particularly toward the end of the decade.

Céline always grants a privileged status to those characters who struggle courageously against engulfment in the filth of existence while, at the same time, making life more bearable for others. The figures of Alcide and Molly in *Voyage au bout de la nuit*, Grandmother Caroline and Uncle Edouard in *Mort à Crédit*, are moral ideals whose essential attitude toward life is also embodied in the profession that Céline's protagonist ultimately adopts, that of the doctor. Here he joins Martin du Gard, for whom Antoine's devotion to his medical duties, rather than Jacques's revolutionary agitation, becomes an ethical model. The figure of the artisan, patiently continuing his humble creative task through the vicissitudes of human existence, plays a central role in Guilloux's fiction, although he is for a time partially obscured by the revolutionary. And Malraux links his soldiers and political militants with the humble peasants and workers who also participate in their struggle. As the warrior characters, like Drieu's Gilles, are destroyed by their own violence at the end of the decade, these less warlike figures come to symbolize the possibilities of action that endure.

Surprisingly, the writers I have examined give little attention in their fiction to the role of the artist. A significant exception is Malraux, whose political militants, like Kassner in *Le Temps du mépris*, make a continual effort to bring artistic order out of the contemporary political chaos; it is to this task that Malraux's narrator returns in *Les Noyers de l'Altenburg*. Sartre, too, suggests in *La Nausée* that artistic creation could provide a means of combatting the absurdity

---

[p] converting as wide a range of experience as possible into conscious thought (p. 396)

that dominates the short stories in *Le Mur*. Other writers are less explicit about the role of the artist. It is clear, however, that the attitudes and work of the doctor in Martin du Gard and Céline are not far distant from their conception of their own literary activities. And Guilloux would later identify himself as an artisan of letters, allying himself with his humble characters. In their attempt to explore the meaning of the events of their time, the characters of Nizan and Brasillach also implicitly validate the artistic endeavor.

The last fictional works of Martin du Gard and Malraux also illustrate the increasing limitation of narrative perspective that seems to characterize the novels of the end of the decade. As we have seen, Martin du Gard has moved from the broad canvas of *L'Eté 1914*, with its many characters and multifaceted discussions, to the solitary reflections of a dying man's journal. In *Les Noyers de l'Altenburg*, Malraux too abandons the scope of his previous novel, *L'Espoir*, where a collective experience of massive proportions had called forth a multiplicity of perspectives. In contrast, the single narrator of *Les Noyers* is spiritually isolated among his fellow prisoners of war, and he tells his father's story as he knows it, from his father's limited point of view. Aragon, too, restricts the omniscience of his narrator in the third volume of *Le Monde Réel*, describing the outbreak of war from the extremely limited perspective of characters who have lost their capacity to understand what is happening. Drieu la Rochelle had consistently made use of limited perspectives in his previous short fiction, but in *Gilles*, the only point of view in almost 700 pages is that of the increasingly isolated protagonist. Even Brasillach's *Les Sept Couleurs*, with its varying modes of narration, moves from the omniscience of the beginning to the interior monologue of an isolated character at the end. Sartre's short stories all use an intentionally limited point of view; indeed, one of the many walls suggested by the collection's title is that which separates one individual's perception of reality from another. The narrator of "Le Mur" is never able to overcome his alienation, and Lucien Fleurier has deepened his own isolation from others while falsely believing himself part of a group. The use of a limited point of view, that of one or more characters, has emerged as a characteristic of the fiction of all the writers examined, with the exception of the Communists, Aragon (before *Les Voyageurs de l'impériale*) and Nizan. The latter often has recourse to an omniscient narrator, and, like Malraux, experiments with the use of a collective point of view. In his last novel, *La Conspiration*, however, Nizan makes much greater use of the limited perspectives of the characters. By the end of the decade, visions of fraternal unity seem largely to have failed, and the notion of a collective vision of reality seems to have been lost, along with other traditional values.

Yet from the isolated perspective of dying or imprisoned characters placed in a collapsing world, Martin du Gard and Malraux are able to draw a statement of reaffirmed faith in humanity. Such a reaffirmation of faith in human possibility, as Frenchmen were experiencing their moment of deepest humiliation, pointed the way toward moral recovery, a necessary prelude to resistance and military liberation. Martin du Gard's tentative faith in a continuing human moral consciousness, and, even more strongly, Malraux's lyrical affirmation of a permanent idea of man showed that deeper and more enduring values could survive the collapse of the superficial and transitory. *Les Noyers de l'Altenburg* already participates in the spirit of a new era, when writers like Camus and Sartre, as well as Malraux himself in his nonfiction, would find new reasons to place hope in human action, even against the background of what would increasingly be perceived as an absurd world.

Notes

Chapter 1: A New Consciousness of History

1. André Malraux, forward to Monique Saint-Claire, *Les Cahiers de la petite dame*, Cahiers André Gide 4 (Paris: Gallimard, 1973), p. xxiv.

2. Paul Nizan, *Pour une Nouvelle Culture*, ed. Susan Suleiman (Paris: Grasset, 1971), p. 143.

3. This was the title of a book written by Henri Daniel-Rops in 1932.

4. Paul Valéry, "La Crise de l'esprit," *Nouvelle Revue Française*, Aug. 1919, p. 325.

5. For an excellent analysis of this group, see Robert Wohl, *The Generation of 1914* (Cambridge, Mass.: Harvard University Press, 1979).

6. Claude-Edmonde Magny, *Histoire du roman français depuis 1918* (1950; reprint, Paris: Points, 1971), p. 18.

7. Jean-Paul Sartre, *Qu'est-ce que la littérature?* (1948; reprint, Paris: Gallimard, Collection Idées, 1972), p. 228.

8. Paul Nizan, *La Conspiration* (1939; reprint, Paris: Folio, 1973), p. 65. All citations in my text refer to this edition.

9. Ibid., p. 66.

10. Magny, *Histoire du roman français*, p. 43.

11. Maurice Sachs, *Le Sabbat* (Paris: Corrêa,.1946), pp. 99–100.

12. Robert Brasillach, "La Fin de l'après-guerre," *La Revue Universelle* 46 (July 15, 1931): 251.

13. Jean-Pierre Maxence, *Histoire de dix ans 1927–1937* (Paris: Gallimard, 1939), p. 63.

14. Magny, *Histoire du roman français*, p. 48.

15. Brasillach, "La Fin de l'après-guerre."

16. Albert Thibaudet, *Histoire de la littérature française de 1789 à nos jours* (Paris: Stock, 1936), p. 522.

17. See especially Magny, *Histoire du roman français*; Pierre-Henri Simon, *Histoire de la littérature française au XXe siècle 1900–1950*, 3d ed. (Paris: Armand Colin, 1957); Gaeton Picon, *Panorama de la nouvelle littérature* (Paris: Gallimard, 1960); Maurice Nadeau, *Littérature présente* (Paris: Corrêa, 1952); R.-M. Albérès, *Bilan littéraire du XXe siècle* (Paris: Aubier, 1956); H. Stuart Hughes, *Consciousness and Society* (New York: Vintage, 1977) and *The Obstructed Path: French Social Thought in the Years of Desperation, 1930–1960* (New York: Harper and Row, 1966).

18. Quoted by Jean Touchard, "L'Esprit des années 1930" in *Tendances politiques dans la vie française depuis 1789* (Paris: Hachette, 1960), p. 100.

19. Ibid., p. 100.

20. Magny, *Histoire du roman français*, p. 49.

21. Sartre, *Qu'est-ce que la littérature?*, p. 257.

22. Maxence, *Dix Ans*, p. 12.

23. Simon, *Histoire de la littérature française*, 2: 78.

24. Brasillach, "La fin de l'après-guerre," p. 251.

25. Maxence, *Dix Ans*, p. 81.

26. Louis Martin-Chauffier, *Marianne*, June 27, 1934, p. 4.

27. Maxence, *Dix Ans*, p. 265.

28. Benda's change in attitude is not as complete a turnabout as it would appear. In *La Trahison des Clercs*, the specific objects of his attack had been those French intellectuals who, in the hysteria of World War I, had abandoned the universal values that Benda felt to be the true concern of intellectuals to become mouthpieces for narrowly nationalistic propaganda. When he found these same values endangered by fascism, however, Benda was glad to lift his own voice in public protest. See the discussion of Benda in David L. Schalk, *The Spectrum of Political Engagement* (Princeton, N.J.: Princeton University Press, 1979).

29. André Gide, "Pages de journal," *Nouvelle Revue Française*, Oct. 1932, p. 492.

30. Claude-Edmonde Magny, *Littérature et critique* (Paris: Payot, 1971), p. 383; Nizan, *Pour une nouvelle culture*, p. 88.

31. The theater, of course, offered another medium of direct communication. Yet few of the writers who attempted to explore contemporary issues wrote plays, and playwrights, for the most part, concentrated on the exploration of timeless themes. Giraudoux's *La Guerre de Troie n'aura pas lieu* is an obvious but rare exception. Some of Anouilh's plays of the 1930s treat the general theme of poverty versus wealth, but he does not relate these problems specifically to the Depression. It was not until the time of the Resistance, with plays like Anouilh's *Antigone* and Sartre's *Les Mouches*, that the theater became an important vehicle for political statements. Perhaps, in the 1930s, the theater appeared to offer too restricted an audience. In addition, during the Depression era, funding must certainly have been difficult to obtain.

32. Sartre, *Qu'est-ce.que la littérature?*, pp. 26–28.

33. Erich Auerbach, *Mimesis* (Garden City, N.Y.: Anchor, 1951), p. 423.

34. Louis Aragon, "Le Roman terrible," *Europe* 48, no. 192 (Dec. 1938): 433–52, quoted by Roger Garaudy, *L'Itinéraire d'Aragon* (Paris: Gallimard, 1961), p. 270.

35. See Pierre Drieu la Rochelle, 1942 Preface to *Gilles* (1939; reprint, Paris: Folio, 1973).

36. Quoted by Pierre Brodin, *Présences contemporaines, Littérature III* (Paris: Debresse, 1957), p. 151.

37. Nizan, *Pour une nouvelle culture*, p. 230

38. Ibid., p. 143

39. For a summary of this activity, see Jean-Louis Saint-Ygnan, *Drieu la Rochelle ou l'obsession de la décadence* (Paris: Nouvelles Editions Latines, 1984).

40. Nizan, *Pour une nouvelle culture*, p. 88.

41. Susan Rubin Suleiman, *Authoritarian Fictions: The Ideological Novel as a Literary Genre* (New York: Columbia University Press, 1983).

42. For example, Thibaudet and Magny. Robert Wohl presents an analysis of the origins and role of generational theory in *The Generation of 1914*.

43. For example, Bernard Bergonzi, *Reading the Thirties* (Pittsburgh: University of Pittsburgh Press, 1978) and Samuel Hynes, *The Auden Generation* (New York: Viking, 1977).

44. Nizan, *Pour une nouvelle culture*, p. 174.

45. See Lucien Goldmann, *Pour une sociologie du roman* (Paris: Gallimard, 1964).

46. Paul Nizan, "Ambition du roman moderne," *Paul Nizan intellectuel communiste*, ed. Jean-Jacques Brochier (Paris: Maspero, 1970), 1: 119.

Chapter 2: Writing About War Between Two Wars

1. Paul Nizan, "Ambition du roman moderne," *Paul Nizan intellectuel communiste*, ed. Jean-Jacques Brochier (Paris: Maspero, 1970), 1: 118.

2. Maurice Rieuneau, *Guerre et révolution dans le roman français de 1919 à 1939* (Paris: Klincksieck, 1974).

3. René Pomeau, "Guerre et roman dans l'entre-deux-guerres," *Revue des Sciences Humaines*, fasc. 109 (Jan.-Mar. 1963): 79.

4. Ibid., p. 84.

5. Rieuneau, *Guerre et révolution*, p. 213.

6. Matthew Arnold, quoted by Robert Wohl, *The Generation of 1914* (Cambridge, Mass.: Harvard University Press, 1979), p. 229.

7. Louis-Ferdinand Céline, *Voyage au bout de la nuit* (1932; reprint, Paris: Folio, 1975), trans. Ralph Manheim as *Journey to the End of the Night* (New York: New Directions, 1983). All citations in my text refer to these editions.

8. "Interview avec Charles Chassé," in *Céline et l'actualité littéraire 1932–1957*, ed. Jean-Pierre Dauphin and Henri Godard (Paris: Gallimard, 1976), p. 88. Colin W. Nettelbeck discusses some affinities between Barbusse and Céline in "Journey to the End of Art: The Evolution of the Novels of Louis-Ferdinand Céline," *PMLA* 87 (1972): 83.

9. One of the earliest critics to mention the picaresque was Nizan. See Paul Nizan, *Pour une nouvelle culture*, ed. Susan Suleiman (Paris: Grasset, 1971), pp. 44–45.

10. This phenomenon is mentioned as an influence on Céline in particular by Nettelbeck in "Journey to the End of Art."

11. Danielle Racelle-Latin, for example, finds that only 4 percent of the lexical units of *Voyage* are terms of "argot spécialisé," while terms drawn from popular speech account for not more than 0.9 percent of the global lexical volume. See Racelle-Latin, "*Voyage au bout de la nuit* ou l'inauguration d'une poétique argotique," *Revue des Lettres Modernes* 462–67 (1976): 57.

12. Leo Spitzer, "Une Habitude de style: Le Rappel chez Céline," *Le Français Moderne* 3 (June 1935): 193–208; Julia Kristeva, *Pouvoirs de l'horreur, Essai sur l'abjection* (Paris: Seuil, 1979).

13. W. M. Frohock, *Style and Temper: Studies in French Fiction, 1925–1960*

(Cambridge, Mass.: Harvard University Press, 1967), pp. 86–91.

14. Robert Brasillach, who was active as a literary critic through the 1930s, later noted, "C'est par le vocabulaire que le *Voyage* a surpris. L'argot s'y déverse avec une abondance qui choqua" ("En relisant le *Voyage*," in *Les Critiques de notre temps et Céline*, ed. Jean-Pierre Dauphin [Paris: Garnier, 1976], p. 101).

15. "Propos sur Fernand Trignol et l'argot, recueillis par *Arts*" in *Céline et l'actualité littéraire*, p. 172.

16. Yves de la Quérière discusses the use of *la vache* in *Céline et les mots* (Lexington: University Press of Kentucky, 1973), p. 141.

17. Erika Ostrovsky notes the tendency of Céline to "blacken and blacken himself" in *Céline and His Vision* (New York: New York University Press, 1967), pp. 29–84.

18. De la Quérière, *Céline et les mots*, p. 133.

19. Kristeva, *Pouvoirs de l'horreur*. See also Jean-Pierre Richard, *Nausée de Céline* (Paris: Fata Morgana, 1973).

20. Kristeva sees the abortion episode as particularly revelatory of Céline's basic attitudes toward women and sexuality (*Pouvoirs de l'horreur*, p. 187).

21. De Beauvoir reports that *Voyage* was in 1932 "the book of the year for us. . . . We knew whole passages of it by heart, and his type of anarchism seemed very close to ours" (Simone de Beauvoir, *La Force de l'âge* [1960; reprint, Paris: Livre de Poche, 1960], p. 157; trans. Peter Green as *The Prime of Life* [Cleveland: World Publishing Company, 1962], p. 113).

Céline's imagery of dissolution and decay is analyzed in detail by Richard in *Nausée de Céline*, and Kristeva offers a psychoanalytic explanation in *Pouvoirs de l'horreur*.

22. Jean-Paul Sartre, *Being and Nothingness*, trans. Hazel Barnes (New York: Philosophical Library, 1956), p. 609.

23. "Interview avec Claude Bonnefoy (*Arts*)," in *Céline et l'actualité littéraire*, p. 212.

24. Gilbert Schilling notes the determining importance of the first fifty pages in "Espace et angoisse dans *Voyage au bout de la nuit*," *Revue des Lettres Modernes* 398–402 (1974): 59.

25. For an analysis of the role of silence in Céline, see Frédéric Vitoux, *Louis-Ferdinand Céline: Misère et parole* (Paris: NRF, Les Essais, 1973).

26. Schilling analyzes Céline's transformation of a place of constraint into one of refuge in "Espace et angoisse."

27. See, for example, Henri Barbusse *Le Feu* (Paris: Flammarion, 1916).

28. See "Interview avec Claude Bonnefoy," p. 212.

29. Lola's ridiculous task is a cruel caricature of the work of the American Salvation Army volunteers, who made donuts to serve with the coffee they offered to combat-weary troops near the front lines. Photographs of these "donut girls" were widely known, and Céline seems to have seen the donuts as identified with the figure of the American volunteer nurse.

30. "Propos recueillis par Pierre Ordioni," in *Céline et l'actualité littéraire*, p. 130.

31. "Hommage à Zola," ibid., pp. 78–83.

32. Louis Guilloux, *Le Sang noir* (Paris: Gallimard, 1935). All citations in my text refer to this edition.

33. See my *Louis Guilloux: An Artisan of Language* (York, S.C.: French Literature Publications [now Summa Publications], 1980).

34. For a study of the mutinies see G. Pedroncini, *Les Mutineries de 1917* (Paris: Presses Universitaires, 1967). Guilloux attempted to document himself on these mutinies, but, even in 1934, information was hard to obtain (see his Journal, reprinted in *Le Sang noir* [Paris: Club Français du Livre, 1964], pp. 457–501).

35. Louis Guilloux, *Carnets 1921–1944* (Paris: Gallimard, 1978), p. 77.

36. Frédéric Lefèvre, "Une Heure avec M. Louis Guilloux," *Les Nouvelles Littéraires*, Dec. 12, 1935.

37. Ibid.

38. Flaubert also had made use of such bovine imagery in *Madame Bovary*.

39. Jean-Louis Bory reports this meeting in his introduction to the 1964 edition of Guilloux, *Le Sang noir* (Lausanne: Editions Rencontre, 1964).

40. See Louis Guilloux, *Souvenirs sur Georges Palante* (Saint-Brieuc: O.L. Aubert, 1931).

41. Victor Brombert, *The Intellectual Hero* (Chicago: Phoenix Books, 1964).

42. See Jean Grenier's introduction to his *La Philosophie de Jules Lequier* (Paris: Les Belles Lettres, 1936).

43. Guilloux, Journal, p. 499.

44. Leon Trotsky, "Novelist and Politician," *Atlantic Monthly* 156 (1935): 420.

45. Other parallels with Roquentin are suggested by Brombert in *The Intellectual Hero*; by Francis J. Greene in "Louis Guilloux's *Le Sang noir*: A Prefiguration of Sartre's *La Nausée*," *French Review* 43 (Dec. 1969): 205–14; and by myself in "The Legacy of *Les Caves du Vatican*," *Kentucky Romance Quarterly* 26, no. 1 (1979): 113–22.

46. Lefèvre, "Louis Guilloux."

47. This feeling about the USSR was clearly expressed by Guilloux's colleague, Jean Guéhenno, in his autobiographical work, *Journal d'un homme de quarante ans* (Paris: Grasset, 1934), p. 241.

48. Lefèvre, "Louis Guilloux."

49. Louis Guilloux, "Notes sur le roman," *Europe* 40, no. 157 (Jan. 1936): 9.

50. Paul Nizan, *Les Chiens de garde* (Paris: Maspero, 1976), p. 108.

51. "A Louis Guilloux," *Commune*, Jan. 1936, p. 546.

52. Guilloux, Journal, p. 487.

53. Ibid., p. 487.

54. Drieu la Rochelle, *Journal*, quoted in Dominique Desanti, *Drieu la Rochelle ou le séducteur mystifié* (Paris: Flammarion, 1978), p. 398.

55. Drieu la Rochelle, "A propos d''A l'Ouest rien de nouveau,'" *Nouvelle Revue Française*, Nov. 1929, p. 727.

56. Pierre Drieu la Rochelle, *L'Europe contre les patries* (Paris: Gallimard, 1931), pp. 143–51.

57. Frédéric J. Grover, *Drieu la Rochelle and the Fiction of Testimony* (Berkeley and Los Angeles: University of California Press, 1958), p. 56. See also his *Drieu la Rochelle* (Paris: Gallimard, La Bibliothèque Idéale, 1962) and *Drieu la Rochelle* (Paris: Gallimard, Collection Idées, 1979); Grover and Pierre Andreu, *Drieu la Rochelle* (Paris: Hachette, 1979).

58. Pierre Drieu la Rochelle, *La Comédie de Charleroi* (1934; reprint, Paris: Livre de Poche, 1970). All citations in my text refer to this edition.

59. The presence of certain oppositions is also noted by Jonathan Dale, "Drieu la Rochelle: The War as 'Comedy'," in *The First World War in Fiction*, ed. Holger Klein (New York: Barnes and Noble, 1977).

60. An imagery based on the viscous was widely used in the fiction of the 1930s, as will be seen in the discussions of Céline and Sartre. This imagery seems to have emerged quite naturally from the mud and putrefaction of the trenches, which became a constant feature in the novels of the Great War. On another level, Kristeva recognizes the importance of this phenomenon, which she terms "the abject," in the work of Drieu when she cites it as "the very example" of a literature that proposes "a perverse denegation of abjection that, deprived of its religious sublimation . . . allowed itself to be seduced by the fascist phenomenon" (*Pouvoirs de l'horreur*, p. 187).

61. See, for example, René Girard, "L'Homme et le cosmos dans *L'Espoir* et *Les Noyers de l'Altenburg* d'André Malraux," *PMLA* 67 (1953): 49−55.

62. Drieu la Rochelle, *Interrogation* (Paris: NRF, 1917), p. 9. This need to unite thought and action certainly helps to account for Drieu's close and enduring relationship with Malraux, for whom this effort was a central one both in life and in art.

63. This theme was also important in the work of other writers of the era. See, for example, Paul Valéry, *Regards sur le monde actuel*, *Oeuvres*, vol. 2, ed. Jean Hytier (Paris: Gallimard, 1958).

64. See Drieu's novel *Gilles* (1939; reprint, Paris: Folio, 1973) and his essay *Socialisme fasciste* (Paris: Gallimard, 1934).

65. Grover notes that Drieu continually reproached the philosophy of bourgeois France for entirely lacking "the sense of the tragic" (*Drieu la Rochelle and the Fiction of Testimony*, p. 6).

66. Her daughter and Drieu's first wife, Colette Jeramec, told Drieu's brother that the portrait of Mme Pragen was "milder than the reality" (Desanti, *Drieu la Rochelle*, p. 79).

67. Drieu la Rochelle, "L'Instinct de la Guerre," *Les Nouvelles Littéraires*, Nov. 25, 1933.

68. These novels of Louis Aragon are: *Les Cloches de Bâle* (1934; reprint, Paris: Livre de Poche, 1966), trans. Haakon M. Chevalier as *The Bells of Basel* (New York: Harcourt Brace, 1936). *Les Beaux Quartiers* (1936; reprint, Paris: Folio, 1972). *Les Voyageurs de l'impériale* (1948; reprint, Paris: Folio, 1972). All citations from these works in my text refer to these editions.

69. Aragon finished writing *Les Voyageurs* in 1939, but, because of the difficulties of publishing literature written by a member of the Communist party at this time, it was not immediately published in France. The novel was first published in English translation as *Passengers of Destiny* and did not enjoy wide distribution in France until 1948.

70. Roger Garaudy notes that in many specific cases, Aragon's views are based on his research on Lenin (*L'Itinéraire d'Aragon*, [Paris: Gallimard, 1961], p. 299).

71. Ibid., p. 276.

72. Gerald Prince analyzes the narrative techniques of *Les Cloches de Bâle* in his article, "Changement de technique romanesque dans *Les Cloches de Bâle*," *Romance Notes* 14, no. 1 (Autumn 1972): 1–6.

73. Susan Rubin Suleiman, *Authoritarian Fictions: The Ideological Novel as a Literary Genre* (New York: Columbia University Press, 1983), pp. 215–16.

74. See Louis Aragon, "La Suite dans les idées," (1965) reprinted as preface to *Les Beaux Quartiers*, p. 47.

75. Quoted by Garaudy, *L'Itinéraire*, p. 327.

76. See Louis Aragon, *J'abats mon jeu* (Paris: Les Editeurs Français Réunis, 1959), p. 92.

77. Quoted by Garaudy, *L'Itinéraire*, p. 306.

78. Suleiman, *Authoritarian Fictions*, p. 210.

79. Aragon, "La Suite dans les idées," pp. 14–15.

80. According to Aragon's preface, one of the murders on which he reported suggested an episode in *Les Beaux Quartiers* (p. 45).

81. Aragon, "La Suite dans les idées," pp. 14–15.

82. See, for example, Aragon's article, "Beautés de la Guerre et leurs reflets dans la littérature," *Europe* 39, no. 150 (Dec. 1935): 474–80; reprinted in *Europe* 421–22 (May-June 1964): 132–37.

83. Garaudy, *L'Itinéraire*, p. 321.

84. Ibid., p. 323.

85. Ibid, p. 323, and Aragon's preface to *Les Voyageurs*, p. 25.

86. Jean-Pierre Azéma, *De Munich à la Libération* (Paris: Seuil, Collection Points, 1979), p. 22.

87. Garaudy, *L'Itinéraire*, p. 300.

88. Aragon, "La Suite dans les idées," p. 20.

89. David R. Schalk, *Roger Martin du Gard: The Novelist and History* (Ithaca, N. Y.: Cornell University Press, 1967), p. 17.

90. René Garguilo, *La Genèse des Thibault de Roger Martin du Gard* (Paris: Klincksieck, 1974).

91. Claude-Edmonde Magny, *Histoire du roman français depuis 1918* (1950; reprint, Paris: Points, 1971), pp. 276–318.

92. Reproduced by Garguilo, *La Genèse*, pp. 169–89.

93. Roger Martin du Gard, *Souvenirs littéraires*, *Oeuvres Complètes* (Paris: Pléiade, 1955), 1: lxxvii.

94. See Martin du Gard's correspondence with Pierre Margaritis, reprinted as "Consultation littéraire," *Nouvelle Revue Française*, Dec. 1958, pp. 1117–35.

95. Martin du Gard, *Souvenirs littéraires*, p. xciv–xcvi.

96. Martin du Gard to Gide, Feb. 5, 1932, cited by Garguilo, *La Genèse*, p. 501.

97. This research has been documented by Jochen Schloback, *Geschichte und Fiktion in "L'Eté 1949" von Roger Martin du Gard* (Munich: Wilhelm Fink Verlag, 1965).

98. This correspondence with Lallemand is published as "Lettres à un ami," *Nouvelle Revue Française*, Dec. 1958, pp. 1137−57.

99. Roger Martin du Gard, *L'Eté 1914*, vols. 3, 4, and 5 of *Les Thibault* (1936; reprint, Paris: Folio, 1973), trans. Stuart Gilbert as *Summer 1914* (New York: Viking, 1941). All citations in my text refer to these editions.

100. Martin du Gard to Gide, Feb. 22, 1933, cited by Rieuneau, *Guerre et révolution*, p. 467.

101. E.g., Garguilo, *La Genèse*, p. 557.

102. Nizan, *Pour une nouvelle culture*, p. 231.

103. Martin du Gard to Sartrieux, Sept. 11, 1927, quoted by Schalk, *Roger Martin du Gard*, p. 97.

104. Martin du Gard to Gide, quoted by Garguilo, *La Genèse*, p. 501.

105. Garguilo, *La Genèse*, p. 197.

106. Albert Camus, Foreword to Martin du Gard, *Oeuvres complètes*, 1: xiv.

107. For a discussion of Martin du Gard's concept of history, see Rieuneau, *Guerre et révolution*, p. 490.

108. Schalk, *Roger Martin du Gard*, p. 156.

109. Maurice Jones, "L'Antihéroisme précurseur de Roger Martin du Gard," *French Review* 42 (May 1969): 834−45.

110. See Schalk, *Roger Martin du Gard*, p. 191.

111. Martin du Gard to Gide, Feb. 23, 1932, quoted by Rieuneau, *Guerre et révolution*, p. 470.

112. Martin du Gard to Lallemand, Nov. 26, 1934, reprinted in *Nouvelle Revue Française*, Dec. 1958, p. 1146.

113. Garguilo, *La Genèse*, pp. 470−71.

114. Ibid., p. 545.

115. Martin du Gard to Ray, Apr. 11, 1915, cited by Rieuneau, *Guerre et révolution*, p. 471.

116. Reprinted in *Nouvelle Revue Française*, Dec. 1958, p. 1150.

117. Camus foreword to Martin du Gard, *Oeuvres complètes*, 1: xvii.

118. Roger Martin du Gard, "Discours de Stockholm," *Nouvelle Revue Française*, May 1959) pp. 956−60.

119. Roger Martin du Gard to Lallemand, Sept. 9, 1936, *Nouvelle Revue Française*, Dec. 1958, p. 1150.

120. Schalk, *Roger Martin du Gard*, p. 102.

121. Martin du Gard to Gaston Gallimard, June 17, 1935, cited by Rieuneau, *Guerre et révolution*, p. 496.

122. See Rieuneau, *Guerre et révolution*, p. 483.

123. See, for example, the article by Nizan in *Pour une nouvelle culture* and the judgment of Georg Lukacs in *Realism in Our Time* (New York: Harper Torchbook, 1971).

124. Martin du Gard to Gide, quoted by Garguilo, *La Genèse*, p. 543.

125. Garguilo, *La Genèse*, p. 540.

Chapter 3: A Literature of the People

1. Robert Brasillach, "La Fin de l'après-guerre," *La Revue Universelle* 46 (July 15, 1931): 251.

2. See my article, "Toward an Analysis of Fascist Fiction: The Contemptuous Narrator in the Work of Brasillach, Céline and Drieu la Rochelle," *Studies in Twentieth Century Literature*, 10, 1 (Fall 1985), 81–97.

3. This is the title of the volume devoted to the years 1918–1931 (vol. 5) of Jacques Chastenet's *Histoire de la Troisième République* (Paris: Hachette, 1960).

4. Brasillach, "La Fin de l'après-guerre," p. 250.

5. See, for example, Jacques Chastenet, *Déclin de la Troisième 1931–1938*, *Histoire de la Troisième République*, vol. 6 (Paris: Hachette, 1962): 143.

6. Brasillach, "La Fin de l'après-guerre," p. 252.

7. Henri Barbusse, "Hommage à Zola," *Monde*, June 10, 1928.

8. Louis Aragon, *Pour un réalisme socialiste* (Paris: Denoël et Steele, 1935), p. 72. However, Aragon remained critical of the naturalists' lack of historical perspective.

9. Aragon indicates his awareness of this influence; see Dominique Aubran, *Aragon parle avec Dominique Aubran* (Paris: Seghers, 1968), p. 114.

10. Louis-Ferdinand Céline, "Hommage à Zola," in *Céline et l'actualité littéraire 1932–1957*, ed. Jean-Pierre Dauphin and Henri Godard, Cahiers Céline, vol. 1 (Paris: Gallimard, 1976).

11. The party membership, reduced by persecution from without and exclusion from within, had dropped steadily from its founding in 1920, reaching a low point of 30,000 in early 1934.

12. For a discussion of the literary theories of French Communists in this period, see Jean-Pierre A. Bernard, *Le Parti communiste français et la question littéraire 1921–1939* (Grenoble: Presses Universitaires de Grenoble, 1972).

13. Many of the theoretical articles Barbusse wrote for *Monde* and *L'Humanité* are collected in his *Russie* (Paris: Flammarion, 1930), especially pp. 155–68.

14. Léon Lemonnier, *L'Oeuvre*, Aug. 27, 1929.

15. Léon Lemonnier, *Manifeste du roman populiste* (Paris: Jacques Bernard, 1929), and *Populisme* (Paris: La Renaissance du Livre, 1930). On populism, see also William Leonard Schwartz, "The Populist School in the French Novel," *French Review* 4 (May 1931): 473–79, and Charles Beuchat, *Histoire du naturalisme français*, vol. 2 (Paris: Corrêa, 1949). Also, David A. Orlando, "The Novels of Eugène Dabit and French Literary *Populisme* of the 1930s," diss., Stanford University, 1972.

16. The Prix Populiste has survived the literary school that gave it birth and has gone on to crown such excellent novels as Guilloux's *Le Pain des rêves* (Paris: Gallimard, 1942) and Christiane Rochefort's *Les Petits Enfants du siècle* (Paris: Editions Bernard Grasset, 1961). It was also, somewhat inexplicably, awarded to Sartre's *Le Mur* in 1939.

17. Henry Poulaille, *Nouvel Age littéraire* (Paris: Librairie Valois, 1930), p. 44.

18. Ibid., p. 104.

19. Both Guilloux and Nizan, for example, made specific statements advocating this approach.

20. The reasons for this are various. The Communists had already resisted the Soviet *rabcors* movement, and they were critical of Poulaille's failure to

insist on the proper ideological stance. In addition, they were suspicious of his financial dependence on Georges Valois, who had participated in various right-wing movements before launching his own brand of syndicalism.

21. There are, however, many similarities, in both form and content, between Guilloux's early novels about working-class characters and *Le Sang noir*. See my *Louis Guilloux: An Artisan of Language* (York, S.C.: French Literature Publications [now Summa Publications], 1980).

22. Gabriel Marcel, review of Louis Guilloux, *Angélina*, *L'Europe Nouvelle* 1, no. 17 (Feb. 10, 1932): 148.

23. Albert Camus, introduction to Louis Guilloux, *La Maison du peuple suivi de Compagnons* (1927, 1931; reprint, Paris: Editions "J'ai lu," 1960), pp. 10–11.

24. Louis Guilloux, review of Henry Poulaille, *Nouvel Age littéraire*, *Europe* 24, no. 95 (1930): 411–13.

25. Louis Guilloux, *Monde*, Oct. 26, 1929.

26. Eugène Dabit, *Journal intime 1928–1936* (Paris: Gallimard, 1939) pp. 23–25.

27. Eugène Dabit, *Commune*, Sept. 1935, p. 60. The one literary group with which Guilloux and Dabit were willing to identify themselves at all was the Association des Ecrivains et des Artistes Révolutionnaires, an organization that grew out of the widely based antifascist spirit of the mid-1930s. The association, however, did not have any official literary theories of its own. The closest it came to taking a theoretical position was in the organization of a meeting entitled "Défense du roman français," called to protest the failure of the Goncourt jury to crown Guilloux's *Le Sang noir*. The platform committee included Dabit, Aragon, Gide, Malraux, and Guéhenno. Aragon noted as the positive qualities of Guilloux's work its realism, its criticism of the existing society, and its thorough grounding in *expérience vécue*. But *Le Sang noir* was one of the few Guilloux novels that did not concern the lower classes, and the association did not seem to have any position on this issue.

28. Eugène Dabit, *Littérature Internationale* 3 (1934): 11.

29. Their first meeting is described in David O'Connell, "La Première Rencontre d'Eugène Dabit avec André Gide: Un Inédit d'Eugène Dabit," *Revue des Lettres Modernes* 374–79 (1973): 107–31.

30. Louis Guilloux, *Compagnons* (1931; reprint, Paris: Editions "J'ai lu," 1960). All citations in my text refer to this edition.

31. André Malraux, "En marge d'Hyménée," *Europe* 29, no. 114 (June 1932): 306.

32. Ibid., p. 306.

33. Guilloux was very active in television in the 1960s, adapting Martin du Gard's *Les Thibault* chronicle in addition to his own work. He seemed to see in this medium the direct communication with a popular audience that he had sought in the novel of the 1930s.

34. Camus foreword to Guilloux, *La Maison du peuple suivi de Compagnons*, p. 11.

35. Louis Guilloux, *Angélina* (Paris: Grasset, 1934). All citations in my text refer to this edition.

36. Almost all of the writers in this study—with the notable exception of Malraux, who refused even to talk about his childhood—wrote novels based on their own childhood memories: Guilloux in *La Maison du peuple*, Dabit in *Petit-Louis*, Céline in *Mort à crédit*, Drieu in *Rêveuse Bourgeoisie*, Brasillach in almost all his novels. Many went even further back into familial history. Aragon's *Voyageurs de l'impériale* is based on the life of his grandfather; Drieu's *Rêveuse Bourgeoisie* focuses on the youth of his mother; Brasillach's *La Conquérante* is based on his mother's experience in North Africa. Even Malraux in *Les Noyers de l'Altenburg* seems to be giving us, in the narrator's grandfather Berger, the life of his own grandfather.

37. See also the discussion of the Commune in Eugène Dabit's autobiographical *Faubourgs de Paris* (Paris: Gallimard, 1934), pp. 79–83, and in Paul Nizan's novel *Le Cheval de Troie* (Paris: Gallimard, 1935); trans. Charles Ashleigh as *Trojan Horse* (1937; reprint, New York: Howard Fertig, 1975). All citations in my text refer to these editions.

38. Paul Nizan, review of Guilloux, *Angélina, Littérature Internationale* 2 (1934): 159.

39. It is hard to see how Nizan could refer to the novel as "intemporal." It is true that Guilloux does not indulge in the magistral economic analysis that forms much of the undigested matter of *Antoine Bloyé*, but precise references are not lacking.

40. Eugène Dabit, "Témoignage," *Train de vies* (Paris: Gallimard, 1936), p. 242

41. Reported in David O'Connell, "Eugène Dabit, A French Working-Class Novelist," *Research Studies* 41, no. 4 (Dec. 1973): 220.

42. O'Connell cites many specific examples in ibid.

43. Ibid., p. 224.

44. André Maurois, "Eugène Dabit," in *Hommage à Eugène Dabit* (Paris: Gallimard, 1939), p. 112.

45. This correspondence is reprinted in *Cahiers de l'Herne*, nos. 3 and 4, réédition intégrale, 1972, pp. 57–61.

46. Eugène Dabit, *Villa Oasis* (Paris: Gallimard, 1932). All citations from this work in my text refer to this edition.

47. Eugène Dabit, *Un Mort tout neuf* (Paris: Gallimard, 1934). All citations from this work in my text refer to this edition.

48. Dabit, *Train de vies*.

49. Eugène Dabit, *L'Ile* (Paris: Gallimard, 1934).

50. The setting, characters and theme of this story are different from Dabit's other work. They seem, indeed, to belong to a novel by Guilloux, who, in fact, makes reference to a similar "Noel des chômeurs" of the 1930s in his 1949 novel, *Le Jeu de patience* (Paris: Gallimard, 1949). Interestingly, Dabit's *Journal intime* reveals that he did, in fact, spend time with Guilloux in Saint-Brieuc in Dec. 1935, although he does not record details of the visit.

51. Robert Brasillach, *L'Enfant de la nuit* (1934), *Oeuvres complètes*, vol. 1 (Paris: Au Club de l'Honnête Homme, 1963). All citations in my text refer to this edition.

52. Robert Brasillach, *Le Marchand d'oiseaux* (1936), ibid. All citations in my text refer to this edition.

53. Maurice Bardèche, forword to Robert Brasillach, *Le Marchand d'oiseaux*, *Oeuvres complètes*, 1: 316.

54. See Brasillach's evaluation of Clair in *Histoire du cinéma*, which he wrote with Maurice Bardèche, *Oeuvres complètes*, vol. 10.

55. Paul Nizan, *Pour une nouvelle culture*, p. 151. He says Brasillach's work is "a sort of flight from the world, a sort of lyrical transposition of daily reality that exempts the reader from any serious, concerned, indignant analysis of that reality."

56. Ramon Fernandez, review of Robert Brasillach, *L'Enfant de la nuit*, *Marianne*, Feb. 13, 1935.

57. Bardèche, foreword, p. 316.

58. Nizan, *Pour une nouvelle culture*, p. 45.

59. In the war, the heart of the frightened Bardamu has been described metaphorically as a caged rabbit (p. 56). The rabbit motif is picked up again later in the lively little Mme Henrouille, who hides out in a shack in the garden like the rabbits her daughter-in-law begins to raise. This image of rabbits fleeing before cruel, rich hunters occurs in at least one other important work of the 1930s, Jean Renoir's film, *La Règle du Jeu*.

60. Céline was no more enthusiastic about the Soviet "workers' paradise" than he was about La Garenne-Rancy. *Mea culpa* (Paris: Denoël et Steele, 1936), the book he wrote on his return, put a definitive end to his courtship by the Communists.

61. Nizan, *Pour une nouvelle culture*, pp. 44–45. The Communist reaction to *Voyage* is discussed by Paul A. Fortier, "Marxist Criticism of Céline's *Voyage au bout de la nuit*," *Modern Fiction Studies* 7 (1971): 268–72.

62. Leon Trotsky, "Novelist and Politician, " *Atlantic Monthly* 156 (1935): 420. This similarity between the Poincaré memoirs and *Voyage* had already been noted by Jean Prévost, review of Louis-Ferdinand Céline, *Voyage au bout de la nuit*, in *Les Critiques de notre temps et Céline*, ed. Jean-Pierre Dauphin (Paris: Garnier, 1976), p. 35.

63. Céline has told interviewers that Dabit's financial success had inspired him to write *Voyage*; see "Interview avec Claude Bonnefoy (Arts)," in *Céline et l'actualité littéraire 1932–1957* ed. Jean-Pierre Dauphin and Henri Godard (Paris: Gallimard, 1976), p. 214. This comment is made half-facetiously, but it is probable that *L'Hôtel du Nord* did suggest to him the feasability of writing about the people with whom he lived and worked.

64. Louis-Ferdinand Céline, *Mort à crédit* (1936; reprint, Paris; Livre de Poche, 1966), trans. Ralph Manheim as *Death on the Installment Plan* (New York: New Directions, 1966). All citations in my text refer to these editions.

65. See, for example, Henri Dubief, *Le déclin de la IIIe République 1929–1938* (Paris: Seuil, Collection Points, 1976), p. 38.

66. In his lingering evocation of this seaside idyll, Céline seems to be expressing his agreement with the call for outdoor activity made by both Right and Left in this era, finally brought to fruition in the Popular Front's legislative program in the summer of 1936.

67. Céline is very conscious of the effects of architecture on human beings, as is seen here and in his description of New York in *Voyage*. Conversely, he analyzes the way in which human attitudes are reflected in architecture.

In both *Voyage* and *Mort à crédit*, he describes the small private houses rising on the outskirts of Paris. These private homes accurately reflect the mentality of their inhabitants, who attempt to wall themselves up in their egoism, defending themselves with shotguns and vicious dogs.

68. De Beauvoir and Sartre immediately reacted against "a certain angry contempt for the little man" they detected in *Mort à crédit* (Simone de Beauvoir, *La Force de l'âge* [1960; reprint, Paris: Livre de Poche, 1966], p. 157, n. 2; trans. Peter Green as *The Prime of Life* [Cleveland: World Publishing Company, 1962], p. 113). Nizan in his review condemned Céline because "he no longer denounces anybody anybody except the poor and downtrodden" (*Pour une nouvelle culture*, p. 209).

69. This corresponds to Céline's own definition of his vocation as a doctor: "I had a medical calling . . . which consists essentially of making life easier and less painful for others" (Marc Hanrez, *Céline* [Paris: Gallimard, 1969], p. 227).

70. Quoted by Frédéric Lefèvre, *Une heure avec. . .*, VIe série (Paris: Flammarion, 1933), p. 130.

71. See Jean Giono, "Lettre aux paysans sur la pauvreté et la paix," *Ecrits pacifistes* (1938; reprint, Paris: Gallimard, Collection Idées, 1978).

72. André Chamson, *L'Année des vaincus* (Paris: Gallimard, 1934), p. 232.

73. Louis Guilloux, "Episode au village," *Commune*, Jan. 1938, 564–81; Feb. 1938, 681–703; Mar. 1938, 815–34; Apr. 1938, 945–65. Much of this material is incorporated in Guilloux's 1960 novel about the Popular Front era, *Les Batailles perdues* (Paris: Gallimard, 1960).

74. Roger Martin du Gard, *Vieille France* (1933; reprint, Paris: Folio, 1974). All citations in my text refer to this edition.

75. Jean Schlumberger, "Art et style," *Nouvelle Revue Française*, Dec. 1958, pp. 1068–73.

76. Roger Martin du Gard, letter, *Nouvelle Revue Française*, June 1933, p. 986.

77. Denis Boak, *Roger Martin du Gard* (Oxford: Clarendon Press, 1963), p. 117.

78. Pierre Drieu la Rochelle, *Gilles* (1939; reprint, Paris: Folio, 1973), p. 489.

79. Eugène Dabit, *La Zone verte* (Paris: Gallimard, 1935).

80. Nizan, *Pour une nouvelle culture*, pp. 138–39.

81. Ibid., p. 35.

82. It should be noted that Nizan reserves his condemnation for the leaders of this school, whom he criticizes for treating the workers as exotic objects of curiosity—ironically, the very charge they themselves had levelled against Zola. On the other hand, he praises novelists who write from within the working class and identify with its values and thus reveals his profound agreement with the type of populism defined by Gabriel Marcel and Nizan himself (see ibid., pp. 138–39).

83. Susan Rubin Suleiman, *Authoritarian Fictions: The Ideological Novel as a Literary Genre* (New York: Columbia University Press, 1983), p. 210.

84. Quoted by Roger Garaudy, *L'Itinéraire d'Aragon* (Paris: Gallimard, 1961), p. 297.

85. Nizan, *Pour une nouvelle culture*, p. 140.

86. Ibid., p. 231.

87. Ibid., p. 36.

88. This doctrine, proclaimed at the Congress of Soviet Writers in 1934, had a devastating effect on Soviet literature under Stalinism. The Soviet version had, however, relatively little effect on the practice of French Communists, who were always careful to distinguish between the needs of a postrevolutionary, socialist society and a prerevolutionary, capitalist society like their own.

89. See, for example, Louis Aragon, "Défense du roman français," *Commune*, Jan. 1936, pp. 562−68.

90. Louis Aragon, *J'abats mon jeu* (Paris: Les Editeurs Français Réunis, 1959), pp. 139−40.

91. Nizan, *Pour une nouvelle culture*, p. 34.

92. Ibid., p. 34.

93. For example, he accurately predicted that Martin du Gard's Thibault chronicle would outlive the many other series novels of the 1930s; he welcomed the stylistic innovations of Céline's *Voyage* but immediately perceived its essentially fascist undertones, etc.

94. Louis Aragon, review of Paul Nizan, *Antoine Bloyé*, *Commune*, Jan.-Feb. 1934, p. 826.

95. Aragon had already written prose works, such as *Anicet* and *Le Paysan de Paris*, during his surrealist period, but he himself took care to differentiate them from those belonging to the cycle he called *Le Monde Réel*, of which *Les Cloches de Bâle* was the first volume.

96. Nizan, *Pour une nouvelle culture*, pp. 175−76.

97. Ibid., p. 91.

98. Paul Nizan, review of Louis Guilloux, *Angélina*, *Littérature Internationale*, 2 (1934): 159.

99. Nizan, for example, criticizes Guilloux for displaying revolutionary ideas both outdated and "poetic," when Guilloux's book had been narrated from a limited point of view close to that of its characters, uneducated nineteenth-century artisans.

100. See, for example, Paul Nizan, "Ambition du roman moderne," *Paul Nizan intellectuel communiste*, ed. Jean-Jacques Brochier, (Paris: Maspero, 1970), 1: 117.

101. Gerald Prince, "Changement de technique romanesque dans *Les Cloches de Bâle*," *Romance Notes* 14, no. 1 (Autumn 1972): 1−6.

102. Jacqueline Leiner notes Nizan's admiration of Romains in *Le Destin littéraire de Paul Nizan et ses étapes successives* (Paris: Klincksieck, 1970), p. 28.

103. André Cuisenier, *Jules Romains: L'Unanimisme et Les Hommes de bonne volonté* (Paris: Flammarion, 1969), p. 12.

104. The city, called Villefranche, is based closely on Bourg-en-Bresse, Villefranche-sur-Saône, and Vienne, where Nizan himself had worked as a lycée professor and engaged in political activity.

105. Paul Nizan, *Antoine Bloyé* (1933; reprint, Paris: Livre de Poche, 1971); trans. Edmund Stevens as *Antoine Bloyé* (New York: Monthly Review Press, 1973).

106. One of the characters of the Sérianne section in Aragon's *Les Beaux Quartiers* is also a "funeral wreath merchant." In the eyes of Communist writers, this was obviously a fitting object of the commerce of capitalist "merchants of death."

107. Louis Aragon, *Les Beaux Quartiers* (1936; reprint, Paris: Folio, 1972), p. 531.

108. Aragon himself notes the metaphorical function of the *Passage-Club* in his essay, "La Suite dans les idées," written in 1965 as a preface to the new edition of *Les Beaux Quartiers*.

109. Doris Kadish notes the irony inherent in Aragon's use of the very term *beaux quartiers* in her article, "L'Ironie et le roman engagé," *French Review* 45 (Feb. 1972), 596–609.

Chapter 4: Political Commitment and Polarization

1. Denis de Rougemont, "A prendre ou à tuer," *Cahier de Revendications*, special issue of *Nouvelle Revue Française*, Dec. 1932, 839.

2. Wohl notes that "generationalism" (the attempt to define social and historical reality in terms of the concept of generation) reached its peak between 1928 and 1933 all over Europe. See Robert Wohl, *The Generation of 1914* (Cambridge, Mass.: Harvard University Press, 1979), p. 208.

3. Paul Nizan, "Les conséquences du refus," *Cahier de Revendications*, p. 810, reprinted in *Paul Nizan intellectuel communiste*, vol. 2, ed. Jean-Jacques Brochier (Paris: Maspero, 1970).

4. See Jean Touchard, "L'Esprit des années trente," in *Tendances politiques dans la vie française depuis 1789* (Paris: Hachette, 1960), p. 89.

5. Jean Loubet del Bayle, *Les Non-Conformistes des années 30* (Paris: Seuil, 1969).

6. Introduction to *Cahier de Revendications*, p. 801.

7. Brasillach describes himself as an anarchist at this period in his memoirs, *Notre Avant-guerre* (1941; reprint, Paris: Livre de Poche, 1973), p. 45. Malraux was allied with the individualist anarchists of the review *Action* in the early 1920s (see Walter Langlois, "Anarchism, Action, and Malraux," *Twentieth Century Literature* 24 [Fall 1978], 272–89) and, as late as 1936, described to a friend his discovery of anarcho-syndicalism, which he said corresponded to his political ideal (see Jean Lacouture, *Malraux, une vie dans le siècle* [Paris: Points, 1973], p. 212).

8. Pierre Drieu la Rochelle, "Malraux, l'homme nouveau," *Nouvelle Revue Française*, Dec. 1930, reprinted in *Les Critiques de notre temps et Malraux*, ed. Pol Gaillard (Paris: Garnier, 1970), pp. 48–50.

9. The stormy relationship between Aragon and Drieu is well described by Dominique Desanti, *Drieu la Rochelle ou le séducteur mystifié* (Paris: Flammarion, 1978).

10. Brasillach, *Notre Avant-guerre*, p. 56.

11. The second volume of Simone de Beauvoir's memoirs, *La Force de l'âge* (1960; reprint, Paris: Livre de Poche, 1966) offers a detailed analysis of the changing political attitudes of Sartre and herself in this period.

12. This slogan appeared on the cover of the association's *Commune* and

was the title of the series of antifascist writers' congresses held in Paris, London, and Madrid in the years 1935–37.

13. André Malraux, *Le Temps du mépris* (Paris: Gallimard, 1935), trans. Haakon M. Chevalier as *Days of Wrath* (New York: Random House, 1936). All citations in my text refer to these editions.

14. The novel not only reflects Malraux's political preoccupations at the time of its composition but also eerily prefigures his own brief imprisonment at the hands of the Germans in 1944 as a leader of the French Resistance. Just as his Nazi captors are unsure of the identity of the protagonist of *Le Temps du mépris*, a confusion that saves him from a harsher fate, the Germans in charge of interrogating Malraux mixed up his dossier with that of his brother, an accident that delayed the discovery of his own important role in the Resistance activity until the Allies had time to liberate the area. Malraux recounts this episode in his *Antimémoires* (Paris: Gallimard, 1967), where he also comments on the strange prefiguration of his Resistance activity offered by *Les Noyers de l'Altenburg*. He might also have mentioned *Le Temps du mépris* in this context.

15. For example, Malraux's pamphlet, *De Dimitrov à Thälmann: Echec au fascisme* (Paris: Bureau d'Editions, 4 rue Saint-Germain-l'Auxerrois, undated). Lacouture speaks of this aspect of Malraux's activity in *Malraux, une vie*, pp. 160–63.

16. This statement is quoted by Lacouture, *Malraux, une vie*, p. 163.

17. This is also the judgment of Lucien Goldmann in *Pour une sociologie du roman* (Paris: Gallimard, Collection Idées, 1964), p. 194.

18. W. M. Frohock, *André Malraux and the Tragic Imagination* (Stanford, Calif.: Stanford University Press, 1967), p. 94.

19. See Henri Peyre, "Friends and Foes of Pascal in France Today," *Yale French Studies* 7 (1953): 8, and my "Pascalian Motifs in the Thought of Camus," *Stanford French Review* 1 (Fall 1977): 229–42.

20. Other famous examples include Malraux's later novel *L'Espoir*, Sartre's *Le Mur*, Camus's *L'Etranger*, Sartre's *Morts sans sépulture* and, of course, the extensive literature of *témoignage* written after the war by returned deportees.

21. See Robert Humphrey, *The Stream of Consciousness in the Modern Novel* (Berkeley and Los Angeles: University of California Press, 1960).

22. Thomas J. Kline, *André Malraux and the Metamorphosis of Death* (New York: Columbia University Press, 1973), p. 93.

23. Kline cites a series of insect images and, at one point, notes a Kafkaesque resonance (ibid., p. 90).

24. Some critics would argue that Kassner, like Garine in *Les Conquérants*, is struggling primarily against the absurd. See Nicola Chiaromonte, "Malraux and the Demons of Action," *Partisan Review* 15 (July 1948): 776–89, and 16 (Aug. 1948): 912–23.

25. André Malraux, "Sur l'héritage culturel," *Commune*, Sept. 1936, 8.

26. This is, to the best of my recollection, the first appearance in Malraux's work of the tree motif, which assumes great importance in his last two novels.

27. Goldmann, *Pour une sociologie*, p. 196.

28. Robert Brasiilach, *Les Sept Couleurs* (1939; reprint, Paris: Livre de Poche, 1973). All citations in my text refer to this edition.

29. Robert Brasillach, *Corneille* (Paris: Fayard, Collection L'Homme et l'Oeuvre, 1938). Pierre-Henri Simon discusses this vogue in *Histoire de la littérature française au XXe siècle 1900–1950*, 3rd ed. (Paris: Armand Colin, 1957), 2: 120–21. To explain this interest in Corneille, Simon quotes Jean Schlumberger: "In periods when civilization seems threatened, when people must get hold of themselves, overcome habits of laxness, reconstitute an ethic, people call for the strong lessons of the affirmatory poets" (p. 120).

30. Robert Brasillach, "Cent Heures chez Hitler," *La Revue Universelle* 71 (Oct. 1937): 55–74. Much of the same material also appears in his memoirs, *Notre Avant-guerre* (1941; reprint, Paris: Livre de Poche, 1973).

31. Some of this material, which describes Brasillach's own visit to Spain, is later reprinted in *Notre Avant-guerre*.

32. Robert Brasillach and Maurice Bardèche, *Histoire de la guerre d'Espagne* (Paris: Plon, 1939).

33. Quoted by Frédéric Grover in *Drieu la Rochelle* (Paris: Gallimard, Collection La Bibliothèque Idéale, 1962), p. 42.

34. For documentation on this event, see Jacques Chastenet, *Histoire de la Troisième République*, vols. 5, 6 (Paris: Hachette, 1962); Max Beloff, "The Sixth of February," in *The Decline of the Third Republic*, ed. James Joll (London: Chatto and Windus, 1959), pp. 9–35; Serge Berslein ed., *Le 6 février 1934*, ed. Serge Berslein (Paris: Gallimard, Julliard, 1975).

35. Statistics on the number of people killed vary. The parliamentary commission of inquiry sets the toll at 14 (see Beloff, "Sixth of February," p. 28), but most accounts of the time give a higher figure.

36. Wilfred Knapp, *France: Partial Eclipse* (New York: American Heritage Press, 1972), p. 21.

37. Louis Aragon, "Les Ouvriers de Paris à làssaut du ciel," *Commune*, Jan.-Feb. 1934, 489.

38. Robert Brasillach, *Les Captifs, Oeuvres complètes* (Paris: Au Club de l'Honnête Homme, 1963), l: 481–659.

39. Maurice Bardèche, foreword, ibid., p. 482.

40. Pierre Drieu la Rochelle, *Gilles* (1939; reprint, Paris: Folio, 1973). All citations in my text refer to this edition.

41. In *Les Captifs*, curiously, Brasillach repeats Drieu's phrase in his "cet étrange ballet du courage et de la peur" (p. 544).

42. Drieu seems to cherish this ideal of the man of intellect allied with the man of action. As Frédéric Grover notes in *Drieu la Rochelle and the Fiction of Testimony* (Berkeley and Los Angeles: University of California Press, 1958), this is the first appearance of this couple in Drieu's work. Later it forms the center of his allegorical novel set in a mythical South America, *L'Homme à cheval* (Paris: Gallimard, 1943). In Drieu's personal life, this ideal seems to lie behind his own involvement with Jacques Doriot and his Parti populaire français.

43. Writing on Drieu's thought in 1935, Nizan comments drily, "Drieu's ideas strike me as less political than erotic" (*Pour une nouvelle culture*, p. 186).

44. Drieu's preface, written in 1942, is reprinted in the Folio edition.

45. Susan Suleiman comments that organic metaphors appear to be the property of right-wing writers (*Authoritarian Fictions: The Ideological Novel as a Literary Genre* [New York: Columbia University Press, 1983], p. 272). I have found, on the contrary, that such metaphors occur in the works of writers at all points of the political spectrum.

46. This was the main point of the article on the events of Feb. 6 and 9 that Drieu wrote for the March *Nouvelle Revue Française*: "in the crowd that rushed toward the place de la Concorde to experience the great 11 o'clock fusillade, people were singing the *Marseillaise* and *L'Internationale* interchangeably. I wish that moment could have lasted forever" (Pierre Drieu la Rochelle, "Air de février 1934," *Nouvelle Revue Française*, Mar. 1934, pp. 568–69).

47. Clérences is probably modeled after the French politician with whom Drieu himself was for a time allied, Gaston Bergery. But in *Drieu la Rochelle and the Fiction of Testimony*, Grover asserts—and I believe rightly—that the characters created by Drieu in *Gilles* go beyond their connections with real contemporary persons to become typical figures who offer the modern reader a real insight into the times. Drieu succeeds in doing what his former friend Aragon, despite his conscious efforts, often does not: creating social "types," like Balzac's characters, who reflect the nature of their society.

48. Ironically, Pierre Andreu and Frédéric Grover, in their most recent biography, *Drieu la Rochelle* (Paris: Hachette, 1979), reveal his unwillingness to accept fatherhood (p. 293). One of his mistresses was forced to undergo two abortions, the second of which rendered her unable to bear children. Thus, the inability to regenerate was in Drieu's personal life a matter of choice rather than situation.

49. Nizan had gone to Brest as a reporter and had seen in the morgue the body of a worker who had been killed by the police. This experience is reflected in the scene where the Communist group goes to identify Paul's body (W. D. Redfern, *Paul Nizan: Committed Literature in a Conspiratorial World* [Princeton, N. J. : Princeton University Press, 1972], p. 123).

50. Cited by Jacqueline Leiner in her excellent article, "La Part de l'actuel dans l'oeuvre de Paul-Yves Nizan," *Revue des Sciences Humaines*, fasc. 129 (Jan.-Mar. 1968): 121.

51. The name Bloyé is consistently given by Nizan to the central figure in each of his three novels, all of which are autobiobiographical to some extent.

52. It is interesting that Nizan has his fascists march down the open space provided them by the boulevard Wilson, as they had historically profited from the arrangements made by Wilsonian internationalist idealists.

53. This image seems to be a constant of Nizan's vision of fascists. In his article on Drieu la Rochelle, he had written: "There are men whose whole lives are dominated by a certain power, a certain unity of affirmation. There are others whose whole law is in dispersion. Such is Drieu" (*Pour une nouvelle culture*, p. 184).

54. De Beauvoir discusses Nizan's obsession with death and notes his disappointment in discovering that the solidarity of life in socialistic society

could not solve this problem: "It had been a great blow for him to discover that, in Russia as in France, the individual was alone when he died and knew it" (*The Prime of Life*, p. 166).

55. Paul Nizan, *La Conspiration* (1938; reprint, Paris: Folio, 1973).

56. Redfern, p. 151.

57. Paul Nizan, *Aden-Arabie* (1932; reprint, Paris: Maspero, 1976), p. 53.

58. Jean-Paul Sartre, foreword to ibid.

59. Jean-Paul Sartre, "La Conspiration," in *Critiques littéraires (Situations, I)* (1947; Paris: Gallimard, Collection Idées, 1974).

60. Another member of this group, Henri Lefebvre, presents his own version of events in *La Somme et le reste* (Paris: La Nef, 1959).

61. For example, David Caute in *Communism and the French Intellectuals* (London: André Deutsch, 1964), p. 95.

62. Nizan broke with the French Communist party, although apparently not with his spiritual allegiance to Communism, at the time of the Germano-Soviet pact of 1939. Ironically, certain party members saw a prefiguration of Nizan's own "betrayal" in the story of Pluvinage.

63. These letters are reprinted in *Paul Nizan intellectuel communiste*, ed. Jean-Jacques Brochier (Paris: Maspero, 1970), 2: 105–41.

64. Quoted by Redfern, *Paul Nizan*, p. 166.

65. See ibid., p. 166.

66. In his review of *La Conspiration*, Nizan's colleague Aragon saw Carré as the "positive element" in the novel (cited in ibid., p. 165).

67. Redfern notes this was the first mass demonstration organized by the Communist party in France (ibid., p. 175).

68. This description of the Communist marchers uses the same metaphors employed in *Le Cheval de Troie* for a similar occasion.

69. Tarmo Kunnas, *Drieu la Rochelle, Céline, Brasillach et la tentation fasciste* (Paris: Les Sept Couleurs, 1972).

70. Frédéric J. Grover, *Drieu la Rochelle and the Fiction of Testimony* (Berkeley and Los Angeles: University of California Press, 1958), p. 193.

71. See Desanti, *Drieu la Rochelle*.

72. This name is somewhat reminiscent of Drieu's actual periodical, *Les Derniers Jours*.

73. Grover points out that the term fascist should be used cautiously with reference to Drieu (*Drieu la Rochelle*, p. 56).

74. According to Grover, Drieu began the composition of *Gilles* in the period immediately following his alienation from the Parti populaire français in 1937.

75. Pierre Drieu la Rochelle, *Une Femme à sa fenêtre* (Paris: Gallimard, 1930), p. 144. Grover (*Drieu la Rochelle*, p. 149) points out the uncanny resemblance of this formulation to Kyo's statement of allegiance in Malraux's *La Condition humaine*. Parallels of this sort indicate a basic similarity in temperament between Drieu and Malraux and help to explain why their friendship survived even the political divisions of the Occupation.

76. Near the end of his life, Drieu had withdrawn from public life and devoted himself increasingly to the study of religious thought.

77. For example, Simone de Beauvoir in *Pour une morale de l'ambiguité* (Paris: Gallimard, Collection Idées, 1968), p. 82.

78. In his review of *La Nausée*, Nizan notes, "The object of anguish in the work of the German philosopher [Heidegger] is nothingness: in M. Sartre's work, it is existence" (*Pour une nouvelle culture*, pp. 285–86).

79. See de Beauvoir, *La Force de l'âge*, p. 272.

80. In his review of *La Nausée*, Nizan, in fact, would indicate a much more positive view of Sartre's attitudes: "*La Nausée* is not a book without a positive element." He cites with particular approval the satiric treatment of the Bouville bourgeoisie and expresses his hope that Sartre will put his gifts to greater use in this direction (*Pour une nouvelle culture*, p. 286).

81. De Beauvoir, *The Prime of Life*, pp. 174–75.

82. It is interesting to note that Bloyé, like Lange, feels a certain pleasure in imagining the prospective cataclysm: "Un monde naissait. La France entrait dans le jeu des nations, pour elle aussi la violence qui refait l'histoire commençait. Plus de projets, d'attentes dans cet avenir incroyable où on ne compterait un jour les victimes qu'en gros" (p. 238). ("A world was in birth. France was entering into the struggle of nations—violence, which remoulds history, was beginning here also. There would be no more vain speculation or inactive waiting in this incredible future where, one day, the victims would be counted in hundreds" [p. 245]) In this passage Nizan, perhaps inadvertently, reveals the spiritual bonds that link the adversaries in this political struggle, a struggle that had led intellectuals of very similar backgrounds to fight on different sides of the political barrier. Nizan may have put certain aspects of himself, in addition to Sartre, Drieu and Brice Parain (whom Nizan had mentioned to Sartre as a model for Lange), into the character Lange.

83. Drieu la Rochelle, "Air de février 1934," p. 568.

84. Nizan, *Pour une nouvelle culture*, p. 187.

85. See de Beauvoir, *Pour une morale de l'ambiguité*, pp. 80–82.

86. William R. Tucker, *The Fascist Ego: A Politial Biography of Robert Brasillach* (Berkeley and Los Angeles: University of California Press, 1975), p. 3.

87. Robert Brasillach, *Notre Avant-guerre*, p. 362.

88. Robert Brasillach, *Lettre à un soldat de la classe 60* (Paris: Les Sept Couleurs, 1960), pp. 30–31.

89. Jean-Paul Sartre, "L'Enfance d'un chef," in *Le Mur* (1939; reprint, Paris: Folio, 1974), trans. Lloyd Alexander as "The Childhood of a Leader," in *The Wall* (New York: New Directions, 1948). All citations in my text refer to these editions.

90. Despite the many parallels between Lucien and himself, Brasillach, in his review of Sartre's story, refers to Lucien as "a dreary character," "a timid soul who lets himself be seduced by all kinds of errors" (*Action Française*, Apr. 13, 1939, reprinted in *Oeuvres complètes*, 12: 280–82.

91. Geneviève Idt makes this point in *Le Mur de Jean-Paul Sartre: Techniques et Contexte d'une provocation* (Paris: Larousse, 1972), p. 156.

92. Ibid., pp. 166–67.

93. On this basis, Gerald Prince, for example, sets the ending in Apr. 1927

(*Métaphysique et Technique dans l'oeuvre romanesque de Sartre* [Geneva: Droz, 1968], p. 71).

94. Freudian thought emerged into the French consciousness in the 1920s. Much of the interest in Freud was due to the enormous importance accorded him by the surrealists, whose leader, André Breton, had been trained in psychiatry and had visited Freud in Vienna after the war.

95. Idt, *Le Mur de Jean-Paul Sartre*, p. 104.

96. In my own experience, which accords with Susan Suleiman's, students have a tendency to miss Sartre's sarcasm and to read the story as a successful apprenticeship. This phenomenon invites speculation.

97. Idt, *Le Mur de Jean-Paul Sartre*, p. 174.

Chapter 5: The Fiction of the Spanish Civil War

1. Simone de Beauvoir, *La Force de l'âge* (1960; reprint, Paris: Livre de Poche, 1966), p. 318; trans. Peter Green as *The Prime of Life* (Cleveland: World Publishing Company, 1962), p. 231.

2. In the wide choice of labels available to writers on the Spanish Civil War, I have chosen the terms Republican for the side that supported the elected Popular Front government and Falangist for the side that supported the uprising led by General Franco. These terms seem to avoid the evident confusion promoted by such labels as Loyalist (to whom?) or Nationalist (which could equally well be applied to either side).

3. For a study that emphasizes these ideological differences, see Pierre Broué, *La Révolution espagnole (1931–1939)* (Paris: Flammarion, 1973).

4. Jean Duvignaud, "Les Petits Cimetières sous la lune," *L'Express*, Nov. 14, 1958.

5. See *Paul Nizan intellectuel communiste*, vol. 2, ed. Jean-Jacques Brochier (Paris: Maspero, 1970) for examples of his reportage on Spain.

6. Reported by Jean Lacouture, *Malraux, une vie dans le siècle* (Paris: Seuil, Collection Points, 1975), p. 228.

7. Robert Brasillach and Maurice Bardèche, *Histoire de la Guerre d'Espagne* (Paris: Plon, 1969).

8. François Mauriac, *Le Figaro*, Aug. 18, 1936. Cited by Maryse Bertrand de Munoz, *La Guerre civile espagnole et la littérature française* (Ottawa: Didier, 1972).

9. For a thorough study of the Spanish Civil War literature produced in French, see de Munoz, *La Guerre civile*.

10. Malraux told Lacouture in response to a question about his identity with Magnin, "Any psychoanalyst will tell you that when a novelist puts a mustache on a hero who represents him more or less, it's because he's looking for a mask" (*Malraux, une vie*, p. 248).

11. For documentation on this phase of Malraux's life, see ibid., Ch. 4; Robert S. Thornberry, *André Malraux et l'Espagne* (Geneva: Droz, 1977); and Walter G. Langlois, "The Novelist Malraux and History," *L'Esprit Créateur* 15, no. 3 (Fall 1975): 345–66. Pierre Broué and Emile Témime, in their classic work, *La Révolution et la guerre d'Espagne* (Paris: Minuit, 1961), state: "But the first example of a serious organization is that of the international avia-

tion unit set up by André Malraux. The *Espagne* squadron rendered enormous services, at least in the first months of the war, at a time when government bombers were totally nonexistent. Despite the small number of planes they had at their disposal—about twenty—the 'Internationals' were the only ones to act with any effectiveness" (p. 348).

12. See Lacouture, *Malraux, une vie*, pp. 220–21.

13. This is particularly true in the classic work in English: Hugh Thomas, *The Spanish Civil War* (New York: Harper and Row, 1961). See, for example, p. 139. The problem occurs as well in Broué and Témime. As I will point out later, there are some minor discrepancies in dating and architectural detail, but Malraux's fictional account of the war generally coincides with that of the historians mentioned. Malraux's history is, of course, the Republican version, and it differs on many points from accounts that accept the facts provided by the fascist side (e.g. that of Brasillach).

14. The role of Ximénès corresponds to that played in reality by Colonel Escobar, whose loyal Civil Guards did, as in the novel, dislodge the Falangists from Barcelona's Plaza de Cataluna. The sculptor Lopez expresses ideas on revolutionary art which would have been appropriate to the Mexican mural painter David Siqueiros (see James W. Greenlee, *Malraux's Heroes and History* [DeKalb: Northern Illinois University Press], 1975, p. 235). The Catholic writer Guernico shows parallels with Malraux's friend Jose Bergamin and expresses sentiments shared by many French Catholics of the era during the bombing of Madrid. Magnin and the men of his international aviation squadron are surprisingly faithful portraits of the Escuadra André Malraux (see Lacouture, *Malraux, une vie*, for a precise account of these characters and their real-life counterparts).

15. The anarchist leader Durruti, some of whose traits are given to the Negus, did, in fact, die during the battle of Madrid, while Ascaso (Puig) had been killed in Barcelona; men like Enrique Lister or the musician-turned-officer Gabriel Duran, both of whom have been suggested as models for Manuel, lived on to have successful military careers.

16. For example, W. M. Frohock, *André Malraux and the Tragic Imagination* (Stanford, Calif.: Stanford University Press, 1967), p. 122.

17. This anecdote is, however, repeated by other left-wing writers of the period.

18. This anecdote has become a Falangist legend, but a historian like Thomas is willing to concede its authenticity (*The Spanish Civil War*, p. 203). To the credit of the Republicans, Moscardo's son was evidently not executed on the spot; however, he apparently was killed, along with many other Falangist prisoners, on the occasion of their evacuation from Madrid.

19. Cecil D. Eby, *The Siege of the Alcazar* (New York: Random House, 1965), p. 189.

20. See Langlois, "The Novelist Malraux." Malraux has also adjusted the date on his Medellin raid to coincide with the Badajoz massacre by the Falangists. See Bernard Wilhelm, *Hemingway et Malraux devant la guerre d'Espagne* (Porrentruy: La Bonne Presse, 1966), pp. 93–94. According to Wilhelm, this underlines the theme that individual action alone cannot win the war.

21. See Thomas J. Kline, "The Tension of Hope in *L'Espoir*," *André Malraux and the Metamorphosis of Death* (New York: Columbia University Press, 1973).

22. Philippe Carrard, *Malraux ou le récit hybride* (Paris: Lettres Modernes, 1976), pp. 86–87.

23. Jean Carduner, *La Création romanesque chez Malraux* (Paris: Nizet, 1968), pp. 59–61, traces the history of point of view theory in France at this time.

24. Ibid., p. 42.

25. André Malraux, *L'Espoir* (1937; reprint, Paris: Folio, 1972), trans. Stuart Gilbert and Alastair Macdonald as *Man's Hope* (New York: Grove Press, 1979). All citations in my text refer to these editions. This reproduces almost exactly the words Malraux used in his speech to the London meeting of the Antifascist Writers' Congress in 1936.

26. Here Manuel's activity coincides with that of Enrique Lister, who is also prominently featured in Hemingway's film.

27. Drieu la Rochelle, "Ce qui meurt en Espagne," *Nouvelle Revue Française*, Nov. 1936, pp. 920–22.

28. Lucien Goldmann, *Pour une sociologie du roman* (Paris: Gallimard, Collection Idées, 1964), p. 222.

29. See especially Broué, *La Révolution espagnole*.

30. This incident is historically authentic (see the articles Louis Delaprée wrote from Toledo for *Paris-Soir*, collected after his death in *Mort en Espagne* [Paris: Editions Tisné, 1937]).

31. Frohock, *André Malraux*, p. 112.

32. See Louis Aragon, "Ne rêvez plus qu'à l'Espagne," *Europe* 42, 167 (Nov. 1936): 353–61.

33. André Malraux used this phrase in "Sur l'héritage culturel," *Commune*, Sept. 1936, p. 7.

34. Dominique Desanti, *Drieu la Rochelle ou le séducteur mystifié* (Paris: Flammarion, 1978), p. 329.

35. Ibid., p. 329.

36. Bernanos seems to be particularly on Drieu's mind in this chapter on Ibiza, as is apparent from his including certain "Catholic novelists" among his list of decadent phenomena. Both Bernanos and François Mauriac, who had vigorously opposed the Falangist policies in Spain, were likely targets of his criticism.

37. See Desanti, *Drieu la Rochelle*, p. 329.

38. Jean-Paul Sartre, "Le Mur," in the collection *Le Mur* (1939; reprint, Paris: Folio, 1974), trans. Lloyd Alexander as "The Wall" in *The Wall* (New York: New Directions, 1948). All citations in my text refer to these editions.

39. Jean-Paul Sartre, press conference, Venice, *Jeune Cinéma* 25 (Oct. 1967): 24.

40. De Beauvoir, *The Prime of Life*, p. 231.

41. Sartre, press conference.

42. Ibid.

43. De Beauvoir, *La Force de l'âge*, p. 335.

44. Sartre, press conference.

45. Ibid.

46. I have analyzed this similarity in greater depth in "Malraux and Sartre: Dialogue on the Far Side of Despair," in *Witnessing André Malraux: Visions and Re-Visions*, ed. Brian Thompson and Carl A. Viggiani (Middletown, Conn.: Wesleyan University Press, 1984), pp. 62–72.

47. De Beauvoir, *La Force de l'âge*, pp. 570–71.

48. Jean-Paul Sartre, *Les Mouches* (1947; reprint, Paris: Folio 1974), p. 236.

Chapter 6: On the Far Side of Despair

1. Robert Brasillach, *Notre Avant-guerre* (1941; reprint, Paris: Livre de Poche, 1973), p. 363.

2. See, for example, the interpretation Louis Guilloux gives of this phenomenon in *Les Batailles perdues* (Paris: Gallimard, 1960).

3. See Denis Marion, *André Malraux* (Paris: Seghers, 1970), p. 24.

4. See Louis Guilloux, "Refuge in Limbo," trans. D. S. Bussy, *Living Age* 354 (July 1938): 440–45, and "The Betrayal of the Refugees," *New Republic* 98 (Feb. 22, 1939), 68–79.

5. See Louis Guilloux, *Salido* (Paris: Gallimard, 1976).

6. Guy de Belleval, "Louis Guilloux: 'Il faut être un témoin de son temps,'" *Arts* 870 (May 23–29, 1962): 3.

7. See Louis Guilloux, *Carnets 1921–1944* (Paris: Gallimard, 1978), pp. 140–41, 153.

8. See David O'Connell, "Eugène Dabit: A French Working-class Novelist," *Research Studies* 4 (Dec. 1973): 222.

9. Louis Aragon, *Les Voyageurs de l'impériale* (1948; reprint, Paris: Folio, 1972), p. 25.

10. Simone de Beauvoir, *La Force de l'âge* (1960; reprint, Paris: Livre de Poche, 1966), p. 431; trans. Peter Green as *The Prime of Life* (Cleveland: World Publishing Company, 1962), p. 300.

11. See Nizan to his wife, *Paul Nizan intellectuel communiste*, ed. Jean-Jacques Brochier (Paris: Maspero, 1970) 1: 105–41. Also W. D. Redfern, *Paul Nizan: Committed Literature in a Conspiratorial World* (Princeton, N.J.: Princeton University Press, 1972), pp. 188–98.

12. Aragon speaks of this period in his preface to *Les Voyageurs de l'impériale*.

13. Aragon, *Les Voyageurs de l'impériale*, p. 9.

14. Brasillach, *Notre Avant-guerre*, p. 441.

15. De Beauvoir, *The Prime of Life*, p. 295–96.

16. Roger Martin du Gard, *Epilogue*, vol. 5 of *Les Thibault* (1940; reprint, Paris: Folio, 1973), trans. Stuart Gilbert in *Summer 1914* (New York: Viking Press, 1941). All citations in my text refer to these editions.

17. See the summary of the book's critical reception given by David Schalk, *Roger Martin du Gard: The Novelist and History* (Ithaca, N. Y.: Cornell University Press, 1967), pp. 173–75.

18. Ibid., p. 205.

19. Jean Paulhan, *Nouvelle Revue Française*, Oct. 1958, p. 579, cited by Schalk, *Roger Martin du Gard*, p. 174.

20. Roger Martin du Gard, "Condamnation de la guerre," *La Dépêche socialiste*, July 30, 1938, p. 2.

21. Roger Martin du Gard, "L'Eté 1939," *Nouvelle Revue Française*, Dec. 1958, p. 1055.

22. Albert Camus, foreword to Roger Martin du Gard, *Les Thibault, Oeuvres complètes* (Paris: Pléiade, 1955), 1: xvii. See my "A Moral Image of Modern Man: The Doctor in the Work of Martin du Gard," in *Medicine and Literature*, ed. E. R. Peschel (New York: Neale Watson Academic Publications, Inc., 1980).

23. André Malraux, *Les Noyers de l'Altenburg* (Paris: Gallimard, 1948). All citations in my text refer to this edition.

24. Claude-Edmonde Magny has suggested Leo Frobenius as a model for Mollberg. Whether or not this character is based on a living person, however, is of relatively little importance. Of greater significance is the fact that his theories show a visible affinity with Spengler's influential work, *The Decline of the West*, and with theories suggested by anthropological discoveries of the time.

25. André Malraux, "L'Homme et la culture artistique," in *Conférences de l'UNESCO* (Paris: Fontaine, 1947), p. 80.

26. Maurice Rieuneau, *Guerre et révolution dans le roman français de 1919 à 1939* (Paris: Klincksieck, 1974), p. 234.

27. W. M. Frohock, *André Malraux and the Tragic Imagination* (Stanford, Calif.: Stanford University Press, 1967), p. 151.

28. Ibid., p. 135.

29. Lucien Goldmann feels that Malraux's disillusionment with Communism is mirrored in Vincent Berger's discovery of the meaninglessness of the Turkish political doctrine of "Touranism" (*Pour une sociologie du roman* [1964; reprint, Paris: Gallimard, Collection Idées, 1973], p. 252).

Selected Bibliography of Individual Writers

Primary Texts

Aragon, Louis. *Les Cloches de Bâle*. 1934; Reprint. Paris: Livre de Poche, 1966. Translated by Haakon M. Chevalier as *The Bells of Basel*. New York: Harcourt Brace, 1936.

———. *Les Beaux Quartiers*. 1936; Reprint. Paris: Folio, 1972.

———. *Les Voyageurs de l'impériale*. 1948; Reprint. Paris: Folio, 1972. Translated by Hannah Josephson as *Passengers of Destiny*. London: The Pilot Press Ltd., 1947.

Brasillach, Robert. *Les Captifs*. *Oeuvres complètes*, vol. 1. Paris: Au Club de l'Honnête Homme, 1963.

———. *L'Enfant de la nuit*. 1934; Reprint. *Oeuvres complètes*, vol. 1. Paris: Au Club de l'Honnête Homme, 1963.

———. *Le Marchand d'oiseaux*. 1936; Reprint. *Oeuvres complètes*, vol. 1. Paris: Au Club de l'Honnête Homme, 1963.

———. *Les Sept Couleurs*. 1939; Reprint. Paris: Livre de Poche, 1973.

Céline, Louis-Ferdinand. *Voyage au bout de la nuit*. 1932; Reprint. Paris: Folio, 1975. Translated by Ralph Manheim as *Journey to the End of the Night*. New York: New Directions, 1983.

———. *Mort à crédit*. 1936; Reprint. Paris: Livre de Poche, 1966. Translated by Ralph Manheim as *Death on the Installment Plan*. New York: New Directions, 1966.

Dabit, Eugène. *Faubourgs de Paris*. Paris: Gallimard, 1934.

———. *L'Ile*. Paris: Gallimard, 1934.

———. *Un Mort tout neuf*. Paris: Gallimard, 1934.

———. *Train de vies*. Paris: Gallimard, 1936.

———. *Villa Oasis*. Paris: Gallimard, 1932.

———. *La Zone verte*. Paris: Gallimard, 1935.

Drieu la Rochelle, Pierre. *La Comédie de Charleroi*. 1934; Reprint. Paris: Livre de Poche, 1970.

———. *Gilles*. 1939; Reprint. Paris: Folio, 1973.

Guilloux, Louis. *Angélina*. Paris: Grasset, 1934.

———. *Compagnons*. 1931; Paris: Editions "J'ai lu," 1960.

———. *Le Sang noir*. Paris: Gallimard, 1935.

———. *Le Sang noir*. Lausanne: Editions Rencontre, 1964.

———. *Le Sang noir*. Paris: Club Français du Livre, 1964.

Malraux, André. *L'Espoir*. 1937; Reprint. Paris: Folio, 1972. Translated by

Stuart Gilbert and Alastair Macdonald as *Man's Hope*. New York: Grove Press, 1979.

———. *Le Temps du mépris*. Paris: Gallimard, 1935. Translated by Haakon M. Chevalier as *Days of Wrath*. New York: Random House, 1936.

———. *Les Noyers de l'Altenburg*. 1942; Reprint. Paris: Gallimard, 1948.

Martin du Gard, Roger. *Epilogue*. *Les Thibault*, vol. 5. 1940; Reprint. Paris: Folio, 1973. Translated by Stuart Gilbert in *Summer 1914*. New York: Viking Press, 1941.

———. *L'Eté 1914*. *Les Thibault*, vols. 3–5. 1936; Reprint. Paris: Folio, 1973. Translated by Stuart Gilbert as *Summer 1914*. New York: Viking Press, 1941.

———. *Vieille France*. 1933; Reprint. Paris: Folio, 1974.

Nizan, Paul. *Le Cheval de Troie*. Paris: Gallimard, 1935. Translated by Charles Ashleigh as *Trojan Horse*. 1937; Reprint. New York: Howard Fertig, 1975.

———. *La Conspiration*. 1939; Reprint. Paris: Folio, 1973.

Sartre, Jean-Paul. "Le Mur" and "L'Enfance d'un Chef." *Le Mur*. 1939; Reprint. Paris: Folio, 1974. Translated by Lloyd Alexander as "The Wall" and "The Childhood of a Leader." *The Wall*. New York: New Directions, 1948.

Other Works and Editions Cited

Aragon, Louis. *J'abats mon jeu*. Paris: Les Editeurs Français Réunis, 1959.

———. *Pour un réalisme socialiste*. Paris: Denoël et Steele, 1935.

Brasillach, Robert. *Corneille*. Paris: Fayard, Collection L'Homme et l'Oeuvre, 1938.

———(with Maurice Bardèche). *Histoire du cinéma*. *Oeuvres complètes*, vol. 10.

———. "La Fin de l'après-guerre," *La Revue Universelle*, 46 (July 15, 1931): 251.

———(with Maurice Bardèche) *Histoire de la guerre d'Espagne*. Paris: Plon, 1939.

———. *Lettre à un soldat de la classe 60*. Paris: Les Sept Couleurs, 1960.

———. *Notre Avant-guerre*. 1941; Reprint. Paris: Livre de Poche, 1973.

———. *Le Siège de l'Alcazar* (originally titled "Les Cadets de l'Alcazar"). *Oeuvres complètes*, vol. 5. 1936; Reprint. Paris: Au Club de l'Honnête homme, 1963.

Céline, Louis-Ferdinand. *Mea Culpa*. Paris: Denoël et Steele, 1936.

Dabit, Eugène. *Faubourgs de Paris*. Paris: Gallimard, 1934.

———. *Journal intime 1928–1936*. Paris: Gallimard, 1939.

Drieu la Rochelle, Pierre. *Avec Doriot*. Paris: Gallimard, 1937.

———. *L'Europe contre les patries*. Paris: Gallimard, 1931.

———. *Une Femme à sa fenêtre*. Paris: Gallimard, 1930.

———. *Interrogation*. Paris: NRF, 1917.

———. *L'Homme à cheval*. Paris: Gallimard, 1943.

———. *Socialisme fasciste*. Paris: Gallimard, 1934.

Guilloux, Louis. *Les Batailles perdues*. Paris: Gallimard, 1960.

———. *Carnets 1921–1944*. Paris: Gallimard, 1978.

————. "Episode au village," *Commune*, Jan. 1938, pp. 564–81; Feb. 1938, pp. 681–703; Mar. 1938, 815–34; Apr. 1938, pp. 945–65.

————. *Le Jeu de patience*. Paris: Gallimard, 1949.

————. "Journal." *Le Sang noir*. Paris: Club Français du Livre, 1963, pp. 457–50.

————. *La Maison du peuple*. 1927; Reprint. Paris: Editions "J'ai lu," 1960.

————. *Le Pain des rêves*. Paris: Gallimard, 1942.

————. *Salido*. Paris: Gallimard, 1976.

————. *Souvenirs sur Georges Palante*. Saint-Brieuc: O. L. Aubert, 1931.

Malraux, André. *Antimémoires*. Paris: Gallimard, 1967.

————. *De Dimitrov à Thälmann: Echec au fascisme*. Bureau d'Editions, 4 rue Saint-Germain-l'Auxerrois. Undated pamphlet.

————. Foreword to Monique Saint-Claire, *Les Cahiers de la Petite Dame*, Cahiers André Gide 4. Paris: Gallimard, 1973.

Martin du Gard, Roger. *Souvenirs littéraires*. *Oeuvres complètes*, vol. 1. Paris: Pléiade, 1955.

Nizan, Paul. *Aden-Arabie*. 1932; Reprint. Paris: Maspero, 1976.

————. *Antoine Bloyé*. 1933; Reprint. Paris: Livre de Poche, 1971. Translated by Edmund Stevens as *Antoine Bloyé*. New York: Monthly Review Press, 1973.

————. *Les Chiens de garde*. Paris: Maspero, 1976.

————. *Chronique de septembre*. Paris: Gallimard, 1978.

————. *Paul Nizan intellectuel communiste*, vols. 1, 2. Edited by Jean-Jacques Brochier. Paris: Maspero, 1970.

————. *Pour une nouvelle culture*. Edited by Susan Suleiman. Paris: Grasset, 1971.

Sartre, Jean-Paul. *Les Carnets de la drôle de guerre*. Paris: Gallimard, 1983.

————. *L'Etre et le néant*. Paris: Gallimard, 1943. Translated by Hazel Barnes as *Being and Nothingness*. New York: Philosophical Library, 1956.

————. *Les Mouches*. 1947; Reprint. Paris: Folio, 1974.

————. *La Nausée*. Paris: Gallimard, 1938.

————. *Qu'est-ce que la littérature?* 1948; Reprint. Paris: Gallimard, Collection Idées, 1972.

Selected Bibliography of Secondary Sources

ABBREVIATION   NRF: Nouvelle Revue Française

Aaron, Daniel. *Writers on the Left*. New York: Oxford University Press, 1977.
Adereth, Maxwell. *Commitment in Modern French Literature: A Brief Study of "Littérature Engagée" in the Works of Péguy, Aragon, and Sartre*. London: Victor Gollancz, 1967.
Albérès, R.-M. *Bilan littéraire du XXe siècle*. Paris: Aubier, 1956.
Andreu, Pierre. *Drieu, témoin et visionnaire*. Paris: Grasset, 1952.
Astier, Pierre A. G. *Ecrivains français engagés*. Paris: Nouvelles Editions Debresse, 1978.
Aubran, Dominique. *Aragon parle avec Dominique Aubran*. Paris: Seghers, 1968.
Auerbach, Eric. *Mimesis*. Garden City, N.Y.: Anchor, 1951.
Azéma, Jean-Pierre. *De Munich à la Libération*. Paris: Seuil, Collection Points, 1979.
Barbusse, Henri. *Le Feu*. Paris: Flammarion, 1916.
———. *Russie*. Paris: Flammarion, 1930.
Bardel, Pierre. "Henry Poulaille et la littérature prolétarienne," *Europe* 575–76 (Mar.-Apr. 1977): 168–78.
Barnes, Hazel E. *Sartre*. Philadelphia: Lippincott, 1973.
Beauvoir, Simone de. *La Force de l'âge*. 1960; Reprint. Paris: Livre de Poche, 1966. Translated by Peter Green as *The Prime of Life*. Cleveland: The World Publishing Company, 1962.
———. *Pour une morale de l'ambiguité*. Paris: Gallimard, Collection Idées, 1968.
Beloff, Max. "The Sixth of February." In *The Decline of the Third Republic*, edited by James Joll. London: Chatto and Windus, 1959.
Benson, Frederick R. *Writers in Arms*. New York: New York University Press, 1967.
Bergonzi, Bernard. *Reading the Thirties*. Pittsburgh: University of Pittsburgh Press, 1978.
Bernanos, Georges. *Les Grands Cimetières sous la lune*. Paris: Plon, 1938.
Bernard, Jean-Pierre A. *Le Parti communiste français et la question littéraire 1921–1939*. Grenoble: Presses Universitaires de Grenoble, 1972.
———. "Le Parti communiste français et les problèmes littéraires (1920–1939)," *Revue Française de Science Politique* 17 (June 1967): 520–44.

Bernard, Philippe. *La Fin d'un monde 1914–1929.* Paris: Seuil, Collection Points, 1975.

Berslein, Serge, ed. *Le 6 février 1934.* Paris: Gallimard, Julliard, 1975.

Beuchat, Charles. *Histoire du naturalisme français,* vol. 2. Paris: Corrêa, 1949.

Bibrowska, Sophie. *Une Mise à mort.* Paris: Denoël, 1972. (On Aragon.)

Boak, Denis. *André Malraux.* Oxford: Clarendon Press, 1968.

―――. *Roger Martin du Gard.* Oxford: Clarendon Press, 1963.

Bodin, Louis, and Jean Touchard. *Front populaire 1936.* Paris: Armand Colin, 1961.

Bonnefous, Edouard. *Histoire politique de la Troisième République,* vols. 5–7. Paris: Presses Universitaires de France, 1962.

Bourgeat, François, ed. *Actualité de Louis Guilloux.* Marseille: Editions Jeanne Laffitte, 1978.

Brée, Germaine, and Margaret Guiton. *The French Novel from Gide to Camus.* New Brunswick, N.J.: Rutgers University Press, 1957.

―――. *Twentieth-Century French Literature.* Chicago: University of Chicago Press, 1983.

Brodin, Pierre. *Présences contemporaines, Littérature III.* Paris: Debresse, 1957.

Brombert, Victor. *The Intellectual Hero: Studies in the French Novel, 1900–1960.* Chicago: Phoenix Books, 1964.

Broué, Pierre. *La Révolution espagnole (1931–1939).* Paris: Flammarion, 1973.

Broué, Pierre, and Emile Témime, *La Révolution et la guerre d'Espagne.* Paris: Minuit, 1961.

Cadwallader, Barrie. *Crisis of the European Mind.* Cardiff: University of Wales Press, 1981. (On Drieu la Rochelle and Malraux.)

Camus, Albert. Foreword to Rogert Martin du Gard, *Les Thibault, Oeuvres complètes,* vol. 1. Paris.: Pléiade, 1955.

Carduner, Jean. *La Création romanesque chez Malraux.* Paris: Nizet, 1968.

Carrard, Philippe. *Malraux ou le récit hybride.* Paris: Lettres Modernes, 1976.

Caute, David. *Communism and the French Intellectuals.* London: André Deutsch, 1964.

Chamson, André. *L'Année des vaincus.* Paris: Gallimard, 1934.

―――. *La Galère.* Paris: Gallimard, 1939.

Chastenet, Jacques. *Histoire de la Troisième République,* vols. 5, 6. Paris: Hachette, 1960, 1962.

Chavardès, Maurice. *Le 6 février 1934, La République en danger.* Paris: Calmann-Lévy, 1966.

Chiaromonte, Nicola. "Malraux and the Demons of Action," *Partisan Review* 15 (July 1948): 776–89; 16 (Aug. 1948): 912–23.

Cohen-Solal, Annie, and Henriette Nizan. *Paul Nizan, communiste impossible.* Paris: Grasset, 1980.

Courcel, Martine de. *Malraux, Life and Work.* New York : Harcourt Brace Jovanovich, 1976.

Crossman, Richard, ed. *The God That Failed.* 1950; Reprint. New York: Harper Colophon, 1963.

Cruickshank, John, ed. *French Literature and Its Background: The Twentieth Century.* London: Oxford University Press, 1970.

Cryle, P. M. *The Thematics of Commitment.* Princeton, N.J.: Princeton University Press, 1985.

Cuisenier, André. *Jules Romains: L'Unanimisme et Les Hommes de bonne volonté.* Paris: Flammarion, 1935.

Dale, Jonathan. "Drieu la Rochelle: The War as 'Comedy.'" In *The First World War in Fiction*, edited by Holger Klein. New York: Barnes and Noble, 1977.

Dauphin, Jean-Pierre, ed. *Les Critiques de notre temps et Céline.* Paris: Garnier, 1976.

Dauphin, Jean-Pierre, and Henri Godard, eds. *Céline et l'actualité littéraire 1932–1957.* Paris: Gallimard, 1976.

Day, Philip Stephen. *Le Miroir allégorique de Louis-Ferdinard Céline.* Paris: Klincksieck, 1974.

Delaprée, Louis. *Mort en Espagne.* Paris: Editions Tisné, 1937.

Desanti, Dominique. *Drieu la Rochelle, le séducteur mystifié.* Paris: Flammarion, 1978.

Dialogues with the Unseen and the Unknown. Saratoga Springs, New York: Skidmore College Department of Modern Languages, 1978. (On Malraux.)

Dubief, Henri. *Le Déclin de la IIIe République 1929–1938.* Paris: Seuil, Collection Points, 1976.

Eby, Cecil D. *The Siege of the Alcazar.* New York: Random House, 1965.

Ermolaev, Herman. *Soviet Literary Theories 1917–1934.* Berkeley and Los Angeles: University of California Press, 1963.

Ferro, Marc. *La Grande Guerre 1914–1918.* Paris: Gallimard, Collection Idées, 1969.

Field, Frank. *Three French Writers and the Great War.* Cambridge: Cambridge University Press, 1975.

Flower, J. E. *Writers and Politics in Modern France.* London: Hodder and Stoughton, 1977.

Fortier, Paul A. "Marxist Criticism of Céline's *Voyage au bout de la nuit*," *Modern Fiction Studies* 57 (1971): 268–72.

Frank, Bernard. *La Panoplie littéraire.* Paris: Julliard, 1958.

Frank, Joseph. *The Widening Gyre.* New Brunswick, N.J.: Rutgers University Press, 1963.

Frohock, W. M. *André Malraux and the Tragic Imagination.* Stanford, Calif.: Stanford University Press, 1967.

———. *Style and Temper: Studies in French Fiction, 1925–1960.* Cambridge, Mass.: Harvard University Press, 1967.

Fussell, Paul. *The Great War and Modern Memory.* New York: Oxford University Press, 1975.

Gaillard, Pol, ed. *Les Critiques de notre temps et Malraux.* Paris: Garnier, 1970.

———. *L'Espoir.* Paris: Hatier, 1970.

Garaudy, Roger. *L'Itinéraire d'Aragon.* Paris: Gallimard, 1961.

Garguilo, René. *La Genèse des Thibault de Roger Martin du Gard.* Paris: Klincksieck, 1974.

George, Bernard. *Brasillach.* Paris: Editions Universitaires, 1968.

Gibault, François. *Céline.* Paris: Mercure de France, 1977.

Gide, André. *Journal 1889–1939*. Paris: Gallimard, 1948.
———. *Littérature engagée*. Paris: Gallimard, 1950.
———. "Pages de journal," *NRF*, Aug. 1932, pp. 161–72; Sept. 1932, pp. 362–71; Oct. 1932, pp. 481–506.
———. *Retour de l'USSR*. Paris: Gallimard, 1936.
Ginsbourg, Ariel. *Nizan*. Paris: Editions Universitaires, 1966.
Giono, Jean. *Ecrits Pacifistes*. 1938; Reprint., Paris: Gallimard, Collection Idées, 1978.
Girard, René. "L'Homme et le Cosmos dans *L'Espoir* et *Les Noyers de l'Altenburg* d'André Malraux," *PMLA* 68 (1953): 49–55.
Girardet, Raoul. "Notes sur l'Esprit d'un Fascisme Français 1934–1939," *Revue Française de Science Politique* 5, no. 3 (July-Sept. 1955): 529–46.
Goldmann, Lucien. *Pour une sociologie du roman*. Paris: Gallimard, 1964.
Gonthier, Fernande. *La Femme et le couple dans le roman (1919–1939)*. Paris: Klincksieck, 1976.
Green, Mary Jean. *Louis Guilloux: An Artisan of Language*. York, S.C.: French Literature Publications (now Summa Publications), 1980.
———. "Toward an Analysis of Fascist Fiction: The Contemptuous Narrator in the Work of Brasillach, Céline and Drieu la Rochelle, " *Studies in Twentieth Century Literature*, forthcoming.
Greene, Francis J. "Louis Guilloux's *Le Sang noir*: A prefiguration of Sartre's *La Nausée*," *French Review* 43 (Dec. 1969), 205–14.
Greenlee, James W. *Malraux's Heroes and History*. DeKalb: Northern Illinois University Press, 1975.
Grover, Frédéric J. *Drieu la Rochelle*. Paris: Gallimard, Collection La Bibliothèque Idéale, 1962.
———. *Drieu la Rochelle*. Paris: Gallimard, Collection Idées, 1979.
———. *Drieu la Rochelle and the Fiction of Testimony*. Berkeley and Los Angeles: University of California Press, 1958.
Grover, M. "The Inheritors of Maurice Barrès," *Modern Language Review* 64, no. 3 (July 1969): 529–45.
Guéhenno, Jean. *Journal d'un homme de quarante ans*. Paris: Grasset, 1934.
———. *Journal d'une révolution, 1937–38*. Paris: Grasset, 1939.
Hamilton, Alastair. *The Appeal of Fascism*. New York: Macmillan, 1971.
Hanrez, Marc. *Céline*. Paris: Gallimard, 1969.
———. ed. *Espagne/écrivains/guerre civile*. Paris: Pantheon Press,Les Dossiers H, 1975.
Harris, Geoffrey T. *L'Ethique comme fonction de l'esthétique*. Paris: Lettres Modernes, 1972. (On Malraux.)
Howe, Irving. *Politics and the Novel*. New York: Meridian Books, 1957.
Hughes, H. Stuart. *Consciousness and Society*. New York: Vintage, 1977.
———. *The Obstructed Path: French Social Thought in the Years of Desperation, 1930–1960*. New York: Harper and Row, 1966.
Humphrey, Robert. *The Stream of Consciousness in the Modern Novel*. Berkeley and Los Angeles: University of California Press, 1960.
Hynes, Samuel. *The Auden Generation*. New York: Viking, 1977.
Idt, Geneviève. *Le Mur de Jean-Paul Sartre: Techniques et contexte d'une provocation*. Paris: Larousse, 1972.

Jackson, Gabriel. *The Spanish Republic and the Civil War 1931–1939*. Princeton, N.J.: Princeton University Press, 1965.

Jameson, Fredric. *Sartre: The Origins of a Style*. New Haven, Conn.: Yale University Press, 1961.

Jones, Maurice. "L'Antihéroisme précurseur de Roger Martin du Gard," *French Review* 42 (May 1969): 834–45.

Jubécourt, Gérard Sthème de. *Robert Brasillach, critique littéraire*. Lausanne: Association des Amis de Robert Brasillach, 1972.

Kadish, Doris. "L'Ironie et le roman engagé," *French Review* 45 (Feb. 1972): 596–609.

Kilborn, Mary C. "The Theme of Suffering in the Works of Louis Guilloux," *Nottingham French Studies* 17, no. 2 (Oct. 1978): 44–59.

Klein, Holger, ed. *The First World War in Fiction*. New York: Barnes and Noble, 1977.

Kline, Thomas J. *André Malraux and the Metamorphosis of Death*. New York: Columbia University Press, 1973.

Knapp, Bettina L. *Céline: Man of Hate*. University of Alabama Press, 1974.

Knapp, Wilfred. *France: Partial Eclipse*. New York: American Heritage Press, 1972.

Kristeva, Julia. *Pouvoirs de l'horreur, Essai sur l'abjection*. Paris: Seuil, 1979.

Kunnas, Tarmo. *Drieu la Rochelle, Céline, Brasillach et la tentation fasciste*. Paris: Les Sept Couleurs, 1972.

Lacouture, Jean. *Malraux, une vie dans le siècle*. Paris: Collection Points, 1973.

Lalou, René. *Le Roman français depuis 1900*. Paris: Presses Universitaires de France, 1941.

Langlois, Walter. "Anarchism, Action, and Malraux," *Twentieth Century Literature* 24 (Fall 1978), 272–89.

———. "The Novelist Malraux and History," *L'Esprit Créateur* 15, no. 3 (Fall 1975): 345–66.

Laqueur, Walter, and George L. Mosse, eds. *The Left-Wing Intellectuals Between the Wars, 1919–1939*. New York: Harper Torchbooks, 1966.

Leal, Robert Barry. *Drieu la Rochelle*. Boston: Twayne, 1982.

Lefebvre, Henri. *La Somme et le reste*. Paris: La Nef, 1959.

Lefèvre, Frédéric. *Une heure avec. . .*, VIe série. Paris: Flammarion, 1933.

———. "Une heure avec M. Louis Guilloux," *Les Nouvelles Littéraires*, Dec. 12, 1935.

Lefranc, Georges. *Les Gauches en France 1789–1972*. Paris: Payot, 1973.

———. *Histoire du Front populaire (1934–1938)*. Paris: Payot, 1965.

———. *Le Mouvement socialiste sous la Troisième République*. Paris: Payot, 1977.

Leiner, Jacqueline. *Le Destin littéraire de Paul Nizan et ses étapes successives*. Paris: Klincksieck, 1970.

———."La Part de l'actuel dans l'oeuvre de Paul-Yves Nizan," *Revue des Sciences Humaines*, fasc. 129 (Jan.-Mar. 1968).

Lemonnier, Leon. *Manifeste du roman populiste*. Paris: Jacques Bernard, 1929.

———. *Populisme*. Paris: La Renaissance du Livre, 1930.

Lewis, R. W. B., ed. *Malraux: A Collection of Critical Essays*. Englewood Cliffs, N.J.: Prentice-Hall, 1964.

Lottman, Herbert R. *The Left Bank*. Boston: Houghton Mifflin, 1982.

Loubet del Bayle, Jean. *Les Non-conformistes des années 30*. Paris: Seuil, 1969.

Lukacs, Georg. *Realism in Our Time*. New York: Harper Torchbook, 1971.

――――. *The Historical Novel*. New York: Penguin, 1976.

McCarthy, Patrick. *Céline*. New York: Penguin, 1977.

Magny, Claude-Edmonde. *Histoire du roman français depuis 1918*. 1950; Reprint. Paris: Points, 1971.

――――. *Littérature et critique*. Paris: Payot, 1971.

Marion, Denis. *André Malraux*. Paris: Seghers, 1970.

Matthews, John H. *Surrealism and the Novel*. Ann Arbor: University of Michigan Press, 1966.

Maurois, André. "Eugène Dabit." In *Hommage à Eugène Dabit*. Paris: Gallimard, 1939.

Maxence, Jean-Pierre. *Histoire de dix ans 1927–1937*. Paris: Gallimard, 1939.

Munoz, Maryse Bertrand de. *La Guerre civile espagnole et la littérature française*. Ottawa: Didier, 1972.

Nadeau, Maurice. *Histoire du surréalisme*. Paris: Seuil 1964.

――――. *Littérature présente*. Paris: Corrêa, 1952.

Nettelbeck, Colin W. "Journey to the End of Art: The Evolution of the Novels of Louis-Ferdinand Céline," *PMLA* 87 (1972): 80–89.

Nolte, Ernst. *Three Faces of Fascism*. New York: Mentor, 1969.

O'Connell, David. "Eugène Dabit: A French Working-Class Novelist," *Research Studies* 41, no. 4 (Dec. 1973): 217–33.

――――. "La Première Rencontre d'Eugène Dabit avec André Gide: Un Inédit d'Eugène Dabit," *Revue des Lettres Modernes*, nos. 374–79 (1973): 107–31.

Orlando, David A. "The Novels of Eugène Dabit and French Literary *Populisme* of the 1930s," Ph. D. diss., Stanford University, 1972.

Ory, Pascal. *Les collaborateurs 1940–1945*. Paris: Seuil, Collection Points, 1976.

――――. *Nizan: Destin d'un révolté*. Paris: Editions Ramsay, 1980.

Ostrovsky, Erika. *Céline and His Vision*. New York: New York University Press, 1967.

Pedroncini, G. *Les Mutineries de 1917*. Paris: Presses Universitaires, 1967.

Peyre, Henri. *The Contemporary French Novel*. New York: Oxford University Press, 1955.

Picon, Gaeton. *Malraux*. Paris: Seuil, Collection Ecrivains de Toujours, 1976.

――――. *Panorama de la nouvelle littérature*. Paris: Gallimard, 1960.

Pike, David W. *Les Français et la guerre d'Espagne*. Paris: Presses universitaires de France, 1975.

Plumyène, J., and R. Lasierra. *Les Fascismes français 1923–1963*. Paris: Seuil, 1963.

Pomeau, René. "Guerre et roman dans l'entre-deux-guerres," *Revue des Sciences Humaines*, fasc. 109 (Jan.-Mar. 1963): 77–95.

Poulaille, Henry. *Nouvel Age littéraire*. Paris: Librairie Valois, 1930.

Prigent, Edouard, ed. *Louis Guilloux*. Saint-Brieuc: Presses Universitaires de Bretagne, 1971.

Prince, Gerald. "Changement de technique romanesque dans *Les Cloches de Bâle*," *Romance Notes* 14, no. 1 (Autumn 1972): 1–6.

———. *Métaphysique et technique dans l'oeuvre romanesque de Sartre*. Geneva: Droz, 1968.

Quérière, Yves de la. *Céline et les mots*. Lexington: University Press of Kentucky, 1973.

Racelle-Latin, Danielle. "*Voyage au bout de la nuit* ou l'inauguration d'une poétique argotique," *Revue des Lettres Modernes*, 462–67 (1976): 53–77.

Racine, Nicole. "L'Association des Ecrivains et Artistes Révolutionnaires 1932–1936," *Le Mouvement Social* 54 (Jan.-Mar. 1966).

Racine, Nicole, and Louis Bodin. *Le Parti communiste français pendant l'entre-deux-guerres*. Paris: Armand Colin, 1972.

Ragon, Michel. *Les Ecrivains du peuple*. Paris: Jean Vigneau, 1947.

———. *Histoire de la littérature ouvrière du moyen âge à nos jours*. Paris: Editions Ouvrières, 1953.

Reck, Rina Drell. *Literature and Responsibility: The French Novelist in the Twentieth Century*. Baton Rouge: Louisiana University Press, 1969.

Redfern, W. D. *Paul Nizan: Committed Literature in a Conspiratorial World*. Princeton, N.J.: Princeton University Press, 1972.

Rémond, René. *La Droite en France de la première Restauration à la Ve République*. Paris: Aubier, 1954.

Richard, Jean-Pierre. *Nausée de Céline*. Paris: Fata Morgana, 1973.

Riegel, Leon. *Guerre et littérature*. Paris: Klincksieck, 1978.

Rieuneau, Maurice. *Guerre et révolution dans le roman français de 1919 à 1939*. Paris: Klincksieck, 1974.

Roche-Calmette, Anne. "Pour un Louis Guilloux et son temps," *Annales de la Faculté des Lettres et Sciences Humaines d'Aix* 44 (1968):7–31.

Sabourin, Pascal. *La Réflexion sur l'art d'André Malraux*. Paris: Klincksieck, 1972.

Sachs, Maurice. *Le Sabbat*. Paris: Corrêa, 1946.

Saint-Claire, Monique. *Les Cahiers de la petite dame*, Cahiers André Gide 4. Paris: Gallimard, 1973.

Saint-Ygnan, Jean-Louis. *Drieu la Rochelle ou l'obsession de la décadence*. Paris: Nouvelles Editions Latines, 1984.

Sartre, Jean-Paul. "La Conspiration," in *Critiques littéraires, Situations, I*. 1947; Reprint. Paris: Gallimard, Collection Idées, 1974.

Savage, Catharine H. *Malraux, Sartre and Aragon as Political Novelists*. University of Florida Monographs, no. 17, Gainsville: University of Florida, 1964.

Schalk, David R. *Roger Martin du Gard: The Novelist and History*. Ithaca, N. Y.: Cornell University Press, 1967.

———. *The Spectrum of Political Engagement*. Princeton, N.J.: Princeton University Press, 1979.

Schilling, Gilbert. "Espace et angoisse dans *Voyage au bout de la nuit*," *Revue des Lettres Modernes* 398–402 (1974): 57–79.

Schwartz, William Leonard. "The Populist School in the French Novel," *French Review* 4 (May 1931): 473–79.

Sérant, Paul. *Le Romantisme fasciste*. Paris: Fasquelle, 1959.

Simon, Pierre-Henri. *L'Esprit et l'histoire*. Paris: Armand Colin, 1954.

————. *Histoire de la littérature française au XXe siècle, 1900–1950*, 3d ed. Paris: Armand Colin, 1957.

————. *L'Homme en procès*. Boudry, Neuchâtel: Editions de la Baconnière, 1950.

————. *Procès du héros: Montherlant, Drieu La Rochelle, Jean Prévost*. Paris: Seuil, 1950.

Spitzer, Leo. "Une Habitude de style: Le Rappel chez Céline," *Le Français Moderne* 3 (June 1935): 193–208.

Suleiman, Susan Rubin. *Authoritarian Fictions: The Ideological Novel as a Literary Genre*. New York: Columbia University Press, 1983.

————. "Ideological Dissent from Works of Fiction: Toward a Rhetoric of the *roman à thèse*," *Neophilologus* 60 (1976): 162–77.

————. "The Structure of Confrontation: Nizan, Barrès, Malraux," *Modern Language Notes* 95, no. 4 (May 1980): 938–67.

Thibaudet, Albert. *Histoire de la littérature française de 1789 à nos jours*. Paris: Stock, 1936.

Thiher, Allen. *Céline: The Novel as Delirium*. New Brunswick, N.J.: Rutgers University Press, 1972.

Thomas, Hugh. *The Spanish Civil War*. New York: Harper and Row, 1961.

Thompson, Brian, and Carl A. Viggiani, eds., *Witnessing André Malraux: Visions and Re-Visions*. Middletown, Conn.: Wesleyan University Press, 1984.

Thomson, David. *Democracy in France: The Third and Fourth Republics*. London: Oxford University Press, 1958.

Thornberry, Robert S. *André Malraux et l'Espagne*. Geneva: Droz, 1977.

Tison-Braun, Micheline. *La Crise de l'humanisme. Le Conflit de l'individu et de la société dans la littérature française moderne*, 2 vols. Paris: Nizet, 1958, 1967.

————. *Ce monstre incomparable. . . Malraux ou l'énigme du moi*. Paris: Armand Colin, 1983.

Touchard, Jean. "L'Esprit des années 1930." In *Tendances politiques dans la vie française depuis 1789*. Paris: Hachette, 1960.

————. *La Gauche en France depuis 1900*. Paris: Seuil, Collection Points, 1972.

————. "Le Parti communiste français et les intellectuels (1920–1939)." *Revue Française de Science Politique* 17 (June 1967): 408–23.

Trotsky, Leon. "Novelist and Politician," *Atlantic Monthly* 156 (1935).

Tucker, William R. *The Fascist Ego: A Politial Biography of Robert Brasillach*. Berkeley and Los Angeles: University of California Press, 1975.

Valéry, Paul. "La Crise de l'esprit," *NRF*, Aug. 1919, p. 325.

————. *Regards sur le monde actuel*. *Oeuvres*, vol. 2. Edited by Jean Hytier. Paris: Gallimard, 1958.

Vandromme, Pol. *Robert Brasillach: L'Homme et l'oeuvre*. Paris: Plon, 1956.

Vitoux, Frédéric. *Louis-Ferdinand Céline: Misère et parole*. Paris: NRF, Les Essais, 1973.

Weber, Eugen. *Action Française.* Stanford, Calif.: Stanford University Press, 1962.

Wilhelm, Bernard. *Hemingway et Malraux devant la guerre d'Espagne.* Porrentruy: La Bonne Presse, 1966.

Wilkinson, David. *Malraux: An Essay in Political Criticism.* Cambridge, Mass.: Harvard University Press, 1967.

Winegarten, Renée. *Writers and Revolution.* New York: New Viewpoints, 1974.

Wohl, Robert. *The Generation of 1914.* Cambridge, Mass.: Harvard University Press, 1979.

Woolf, S. J., ed. *European Fascism.* New York: Vintage, 1969.

Index